Environmental Policy in the European Union

SECOND EDITION

**To
Bessie**

Environmental Policy in the European Union

SECOND EDITION

Edited by

Andrew Jordan

London • Sterling, VA

Second edition first published by
Earthscan in the UK and USA in 2005

First edition 2002

ISBN: 1-84407-158-8 paperback
         1-84407-157-X hardback

Typesetting by Composition and Design Services, Belarus
Printed and bound in the UK by Bath Press, Bath
Cover design by Ruth Bateson

For a full list of publications please contact:

Earthscan
8–12 Camden High Street
London, NW1 0JH, UK
Tel: +44 (0)20 7387 8558
Fax: +44 (0)20 7387 8998
Email: earthinfo@earthscan.co.uk
Web: **www.earthscan.co.uk**

22883 Quicksilver Drive, Sterling, VA 20166-2012, USA

Earthscan is an imprint of James & James (Science Publishers) Ltd and publishes
in association with the International Institute for Environment and Development

A catalogue record for this book is available from the British Library

Library of Congress Cataloging-in-Publication Data
has been applied for.

Printed on elemental chlorine-free paper

Contents

List of Illustrations

Figures

Tables

List of Contributors

Tanja Börzel is Professor of Political Science, Institute of Political Science, University of Heidelberg, Heidelberg, Germany.
Email: boerzel@uni-hd.de

Lars Brückner works as an environmental affairs adviser for a global ICT (information and communication technology) company in Brussels, Belgium.
Email: larsbruckner@yahoo.com

Charlotte Burns is Lecturer in European Politics, Department of International Politics, University of Wales at Aberystwyth, Aberystwyth, Wales, UK.
Email: ctb@aber.ac.uk

Jo Ann Carmin is Assistant Professor of Environmental Policy and Planning, Department of Urban Studies and Planning, Massachusetts Institute of Technology (MIT), Cambridge, MA, USA.
Email: jcarmin@mit.edu

Chad Damro is Lecturer in Politics, School of Social and Political Studies, University of Edinburgh, Edinburgh, UK.
Email: chad.damro@ed.ac.uk

Jenny Fairbrass is Lecturer in Business Strategy, School of Management, University of Bradford, Bradford, UK.
Email: j.fairbrass@bradford.ac.uk

Philipp Hildebrand works at the World Economic Forum in Geneva, Switzerland.

Andrew Jordan is Reader in Environmental Politics and Philip Leverhulme Prize Fellow, School of Environmental Sciences, University of East Anglia, Norwich, UK.
Email: a.jordan@uea.ac.uk

Tim Josling is Professor Emeritus and Senior Fellow, Stanford Institute for International Studies (SIIS), Stanford University, Palo Alto, CA, USA, and a consultant at Agricola Trade.
Email: josling@agricolatrade.com

Ida Koppen teaches at the University of Siena and the Johns Hopkins University Bologna Centre. She is also Director of the Sustainability Challenge Foundation.
Email: koppen@unisi.it

Andrea Lenschow is Junior Professor in Political Science, University of Osnabrück, Osnabrück, Germany.
Email: andrea.lenschow@uos.de

Duncan Liefferink is Senior Researcher, Department of Political Sciences of the Environment, Radboud University Nijmegen, Nijmegen, The Netherlands.
Email: d.liefferink@nsm.kun.nl

Pilar Luaces Méndez is a PhD candidate, Department of Political Science, University of Santiago de Compostela, Santiago, Spain.
Email: pilarluaces@mundo-r.com

Sonia Mazey is Senior Tutor, Keble College, University of Oxford, Oxford, UK.
Email: sonia.mazey@keb.ox/ac.uk

Lee Ann Patterson is Research Associate, Center for West European Studies, University of Pittsburgh, Pittsburgh, PA, USA, and a consultant at Agricola Trade.
Email: patterson@agricolatrade.com

Jeremy Richardson is Emeritus Fellow, Nuffield College, University of Oxford, Oxford, UK.
Email: jeremy.richardson@nuffield.ox.ac.uk

Alberta Sbragia is Director, Centre for West European Studies, University of Pittsburgh, Pittsburgh, PA, USA.
Email: sbragia+@pitt.edu

Mikael Skou Andersen works in the Department of Policy Analysis, Danish National Environmental Research Institute, Rosskilde, Denmark.
Email: msa@dmu.dk

Stacy D. VanDeveer is the 2003–2006 Ronald H. O'Neal Associate Professor, Political Science Department, University of New Hampshire, Durham, New Hampshire, USA.
Email: stacy.vandeveer@unh.edu

David Vogel is George Quist Professor of Business Ethics, Haas School of Business, University of California at Berkeley, CA, USA.
Email: vogel@haas.berkeley.edu.

Albert Weale is Professor of Government, Department of Government, University of Essex, Colchester, UK.
Email: weala@essex.ac.uk

Rüdiger Wurzel is Senior Lecturer in Politics, Department of Politics and International Studies, University of Hull, Hull, UK.
Email: r.k.wurzel@hull.ac.uk

Anthony Zito is Reader in Politics, School of Geography, Politics and Sociology, University of Newcastle, Newcastle upon Tyne, UK.
Email: a.r.zito@newcastle.ac.uk

List of Sources

Earthscan and the editor would like to thank the authors and copyright holders for permission to reprint the contributions appearing in this volume.

Chapter 2: 'The European Community's Environmental Policy, 1957 to 1992: From Incidental Measures to an International Regime?', from the journal *Environmental Politics*, 1993, Vol.1, No.4, pp13–44, Frank Cass Publishers.

Chapter 3: 'European Union Environmental Policy after the Nice Summit', from the journal *Environmental Politics*, 2001, Vol.10, No.4, pp109–114, Frank Cass Publishers.

Chapter 4: 'Strategies of the "Green" Member States in EU Environmental Policy-making', from the *Journal of European Public Policy*, 1998, Vol.5, No.2, pp254–270, Routledge/Taylor & Francis Ltd.

Chapter 5: 'The Role of the European Court of Justice', from J. D. Liefferink, P. D. Lowe and A. P. J. Mol (eds), *European Integration and Environmental Policy*, 1993, pp126–149, John Wiley & Sons.

Chapter 7: 'Environmental Groups and the EC: Challenges and Opportunities', from the journal *Environmental Politics,* 1992, Vol.1, No.4, pp109–128, Frank Cass Publishers.

Chapter 8: 'Environmental Rules and Rule-making in the European Union', from the *Journal of European Public Policy*, 1996, Vol.3, No.4, pp594–611, Routledge/Taylor & Francis Ltd.

Chapter 9: 'Task Expansion: A Theoretical Overview', from the journal *Environment and Planning C,* 1999, Vol.17, No.1, pp19–35, Pion Ltd.

Chapter 10: 'Pace-setting, Foot-dragging and Fence-sitting: Member State Responses to Europeanization', from the *Journal of Common Market Studies*, 2002, Vol.40, No.2, pp193–214, Blackwell Publishers Ltd.

Chapter 12: 'Institution-building from Below and Above: The European Community in Global Environmental Politics' from A. Stone Sweet and W. Sandholtz (eds), *European Integration and Supranational Governance*, 1998, pp283–303, Oxford University Press.

Chapter 13: 'The Hare and the Tortoise Revisited: The New Politics of Consumer and Environmental Regulation in Europe', from the *British Journal of Political Science*, 2003, Vol.33, pp557–580, Cambridge University Press.

Chapter 14: 'Emissions Trading at Kyoto: From EU Resistance to Union Innovation', from the journal *Environmental Politics*, Vol.12, No.2, pp71–94, Frank Cass Publishers.

Chapter 16: 'New Regulatory Approaches in "Greening" EU Policies', from the *European Law Journal*, 2002, Vol.8, No.1, pp19–37, Blackwell Publishing Ltd.

Chapter 17: 'European Governance and the Transfer of "New" Environmental Policy Instruments in the European Union', from the journal *Public Administration*, 2003, Vol.81, No.3, pp555–574, Blackwell Publishing Ltd.

Chapter 18: 'European Environmental Policy by Stealth: The Dysfunctionality of Functionalism?', from the journal *Environment and Planning C,* 1999, Vol.17, No.1, pp37–51, Pion Ltd.

List of Acronyms and Abbreviations

AFSSA	L'Agence Française de Securité Sanitaire des Aliments
AIDS	Acquired Immune Deficiency Syndrome
BAT	Best Available Technology/Techniques
BS	British Standard
BSE	Bovine Spongiform Encephalopathy
BST	Borine Somatotropin
CAP	Common Agricultural Policy (EU)
CCPM	Common and Co-ordinated Policies and Measures (EU)
CDM	Clean Development Mechanism
CEE	Central and Eastern Europe(an)
CEFIC	European Chemical Industry Council
CFC	Chlorofluorocarbon
CFSP	Common Foreign Security Policy (EU)
CH_4	Methane
CITES	Convention on International Trade in Endangered Species (UN)
CO_2	Carbon Dioxide
CoM	Council of Ministers (EU)
CoP	Conference of the Parties (UN)
COREPER	Committee of Permanent Representatives
CSD	Commission on Sustainable Development (UN)
DDT	Dichlorodiphenyltrichloroethane
DETR	Department of the Environment, Transport and the Regions (UK)
DG	Directorate General (EU)
DG XI	Directorate General for the Environment (now 'DG Environment') (EU)
DG Environment	Directorate General for the Environment (formerly 'DG XI') (EU)
DNA	Deoxyribonucleic (acid)
DoE	Department of the Environment (UK)
EAGGF	European Agricultural Guidance and Guarantee Find
EAP	Environment Action Programme (EU)
EATP	European Association for Textile Polyolefins
EC	European Community (now part of the EU)
ECJ	European Court of Justice (EU)
ECOFIN	Council of Finance Ministers (EU)
ECSC	European Coal and Steel Community (now part of the EU)
EEA	European Environment Agency (EU)
EEB	European Environmental Bureau
EEC	European Economic Community (now part of the EU)
EFSA	European Food Safety Authority (EU)

ELO	Environmental Label Organization
ELR	European Law Report (EU)
ELV	End of Life Vehicles (Directive) (EU)
EMAS	Eco-Management and Audit System
EMU	European Monetary Union (EU)
ENDS	Environmental Data Services
EP	European Parliament
EPA	Environmental Protection Agency (US)
EPI	Environmental Policy Integration
EPP	European People's Party
EPRG	Environmental Policy Review Group
ERDF	European Regional Development Fund
ESRC	Economic and Social Research Council
EU	European Union
EUEB	European Union Ecolabelling Board
FDA	Food and Drug Administration (US)
FoE	Friends of the Earth
FRG	Federal Republic of Germany
G77	Group of 77 (developing countries)
GATT	General Agreement on Tariffs and Trade
GDP	Gross Domestic Product
GM	Genetically Modified
GMO	Genetically Modified Organism
GNP	Gross National Product
HCFC	Hydrochloroflourocarbon
HIV	Human Immunodeficiency Virus
HL	House of Lords
HOLSCEC	House of Lords Select Committee on the European Communities
IGC	Intergovernmental Conference (EU)
IMPEL	Network for the Implementation and Enforcement of Environmental Law (EU)
INC	Intergovernmental Negotiating Committee
INCPEC	Industrial Council for Packaging and the Environment
IPC	Integrated Pollution Control
IPP	Integrated Product Policy
IPPC	Integrated Pollution Prevention and Control
LEG	Liquefied Energy Gas
MEP	Member of European Parliament (EU)
NGO	Non-governmental Organization
NEPI	New Environmental Policy Instrument
NO_2	Nitrogen Dioxide
NO_X	Nitrogen Oxides
N_2O	Nitrous Oxide
OECD	Organisation for Economic Co-operation and Development
OECD GNE	OECD Group of National Experts
OI	Own Initiative

OJ	Official Journal (EU)
PCP	Pentachlorophenol
PES	Party of European Socialists
PT	Policy Transfer
QUELROS	Quantified Emissions Limitations and Reduction Objectives
QMV	Qualified Majority Voting (EU)
rDNA	Recombinant DNA
REACH	Registration, Evaluation and Authorization of Chemicals
SEA	Single European Act (EU)
SEM	Single European Market
SO_2	Sulphur Dioxide
SPS	Sanitary and Phytosanitary
TABD	Transatlantic Business Dialogue
TACD	Transatlantic Consumer Dialogue
TAED	Transatlantic Environmental Dialogue
TBT	Technical Barriers to Trade
TEP	Transatlantic Economic Partnership
TEU	(Maastricht) Treaty on European Union (EU)
ToN	Treaty of Nice (EU)
TSCA	Toxic Substances Control Act (US)
UN	United Nations
UNCED	UN Conference on Environment and Development
UNCTAD	United Nations Conference on Trade and Development
UNECE	United Nations Economic Commission for Europe
UNEP	United Nations Environment Programme
USSR	Union of Soviet Socialist Republics
VA	Voluntary Agreement
VAT	Value Added Tax
WEEE	Waste from Electrical and Electronic Equipment (EU Directive)
VOC	Volatile Organic Compound
WWF	World Wide Fund for Nature
WTO	World Trade Organization

Preface

If 'a week is', to use former UK Prime Minister Harold Wilson's well-worn phrase 'a long time in politics', then four years seem like a lifetime in the relatively short history of European integration. On one level, everything is different. Back in 2000–2001 when I was assembling the material for the first edition of this book on European Union (EU) environmental policy, the EU was just coming to terms with the new rules and procedures contained in the Amsterdam Treaty. Now it is about to put into effect revisions agreed at Nice in 2001, and is savouring (or should that be 'worrying about'?) the prospect of implementing a unified European constitution – should it ever, of course, be ratified. Back then there were 15 Member States; now there are 25. Environment was still the dominant frame of reference four years ago; the 2002 Johannesburg Summit made the European Commission DG Environment recognize that sustainability – not only within, but increasingly also outside Europe – was the only effective way to think about the future of EU environmental policy. And in 2000–2001, US–EU environmental relations were tense; now there is a real danger of them escalating into a damaging trade war.

But in many other respects, many things remain the same. Aside from the ten new Member States of Central and Eastern Europe, much the same cast of actors 'make' EU policy today as they did in 2001, although the rules governing their interaction have changed. Many of the challenges also remain the same. In its very first strategic Environmental Policy Review (COM 745, 3-12-03), the European Commission stressed the importance of the three 'I's: policy implementation; integration of environmental concerns into sectoral policies; and public information and involvement. These would not have looked out of place in the Fifth (1993–2000) or even the Fourth (1987) Environmental Action Programmes.

Putting together the second edition of this book has proved both stimulating and a challenge. It has been stimulating to have a reason to read all those papers and book chapters that I had always meant to read but never had time. It has also been a challenge to find 18 chapters that encapsulate the basic 'nuts and bolts' of EU environmental policy, such as the main actors, institutions and legal provisions, but that also look forward to current and future challenges, such as enlargement. On reflection, I therefore decided to reduce the lengths of Parts 1 and 2 of the first edition to create space for fresh material to be added to Parts 4 and 5 of this new edition. Those seeking information on, for example, basic decision rules, would be wise to read some of the initial chapters of the first edition before picking up this one.

This edition contains three specially commissioned chapters on the European Parliament, biotechnology/genetically modified organisms (GMOs) and enlargement. I am extremely grateful to the respective authors for responding eagerly to my invitation to contribute and to my subsequent comments on their first drafts.

I would also like to thank my publishing editor, Jonathan Sinclair Wilson, for giving me the opportunity to have a second go at distilling the essence of EU environmental policy into one book. Finally, thanks to Catherine Day for kindly agreeing to write the Foreword and to David Benson for helping me compile the index.

Andrew Jordan
Norwich
November 2004

Foreword

Catherine Day

Director-General, DG Environment,
European Commission

It is a commonplace that 'the environment knows no borders', but it is no less true for that. When the environment as an issue came to the fore of public debate in the late 1960s and early 1970s, the European Economic Community – as it was then – recognized immediately the significance of cross-border co-operation to address common problems. In 1973, the European Commission presented a first Environment Action Programme that was approved by the Council.

Over 30 years later, the European Union (EU) continues to take the initiative in protecting and restoring our common environment. Benefiting from an array of proposals adopted since then, the Member States of the EU have experienced significant improvements in air and water quality as a consequence of legislation on industrial emissions and waste-water and sewage treatment. Dangerous substances, such as heavy metals, are subject to strict controls. The 1979 Birds Directive – at the heart of the EU's species and habitats protection regime – has just celebrated its 25th anniversary. Indeed, the standards and policies agreed within the EU act as a benchmark against which countries around the world assess and formulate their own environmental polices.

As we learn more about the environment in which we live, the more we realize that new challenges are facing us all the time. In the first Environment Action Programme, climate change was not even on the radar screen. Now, we see it as the single greatest long-term threat facing the global community, and the EU is in the vanguard of discussions at both the European and global level. The EU has argued forcefully and successfully for the ratification of the Kyoto Protocol while recognizing that this is but a first step on the path to combating global warming.

If the issues are changing, so is the public mood. Environmental policy has to be increasingly justified in the language of economics, of costs and benefits. While some see this as a means to thwart the adoption of further environmental legislation, it is increasingly clear that failing to take account of environmental aspects in policy formulation now will only postpone the day of reckoning – a point that is recognized by business as well as government. Fortunately, our increasingly sophisticated understanding of environmental impacts provides us with a sound base from which to counter short-term quick fixes in favour of the long-term goal of sustainable development.

Opinion poll surveys reveal time and time again the widespread public support for EU initiatives that seek to protect the environment. Surveys show that European citizens rank environmental factors as more important than economic or social issues for their quality of life as well as indicating public support for addressing environmental problems at the European level.

I welcome this second edition of *Environmental Policy in the European Union* because it reflects certain guiding principles of the EU's environment policy: environmental aspects must be integrated into other policy areas and information about the policy must be widely available to facilitate its implementation. In doing so, it responds to the appetite of both the general public and the policy-maker to know what decisions are being made, and how they are made, at European level.

1

Introduction: European Union Environmental Policy – Actors, Institutions and Policy Processes

Andrew Jordan

Analytical Puzzles

At its founding in 1957, the European Union (EU) had no environmental policy, no environmental bureaucracy and no environmental laws. The European Economic Community (EEC), as it then was, was primarily an *intergovernmental* agreement between six like-minded states to boost economic prosperity and repair political relations in war-torn Europe. When Britain joined in 1973, the EEC had adopted a very limited number of environmental policies, but they were primarily directed at safeguarding human health and removing internal barriers to trade.

Today, the EU has some of the most progressive environmental policies of any state in the world, despite the fact that it does not possess many of the formal attributes of a sovereign state such as an effective, commonly organized army or a formal constitution. In fact, over the course of the last 40 years, EU environmental policy has gradually expanded to an extent that is unique among international organizations, although of course the EU is not a conventional international organization dominated by states. The purpose of this book is to act as a guide to the history and constituent institutions of EU environmental policy, to explain how the EU makes and implements environmental policy, and to introduce some of the main current and future debates within the academic study of EU public policy and politics to students of environmental management.

One of the more puzzling characteristics of EU environmental policy is its remarkable capacity for steady growth. For the most part, it has been (and remains) largely unaffected by the political and economic vicissitudes, periodic budgetary crises and recurrent waves of Euro-pessimism that have continually frustrated European integration in cognate policy fields such as social, transport or energy policy. Another puzzling feature is that EU environmental policy now adds up to considerably *more* than the sum of national environmental policies. In fact, as far as environmental policy is concerned, the EU currently enjoys powers such as the ability to negotiate externally with other states in international meetings and to levy financial sanctions on those actors (ie states) that do not uphold its laws and policies, that are normally the sole preserve of states. The third analytical puzzle is that the pre-existing environmental policies of the Member States are no longer politically or legally separate from EU environmental policy. In fact, they have undergone a progressive change ('Europeanization') through their involvement in EU policy-making. In other words, the Member States have created an institutional entity to perform certain tasks which has, in turn, deeply affected the way they perceive and act against environmental problems. The relationship between the two main levels – international and national – of this unique system of *multilevel* environmental governance, has been and remains genuinely *two-way*, creating new opportunities and constraints for the various state and non-state actors involved.

An Overview

Against the odds, environmental policy has come a very long way since the EEC adopted the First Environmental Action Programme (EAP) in 1973. This book charts and tries to explain the startling transformation of EU environmental policy from what Philipp Hildebrand in Chapter 2 describes as a series of 'incidental measures' to a sophisticated, multilevel governance system in which policy-making powers are shared between supranational, national and subnational actors (Jordan, 2001; Marks et al, 1996; Sandholtz and Stone Sweet, 1998). Throughout the 1970s and early 1980s, items of EU environmental policy were agreed by the Council of Environment Ministers on the basis of proposals submitted by the Commission. In the 1980s, this bilateral arrangement gradually gave way to a more diffuse web of activities centred on a set of trilateral links between the Council, the Commission and the European Parliament's Environment Committee. Matters which had been successfully contained in discrete intergovernmental committees of national bureaucrats and state-sponsored scientists quickly entered the political mainstream, energizing national and international pressure groups, disrupting national practices and exciting public interest. In turn, these groups have had to be accommodated in the EU policy-making process through extensive systems of consultation, negotiation and lobbying (see Chapter 7). Consequently:

> *Just as policy-making in the Member States can no longer be explained exclusively in national terms, so it is impossible to understand the development of [EU] regulatory policy-making as if the only important political actors were the national governments* (Majone, 1991, p98).

This book draws together in one volume a number of influential accounts of the making of EU environmental policy, written from different disciplinary and theoretical perspectives. The chapters are grouped into five parts. Part 1 ('The Historical and Institutional Context') describes the history and institutions of EU environmental policy, and explains the formal rules for making policy. Different actors (some state, some non-state) work within these rules to attain their policy objectives, as shown in Part 2 ('Actors'). A number of commentators have sought to identify general patterns and processes using theories of national and international politics, which is the subject of Part 3 ('Policy Dynamics'). However, far and away the best (and perhaps the only) way fully to appreciate how the EU environmental policy process really works is to undertake detailed empirical and theoretical studies of 'real-world' political issues and policies. Part 4 ('Making EU Environmental Policy') contains four in-depth case studies of how particular environmental policies were made in the EU. Finally, Part 5 ('Future Challenges') explores a number of old and emerging policy problems and looks forward to the next phase in the development of EU environmental policy. This collection assumes some prior knowledge of the EU. Those entirely new to the study of the EU, or who require a more detailed review of the history, law and institutions of the EU, may therefore wish to start by consulting some of the excellent introductory textbooks on the EU listed in the Further Reading section.

Before moving on, it is important to clarify the meaning of some of the confusingly similar terms used to describe the EU. Until the ratification of the Single European Act (SEA) in 1987, the European Union was officially known as the EEC. The SEA officially re-christened this entity the European Community (EC), a term which remained in popular use until 1993 when the Maastricht Treaty created the European Union with a new, three 'pillar' structure. Strictly speaking, environmental policy is still made within the first 'pillar' of the EU (ie the EC). Although it is still correct to use either EC or EU, most people now use the acronym 'EU' to cover all of its policy responsibilities. Just to confuse matters still further, many of the legal articles of the Treaty referred to in the text below were re-numbered by the 1999 Amsterdam Treaty. So, for example, the environmental Article 130r, s and t (SEA) is now Articles 174–6 of the Amsterdam Treaty, and so on (for a handy summary, see Haigh (2004, Figure 2.1.1)). By and large, the Nice Treaty (Chapter 3) did not disrupt these arrangements, but if it is ever adopted and fully ratified, the EU constitution will make some small changes.

Part 1: The Historical and Institutional Context

It seems almost remarkable today, but the word 'environment' was not even mentioned in the 1957 Treaty of Rome. As Philipp Hildebrand explains in Chapter 2, there was no formal recognition that there might be environmental limits to economic growth, or that environmental factors should be a necessary component of policy-making in cognate sectors such as agriculture and energy. It was only after the surge of environmental awareness in the late 1960s and early 1970s, which culminated in the 1972 United Nations Environment Conference in Stockholm, that the Member States of the EEC started to deal purposively and intensively with the environmental repercussions of European integration.

As is so often the case in Europe, it was the Commission that first seized the initiative, submitting a proposal to the Council of Ministers (CoM) on the need for a formal programme of action. Acting on the political direction of the

European Council of Member State leaders, the Commission subsequently drew up a short but detailed Programme of Action on the Environment in 1973, which covered the period 1973–1976 (OJ, C112, 20.12.73). Although a few legal measures on chemicals had been adopted as long ago as 1967, and other actions were taken to combat noise and vehicle emissions in 1970, this programme is now widely regarded as marking the beginning of a co-ordinated and purposeful European environmental policy. Throughout the 1970s policy continued to develop but in a very ad hoc and incremental manner, according to the whims of different states (Lenschow, 2004; 2005). In many crucial respects, the EEC functioned just like any other international organization. States held a 'double veto' over all affairs: one during the process of policy adoption in the CoM; the other during the subsequent process of implementation (Puchala, 1975, p510). In theory, this two-pronged constraint on the development of the *acquis communautaire* – that is the corpus of principles, policies, laws, treaties and practices adopted by the EU – should have allowed states to cherry-pick their preferred policies. After all, proposals had to secure the support of every state in the CoM before they could be adopted. But this expectation proved to be wide of the mark as EU environmental policy continued its gradual but seemingly continuous accumulation.

Having formally established an environmental role for the EEC in 1972, state leaders moved on to address other, more pressing economic political issues of which there were many. In 1973 the Yom Kippur war broke out and the first oil shock soon followed in its wake. In Europe, the ensuing economic recession coincided with declining levels of political support for political integration (that is the shifting upwards of decision-making powers to supranational bodies) in the wake of the 1965 'empty-chair' crisis. This crisis, which brought Community business to a virtual standstill, was precipitated by the French President General De Gaulle's reluctance to cede more powers to the EU. Politically speaking, the decade from the mid-1970s to the launch of the Single Market Programme in the mid-1980s was a lost 'stagnant epoch' in the history of the EU (Weiler, 1991, p2431. But in much less overtly political areas of policy-making such as the environment, European integration continued slowly to inch forwards. In the 1980s, the trickle of legislation turned into a stream as EU environmental policy underwent a relatively rapid and profound transformation, spurred on by rising levels of public concern for environmental matters in 'greener' states such as Germany, The Netherlands and Denmark.

Philipp Hildebrand shows how the SEA helped both to entrench and formalize the EU's existing involvement by placing environmental policy on a firm legal footing and creating the necessary springboard for the next phase in its development. Crucially, the SEA provided the institutional means to achieve still higher standards by altering the decision rule in the CoM to qualified majority voting for proposals linked to the single market (Article 100a). It also called for greater intersectoral (or environmental policy – see below) integration and for new standards to be based on a high level of protection. These changes were subject to further amendment when states negotiated and ratified the 1993 Maastricht and 1999 Amsterdam Treaties. Andrew Jordan and Jenny Fairbrass (Chapter 3) bring the story right up to date with an analysis of the amendments introduced by the 2001 Nice Treaty. They show that while the Nice Treaty did not make any substantive changes to the 'environmental' parts of the founding treaties, it introduced subtle but potentially important changes to the formal rules governing decision-making. These changes to national voting weights finally entered into force in November 2004. According to Jordan and Fairbrass, when coupled with the recent Eastern enlargement of the EU in May 2004, they may alter the balance of political power in the CoM towards those states favouring the status quo (ie against new and more environmentally ambitious policies).

Part 2: Actors

The system of rules described in Part 1 comprises the legal 'hardware' of EU environmental policy. However, the development of the environmental *acquis* has often run ahead of the formal (ie state-directed) process of amending the founding treaties, inviting us to speculate about whether and to what extent this sequence of changes was ever fully under state control. In order to explain this puzzle, analysts must first examine the motives and activities of the different actors that populate the institutional venues of EU policy-making. In the 1970s, the cast list of actors was a relatively short one. Political leaders paid little sustained attention to environmental issues and European environmental pressure groups were conspicuous by their absence. Nigel Haigh (1996) has described the early 1970s as the 'dark ages' of EU environmental policy, when unanimous voting meant standards developed at the pace of the most reluctant state or coalition of states. Supranational institutional and legal structures were weakly developed and in several key respects EEC environmental policy functioned like a normal international organization, with lowest common denominator decision-making in the CoM. By the early 1980s, there were only around 60 legislative texts dealing with the environment.

However, beneath the surface a series of powerful 'subterranean mutations' were gradually shifting the delicate balance of political power between states and supranational bodies (Weiler, 1991, p2408). Weiler argues that a gradual extension of Community competence in areas of 'low politics' produced a powerful political undertow:

> *The momentum [of political integration] was directed at a range of ancillary issues, such as environmental policy, consumer protection, energy and research, all important of course, but a side game all the same. Yet, although these were not taken very seriously in substance (and maybe because of that) each ... represented part of the brick-by-brick demolition of the wall circumscribing Community competences* (ibid, p2446).

These processes most certainly did not emerge by chance. The founders of the EEC, notably Jean Monnet and Robert Schuman, firmly believed that the cause of political integration would be best served if the EEC's bureaucratic arm, the European Commission, focused its limited energies and political power on building transnational co-operation in areas of 'low politics' like environmental, health and safety or internal market policy. By employing the 'Monnet method' to pursue

'European integration by stealth' (see Chapters 8 and 18), the Commission hoped that enthusiasm for European solutions would eventually 'spill over' into more sensitive areas such as the economy and foreign and defence policy where state support for deeper integration was weak or non-existent. In these most technical of policy areas, the Commission found it could work up proposals for new European legislation relatively unsupervised by pressure groups and national bureaucracies. With some notable exceptions, democratic oversight by the European Parliament (see Chapter 6) and national parliaments remained weak and inconsistent. Every now and again a particular proposal would provoke conflict between states, but for the most part, the EEC remained a very weakly developed polity. National pressure groups concentrated on domestic affairs because that was where the locus of environmental policy was thought to lie (Chapter 7).

Although the environmental *acquis* expanded to fill the political space created by the Monnet method, overriding legal constraints meant that the aims of very early environmental measures such as the common classification, labelling and packaging of dangerous substances, remained relatively modest in the sense that they did not depart significantly from the EEC's core mission, which was to achieve a common market in goods and services. But in the 1980s, the number of policies began to expand much more rapidly, rising to over 200 by 1987. Moreover, many of the new policies, which related inter alia to seals, natural habitats, sewage treatment, genetically modified organisms and climate change, went well 'beyond any conceivable standards that would be strictly necessitated by a concern to ensure a single functioning market' (see Weale, Chapter 8). The Commission successfully took the standards promoted by the leader states and used them to build a set of proposals for common European legislation that went considerably further than the lowest common denominator of state preferences. It was neither the most elegant nor the most rapid way of making joint decisions; rather, an odd but highly potent mixture of opportunism and political pragmatism. But gradually, 'active [entrepreneurship] combined with the use of Treaty games [whereby] the Commission "picked" the legal basis for its proposals according to procedure rather than substance' gradually generated an extensive corpus of common policies (Lenschow, 2005). The environmental *acquis* now comprises well over 500 legislative items and, until recently, was one of the fastest-growing areas of EU activity. Between 1989 and 1991 the EU adopted more environmental statutes than in the previous 20 years combined.

What explains the sudden step change in the scope and stringency of the EU environmental policy that occurred in the period after the mid-1980s? Many chapters of this book contain examples of the 'greener' (or 'leader') states such as Germany, The Netherlands and Denmark pushing the EU to adopt standards that are as high if not higher than their own national standards. Having unilaterally adopted high standards in their own territories, these states had an obvious incentive to share the political and economic pain (as well as reap 'first mover' advantages) by 'exporting' them to other, less environmentally progressive EU states. In Chapter 4, Duncan Liefferink and Mikael Skou Andersen describe the various mechanisms used by 'leader' states to achieve this. In the southern Member States, the pressure to conform to increasingly stringent environmental standards pursued by the northern states has often felt like a 'cold if bracing wind from the north' (Pridham, 2002, 96). While, as Pridham (2002) and others (eg Börzel, 2002) have claimed, the Mediterranean states are not as environmentally 'backward' or 'laggardly' as is sometimes assumed, basic deficiencies in their domestic environmental management systems have undoubtedly left them struggling to keep up in the regulatory 'competition' to set environmental standards in Europe (see Chapter 10).

The European Court of Justice (ECJ) has also played an important but greatly overlooked role in raising and also maintaining high environmental standards in the EU. In Chapter 5, Ida Koppen usefully describes how important Court rulings in the 1960s and in 1970 helped to legitimize the Commission's opportunistic activities, create new entry points for the European Parliament (EP) and tighten the legal framework of compliance with EU rules. Although it was originally very weakly represented, the European Parliament's role has also grown substantially since the late 1970s, to the extent where it shares responsibility for setting new standards with the CoM under a complicated institutional procedure known as co-decision-making. As Charlotte Burns explains in Chapter 6, the EP has fought to become a persistently powerful advocate of higher environmental standards in Europe. It has done so by utilizing both formal (ie Treaty changes) and more informal means at its disposal. In so doing, it has opened up the EU policy process to actors (eg environmental pressure groups) that would otherwise have been neglected or deliberately excluded. Finally, national environmental pressure groups have, as Sonia Mazey and Jeremy Richardson explain in Chapter 7, also successfully learned to exploit the political opportunities presented by European integration to achieve considerably higher environmental standards than might otherwise have emerged through nationally focused action.

Part 3: Policy Dynamics

Putting these different actors together with the rules and the institutions described in Part 1 produces an extremely complicated and dynamic picture, which does not correspond to any commonly accepted model of how policy is made in sovereign states (Richardson, 2001). In Chapter 8, Albert Weale tries to make sense of the whole. He concludes that the process is too densely populated with veto players (ie actors whose views have to be taken into account) for any actor or group of actors (including states) consistently to dictate the direction of political and economic integration. More often than not, detailed case studies of individual EU environmental standards reveal them to be 'the aggregated and transformed standards of their original champions modified under the need to secure political accommodation from the powerful veto players'. In other words, they bear some resemblance to pre-existing national standards, but are rarely totally similar to any national model, ie the overall picture resembles what Héritier (2002) refers to as a constantly evolving 'policy patchwork' which cannot easily be absorbed into national systems without some prior adjustment.

In order to identify and test underlying explanations, EU scholars have employed different explanatory theories. At first, the main question which preoccupied them was whether and to what extent state and/or non-state actors controlled the expansion of the environmental *acquis*. In an early contribution, Rehbinder and Stewart argued that it was not states (who remained fairly passive), but the very supranational agents that they had established to perform relatively routine tasks, that engineered the shift in governance described above:

> *Using a pragmatic, incrementalist approach and concentrating on problems where the benefits of common action were evident, [the Community institutions] have, step by step, established a network of ... legislative texts for the protection of the environment, thereby creating a mosaic of precedents ... which will be hard to overrule. The deficiencies in the legal basis ... were compensated by the polit-ical will of the Member States* (Rehbinder and Stewart, 1985, p400).

Other commentators fundamentally disagreed with this interpretation, believing that the *acquis* represents the lowest common denominator of state preferences (Huelshoff and Pfeiffer, 1991). In Chapter 9, Anthony Zito weighs the evidence in support of both sides. Not surprisingly, he finds no clear 'winner'. Instead, some theories appear to work better at certain levels and stages of the policy pro-cess than at others. Specifically, macro-level theories such as intergovernmental-ism appear to offer a more credible account of the creation of a new policy area such as the environment, whereas meso-level theories such as policy networks or aspects of the new institutionalism are more appropriately used if the aim is to understand the genesis and administrative implementation of specific directives or regulations.

In recent years, attention has shifted from studying the creation and develop-ment of the EU to its internal operation as a rapidly maturing political and eco-nomic system. Under the banner of 'multilevel governance' (Jordan, 2001), scholars have sought to import standard tools and concepts (eg policy learning and transfer, policy convergence and co-ordination) from mainstream political science and public policy, and apply them to the EU. Examples of this type of work can be found in Chapters 14, 16 and 17. The overall pattern, therefore, is one in which EU analysis is being progressively 'normalized' ie brought into the mainstream of political science.

Chapter 10 is typical of the governance 'turn' in EU scholarship. Instead of studying how the Member States have affected the (creation and functioning of) the EU, Tanja Börzel turns the analytical telescope the other way and asks 'how has the EU's patchwork of environmental policy affected its Member States?' This question provides the analytical starting point for a rapidly developing body of literature which seeks to analyse the causes and consequences of Europeaniza-tion (for a recent review, see Jordan and Liefferink (2004)). Börzel successfully reveals that in the environmental sector, Europeanization is neither an entirely top-down nor a bottom-up process, but a complex amalgam of the two. However, detailed empirical work reveals that there are patterns in the data. On this basis, she differentiates between 'pace-setters' (ie states like Sweden, Austria, Germany and Denmark that have the capacity both to shape the EU and implement its pol-icies) and 'foot-draggers' like Portugal, Greece, Spain and Italy (whose capacity to shape the EU and implement its common policies is relatively weak). Drawing on an impressive range of empirical examples, she shows that, with some exceptions, this line-up of pace-setters and foot-draggers has remained relatively constant since the dawn of EU environmental policy. As well as explaining one of the most significant and ensuring motors of EU environmental politics (namely differences in inter-state preferences), she also goes some way towards explaining how these feed back and alter Member State responses ('Europeanization'). As important, if not more so, is her more policy-relevant claim that these basic differences arise from differences in economic wealth that are not easily washed away by several decades of European integration. To try (as the EU has) to secure a common set of environmental policies is to risk exacerbating these basic capacity problems. Ultimately, this may produce a forceful backlash as the willingness of some states to comply with common standards declines. Given this, she suggests, the EU must learn to accept a less harmonized and more differentiated form of environmental policy.

Part 4: Making Environmental Policy

In an effort better to understand the process through which day-to-day policy is made, EU scholars have continued to look at how key pieces of legislation emerge on the political agenda, are bargained over and then implemented. The chapters in Part 4 give a brief flavour of the directions in which this sort of work is going in relation to a number of politically salient issue areas. Thus in Chapter 11, Lee Ann Patterson and Tim Josling analyse the politics emerging around influential new biotechnologies, in particular genetically modified foods and feed products. They show that the EU has adopted a somewhat different approach to regulating these new technologies from that of its main trading partner, the US. They show that this issue area is densely populated with many different types of actors. States, while dominant, struggle to manage the multilevel interactions that have emerged in the last decade or so. The authors uncover the roots of the growing conflict between these two trading blocs and then propose their own solution, drawing upon different types of product labelling devices.

Interestingly, the only chapter in Part 4 to find strong evidence of supranational entrepreneurship by the Commission is Alberta Sbragia's (Chapter 12) on the EU as an emerging international environmental actor. As well as dealing with environmental problems within its own borders, she explains that the EU has also steadily enhanced its role in global environmental policy-making ('parallelism' in EU speak). Picking up on points aired in Chapters 5 and 8, she identifies the ECJ as a prime mover in granting the Commission a stronger external presence. In developing the doctrine of implied (or 'parallel') powers, the Court effectively rejected a state-sanctioned approach to integration. Thereafter, the Community's powers could expand automatically, even without the express approval of the Member States (Nollkaemper, 1987). Although the Commission's environmental directorate, DG Environment, does not (at least yet) enjoy quite the same level of responsibility (or competence) as the Trade Directorate (which represents rather than sits alongside the Member States in international trade negotiations), the emergence of the EU as a creative force in international environmental diplomacy must rank as one of its greatest and most unexpected achievements since 1970.

Throughout the late 1990s and early 2000s, US–EU relations re-emerged as a focal point of political and economic conflict. In Chapter 13, David Vogel argues that in the 1970s and 1980s, the main source of conflict was the differential between the standards set by the US and the EU. At this time, he writes, 'American regulatory standards tended to be more stringent, comprehensive and innovative than in individual European countries or in the European Union.' But, starting in the late 1980s, the US and the EU have gradually 'traded places', with policy innovation increasingly being confined to Europe. Across a broad array of different issue areas from food safety through to climate change and waste recycling, 'the locus of policy innovation … has passed from the United States to Europe.' In a wide-ranging assessment, he argues that the precautionary principle has become a lightning conductor for a number of emerging transatlantic political disputes in relation to these topics (Jordan, 2001). He identifies the underlying roots of these conflicts and suggests how they may evolve in the future. More controversially, in a re-statement of the classical cyclical model of environmental policy first expounded by Downs (Downs, 1972), he argues that that the current period of environmental policy innovation in Europe will gradually peter out, just as it did in the US in the 1980s. In other words, at the same time as environmentalists in Europe are eagerly anticipating the dawning of a new era of ecological modernization, the steady accumulation of regulatory costs and increasing policy gridlock within Brussels will be gradually turning off the taps of new policy initiatives. There is, as Charlotte Burns shows in Chapter 6, already some evidence that EU environmental policy is experiencing a backlash, in which economic and competitiveness concerns are gradually rising to the fore in relation to the Lisbon process of economic renewal and the recent (2004) appointment of a pro-economy Commission, headed by the former Portugese politician, José Manuel Barroso.

Finally, in Chapter 14 Chad Damro and Pilar Luaces Méndez employ theories of policy learning and transfer to explain recent changes in US and EU climate change policies. Climate change is one of, if not the most, pressing environmental issues today. But while the EU has adopted a precautionary stance embracing ambitious emissions reduction targets, the US has effectively exited the main international environmental agreement, the 1997 Kyoto Protocol. However, beneath the surface, Damro and Luaces find evidence of more complex patterns of policy innovation and inertia. In particular, they show how the EU has significantly shifted position from a position of initially (and very strongly) opposing the adoption of a US-sponsored policy tool (termed 'emissions trading') that will allow polluters to buy and sell greenhouse gas emissions, to being its most enthusiastic and committed advocate. In fact, the EU has undergone such a significant Damascene conversion to this tool that it has just (2005) implemented a pan-European emissions trading system of its own, well in advance of UN agreement on its use at a global level. The evidence presented in this chapter strongly suggests (cf Vogel, Chapter 13) that the EU's capacity to implement environmental innovations – at least in this sub-sector – is alive and well.

Part 5: Future Challenges

Irrespective of their theoretical position, most analysts now agree that EU environmental policy has come a very long way since the 1970s. Politicians both national and European are also all too ready to proclaim environmental policy as one of the EU's greatest 'success stories' (Lenschow, 2004). But in spite of the progress made, several important challenges remain. These include enlargement, (environmental) policy integration and implementation (for a comprehensive and self-critical stocktake, see the First (2003) *Environmental Policy Review* (COM (2003) 745, 3-12-03)).

In Chapter 15, Stacy VanDeveer and Jo Ann Carmin unpack and explore the various challenges posed by the EU's recent expansion from 15 to 25 Member States. The EU is a constantly expanding political entity, having started out in life as a six-country economic trading bloc. But Chapter 15 shows that simply in terms of speed and scale, the 2004 enlargement was several orders of magnitude more complex than anything that had gone before. The authors show that enlargement has severely challenged the new entrant states by forcing them to invest in new institutional, technological and administrative capital to cope with the environmental *acquis*. The transposition of the *acquis* is, they claim, largely on track to be achieved, but time will tell whether the ten new states can implement it in practice as well as the EU 15. Above and beyond these immediate challenges, the new Member States face an uphill struggle to integrate themselves into and make the most effective use of the complex decision-making arrangement in the EU.

However, VanDeveer and Carmin are at pains to argue that the challenges posed by enlargement work both ways: ie enlargement calls for adjustments to be made within the EU 15 as well as in the new entrants. Thus at the same time as the new states are struggling to adapt to the EU, the EU is struggling to adapt itself to the political demands and practices of the new Member States. This applies as much to the internal operation of the European Commission and the European Parliament (see Chapter 6), as it does to the highly formalized process of policy decision-making in the Council of Ministers. In the medium-to-long term, enlargement will significantly increase the pressure on the EU to overhaul politically important but also environmentally damaging common policies such as the structural funds and the Common Agricultural Policy. It will doubtless add to recent calls (reviewed and interrogated in the recent White Paper on Governance (COM (2001) 428, 25-7-01), for EU policy to become less prescriptive, less intrusive, less harmonized and more flexible in its incorporation of national circumstances and peculiarities. So, one way or another, EU environmental policy looks set to remain in a state of flux well after the completion of the formal arrangements in 2004.

A second challenge is how best to ensure that *all* the EU's activities (and not just the environmental *acquis cummunautaire*) take account of and support fully the achievements of its environmental policy via a step-wise process known as 'environmental policy integration' (Jordan and Lenschow, 2000; Lenschow, 2002; Schout and Jordan, 2005). In Chapter 16, Andrea Lenschow reveals that the first 30 years of EU policy were arguably spent crafting an identifiable environmental policy. That task is close to being completed. However, since the 1970s environmentalism has gradually mutated into the more diffuse and politically complicated concept popularly known as 'sustainability'. This change has forced many actors, including the EU, to devise sustainability strategies and policies (see COM (2001) 264, 15-5-01). The EU's sustainable development strategy is supposed to work in tandem with the Sixth EAP (2002–2012), which, like its predecessor the Fifth EAP, adopts a thematic rather than a sectoral approach to environmental issues. A series of thematic strategies covering cross-cutting challenges such as soil protection, marine environment and air quality are currently being prepared in consultation with relevant stakeholders. These are underpinned by several strategic (or 'horizontal') co-ordination measures (for details, see Kraemer et al (2002) and Jordan et al (2005)). Evidently, the days when the European Commission moved incrementally, deliberately avoiding societal debate to push through joint policies (the 'Monnet method' – see above) are very much on the wane.

Sustainable development challenges the advocates of strong environmental rules to be less isolated and introspective in their outlook by building alliances with actors in cognate policy domains. It entails much greater societal dialogue and more open and critical self-reflection on behalf of the European Commission. More specifically, sustainability means finding ways to integrate the environmental *acquis* into the wider and long-term political, social and economic priorities of the EU (EEA, 2004): not easy. Andrea Lenschow argues that environmental policy integration (EPI) provides a handy 'first-order operational principle to implement and institutionalize the idea of sustainable development' in the EU. She notes that the 1992 Fifth EAP (1993–2000) marked a turning point in the EU's attempt to achieve EPI, but explains that there are many significant obstacles to further progress, not least the unwillingness of most 'non'-environmental sectors to share responsibility for remedying environmental damage with the environmental sector. Interestingly, she proposes a 'belt-and-braces' approach in which 'new governance' approaches such as reporting, target-setting, peer review and benchmarking exercises, are combined with the 'old governance' tools of regulation and subsidies (to compensate the losers) so as to ensure that EPI is implemented where it is most needed. The oft-heard claims that the EU should become less involved in regulating societal affairs (see the EU White Paper on Governance – above) (ie more governance), should, she implies, be treated with caution as governance and government are (potentially) mutually reinforcing.

Either way, as the legal and political pressure for greater EPI continues to ebb and flow (witness the changing political fortunes of the Cardiff process of integration reporting and target-setting (see COM (2004) 394 final)), the axis of future political conflict in Europe will continue to become more and more inter-sectoral in nature (eg Environment Council vs Agriculture Council), and less inter-actor (eg Commission vs Council of Ministers). This should create interesting new political alliances, possibly spanning the traditional state–supranational (eg the CoM vs the Commission or the Parliament) divide. If the 1980s and 1990s were dominated by conflicts between different *levels* of governance, then the 2000s look set to be characterized by more and more conflicts between different *parts* of the Commission and different sectoral formations of the Councils of Ministers, much as they do at the national level. This is not necessarily a bad thing. In fact, it will demonstrate that the EU has matured into a political system that shares many similarities with national systems.

The third problem is how to improve the implementation of EU environmental policy at the national level. Jordan (2002) argues that because EU policy is 'European' – ie born of ideas and practices plucked from many states – and not purely 'national', it is more likely to be refracted and mutated when it is implemented in the diverse political and legal circumstances of the Member States. Echoing points raised by Tanja Börzel in Chapter 10, he explains why EU policy is particularly prone to implementation 'deficits' or 'gaps', and appraises the Commission's recent efforts to address them. One (possible) response is to adopt more and more 'new' environmental policy instruments (NEPIs) in preference to regulation. NEPIs include emission trading systems (see, for example, Chapter 14), as well as eco-labels, voluntary agreements and eco-taxes (Jordan et al, 2003). However, their use at EU level has been constrained by a number of factors, not least the requirement (preserved by the Nice Treaty) for unanimity in the Environment Council for eco-taxes (see below). There are, of course, various funding streams that finance environmental investments, for example the structural and cohesion funds, and the Common Agricultural Policy (notably the European Agricultural Guidance and Guarantee Fund – the EAGGF). Crucially, however, none of these is directly controlled by the Commission's DG Environment.

So how well prepared is the EU to overcome these challenges? On the face of it, the EU is in remarkably good shape: the environmental *acquis* is much more deeply rooted in the law and institutions of the EU, and the national societies of the Member States, than it ever was in the early 1970s; DG Environment is pursuing ambitious and politically daring solutions to emerging challenges such as climate change, biodiversity loss and the development of biotechnologies; and many old laws are now in the process of being adapted and updated (most notably chemicals policy via a complex process known as REACH – Registration, Evaluation and Authorization of Chemicals (COM (2001) 88)). But important – some would say fundamental – weaknesses remain in the EU's modus operandi. In Chapter 18, Albert Weale argues that until now, the environmental *acquis* has tended to develop 'by stealth' rather than via a series of strategic decisions explicitly taken by political leaders. Commission officials have, as described in Parts 1 and 2, become adept at working behind the scenes in technical committees, employing the 'Monnet method'. This may have successfully produced an impressively large corpus of environmental policies, but it is 'pervaded by pathologies'. Thus, for Weale, the EU is very good at doing some things, but weak at doing others. Unfortunately, the problem is that it is now being prevented (mainly by states) from doing more of the things it is good at, while continuing to do the things it is weaker at.

Consider, for example, the adoption of NEPIs. In Chapter 17, Jordan et al assess the extent to which promises dating back to the late 1980s to adopt more NEPIs and less regulation have been realized in practice. They find that NEPIs have not supplanted regulation in the EU, largely because of opposition from Member States and other actors. In fact, they show that regulation remains the main instrument of choice in the EU, although there has been significant NEPI adoption at national and subnational levels. On balance, the EU's ability to innovate in relation to the selection and adoption of instruments is quite modest; '[t]he most significant strides in the use of 'soft' NEPI innovation seem to be occurring in particular Member States'. Consider also the struggle to implement

EPI. Thus, of the three main modes of policy co-ordination (markets, hierarchies and networks), the Commission is under political pressure to make significantly less use of one of these (hierarchy) by adopting less regulation, and continues to lack the legal competence to adopt new, market-based instruments such as eco-taxes. So, almost by default, the Commission is driven to rely on cross-sectoral networks, which it has neither the political nor the legal resources to create and sustain. Consequently, the Member States continue to look to the Commission to take the lead on EPI, at the same time as the DG Environment is telling them that successful integration requires simultaneously co-ordinated actions at the national level (Schout and Jordan, 2005; Jordan and Schout, 2006). The end result is a dialogue of the deaf.

So what EU environmental policy really needs at the dawn of a new millennium is a genuinely thoroughgoing debate about its structure and purpose to prepare itself fully for the transition to sustainability. Lenschow (2004) even goes so far as to suggest that the EU has reached a 'crossroads', where such a debate can no longer be evaded. The unfortunate paradox is that until now, EU environmental policy has expanded by avoiding, delaying or finding ways of working around profound questions such as these. One could even argue that it has become too good at 'muddling through' problems in its youth easily to embrace the more strategic and comprehensive approach to future problem-solving now being demanded by the sustainability agenda. Time will tell whether the EU has the capability to unlearn the habits of the past in order to adjust to the progressive politics of sustainable development in an enlarging Europe.

References

Börzel, T. (2002) *On Environmental Leaders and Laggards in the EU: Why There is (Not) a Southern Problem*, Aldershot: Ashgate.

Downs, A. (1972) 'Up and Down with Ecology: The Issue Attention Cycle', *Public Interest*, Vol.28, pp38–50.

EEA (European Environment Agency) (2004) *Environmental Policy Integration: Looking Back, Thinking Ahead*, Copenhagen: European Environment Agency.

Haigh, N. (1996) 'A Green Agenda for the IGC: The Future of EU Environmental Policy', paper presented at a conference at Kings College, London, March, copy available from Institute of European Environmental Policy, 52 Horseferry Road, London SW1P 2AG.

Haigh, N. (ed) (2004) *Manual of Environmental Policy*, Leeds: Maney Publishing.

Héritier, A. (2002) 'The Accommodation of Diversity in European Policy-making and its Outcomes: Regulatory Policy as a Patchwork' in Jordan, A. (ed) *Environmental Policy in European Union*, London: Earthscan.

Huelshoff, M. and Pfeiffer, T. (1991) 'Environmental Policy in the EC: Neo-functionalist Sovereignty Transfer or Neo-realist Gatekeeping?' *International Journal*, Vol.47, pp136–158.

Jordan, A. (2001) 'The European Union: An Evolving System of Multi-level Governance... or Government?', *Policy and Politics*, Vol.29, No.2, April, pp193–208.

Jordan, A. (2002) 'The Implementation of EU Environmental Policy: A Policy Problem without a Political Solution?', in Jordan, A. (ed) *Environmental Policy in European Union*, London: Earthscan.

Jordan, A. and Lenschow, A. (2000) '"Greening" the European Union: What Can Be Learned from the Leaders of EU Environmental Policy?', *European Environment*, Vol.10, No.3, pp109–120.

Jordan, A. and Liefferink, D. (eds) (2004) *Environmental Policy in Europe: the Europeanization of National Environmental Policy*, London: Routledge.

Jordan, A. and Schout, A. (2006) *The Coordination of the European Union: Exploring the Capacities for Networked Governance*, Oxford: Oxford University Press.

Jordan, A., Wurzel, R. and Zito, A. (eds) (2003) *New Instruments of Environmental Governance*, London: Frank Cass.

Kraemer, A. et al (2002) *EU Environmental Governance: A Benchmark of Policy Instruments*, Berlin/London: Ecologic/IEEP.

Lenschow, A. (ed) (2002) *Environmental Policy Integration*, London: Earthscan.

Lenschow, A. (2004) 'Environmental Policy: At a Crossroads' in Green Cowles, M. and Dinan, D. (eds) *Developments in the European Union 2*, Basingstoke: Palgrave.

Lenschow, A. (2005) 'Environmental Policy', in Wallace, H., Wallace W. and Pollack, M. (eds) *Policy Making in the European Union* (5e), Oxford: Oxford University Press.

Majone, G. (1991) 'Cross-national Sources of Regulatory Policy-making in Europe and the US', *Journal of Public Policy*, Vol.11, Part 1, pp79–106.

Marks, G., Scharpf, F., Schmitter, P. and Streek, W. (1996) *Governance in the EU*, London: Sage.

Nollkaemper, A. (1987) 'The European Community and International Environmental Co-operation: Legal Issues of External Community Business', *Legal Issues of European Integration*, Vol.2, pp55–91.

Pridham, G. (2002) 'National Environmental Policy Making in the European Framework: Spain, Greece and Italy in Comparison', in Jordan, A. (ed) *Environmental Policy in the European Union*, London: Earthscan.

Puchala, D. (1975) 'Domestic Politics and Regional Harmonisation in the European Communities', *World Politics*, Vol.27, pp496–520.

Rehbinder, E. and Stewart, R. (1985) 'Legal Integration in Federal Systems: European Community Environmental Law', *The American Journal of Comparative Law*, Vol.33, pp37–447.

Richardson, J. (ed) (2001) *European Union: Power and Policy Making* (2e), London: Routledge.

Sandholtz, W. and Stone Sweet, A. (1998) *Supranational Governance: the Instutionalization of the European Union*, Cambridge, MA: MIT Press.

Schout, A. and Jordan, A. (2005) 'Co-ordinating European Governance: Self-organising or Centrally Steered?' *Public Administration*, Vol.83, No.1, pp201–220.

Weiler, J. (1991) 'The Transformation of Europe', *The Yale Law Journal*, Vol.100, pp2403–2483.

Part 1
THE HISTORICAL AND INSTITUTIONAL CONTEXT

2

The European Community's Environmental Policy, 1957 to '1992': From Incidental Measures to an International Regime?

Philip M. Hildebrand

This chapter describes and analyses the evolution of the European Community's (EC's) environmental policy. The chosen time frame covers the period from January 1958, when the Treaty of Rome came into effect, to '1992', the target date for the completion of the Single European Act (SEA) which entered into force on 1 July 1987.[1]

It is often stated that, prior to 1973, there was no EC environmental policy. In principle this assessment is correct. Nevertheless, a number of pieces of environmental legislation had been adopted during that period. For that reason and in order to present an historically and analytically complete picture, the entire period will be assessed here.

At the outset it is necessary to ask two questions. First, how did the EC environmental policy evolve? Second, what were the determining factors of this evolution? At a time when the EC's environmental policies are increasingly being followed by the public, private corporations as well as various interest groups (Sands, 1990, p2), it is important to gain a thorough understanding of the historic evolution of European[2] environmental policies as a whole. The introduction of the Single European Act has brought about significant changes. Yet, relatively little has been written on the subject and, although '1992' has become every European's catchword, few seem to be aware of the potential environmental consequences of these recent developments.

Before laying out the structure of this chapter, it is necessary to discuss briefly the legal instruments that the relevant Community institutions are equipped with, in 'order to carry out their task'.[3] They are applicable to all issue areas within the competence of the European Community and have not been changed by the amendments introduced by the Single European Act or the Maastricht Treaty creating the European Union. Article 189 of the European Economic Community (EEC) Treaty sets out five different types of legal instruments. The first paragraph states: 'In order to carry out their task the Council and the Commission shall, in accordance with the provisions of this Treaty, make regulations, issue directives, take decisions, make recommendations or deliver opinions.' The last two have no binding force and should therefore not 'properly be regarded as legislative instruments' (Haigh, 1990, p2).

A regulation has general application and is 'binding in its entirety and directly applicable in all Member States' (Article 189/2). It has generally been used for precise purposes such as financial matters or the daily management of the Common Agricultural Policy (CAP). Only rarely has it been used for environmental matters (Haigh, 1990, p2).

A directive is 'binding, as to the result to be achieved', while it leaves it to the national authorities as to the 'choice of form and method' (Article 189/3). According to Nigel Haigh, 'it is therefore the most appropriate instrument for more general purposes particularly where some flexibility is required to accommodate existing national procedures and, for this reason, is the instrument most commonly used for environmental matters' (Haigh, 1990, p2).[4]

Finally a decision is 'binding in its entirety upon those to whom it is addressed' (Article 189/4). With respect to environmental protection, decisions have been used in connection with international conventions and with certain procedural matters.

For analytical purposes I have divided the period to be covered here into three different phases. The first one begins with the entry into force of the Treaty of Rome and the establishment of the European Economic Community in 1957 and ends in 1972 with the Stockholm Conference on the Human Environment. With the approval of the first Community Action Programme on the Environment by the Council of Ministers in November 1973, the second phase begins which, according to this chronology, lasts until the adoption of the Single European Act in Luxembourg in December 1985. On 17 and 28 February the SEA was signed in Luxembourg and The Hague and, after ratification by the 12 national parliaments (and referenda in Denmark and Ireland), it came into force on 1 July 1987. The ratification of the SEA represents the onset of the third phase, in the midst of which the European Community's environmental policy is presently unfolding.[5]

I have attempted to describe and label each of the three phases in a distinct manner. According to this typology, the first one, from 1956 to 1972 is best understood as a time of pragmatic measures as opposed to proper policy. The overriding objective of the European Community during that time was to harmonize laws in order to abolish trade impediments between the Member States. The pieces of environmental legislation that were adopted throughout those years were, as one observer has described them, 'incidental' to the overriding economic objectives (McGrory, 1990, p304).

After 1972 one begins to witness the emergence of an EC environmental policy. Specific actions and measures were initiated in a response to a number of circumstances and events. First, mounting public protest against environmental destruction exerted a considerable degree of pressure upon elected government officials. This pressure, in turn, seems to have had a positive effect on the dynamics and innovation of official EC policy. Second, during the 1970s and the early 1980s the world was witness to a number of environmental disasters which provided a dramatic backdrop to the emerging environmental sensitivity. Last but by no means least, Member States became concerned about unco-ordinated local environmental protection measures causing intra-community trade distortions.

With the third phase, which essentially coincides with the SEA, EC environmental policy becomes more substantive. The Title VII amendment to the original Treaty of Rome introduced important new ideas and methods of environmental policy. Within this context, it is important to keep a proper perspective and avoid a sense of 'Europhoria'. The new provisions of the Single European Act are, although potentially far-reaching, rather abstract. Dirk Vandermeersch (1957, p407) describes them as giving a 'constitutional' base to the Community's environmental policy, and as defining its objectives. Nigel Haigh and David Baldock (1989, p20) take this line of thought one step further arguing that, depending on how one views the relevant articles of Title VII, they may 'do no more than legitimize what was happening anyway'. Yet, at the end, their final judgement is a positive one. They conclude that the new provisions contain interesting elements and result in subtle consequences.

This brings me to the concept of an international regime, to which I referred in the title of this chapter. Throughout the past decade, a significant amount of international relations and political science literature has been concerned with the concept of international regimes. As a result, a whole range of different definitions and approaches has emerged. Arguably, the most promising path is the one that perceives an international regime as a form of international institution or 'persistent and connected sets of rules (formal and informal) that prescribe behavioural roles, constrain activity, and shape expectations' (Keohane, 1989, p3). Within this tradition, Robert Keohane defines international regimes as institutions with explicit rules, agreed upon by governments, that pertain to particular sets of issues in international relations'. Similarly, Oran Young (1992, p165) defines international regimes as 'institutional arrangements that deal with specific issue areas'.

Another recent and related definition stems from Otto Keck (1991, p637) who views an international regime as an institutional arrangement for the collective management of problematic interdependencies of action, meaning problems that simultaneously touch upon the interests of several states and that cannot, or can only inadequately, be resolved by individual states without resorting to co-ordination or co-operation with other states.[6] Applying this kind of concept of an international regime to the EC's environmental policy allows us to embark upon a dynamic analysis. Regimes do not just come into existence; they develop over time. The same applies to the EC's environmental policy. This development takes place via a process of increasing institutionalization, which is the gradual recognition of participants that their behaviour reflects, to a considerable extent, the established rules, norms and conventions and that its meaning is interpreted in light of this recognition (Keohane, 1989, p1).

Throughout the following discussion of the evolution of the environmental policy of the European Community I shall pause at the end of each of the three phases mentioned above in order to assess to what extent this process of institutionalization can be said to have taken place. In the conclusion I shall briefly address the question of the benefits of using a regime or institutional framework in an analysis of the European Community's environmental policy.

1957–1972: 'Incidental' Measures

When the Treaty of Rome, establishing the European Economic Community (EEC), was signed on 25 March 1957, it did not include any explicit reference to the idea of environmental policy or environmental protection. The primary aim of the six founding Member States was to establish a 'common market' in which goods, people, services and capital could move without obstacles (Article 3). There are two articles in the original treaty that can be regarded as a direct indicator that, as Rolf Wägenbaur (1990, p16) has pointed out, 'the ambitions of the founding fathers went far beyond' the objective of the common market. First, Article 2 of the Treaty of Rome calls for the promotion throughout the Community of 'a harmonious development of economic activities, a continuous and balanced expansion, an increase in stability, an accelerated raising of the standard of living and closer relations between the states belonging to it'. The Community institutions tend to interpret this mandate to include not only an improved standard of living but also an improved quality of life (Rehbinder and Stewart, 1985, p21). Although this interpretation, which suggests that environmental protection might be among the Community's objectives, is not uncontroversial, the general view of the literature seems to be that it is 'reasonable to interpret the Preamble and Article 2 of the EEC Treaty as including economic concepts of environmental pollution, such as those of external cost and of the environment as a common good' (Rehbinder and Stewart, 1985, p21).

Secondly, Article 36 refers, at least implicitly, to the protection of the environment. It states that it is justifiable to restrict imports, exports or goods in transit on grounds of 'public morality, public policy or public security; the protection of health and life of humans, animals or plants; the protection of national treasures possessing artistic, historic or archaeological value'. In both cases, therefore, there exists a certain obligation to safeguard the environment. However, given the very general phrasing of Article 2 and the negative provision of Article 36, allowing for trade restrictions for reasons of public health and the protection of humans, animals and plants only as a derogation from the supreme principle of freedom of exchange, it is obvious that it was the 'common market' and the four 'freedoms' that constituted the core of the treaty's objectives (Wägenbaur, 1990, p16). Within this context it is worth noting that the European Court of Justice made an attempt to define the substance of the common market, stating that it involves 'the elimination of all obstacles to intra-Community trade in order to merge the national markets into a single market bringing about conditions as close as possible to those of a genuine internal market'.[7] Again, there is some room to perceive environmental protection as being related to the objective of such a common market but only insofar as it touches upon intra-Community trade obstacles, particularly non-tariff barriers.

During those early years, EC environmental legislation was therefore subject to a twofold restriction. First, there were no explicit, formal legal provisions to support any Community-wide action and, secondly, whatever action could be taken under the available general provisions had to be directly related to the objective of economic and community harmonization (McGrory, 1990, p304). This meant that the pace of environmental protection was essentially set by strongly environmentally oriented Member States as opposed to anyone on the Community level.

As a result of the uncertainty about the jurisdictional basis for Community environmental protection measures, the Community institutions have, at least until the Single European Act, based their environmental policy primarily on Article 100 and, to a lesser extent, on Article 235 of the Treaty of Rome. Article 100 authorizes the Council, provided it acts unanimously, to 'issue directives for the approximation of such provisions laid down by law, regulation or administrative action in Member States as directly affect the establishment or functioning of the common market'. Article 235 is also based on unanimous decision. It accords the Council the authority to take 'appropriate measures' to 'attain, in the course of the operation of the common market, one of the objectives of the Community' where the Treaty has not provided the necessary powers' to do so. Obviously the 'justification for using these two articles as the foundation of a common environmental policy depends ultimately on basic Community goals' (Rehbinder and Stewart, 1985, p20). According to Article 3 of the EEC Treaty, 'approximation of the laws of the Member States' is to 'promote the proper functioning of the Common Market and the Community's objectives set out in Article 2' (Rehbinder and Stewart, 1985, p20). As a result, the use of Article 100 and Article 235 was essentially dependent on a generous reading of Article 2.[8] To sum up, while politically it was possible to use Article 100 and Article 235 for environmental objectives, these provisions were, as Rehbinder has pointed out, originally:

designed to give Community institutions powers to ensure the establishment and functioning of the Common Market as an economic institution and were not aimed at environmental protection as such (Rehbinder and Steward, 1985, p16).

Despite the absence of a coherent framework, the Council passed several concrete pieces of environmental legislation prior to the First Action Programme on the Environment (EAP). Between 1964 and 1975 a number of initiatives were adopted under Articles 30, 92, 93 and 95 of the EEC Treaty to prevent excessive subsidization of the regeneration or incineration of used oil (Rehbinder and Steward, 1985, p16). In 1967 a directive was used for the first time to deal with environmental matters, establishing a uniform system of classification, labelling and packaging of dangerous substances.[9] The jurisdictional basis for Directive 67/548 was Article 100 of the Treaty of Rome. In March 1969 this directive was modified, again on the basis of Article 100.[10] In 1970, Directives 70/157, regulating permissible sound level and exhaust systems of motor vehicles, and 70/220, limiting vehicle emissions, were again passed with reference to Article 100 of the EEC Treaty, while Regulation 729/70 with respect to countryside protection in agriculturally less favoured areas was based on Articles 43 and 209. In 1971, the only 'environmental' directive that was passed extended the deadline for the implementation of the 1967 Directive on dangerous substances. In the last year of the first phase, the Council passed three directives that can be considered to have an environmental impact, two of which were related to agricultural issues and therefore took their jurisdictional basis from Articles 42 and 43 of the EEC Treaty. Directive 72/306, regulating vehicle emissions caused by diesel engines, once again referred to Article 100.

While environmental measures were not altogether absent during the first 15 years of the European Community's history, they cannot be regarded as adding up to any sort of proper and coherent policy. Only nine directives and one regulation were adopted during that time and, on the whole, these measures were incidental to the overriding economic objective (McGrory, 1990, p304). This is reaffirmed by the fact that all 'environmental' directives, with the exception of the ones pertaining to agriculture, were adopted on the basis of Article 100 and thus perceived as approximation measures with respect to the 'establishment or functioning of the common market'.

During this first phase, it is inappropriate to speak of an institutionalization process in terms of environmental protection. A limited number of pieces of legislation were passed but these were not based on an established set of rules pertaining to the protection of the environment. In fact, the issue area of the environment did not yet exist per se. It was therefore impossible for the participants to perceive their behaviour as a reflection of a set of rules within this issue area.

1972–1986: The 'Responsive' Period

The Paris Summit Conference on 19 and 20 October 1972 marks the onset of the second phase in the evolution of Community environmental policy. In Versailles, the heads of state or government of the six founding Member States and of the new members (United Kingdom, Denmark and Ireland) called upon the institutions of the Community to provide them with a blueprint for an official EC environmental policy by 31 July 1973. Accordingly, the Commission forwarded a 'Programme of environmental action of the European Communities' to the Council on 17 April 1973. Pursuant to this Commission initiative, the First Community Action Programme on the Environment was formally approved by the Council and the representatives of the Member States on 22 November 1973.[11] The programme must be regarded as a landmark in the evolution of Community environmental efforts. It marked the beginning of an actual policy in that it set the objectives, stated the principles, selected the priorities and described the measures to be taken in different sectors of the environment for the next two years. As Eckhard Rehbinder (Rehbinder and Steward, 1985, pp17–18) states, it 'opened up a field for Community action not originally provided for in the treaties' and, according to the Commission, 'added a new dimension to the construction of Europe'.[12]

The objective of Community environmental policy, as expressed in the First Action Programme, was 'to improve the setting and quality of life, and the surroundings and living conditions of the Community population'.[13] In order to achieve this objective, the Council adopted 11 principles, determining the main features of the policy. Three of these principles deserve particular mention here. First, the emphasis was laid on preventive action. Secondly, it was asserted that 'the expense of preventing and eliminating pollution should, in principle be borne by the polluter'.[14] Finally, the programme stipulated that 'for each different type of pollution, it is necessary to establish the level of action' befitting the type of pollution and the geographical zone to be protected.[15] With respect to the Commission this meant that it had the authority to act 'whenever lack of action would thwart the efforts of more localized authorities and whenever real effectiveness is attainable by action at Community level'.[16] Overall, the First Action Programme called for measures in three different categories: the reduction of pollution and nuisances as such; the improvement of the environment and the setting of life as well as the joint action in international organizations dealing with the environment. The second category of measures essentially fell under common policies, such as the common agricultural policies (CAP), social policy, regional policy, and the information programme.[17]

The first Action Programme was followed in 1976 by a second, more encompassing programme covering the period from 1977 to 1981. It was approved by the Council on 9 December 1976 and formally adopted on 17 May 1977.[18] With the transition from the first to the Second Action Programme coincided the publication of the first report by the Commission on the state of the environment in the Community, as provided for in the 1973 programme, reviewing all the environmental measures taken up to the end of 1976.[19] The aim of the Second Action Programme was to continue and expand the actions taken within the framework of the previous one. Special emphasis was laid on reinforcing the preventive nature of Community policy. Furthermore the programme paid special attention to the non-damaging use and rational management of space, the environment and natural resources. With respect to the actual reduction of pollution, the programme accorded special priority to measures against water pollution. Prior to the adoption of the third environmental programme in 1983, the second programme was extended by one and a half years. Due to the problems of institutional transition caused by the accession of Greece and the upgrading of the Environment and Consumer Protection Service to a Directorate General for Environment, Consumer Protection and Nuclear Safety, the extra time was needed to make the necessary adjustments (Rehbinder and Steward, 1985, p18).

The continuity of Community environmental policy was assured on 7 February 1983 when the Council adopted a resolution on a Third Community Action Programme covering the years 1982 to 1986.[20] While the third programme certainly remained within the general framework of the policy as outlined in the previous two, it introduced a number of new elements. Most importantly, it stated that, while originally 'the central concern was that, as a result of very divergent national policies, disparities would arise capable of affecting the proper functioning of the common market',[21] the common environmental policy is now motivated equally by the observation that the resources of the environment are the basis of – but also constitute the limit to – further economic and social development and the improvement of living conditions. It therefore advocated 'the implementation of an overall strategy which would permit the incorporation of environmental considerations in certain other Community policies such as those for agriculture, energy, industry and transport'.[22] According to the resolution, the EC environmental policy could, in fact, no longer be dissociated from measures designed to achieve the fundamental objectives of the Community.

This acceptance of environmental policy as a component of the Community's economic objectives was fundamental in that it was the first attempt to do away with the clear subordination of environmental concerns vis-à-vis the overriding economic goal of the common market. Admittedly, the wording of the resolution was carefully chosen. Yet, with the Third Action Programme, environmental policy had clearly gained in terms of its political status. Besides the integration of an environmental dimension into other policies, the programme again reinforced the preventive character of Community policy, specifically referring to the environmental impact assessment procedure. It also established a list of actual priorities, ranging from atmosphere pollution (Directive 89/779/EEC), fresh-water and marine pollution (Directive 76/464/EEC; Directive 78/176/EEC), dangerous chemical substances (Directive 79/831/EEC; Directive 67/548/EEC), waste management (Directive 78/319/EEC) to the protection of sensitive areas within the Community and the co-operation with developing countries on environmental matters. Finally, the programme also included a commitment by the Commission to use certain considerations as a basis for drawing up their proposals such as, for instance, the obligation to evaluate, as much as possible, the costs and benefits of the action envisaged.[23]

Not surprisingly, these novelties resulted in a significant increase in terms of environmental legislation. Between February 1983 and the adoption of the SEA in December 1985, over 40 directives, eight decisions and ten regulations that all had at least some regard to the environment were adopted by the Council.

1986 was the designated final year of the Third Action Programme. The negotiations about a follow-up fourth programme were well under way by 1985, at which time it had become clear that the EEC Treaty would be supplemented by the SEA by way of which a separate chapter on the environment would be introduced in the Treaty. Although the Fourth Action Programme was not formally adopted until October 1987,[24] a new phase in the evolution of Community environmental policy was about to begin by the end of 1985, the legal basis of which would be provided by the Single European Act.

The preceding paragraphs have outlined how the Community's environmental policy evolved quite significantly during the second phase; both in terms of the underlying political attitude towards environmental protection as well as the actual number of adopted pieces of legislation. It must be remembered, however, that the actual legal basis for the policy remained relatively weak. In other words, even by the mid-1980s the Community lacked the formal competences to deal with many environmental problems. Two writers have evoked the image of a 'grey zone' of Community competences in this respect (Teitgen and Mégret, 1981, p69). Rehbinder and Steward (1985, p19) have gone even further by stating that the 'Community's expansion into this policy area is a considerable extension of Community law and policy at the expense of Member States without any express authorization'. To put it differently, until the SEA, the evolution of Community environmental policy took place in the absence of an evolution of its formal legal basis.

All said, the second epoch of the EC environmental policy portrays a peculiar image. On the one hand, the jurisdictional basis, being limited from the outset, did not evolve until the adoption of the SEA. On the other hand, the development towards a common environmental policy framework was, though arguably far from satisfactory, remarkable. Within the context of this dichotomy, I shall, in the following paragraphs, make an attempt to shed some light upon the driving forces behind Community environmental policy during these years.

With the unequivocal establishment of economic growth as the goal for post-war Europe, there was simply no room for environmental concerns at the time of the foundation of the European Economic Communities. This situation was accentuated by the fact that, at the time, the majority of the public and certainly most politicians probably did not perceive the need for particular efforts in the domain of the environment. The general degree of environmental degradation had not yet reached today's dimensions and even where that was not necessarily true, relatively little reliable scientific information was available. Within this context, it is interesting to note that even progressive politicians such as, for example, Lester Pearson had little doubt as to the political supremacy of economic growth.[25]

By the early 1970s, this premise was no longer uncontested. In many parts of the developed world, environmental concerns started to surface on political agendas. In the US, the Environmental Protection Agency was founded in 1970, accompanied by the Clean Air Act and the subsequent Clean Water Act of 1972. American public opinion was mobilized through organizations such as Friends of the Earth and the Conservation Foundation which later merged with the WWF-USA. During the late 1960s Europe witnessed the emergence to prominence of environmentalists such as Bernhard Grzimek in Germany and Jacques Cousteau in France. They made effective use of the mass media to sensitize the public to their causes. Greenpeace International also started to make an important impact with its much-publicized and often spectacular missions on behalf of the environment. In the Federal Republic, Willy Brandt put environmental protection on his 1969 election platform. As Chancellor, he then set a precedent by granting environmental protection a high political priority. In fact, in October 1971, his government launched an official environmental programme (Hartkopf and Bohme, 1983, pp84–118; Bechmann, 1984, pp55–65; Müller, 1986, pp57–96). At least formally, France went even further, becoming the first European country to establish its own environmental ministry. Finally, in the summer of 1972, the United Nations convened the Stockholm Conference on the Human Environment with the extensive acid rain damage to a large number of Swedish lakes as a dramatic backdrop. Under the leadership of Maurice Strong the conference succeeded, despite diplomatic isolation of the West, in establishing a United Nations Environmental Programme (UNEP).

Within the context of this newly emerging international sensitivity towards environmental protection, France seized the opportunity of her EC presidency to bring about the decision to establish the First Environmental Action Programme on the Environment at the 1972 Paris Summit in Versailles. Juliet Lodge has pointed out that the Member States' interest in an EC environmental policy was *spurred not so much by upsurge of post-industrial values and the Nine's[26] endeavours to create a 'Human Union' or to give the EC a 'human face' as by the realization that widely differing national rules on industrial pollution could distort competition: 'dirty states' could profit economically by being slack (Lodge, 1989, p320).*

The Federal Republic of Germany and The Netherlands were among the strongest supporters of a concerted Community environmental policy. Their actual and foreseen national environmental standards were relatively strict, causing some concern about the resulting economic burdens. The German and Dutch industrial lobbies therefore argued for equal economic cost of environmental protection throughout the EC via the adoption of their standards on a Community-wide basis.

To sum up, the impetus for the First Action Programme was essentially threefold. First and, as we have seen, most importantly, there prevailed an increasing concern among the Member States about the relationship of environmental protection and trade distortions. Secondly, governments felt the need to initiate a coherent response to the increasing political pressure from environmentalists both on the national as well as on the international level. Finally, considering the inherently transnational characteristics of much of Europe's pollution, it was recognized that, in order to be effective, concerted supranational efforts were needed which could be based on the existing political structures of the European Community (McCarthy, 1989, p3).

In the years following 1972, there is another factor that affected the further course of Community environmental policy. Environmental disasters demonstrated the urgent need for further strengthening of the existing principles of environmental protection. Flixborough in 1974 and Seveso in 1976 were perhaps the most dramatic representations of the 'daily environmental abuse by petrochemical and other industries, urban programmes and "high-tech" agricultural methods' that grew exponentially during the 1970s and 1980s (Lodge, 1989, p319). The oil shocks of the 1970s resulted in a temporary deceleration of environmental policy.[27] At the latest by the late 1970s, however, environmental protection had once again become an important item on Europe's political agenda. Several European countries experienced fierce debates about the expansion of civil nuclear capacities and by 1982, with the disclosure of the widespread forest destruction in Germany, environmental policy had become a matter of first priority, a status that even surpassed the one it enjoyed in the early 1970s (von Weizsäcker, 1989, p27).[28]

Not surprisingly, the 1983 Stuttgart European Council reacted to these developments. Reviewing the state of Community environmental policy, it concluded that there is an 'urgent need to speed up and reinforce action', drawing special attention to the destruction of the forests (Johnson and Corcelle, 1989, p3). With the 1985 Brussels session of the European Council, the status of environmental protection policy was once again upgraded in so far as it was now perceived as a fundamental part of economic, industrial, agricultural and social policies within the Community (Johnson and Corcelle, 1989, p3). What this meant is that, by the mid-1980s, the view had emerged that environmental protection was an 'economic and not simply a moral imperative' (Lodge, 1989, p321). This final step in the evolution of Community policy during the second phase must be understood as a result of the increasing realization of the link between economic growth stimulated by further integration and the resulting costs in terms of adverse environmental encumbrances (Haigh and Baldock, 1989, p45). The ensuing integrated approach towards environmental protection leads directly to the last of the three phases that were outlined at the outset.

The second phase of Community environmental policy can be summarized as an active one that undoubtedly furthered environmental protection in the European Community. At the same time, however, it was characterized by a considerable degree of uncertainty. It lacked the truly integrated approach based on a sound legal basis that emerged in the third phase with the Fourth Action Programme and the SEA. The policy until 1985 was a 'responsive' one in that it evolved according to the momentary economic, political and social circumstances. Its initial and probably most important impetus was, as described above, the general concern of environmental protection as a potential cause for trade distortions. Public pressure and the direct effects of environmental accidents later accelerated the process. Finally, there was the realization that economic progress and the protection of the environment are so closely interlinked that one cannot be considered without the other. The nature of the policy evolved at each stage depending on the given set of circumstances. Generally speaking, the circumstances as they presented themselves during the second phase favoured a progressive evolution of the policy although, in the case of the 1973 oil shock, they temporarily worked in the opposite direction.

This type of policy had certain advantages. As a whole it remained flexible, not having to rely on rigid principles that quickly become outdated. In other words, it was possible to readjust quickly the policy to a newly arisen situation or set of circumstances. The disadvantage rested in the fact that under these conditions, environmental protection would always be relegated to a subordinate position in relation to Community economic aims. Whether this disadvantage has successfully been eliminated without undermining some of the positive aspects of the second phase will be discussed in the following section. Before that, however, I shall briefly review the most important pieces of legislation of the second phase. Given the significant number of environmental directives, regulations and decisions between the First Action Programme and the Single European Act, it would, of course, exceed the limits of this study to review them all. I have therefore chosen a small representative selection.

Ernst von Weizsäcker (1989, p42) has identified just over 20 directives as being the most important pieces of Community environmental legislation between 1973 and 1985. For the sake of simplicity I shall base my review on this selection.[29] The relevant directives can conveniently be grouped together in six different categories according to the environmental problem they are addressing:

1 Water
2 Air
3 Noise
4 Waste
5 Emissions
6 Lead in petrol.

In addition there are a number of other directives that do not readily fit into any of these categories: the 'Seveso' Directive, a directive on chemicals, one on birds and their habitat and one on sewage sludge. von Weizsacker's selection of directives is useful in that it more or less represents the full spectrum of EC environmental activities.

In the fight against water pollution, there are four directives, all of which are based both on Article 100 and Article 235 of the EEC Treaty. Directives 75/440 and 80/778 are concerned with drinking water while Directive 76/160 regulates bathing water.[30] Directive 76/464 deals with dangerous substances in water.[31] The air quality efforts are represented by three directives: 80/779 on smoke and sulphur dioxide, 82/884 on lead and 85/203 on nitrogen dioxide.[32] Again the legal basis for all three directives rests in Article 100 and Article 235 of the Treaty of Rome. The same applies to the three directives on waste: 75/442 outlines a general waste framework while 78/319 and 84/631 deal with toxic waste and transfrontier shipment of waste respectively.[33] In terms of emission standards, Directive 83/351 on vehicle emission only refers to Article 100, whereas Directive 84/360 on emission from industrial plants is again based on Article 100 and Article 235.[34] The two directives on the approximation of laws of Member States concerning lead content in petrol (85/210 and 78/611) are solely based on Article 100 of the Treaty of Rome.[35] The same is true of Directive 79/831, amending for the sixth time Directive 67/548 on the approximation of the laws, regulations and administrative provisions relating to the classification, packaging and labelling of dangerous substances, as well as Directive 79/117 on use restrictions and labelling of pesticides.[36]

Directive 79/409 on birds and their habitat, on the other hand is exclusively based on Article 235. This is, of course, to be expected, since animal protection has hardly any direct effect on the 'establishment or functioning of the common market' as expressed in Article 100 of the Treaty of Rome.[37] Finally, there are two more directives that need to be mentioned here, both of which were adopted under Article 100 and 235. Directive 82/501 on the major accident hazards of certain industrial activities was a Community response to the dioxin disaster in Seveso, and Directive 85/337 on the assessment of the effects of certain public and private projects on the environment set out an important new priority of Community environmental policy.[38]

This selective review of EC environmental 'legislation' between 1973 and 1985 re-emphasizes a point made earlier. Although the Community institutions were engaged in a considerable amount of environmental activity, the available legal foundations remained limited. There was no explicit jurisdictional mandate for the protection of the environment; the Community therefore proceeded with its environmental efforts on the basis of what Ernst von Weizsäcker has called a '*Kunstgriff*', or knack, using Articles 100 and 235 of the original EEC Treaty. This is, of course, the most fundamental difference with respect to the final phase of Community environmental policy as it has been unfolding since the adoption of the SEA.

During this second phase, the institutionalization process mentioned at the outset is becoming discernible. Member States begin to understand that certain collective actions are necessary in order to address a more or less specific set of problems in the newly defined issue area of the environment. As I have pointed out, however, the environment does not stand on its own feet yet. It is still at least partly subordinated to the paramount objective of economic growth. Furthermore, although explicit rules exist in the form of the various directives passed, their ability to prescribe behavioural roles, constrain activity and shape expectations is limited because of the absence of an unambiguous legal foundation. Despite an ongoing gradual process of institutionalization, no proper EC environmental regime can therefore be in place. Though explicit and agreed upon by the Member States' governments, the rules in fact remain weak and exert little independent compliance pull.

1985–'1992': The 'Initiative' Phase

An analysis of EC environmental policy after 1985 is rendered more complicated by the fact that, although there exists an element of continuity, it would be too simplistic to regard it as a mere continuation of previous policy developments. In terms of its general approach, the Fourth Action Programme is certainly related to the previous one, despite the fact that it was differently structured and that it initiated a number of new policy directions such as environmental educational efforts and a focus on gene technology. It essentially completed and formalized the notions of earlier Community policy. In fact, EC policy, as laid down in the programme, is virtually all-encompassing. It demands integration of social, industrial, agricultural and economic policies, an objective that, as mentioned earlier, began to emerge with the Third Action Programme in 1983. Besides this factor of continuity, however, post-1985 EC environmental policy is shaped by a second strand of influence which manifests itself in the SEA amendment to the Treaty of Rome. Interestingly enough, the forces behind the emergence of the SEA have little to do with the environment. As Rolf Wägenbaur (1990, p17) has stated, the impetus stemming from the original EEC Treaty gradually weakened in the 1980s and 'it was felt that a new initiative was necessary. The so-called Single European Act came to the rescue.' The initiative was also related to the enlargement of the Community from the original six Member States to the present 12 (UK, Ireland, Denmark: 1973; Greece: 1981; Spain and Portugal: 1986). In light of the extended membership, the original treaty was clearly in need of revision. There were intensive discussions as to what sort of reform the treaty should undergo: a social charter, an environmental chapter, research and development programmes, a regional policy, the strengthening of the European Parliament, majority voting in the Council: all these issues were brought onto the agenda. The most important outcome of these negotiations, however, was the decision to go ahead with the completion of the internal market.

The commitment to achieve this goal within a specific time limit was laid down in Article 8a of the Treaty. This states that the Community 'shall adopt measures with the aim of progressively establishing the internal market over a period expiring on 31 December 1992'. The internal market is defined as 'an area without internal frontiers in which the free movement of goods, persons, services and capital is ensured'. In Lord Cockfield's White Paper, the Commission presented a plan as to what it perceived to be the specific measures that needed to be adopted in order to complete the internal market (COM 85/310).[39] This relatively sudden acceleration in the process of European integration put an end to perceptions of 'Euro-sclerosis' and caused great optimism as to the economic effects of the Single European Market.[40] The Cecchini Report on 'The Economics of 1992' estimated that the internal market would result in an economic gain of 4.5–7 per cent of the Community's gross national product (GNP). Such an increase in economic activities would affect the state of the environment. In the absence of any changes in policies or technologies, the environment could clearly be expected to deteriorate. It is within this context that, in 1989, a Commission Task Force published a report on 'The Environment and the Internal Market' in which it stated that the creation of a single market, as well as the need to decouple economic growth from environmental degradation requires a fundamental review of existing environmental policy at EC level and in the Member States (Wägenbaur, 1990, p18). By including Title VII on 'Environment' in the new EEC Treaty, the authors of the SEA provided the formal legal foundation on the basis of which such a fundamental review could take place.

Figure 2.1 shows the two strands that define the post-1985 EC environmental policy. As mentioned earlier, it is the formal legal foundation as expressed in the SEA that distinguishes Community policy after 1985 from the earlier one. The chart indicates that the dynamics of the first and second phase are still operating (b). However, it is strand (a) that is the primary determinant of the third phase of Community environmental policy.

Obviously the distinction between the two strands is somewhat schematic and therefore not entirely correct. The connecting line between the two strands suggests that the SEA amendment is also a result of Community environmental policy as it had been developing since 1972, culminating in the Fourth Action Programme in 1987. Nigel Haigh and David Baldock (1989, p20) make this point, arguing that the lack of a clear legal base for the EC's environmental policy had been much criticized. Within this context they see the 'Environment' title as

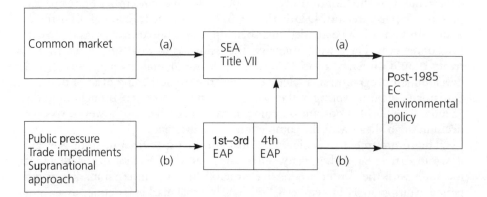

Figure 2.1 *Factors that Shaped EC Environmental Policy Post-1985*

a 'response to this criticism'. Nevertheless, the distinction is analytically useful if one works with the hypothesis that the adoption of the SEA had a significant effect on the nature of EC environmental policy. The following pages attempt to shed some light upon the question of whether or not this hypothesis is valid.

The SEA affects Community environmental policy in three different ways: First, through the general institutional changes – majority voting and the co-operation procedure; secondly, through the objective of completing the internal market; and thirdly through the new legal provisions that actually define Community environmental policy (Haigh and Baldock, 1989, p12).

Institutional Changes

The first of the two institutional changes instigated by the SEA is the 'co-operation procedure' with its second reading by Parliament as expressed in Article 149 of the EEC Treaty. In response to criticism of lack of openness of the EC legislation process and charges of a 'democratic deficit', the 'co-operation procedure is designed to allow the European Parliament to play an effective but qualified role in the legislative process' (Lodge, 1989: 69).[41] In terms of environmental protection, there is some significance to Article 149 in that it effectively allows public opinion, represented by the Parliament, to have more of an impact on the process of environmental policy formation. Considering that environmental consciousness has undoubtedly been heightened throughout the Community in the past few years, this source of public influence could prove to become quite relevant.[42]

The co-operation procedure is limited in that it only applies when a vote is taken in Council by qualified majority. Qualified majority voting, as laid down in Article 148 of the EEC Treaty, is not a new phenomenon; it was already contained in the original Treaty. What is new, however, is that under Article 100A, it is now possible to use it for environmental purposes (Haigh and Baldock, 1989, p14), This stands in contrast to Article 100 and Article 235 on which most pre-1985 pieces of environmental legislation were based, as well as to the new Article 130s which I will discuss below. In all three cases, unanimity is a requirement for any action. As Nigel Haigh and David Baldock (1989, p15) point out, one of the problems with majority voting in the context of the environment is the uncertainty that prevails about how 'a choice is made for environmental measures between Article 130s (unanimity) and Article 100a (majority voting)'. Although Article 100a is, in principle, reserved for traded products, it is difficult to categorize all cases along these lines. Not surprisingly, the Commission and the Council do not see eye to eye on this question. The Commission's view is that Article 100a is the proper legal base whenever the specified conditions are fulfilled. According to this view, Article 130s 'only comes into consideration when the conditions of Article 100a are not fulfilled or when, for instance, the impact of the product on competition is very small as compared with the impact on the environment as such' (Wägenbaur, 1990, p21).

The European Court of Justice had been expected for some time to clarify the legal confusion arising out of the tension between these two articles. With the June 1991 ruling in the titanium dioxide[43] case 300/89, it has finally done so.

The Court clearly gives preference to Article 100a, thus supporting majority voting. This could well set the path for future EC environmental legislation. In anticipation of the actual effect of the Court's position, Nigel Haigh's conclusion can be accepted that, while majority voting may not have revolutionized environmental policy, it has made it more difficult for one or two countries to block certain proposals, as Denmark discovered when it failed to prevent the adoption of Directive 88/76 on emission from large cars (Haigh and Baldock, 1989, p15).

Completion of the 'internal market'

In order to achieve the objective of completing the internal market by 31 December 1992 (Article 8a), the SEA introduced Articles 100a and 100b concerning the harmonization of national laws, including environmental laws. Article 100a(3) states that the Commission essentially takes as a base a 'high level of protection' in its harmonization efforts. Article 100a(4) allows Member States to apply more stringent national environmental standards provided they are 'not a means of arbitrary discrimination or a disguised restriction on trade between Member States'. There is also a safeguard clause (Article 100a(5)) that allows Member States to opt out of harmonization efforts in appropriate cases as provided for in Article 36. Article 100b requires the Community to draw up an inventory of national measures 'which fall under 100a and which have not been harmonized pursuant to that Article'. By majority voting, the Council then is to decide which of these can 'be recognized as being equivalent'. All others presumably have to be harmonized at that point (Haigh and Baldock, 1989, p18). These harmonization measures designed to complete the internal market have an impact on environmental policy to the extent that most environmental protection standards that affect the functioning of the internal market will be set at EC level. Whether or not the EC will seek to harmonize standards for emission (to air or water) or for environmental procedures (eg safety requirements at factories, disposal standards at vast sites), which 'have the potential to affect the "functioning of the common market" (Article 100) or the "establishment of the internal market" (Article 8a) remains uncertain' (Haigh and Baldock, 1989, p19).

Environmental title

The SEA inserted Title VII entitled 'Environment' in part III of the EEC Treaty which is concerned with the 'policies' of the European Community. This is worth noting since it suggests that with the SEA it is no longer just de facto but de jure correct to speak of an environmental policy. The relevant treaty provisions are numbered 130r to 130s. Article 130r specifies the objectives of Community environmental policy and lays down the principles and guidelines that such a policy must follow. It also deals with Member State versus Community competences in terms of environmental protection and finally calls for co-operation with third countries and international organizations in matters involving the environment. Article 130s, as discussed earlier, stipulates the legislative process for the formulation of environmental laws and Article 130t allows states to introduce more stringent protective measures as long as they are compatible with the rest of the Treaty.

There are a number of ways in which these new provisions have affected Community environmental policy. First, Title VII has given symbolic importance to environmental protection policy, reinforced by the preamble to the SEA in which the Community commits itself to 'promote democracy on the basis of the fundamental rights recognized in the constitutions and laws of the Member States'. As Haigh and Baldock (1989, p21) have pointed out, 'more than a third of the Member States have accorded constitutional status to the protection of the environment or recognize environmental rights'. Second, the Community environmental policy objectives outlined in Article 130r(1) are sufficiently broad – to preserve, protect and improve the quality of the environment; to contribute towards protecting human health; to ensure a prudent and rational utilization of national resources – to bring almost any environmental issue within the competence of Community legislation. Third, Article 130r(2) gives legal force to the principle which, as discussed earlier, gradually evolved in the 'Action Programmes on the Environment': principle of prevention, rectification at source and polluter pays. In addition. Article 130r(2) formalizes the new principle that environmental 'protection requirements shall be a component of the Community's other policies'. Fourth, Article 130r(3) states four basic factors that the Community needs to consider in its policy adoption: (a) available scientific data, (b) environmental co-ordination in the various regions of the Community, (c) the potential benefits and cost of action or lack of action and (d) the economic and social development of the Community as a whole and the balanced development of its region. Fifth, Article 130r(4) lays down the principle of subsidiarity which determines whether appropriate action is to be taken at the Community or at the Member States level. The Article states:

> *The Community shall take action relating to the environment to the extent to which the objectives referred to in paragraph I can be attained better at Community level than at the level of the individual Member States, thus expressly reserving residual jurisdiction to the Member States* (Vandermeersch, 1987, p422).

Before addressing the question of whether or not these effects are negative or positive in terms of actual environmental protection, I shall, once again, turn to a brief review of environmental legislative measures of the third phase. As was the case for the second phase, this review is highly selective. I have, however, tried to make the selection as representative as possible of the totality of measures adopted. The survey begins with the entry into force of the SEA on 1 July 1987 and ends in August 1990.

Of the nine directives and two regulations that I have selected to review, there is not a single one that is based on Article 100 and/or Article 235. Regulation 3143/87, amending Regulation 3626/82 on the implementation in the Community of the Convention on International Trade in Endangered Species of Wild Fauna and Flora (CITES), and Directive 88/302, amending for the ninth time Directive 67/548 relating to the classification, packaging and labelling of dangerous substances, make no reference to any specific legal foundations at all. They simply have 'regard to the Treaty of the EEC'.[44] There are four directives and one regulation that take Article 130s as their legal basis: Directive 87/416 amending

Directive 85/210 on approximation of the laws of the Member States concerning lead content of petrol;[45] Directive 88/347, an amendment of Directive 86/280 on DDT, carbon tetrachloride and pentachlorophenol;[46] Regulation 3322/88 on certain chlorofluorocarbons and halons which deplete the ozone layer;[47] Directive 90/219 on the contained use of genetically modified micro-organisms[48] and Directive 90/415 on dangerous substances in water.[49] The remaining four directives – 88/76 and 88/77, both on emissions from vehicles; 88/436, amending an earlier directive on vehicle emission (70/220); and 90/220 on the deliberate release into the environment of genetically modified organisms[50] – were adopted on the basis of Article 100a of the EEC Treaty which, of course, implies that they were essentially harmonization measures agreed on by qualified majority voting and subject to the co-operation procedure.

This limited survey reveals a number of interesting points. First, it is clear that the legal basis used during the first and second phase – mainly Article 100 and Article 235 – have been replaced by the new provisions provided by the SEA amendments to the Treaty of Rome. Second, it reaffirms the fact that, prior to the titanium dioxide case, there reigned uncertainty about which article – 100a or 130s – was to serve as the legal foundation for a given piece of environmental legislation. The range of problems that qualify as having an effect on the 'establishment of the internal market' does not seem to have been rigorously established. Finally, the evidence from our review indicates that Article 100a, implying majority voting and the co-operation procedure, was not used as frequently as one might have expected. Thus, at least until late 1991, much of the Community's environmental policy continued to be contingent on a unanimous decision by the Council.

While it is difficult to assess unfolding events, there are, however, a number of observations about European Community environmental policy since the Single European Act that can already be made. For this purpose it is useful to recall that I set out to examine the hypothesis that the SEA is likely to result in a dramatic change of EC environmental policy. There are a number of indications that would validate such a hypothesis. Community environmental policy has undoubtedly gained momentum since the SEA. Title VII of the EEC Treaty has important symbolic consequences. The protection of the environment is now formally of equal or even superior status to all other Community objectives. The possibility of majority voting provides a framework for adopting a much greater amount of environmental legislation. The principle of subsidiarity, as expressed in Article 130r(4), may well have significant psychological effects on Member States. Using the example of the United Kingdom, Nigel Haigh and David Baldock (1989, p24) have demonstrated how, in terms of the environment, Europe, including its subnational units, is likely to increasingly perceive itself as a whole, thus moving ever closer to the 'union among the peoples of Europe' called for in the preamble to the Treaty of Rome. From such a point of view, the SEA has indeed had dramatic effects; not only in terms of a much broader and more effective environmental policy but also in terms of accelerating the process of integration among the European people in general.

As so often in international politics, there is, however, a perspective that points in the opposite direction. It is conceivable that the new provisions on majority voting could have negative effects in that they allow some Member States to overrule others which will then, in the absence of an effective European enforcement agent, be tempted to simply ignore their implementation obligations. Anxiety has also been expressed with respect to the subsidiarity principle, arguing that, from a Community perspective, it is clearly a step backwards (Vandermeersch, 1987, p422), while, prior to the SEA:

> *the issue was whether or not the EC had competence to act or not, now measures can be challenged in terms of whether or not the EC or the Member States could better deal with the issue* (Lodge, 1989, p323).

In that sense, the SEA has widened the possibilities for challenging EC environmental action which could result in an overall weakened and less effective Community environmental policy.

These examples should suffice to demonstrate that there is indeed significant potential in the Community environmental policy as laid down in the SEA amendments to the EEC Treaty. At the same time, many of the provisions are abstract and leave much room for manoeuvring the thrust of the policy in either direction. Much will therefore depend on the political interpretation of the policy and the nature of future amendments to its jurisdictional basis.

Conclusions

Is it possible to argue that the institutionalization process as described at the start of this study has progressed to the point where it is useful to describe the present state of the European Community's environmental policy in terms of an international regime? Let us once again look at Robert Keohane's definition of an international institution as 'persistent and connected sets of rules (formal and informal) that prescribe behavioural roles, constrain activity, and shape expectations'. The rules are clearly established. There is a large and growing body of legislation in the various areas of European environmental protection. This legislation is based on a relatively unambiguous jurisdictional basis. Formally, there is no doubt that it prescribes behavioural roles, constrains activities and shapes expectations. In fact, its tendency to shape expectations has even reached beyond the present Community Member States. The Central and Eastern European countries which are aspiring to an eventual accession to the European Community are already involved in adjusting or, in some cases, establishing their domestic environmental legislative bodies in such a way as to make sure that they will eventually be compatible with the expectations as expressed in the Community rules. Within this context the conclusion imposes itself that the institutionalization process of the European Community's environmental policy, notwithstanding the above-mentioned weaknesses, has progressed far enough to warrant the description of an international environmental regime.

The conclusion that the European Community's environmental policy has reached the state of an international regime is therefore no cause for complacency. In many ways the task has only just begun. We are, after all, not dealing with an obscure intellectual puzzle. The issue at hand is the increasing threat to our environment. It is in our immediate interest to start examining the effectiveness of the European Community's environmental regime as one of the available institutional arrangements to address this situation. The first set of conceptual guideposts has been provided by the advocates of international institutional approaches. It certainly seems worthwhile and, for the time being, promising to try to build on them.

Acknowledgements

The author wishes to thank Andrew Hurrell, Andrew Walter, David Wartenweiler and David Judge for their helpful comments on earlier versions of this study.

Notes

1   The first time '1992' was officially mentioned was in the Commission president's statement to the European Parliament on 14 January 1985. Referring to the next European Council, he said: 'now that some heads of state and government have decided to set an example ... it may not be overoptimistic to announce a decision to eliminate all frontiers within Europe by 1992 and to implement it' (Commission of the European Communities (1985b), 'The Thrust of Commission Policy', Bulletin of the European Communities, Supplement 1/85, 14 and 15 January). The idea was formally approved by the Brussels European Council on 29–30 March 1985 and adopted in December 1985 in Luxembourg (see Lodge, 1989, p9).

2   The terms 'European' and 'European Community' are used interchangeably throughout this chapter. When referring to other parts of Europe, the proper specification will be made; ie 'Eastern European', 'Southern Europe', and so on.

3   Article 189, Treaty Establishing the European Economic Community as Amended by Subsequent Treaties, Rome, 25 March, 1957; subsequently referred to as Treaty of Rome.

4   See also House of Lords' Select Committee on the European Communities Transfrontier Shipment of Hazardous Wastes, 9th Report Session 1983–1984, HMSO.

5   It remains to be seen whether the changes incorporated in the Maastricht Treaty, creating a European Union will, in itself, represent a new phase of Community environmental policy or follow in the footsteps of this third phase. I will briefly comment on this question in the final section on Maastricht.

6   Citation translated by author.

7   Gaston Schul Judgment of 1982, Case 15/18, 1982 ECR 1409, p1431.

8   For a thorough discussion of the legal details of Article 100 and Article 235 see Rehbinder and Steward (1985, pp21–28).

9   Directive 67/548 EEC of 27 June 1967 on classification, packaging and labelling of dangerous substances, JO No.196, 16.8.1967, p1 (French edn).

10 Directive 69/81 EEC of 13 March 1969 modifying the Directive of 16.8.1976 on classification, packaging and labelling of dangerous substances, JO No.L68, 19.3.1969, p1 (French edn).

11 OJ No.C112. 20.12.1973, p3. See also Seventh General Report of the EC (Brussels, 1973), point 258; Bulletin of the EC, 11–1974, point 1203, pp11–12.

12 7th Report EC, 1973, point 258, p235.

13 See OJ No.C112, 20.12.73, p5.

14 7th Report EC, 1973, point 262.

15 OJ No.C112, p7.

16 7th Report EC, 1973, point 263.

17 Ibid, point 264.

18 OJ No.C139, 13.6.1977; Bulletin EC 5-1977, point 2.1.40.

19 See 'State of the Environment: First Report', 1977.

20 Action Programme of the European Communities on the Environment (1982 to 1986) in OJ No.C46, 17.2.1983, p1.

21 OJ No.C46, 17.2.1983, p3.

22 Seventeenth General Report on the Activities of the European Communities, 1983, point 372, p158.

23 See OJ No.C46, p2.

24 In December 1986 the Council adopted a resolution on the strengthening of Community action in favour of the environment in which it welcomed 'the submission by the Commission of detailed proposals for a Fourth Environmental Action Programme and considers that such a programme provides an opportunity to strengthen decisively Community action in this area, building on the achievements of the past, and to determine a coherent framework within which specific Community actions can be formulated, co-ordinated and implemented over the period of 1987–1992'. It also refers to the SEA which 'will constitute a new legal basis for the Community environmental policy'. OJ No.C3, 7.1.1987, p3.

25 See Pearson Report, 1969, 'Bericht der Kommission fur Internationale Entwicklung', München, Zurich: Wien, pp48–51.

26 By the time of the Paris Summit, the adherence to the Community of the United Kingdom, Ireland and Denmark was already decided. Weizsacker argues that one of the objectives of the 1972 Action Programme was to get it through and then present it to the new Member States as a 'fait accompli'.

27 For a discussion of the German example see Müller (1986, pp97–102).

28 It is worth noting that 1982 was also the year when the Greens were first elected to the German 'Bundestag'.

29 The total number environmental legislative pieces for the entire second phase amounts to 120 directives, 27 decisions and 14 regulations.

30 Directive 75/440, OJ No.L194, p26; Directive 80/778. OJ No.L229, 30.08.1980, p11; Directive 76/160, OJ No.L31, 05.02.1976, p1.

31 Directive 76/464, OJ No.L129, 18.05.1976, p23.

32 Directive 80/779, OJ No.L229, 30.08.1980; Directive 82/884, OJ No.L378, 31.12.1982; Directive 85/203, OJ No.L87, 27.03.1985, p1.

33 Directive 75/442, OJ No.L194, 25.07.1975, p39; Directive 78/319, OJ No. L84, 31.03.1978, p43; Directive 84/631, OJ No.L326, 13.12.1984, p31.

34 Directive 83/351, OJ No.L197, 20.07.1983, p1; Directive 84/360, OJ No.L188, 16.07.1984, p20.
35 Directive 85/210, OJ No.L96, 03.04.1985, p25; Directive 78/611, OJ No.L197, 22.07.1978, p19.
36 Directive 79/831, OJ No.L259, 15.10.1979, p10; Directive 67/548, OJ No.L196, 16.08.1967; Directive 79/117, OJ No.L33, 08.02.1979, p36.
37 Directive 79/409, OJ No.L103, 25.04.1979, p1.
38 Directive 82/501, OJ No.L230, 05.08.1982, p1; Directive 85/337, OJ No.L175, 05.07.1985, p40.
39 Commission of the EC, Completing the Internal Market: White Paper from the Commission of the European Council (the Cockfield White Paper), Luxembourg, 1985.
40 Although the phrase 'Single European Market' has come into widespread use, it is not used in the SEA. It simply combines the SEA and the internal market, at the expense of conferring the original meaning of the word 'Single' in the SEA 'which was so called because it combined in a single legal instrument two texts that had different origins, one amending the Treaty of Rome (Title II) and one dealing with co-operation in the sphere of foreign policy'. See Haigh and Baldock (1989, p10).
41 For a detailed discussion of the 'co-operation procedure' see Lodge (1989, pp68–79).
42 This is illustrated by the case of Directive 88/76 on emissions from small cars. See Haigh and Baldock (1989, pp51–54).
43 Titanium dioxide is a white pigment, generally thought to be harmless. It is used in paints, plastic and other products in order to reduce reliance on toxic substances such as lead and zinc. The problem is that its manufacture results in the discharge of acid waste contaminated by metals. EC legislation on titanium dioxide dates back as far as the early 1970s.
44 Regulation 3143/87 OJ No.L299, 22.10.1978, p33; Regulation 3626/82 OJ No.L3K4.31.12.1982, p1; Directive 88/302 OJ No.L133, 30.05.1988, p1.
45 Directive 87/416 OJ No.L225, 13.08.1987, p33; Directive 85/210 OJ No.L96, 03.04.1985. p25.
46 Directive 88/347 OJ No.L158, 25.06.1988, p35; Directive 86/280 OJ No.L181, 04.07.1986. p16.
47 Regulation 3322/88 OJ No.L297, 31.10.1988. p1.
48 Directive 90/219 OJ No.L117, 08.05.1990, p1.
49 Directive 90/415 OJ No.L219, 14.08.1990, p49.
50 Directive 88/76; Directive 88/77; Directive 88/436; Directive 70/220; Directive 90/220.

References

Bechmann, A. (1984) *Leben wollen,* Cologne.
Haigh, N. (1990) *EEC Environmental Policy and Britain,* 2nd revised edition, Essex: Longman.

Haigh, N. and Baldock, D. (1989) *Environmental Policy and 1992*, London: British Department of the Environment.

Hartkopf, G. and Bohme, E. (1983) *Umweltpolitik, Band 1: Grundlagen, Analysen und Perspektiven*, Opladen: Westdeutscher.

Johnson, S. P. and Corcelle, G. (1989) *The Environmental Policy of the European Communities* (International Environmental Law and Policy Series), London: Graham & Trotman.

Keck, O.(1991) 'Der neue Institutionalismus in der Theorie der Internationalen Politik', *Politische Vierteljahresschrift*, 32, Jahrgang, Heft 4, pp635–653.

Keohane, R. O. (1989) *International Institutions and State Power: Essays in International Relations Theory*, Boulder, Co: Westview Press.

Lodge, J. (1989) 'Environment: Towards a Clean Blue-Green EC', in J. Lodge (ed) *The European Community and the Challenge of the Future*, London: Pinter.

McCarthy, E. (1989) *The EC and the Environment*, European Dossier Service II.

McGrory, D. P. (1990) 'Air Pollution Legislation in the United States and the European Community', *European Law Review*, Vol.15, No.4, Aug.

Müller, E. (1986) *Innenwelt der Umweltpolitik*, Opiaden: Westdeutscher.

Rehbinder, E. and Steward, R. (eds) (1985) *Environmental Protection Policy, Volume 2, Integration Through Law: Europe and the American Federal Experience*, Firenze: European University Institute.

Sands, P. (1990) 'European Community Environmental Law: Legislation, the ECJ and Common Interest Groups', *Modern Law Review*, Vol.53, No.5, Sept., p685.

Teitgen, P.-H. and Mégret, C. (1981) 'La fumée de la cigarette dans la "zone grise" des competences de la C.E.E.', *Revue Trimestrielle de Droit Européen*, 68.

Vandermeersch, D. (1987) 'The Single European Act and the Environmental Policy of the European Economic Community', *European Law Review*, Vol.12, No.6.

Wägenbaur, R. (1990) 'The Single Market Programme and the Protection of the Environment', in *Environmental Protection and the Impact of European Community Law*, Papers from the Joint Conference with the Incorporated Law Society of Ireland, Dublin: Irish Centre for European Law.

Weizsäcker, E. U. von (1989) *Erdpolitik. Oekologische Realpolik an der Schwelle zum Jahrliundert der Umwelt*, Darmstadt: Wissenschaftliche Buchgesellschaft.

Young, O. R. (1992) 'The Effectiveness of International Institutions: Hard Cases and Critical Variables', in J. N. Rosenau, and Czempiel, E.-O. (eds) *Governance without Government: Order and Change in World Politics*, Cambridge: Cambridge University Press.

3

European Union Environmental Policy after the Nice Summit

Andrew Jordan and Jenny Fairbrass

The primary rationale for the new treaty was to deal with matters that were unresolved by the previous amendment, the 1999 Amsterdam Treaty, and prepare the European Union (EU) for enlargement. If and when it is ratified, the Treaty of Nice will be the fourth major reform of the founding treaties of the EU since 1957. The Treaty follows the pattern of previous treaty amendments (Jordan, 2002) in that it was not negotiated for environmental reasons (although environmentalists were quick to submit proposals) (European Environment Bureau (EEB), 2000a), but it could significantly affect the way in which the EU makes environmental policy. Unlike the 1987 Single Act and the 1993 Maastricht Treaty, both of which fundamentally altered the 'rules for making EU environmental rules' (Weale, 1996), the new treaty will only make a number of fairly minor changes to the actual wording of the environmental sections of the Treaty. But it may have important indirect effects on the dynamics of policy-making, although these could take a lot longer to feed through.

The Nice Negotiations (or 'Here We Go Again!')

The new treaty was negotiated and signed by the 15 European political leaders at the December 2000 European Council (Galloway, 2001), following a nine-month intergovernmental conference (IGC). Why did the EU embark upon another round of tortuous negotiations so soon after the ratification of the Amsterdam Treaty? The simple answer is that Amsterdam failed to resolve a number of important issues needed to ensure the effective functioning of the EU as it seeks to expand to almost twice its current size. Currently, the plan is to enlarge the EU 15 to incorporate up to 12 countries from the former Eastern Bloc. In order to do that, the Nice IGC had to address three key issues: the size and composition of the Commission; the weighting of votes in the Council; and the possible extension of qualified majority voting (QMV) to new areas. Pro-integrationists argued that if these issues were not properly resolved, an enlarged EU would simply grind to a halt. The EU spent most of the 1990s in one long constitutional discussion. That a new treaty change has already been scheduled for 2004 suggests that Nice did not complete the reform of the EU.

Substantive Changes

Amsterdam did not trigger a 'step change' (Jordan, 1998) in EU environmental policy-making, but it did strengthen the commitment to achieving sustainable development and environmental policy integration (Jordan and Lenschow, 2000; Lenschow, 2001), and it greatly empowered the European Parliament by extending its co-decision-making powers. However, Nice's impact on the substantive wording of the environmental sections of the Treaty is considerably less significant than Amsterdam's.

Qualified majority voting

The new treaty extends QMV to 31 new areas, including a few that are not legislative (for example, appointments to political posts). But it will not extend QMV or co-decision-making within the scope of the environmental articles (that is, 174–176). Prior to Nice, all environmental policy was subject to QMV except in five specific areas (Jordan, 1998). At Nice, one of those areas, environmental taxation, emerged as the most popular candidate for reform. The Commission, which has long coveted states' ability to experiment with new (that is, non-regulatory) instruments, was supported by Austria, Belgium, Denmark and The Netherlands. But the initiative died in the face of deep opposition from the UK, Sweden and Ireland. So, instead, states negotiated a declaration annexed to the new treaty, which states that 'full use' should be made 'of incentives and instruments which are market-oriented and intended to promote sustainable development'. In the short term, this is likely to unblock the impasse within the Environment Council (Spain in particular has used the unanimity rule to veto EU energy taxes), but it will add weight to those calling for the EU to extend its tool-kit.

Limited changes were also made to three of the other four areas that are still subject to unanimity under Article 175 (2), namely land use, planning and water resources. The new treaty requires that all measures 'affecting' rather than 'concerning' these areas must be agreed by unanimity. It is possible that this amendment may be used to restrict the EU's ability to act in these areas.

Enhanced co-operation

Flexibility or 'enhanced co-operation' (that is, rules allowing a small group of states to go ahead with new forms of co-operation without all the EU's states being involved) was first introduced by the Amsterdam Treaty. However, it has not had any significant effects because it is hedged around by so many conditions (for example, new measures should not undermine the single market or the existing *acquis*) (Bär et al, 2000). The Nice Treaty aims to make the procedure much easier to use. However, it is only to be used as a matter of last resort and is thought unlikely to have much effect on the environmental sector.

The Charter of Fundamental Rights and precaution

Prepared outside the IGC by a group of experts and tabled at the Nice Council, the Charter does not have legal force. Environmentalists wanted it to contain individual rights to a clean environment (EEB, 2000a), which they could then exploit by mounting legal challenges if and when states fail to protect the environment. But for the time being, most states are understandably reluctant to proceed too far down this path.

Finally, European leaders also adopted a Resolution on the application of the precautionary principle. Although it is also not legally binding, it is more progressive than the Commission's 2000 Communication on the application of the precautionary principle (Jordan, 2001). It could also be a portent of more intense US–EU conflicts in relation to issues such as genetically modified organisms (GMOs), where the scientific basis of policy-making is deeply contested.

Procedural Changes

The two most contentious issues that arose during the IGC were the allocation of votes in an enlarged Council of Ministers (CoM) and the voting rules governing the application of QMV.

Voting power

The number of votes held by each state was increased for all existing (EU 15) Member States, with the most populated enjoying the largest relative increase. Post-Nice, the five biggest states will have 60 per cent of votes compared to their current share of 55 per cent. On this basis it will be easier for the four largest Member States (the UK, France, Germany and Italy) to block proposals.

Voting rules: thresholds and the triple lock

Prior to Nice, legislation subject to QMV was adopted if it received 62 out of 87 votes in the CoM (that is, 71.2 per cent). From January 2005, a proposal must achieve 169 votes out of 237 (that is, 71.3 per cent). Thereafter, the QMV threshold will change (via a number of incremental steps which are still unclear), depending on the rate of enlargement. According to the current allocations of votes, when the EU reaches 27 states, the QMV threshold will rise to 74 per cent. This change will also make it easier for a minority of states to block policy-making.

Nice also added two other elements to form a 'triple lock' on any QMV. First, any decision will have to receive at least a specified number of votes (the QMV threshold), as outlined above. Second, any qualified majority will have to be supported by at least half the Member States. Third, any state will be able to request verification that the QMV represents at least 62 per cent of the total population of the EU (equivalent to three of the largest states plus one other). If this last condition is not met (the so-called 'demographic cushion'), the policy will fail.

In return for more votes, the big Member States agreed to surrender their right to nominate a second commissioner. The deal struck at Nice maintains this formula up to a ceiling of 27 commissioners/Member States. Thereafter a rotation system will apply, the exact modalities of which were 'left over' to the next IGC.

Environment Policy Post-Nice

Dedicated 'EU-watchers' always find IGCs enthralling, but Nice was a real cliff-hanger that went right down to the wire. Admittedly, the topics under discussion were always going to be difficult to resolve, but the EU hoped to look forward and project a positive image to the new entrants. Unfortunately, the endgame of the negotiations descended into an unseemly 'vote grab' led (rather unedifyingly) by the French presidency of the EU. In the process (and to the dismay of pro-integrationists), all the old inter-state power politics that the EU was meant to tame surfaced with such force that the experience could well poison Member States' relations for years to come. It also sent a very powerful signal to the new entrants about what is deemed to be 'acceptable' behaviour in an enlarged EU of 27.

Admittedly, in a narrow technical sense, Nice has successfully paved the way for EU enlargement. In fact, some of the candidate states could even be full members when the EU completes the next IGC. This began in 2004 and its task is to sift through the 'Nice leftovers', discuss the status of the Charter, find ways to simplify the treaties and improve the role of national parliaments. It is already being dubbed the 'competences conference' as one of the main aims will be to delineate the respective powers of the EU and the Member States. If you found the subsidiarity debate of the early 1990s rather tiresome, stay well clear!

Major European environmental groups condemned the Treaty of Nice as a 'failure for the environment' (EEB, 2000b). They were especially dismayed at the inability to extend QMV, believing that the imminent addition of new Member States with relatively weak environmental protection policies will hobble the EU's ability to do what it has done in the past – develop ambitious environmental policies. But Nice was primarily an exercise in preparing the EU for enlargement and so, aside from revising Article 175, the scope for amending the wording of the environmental parts of the Treaty was never really that great. Environmental policy is now a comparatively mature area of EU action, and much of the early work (for example, giving the environmental *acquis* a legal base; enshrining sustainable development as a legal goal) was completed at Amsterdam. The bigger and much thornier question of how the enlargement process is to be reconciled with the EU's sustainability strategy was not on the agenda at Nice. Many environmentalists will rightly regard this as a non-decision of titanic proportions.

Those seeking to understand the environmental impacts of Nice have to look at its 'non-environmental' or procedural aspects, not least the Byzantine rules governing voting in the CoM. The problem is that the long-term impact of these changes on the dynamics of environmental policy-making are immensely difficult to predict. Clearly, the real winners at Nice were the three big states – the UK, France and Germany – whose power to block integration grew substantially. The smaller (and often 'greener') states found themselves elbowed out of the way, and the Commission's agenda for wide-sweeping reform was relegated to a very minor role. Overall, it will be more difficult post-Nice to achieve the qualified majority needed to force through a new policy. At the same time the new rules will make it easier for a minority to block progress, although, in practice, only a minority of EU policies are formally voted upon (Wessels, 2001, p209).

But the real unknown is how the new entrants will behave in the Environment Council (see Chapter 15). Until now, the main focus has been on their attempts to adjust to the existing environmental *acquis*, but as members, they will enjoy significant voting power in the Council and a new voice in the European Parliament. On paper, they are more likely to find common cause with the 'laggards' than the 'leaders' although their exact negotiating positions are still in a state of great flux.

References

Bär, S., Gehring, T., von Homeyer, I., Kraemer, R. A., Mazurek, A.-G., Klasing, A. and Tarasofky, R. G. (2000) 'Closer Co-operation: A New Instrument for European Environmental Policy?' *European Integration Online Papers 14*, http://olymp.wu-wien. ac.at/erpa/eiop.htm

Commission of the European Communities (2001), *Memorandum to the Members of the Commission. Summary of the Treaty of Nice*, SEC (2001) 99, http://www. europa.eu.int/igc2000/

EEB (2000a) *Greening the Treaty III: Proposals for the 2000 IGC*, Brussels: EEB.

EEB (2000b) *Nice – Failure for the Environment*, EEB Press Release, 13 December 2000, Brussels: EEB.

Galloway, D. (2001) *The Treaty of Nice and Beyond*, Sheffield: Sheffield Academic Press.

Jordan, A. J. (1998) 'Step Change or Stasis? EC Environmental Policy after the Amsterdam Summit', *Environmental Politics*, Vol.7, No.1, pp227–36.

Jordan, A. J. (2001) 'The Precautionary Principle in the EU', in O'Riordan, T., Cameron, J. and Jordan A. J. (eds), *Re-interpreting the Precautionary Principle*, London: Cameron May.

Jordan, A. J. (2002) *The Europeanisation of British Environmental Policy: A Departmental Perspective*, Basingstoke: Palgrave.

Jordan, A. J. and Lenschow, A. (2000) '"Greening" the European Union: What Can Be Learned from the Leaders of EU Environmental Policy?', *European Environment*, Vol.10, No.3, pp109–20.

Lenschow, A. (ed) (2001) *Environmental Policy Integration: Greening Sectoral Policies in Europe*, London: Earthscan.

Weale, A. (1996) 'Environmental Rules and Rule Making in the EU', *Journal of European Public Policy*, Vol.3, No.4, pp594–611.

Wessels, W. (2001) 'Nice Results: The Millennium IGC in the EU's Evolution', *Journal of Common Market Studies*, Vol.39, No.2, pp197–220.

Part 2
ACTORS

4

Strategies of the 'Green' Member States in EU Environmental Policy-making

Duncan Liefferink and Mikael Skou Andersen

Introduction

Environmentally progressive 'pioneers' are important forces behind the development of international and European Union (EU) environmental policy. On the basis of their own domestic regulations they promote the adoption of stringent environmental policies at the international level. This serves a dual goal. On the one hand, strict international measures lead to the reduction of transboundary flows of pollution and thus contribute to achieving national environmental policy goals. On the other hand, competitive disadvantages for industry in the 'pioneer' countries will diminish if others have to take similarly costly measures. The 'leader–laggard' dynamic in international environmental policy currently enjoys considerable academic interest (eg Haas, 1993; Héritier, 1994; Héritier et al, 1994; Sbragia, 1996; Holzinger, 1997; Andersen and Liefferink, 1997a).

In the specific case of the EU, the increasing attention paid to the role of 'leaders' versus 'laggards' can be linked to shifts in the political context of environmental policy-making. Until recently, Germany, Denmark and The Netherlands were generally regarded as the most environmentally minded Member States, acting as the 'motors' of EU environmental policy-making. This view was held not only by political scientists (cf for instance the references above) but also by authors more directly involved in the policy-making process in Brussels (eg Krämer, 1992, pp52–53; Johnson and Corcelle, 1995, p8). On 1 January 1995 Sweden, Finland and Austria entered the Union. Domestic environmental standards in those countries are at a level comparable to or even higher than those of the former 'green troika'. They were therefore broadly expected to strengthen the group of 'pushers' in EU environmental policy-making (cf Sbragia, 1996; Axelrod, 1997; Aguilar Fernández, 1997). The future enlargement of the Union by a number of Central and Eastern European countries may further increase the importance of the 'leader–laggard' dynamic by making the EU (even) more diverse than it is now. Although the precise mechanisms are as yet uncertain, this will almost inevitably lead to greater flexibility with regard to the differentiation of standards in the EU and thus to more freedom for environmentally progressive Member States to develop their own policies.

In most studies of 'leaders' and 'laggards', however, there is a tendency to treat the categories[1] in a rather undifferentiated way. The main point of interest being the dynamic of the policy process in Brussels, differences within the groups are hardly taken into account. In this chapter we will argue that such differences do exist and that they are indeed relevant for understanding the two-level game being played in the EU. In doing so, we will focus on the group of environmental 'leaders'.

In the following, we will first propose a typology of 'green' strategies in the EU, distinguishing between different kinds of pushers and forerunners. Based on that, we will consider in detail the positions and strategies of the 'green' Member States in the first year after the accession of Sweden, Finland and Austria. The exploration will address policy-making in the Council and its subordinate bodies as well as relations with the Commission and the European Parliament (EP). Apart from policy documents and secondary literature, empirical data derive from a series of interviews with key policy-makers in the six countries under consideration.[2]

Strategies of Influencing EU Environmental Policy

Domestic policies have often been designed on a predominantly domestic background, with limited attention paid to the impact that such policies may have abroad. More than any other form of international policy-making, however, regulatory policy-making in the EU has a reciprocal, two-level character (Putnam, 1988; Andersen and Liefferink, 1997b). On the one hand, negotiations in Brussels are to a large extent determined by the 'input' from the Member States (eg Weale, 1996, p607). On the other hand, processes and outcomes at the EU level often have an impact on domestic policies. This leads to a continuous interrelation and exchange between policy-making processes at both levels. Considering the growing importance and impact of EU environmental policy, this also implies that domestic policies in this field are increasingly designed with a deliberate view to the possible impact on EU policy-making. In the national context, far-reaching domestic measures have sometimes even been justified by their expected impact at the EU or international level.

It is possible to range the various types of 'green' positions on a spectrum, ranging from defensive forerunner to active pusher strategies, as we have done elsewhere (Andersen and Liefferink, 1997b; Liefferink and Andersen, forthcoming). However, this simple distinction does not leave room for the observation that progressive forerunner positions may be taken either with or without an explicit view to the impact in Brussels. In the former case, a forerunner position can (but does not necessarily have to) be combined with active pusher efforts at the EU level. Moreover, even if stringent national policies are implemented for

Table 4.1 *Strategies of Influencing EU Environmental Policy*

Forerunner:	Purposeful	Incremental
Pusher:		
Direct	(a) Pusher-by-example	(b) Constructive pusher
Indirect	(c) Defensive forerunner	(d) Opt-outer

purely domestic reasons, they may still trigger activity in Brussels. In this context it is useful to distinguish between pusher effects that are channelled directly into *environmental* policy-making, and effects that occur via *internal market* policies. In order to accommodate this kind of gradation in the possible strategies applied by 'green' Member States for influencing EU environmental policy-making, we propose a more systematic classification.

Table 4.1 presents a scheme according to which a Member State can act as a 'pioneer' in principally four different ways, with varying emphasis on the aspects of being a forerunner and a pusher. A 'forerunner' is defined as a Member State which is 'ahead' of EU environmental policy in the sense of having developed more advanced policies with a higher level of protection. The table distinguishes between forerunner policies developed in a more incremental, historical process, and those which have been adapted more purposefully with an eye to the EU policy-making process. 'Pushing' can take place directly with regard to environmental policy-making or, more indirectly, usually by interfering with internal market policies. Our approach thus provides a refinement of the 'first mover' strategy as recently described by Héritier (1996), particularly by raising the possibility of less intentional pusher and forerunner roles. The first field (a), where a Member State acts as a purposeful forerunner and pushes directly, is the situation where unilateral action is taken in order to influence EU environmental policy-making. This can be referred to as a *pusher-by-example*. A good example is Denmark's unilateral introduction of a CO_2 tax, introduced not least to promote an EU-wide CO_2 tax (Andersen and Liefferink, 1996, pp114–115).

In the second field (b), the forerunner position of a Member State has been achieved incrementally, without a view to the EU process and usually primarily for domestic reasons. The Member State may nevertheless seek to push EU environmental policy-making directly by building alliances with the Commission's experts or with other Member States. This type of impact is often referred to as the *constructive pusher* strategy, because it is basically oriented towards finding a compromise, possibly at the expense of slightly lower EU standards than domestic ones. An example is the influence exerted by Germany, The Netherlands and Denmark regarding the rather ambitious level of waste water treatment agreed upon in the Urban Waste Water Directive, which followed, to a great extent, the standard in water treatment achieved in these countries over many years.

In the third field (c), the forerunner position of a Member State has been adopted deliberately, but the pushing of EU policy-making is done more indirectly, at least from the point of view of the Member State. It does not explicitly present its unilateral action as a model for environmental policy in the EU. Instead, the pushing effect is a result of interference with EU policies in other fields, mostly internal market policy. This type of impact can be referred to as the *defensive forerunner,* because the Member State is more concerned with protecting its own environment, rather than that of the EU as a whole. The implications for the EU may nevertheless be considerable. The classical example is the Danish bottle system and the matching ban on cans, which was introduced in 1982 (cf Koppen, 1993). The ban was perceived by the Commission as being in conflict with the single market. Denmark never proposed introducing the system at the level of the EU, but after the European Court of Justice had basically acquitted Denmark, the issue formed a significant part of the background for the drafting of the present Packaging Waste Directive.

In the fourth field (d), the pushing of EU environmental policy is indirect too, but the forerunner position has been developed more incrementally. As in the previous category, the impact on EU policy-making is caused by conflicts between domestic environmental standards and the functioning of the internal market. The difference is that national measures in these cases somewhat unexpectedly turn out to be out of step with EU measures, something which may lead the Member State to *opt out.* As an example of this category, we refer to the German and Dutch bans on the wood-preservative pentachlorophenol (PCP). As the EU established a more lax standard for PCP, it led both countries (and later also Denmark) to invoke Article 100a(4) of the Treaty in order to uphold the forerunner position achieved. France successfully challenged the use of Article 100a(4) at the Court of Justice. The impact of the PCP issue on EU policy-making was not really oriented towards a specific directive, but it helped to revitalize an ongoing discussion among the Member States about the freedom to act nationally in the context of EU environmental policy.

With regard to a concrete issue, the above strategies may in fact be combined. It is also conceivable that strategies shift in time. In the case of the introduction of catalytic converters in cars in the 1980s, for instance, Germany successfully combined the role of pusher-by-example with the threat of becoming a defensive forerunner by making advanced preparations for the unilateral introduction of catalytic converters (Holzinger, 1994). The scheme provides us with a tool to distinguish the different strategies analytically.

Strategies of the 'Green' Member States

In this section, we will discuss the strategies of the six allegedly 'green' Member States in the first year after the accession of Sweden, Finland and Austria, ie in 1995. We will start by focusing on forms of indirect pushing (fields (c) and (d)). As we will see, some countries seek to combine these with more direct pushing-by-example (field (a)). Finally, we will examine to what extent various ways of constructive pushing (field (b)) are practised by the environmental 'leaders'. This may involve working through the Council and its subordinate bodies and building alliances with like-minded Member States, but also, for instance, influencing the Commission or lobbying the EP.

Indirect pushing

Under EU law, the room for introducing or maintaining strict national legislation is limited by the effects of such measures on the functioning of the internal market. Article 36 of the Treaty states this principle in general terms for situations where no specific EU legislation exists or where measures have been taken under the Treaty's environmental section (Article 130r–t). The exact balance between environmental and market interests, however, has to be struck in each individual case. The Danish bottle case, referred to above, was one such case that went all the way to the Court of Justice. It showed that some trade barriers may be allowed for pressing environmental reasons (see further, eg Krämer, 1992; Koppen, 1993). If harmonization measures already exist at the EU level, Article 100a(4) of the Treaty further specifies the conditions under which Member States may be permitted to apply stricter national provisions.[3] Particularly in Denmark and Sweden, Article 100a(4) has gained considerable political importance and has become known as the 'environmental guarantee'.

In Denmark, Article 100a(4) became a major issue in the period of the referendum about the Single European Act in 1986. It was a concession from the other Member States to Denmark and used by the Danish government as an argument against the widespread fear of a loss of national control and autonomy owing to the introduction of qualified majority voting in the environmental field. If Denmark were outvoted in the Council, it was argued, the 'environmental guarantee' would release Denmark from the obligation to accept a relaxation of domestic standards. The implication of this argument was entirely defensive. And in fact, also one year earlier when it blocked the so-called Luxembourg compromise on car exhaust standards for small cars (cf Holzinger, 1994, pp258–261; Liefferink, 1996, Chapter 6), Denmark had shown a readiness to jeopardize a compromise at the European level in order not to belie national policy objectives. Against this background, there can be little doubt that the Court's ruling in the PCP case in 1994 (see above) came as a disappointment to the Danish government. In this judgment, the Court of Justice nullified the Commission's authorization of a German ban on the use of PCP on the grounds of insufficient motivation of environmental necessity. Although the Court had chosen a very careful wording and left open the possibility of the application of Article 100a(4) under other circumstances,[4] the judgment made clear that Article 100a(4) can indeed not be taken as a 'guarantee'. As Koppen (1993, p141) points out, its interpretation is a political rather than a juridical matter. This insight does not necessarily reduce the importance of Article 100a(4), however. Recently, a shift has been observed in Denmark in the direction of a somewhat less defensive and more 'activist' approach to EU environmental policy-making owing, among other things, to the key role of environmental issues in the domestic EU debate and the growing ambition to act as the leader of at least the Nordic core of a new 'green' group in the EU. While the minimization of the EU's impact on the domestic policy space will no doubt continue to be a strong focus, the dynamic potential of going-it-alone in the European policy process, either with or without invoking Article 100a(4), may come somewhat more to the fore.

Pushing-by-example

Among the new Member States, concern about the possible consequences of membership for national environmental policy is probably greatest in Sweden. In the accession debate, therefore, the 'environmental guarantee' played a role quite similar to the one it played in Denmark, but beyond defending domestic arrangements for their own sake, Sweden appeared to want more. Both the Swedish government and the environmental movement linked the room for national policies to the ambition of showing a 'good example' to other countries (Naturvårdsverket, 1993; Nielsen, 1994). The government emphasized the need to combine the example strategy with more constructive pushing within the Union. As potential 'good examples' in the EU context, they particularly referred to the system of producer liability for car exhaust cleaning equipment (EU, EES och miljön, 1994, pp140–141) and to ozone-depleting substances (Det svenska miljöarbetet i EU, 1994–5, pp43–44). In both areas, however, the accession agreement had already explicitly permitted Sweden to be a forerunner (EU, EES och miljön, 1994, Chapter 10). More interesting in this respect is the field of chemicals. Here Sweden was granted a four-year transition period, whereas the EU committed itself to reviewing its own legislation in this field during this period. It is quite obvious that Sweden's strict policies, for instance with regard to pesticides, can serve as an example for the EU (Det svenska miljöarbetet i EU, 1994–5, pp21–23). It is unclear, however, what will happen if a gap between Swedish and EU requirements remains after the transition period. For the time being, the Swedish government appears to be quite reluctant about the option of going-it-alone and to prefer a strategy based on discussion and co-operation (EU, EES och miljön, 1994, pp141–145; Det svenska miljöarbetet i EU, 1994–5, pp21–23), but a conflict is likely to evolve on this point in the years to come.

Also, Austria and Finland, as well as the 'old' members Germany and The Netherlands, acknowledge the relevance of national experiences as examples of practicable, feasible policy alternatives during negotiations about specific measures in Brussels. Contrary to Sweden, however, they hardly regard them as vehicles to instigate new policies at the EU level. Considering this, it may be questioned how relevant the more provocative variants of a forerunner strategy, ie the unilateral introduction of stricter national measures, still are at this moment. Germany used to be the champion of this strategy in the 1980s (eg the 'clean' car case, cf Holzinger, 1994), but is not likely to resume this role soon. With its 'good example' ambitions, Sweden may be regarded as Germany's most obvious successor, but so far has not stressed this type of approach. As noted above, Denmark has recently turned to a more 'activist' attitude in EU environmental policy-making. In the view also of its highly committed Environment Minister, Svend Auken, this country now seems to be the Member State most inclined to embark upon confrontational pusher-by-example or defensive forerunner strategies.

Constructive pushing 'inside' Brussels

After having discussed strategies based on the direct or indirect impact of domestic policies in the EU context, we will now turn to strategies applied by the six when they take part in the policy process in Brussels, ie the more constructive approach distinguished above. We will subsequently do so by examining the Member States' dealings in the Council and its subordinate bodies, the opportunities for building alliances in the Council and their various ways of influencing the Commission and the EP.

The Council

Agendas for meetings of the Council of Ministers are set by the Member State holding the Presidency of the Council. In the EU 15, however, Member States are in this position only once in seven-and-a-half years. Moreover, the Presidency is restricted by the fact that a large portion of the agendas are predetermined by proposals already under way in the EU machinery and by external influences, such as major international negotiations in which the EU has to take a common position. During the six months' term of a Presidency, in other words, a Member State is mainly able to affect the order rather than the content of the work of the Council (cf Wurzel, 1996, pp277, 280). In addition, all Member States have the right to submit items to the Council agenda on an ad hoc basis. In the environmental field, Denmark in particular often makes use of this option in order to demand attention for topical issues. Often, however, such interventions are primarily aimed at the domestic audience, as the environment plays a relatively important role in Danish politics (Andersen, 1997). Our study confirms the finding by Pellegrom (1997), however, that other Member States are prepared to go along with this only to a limited extent. A Member State repeatedly overloading the Council agenda with 'other business' runs the risk of losing the goodwill of its partners.

The most conspicuous element of the workings of the Council is their voting procedure. In the Single Act, qualified majority voting (QMV) was introduced for environmental decisions directly related to internal market harmonization (Article 100a). The Maastricht Treaty on European Union extended this, with a number of exceptions, to the entire environmental policy field (Article 130s).

Unlike the former 'troika', the present six 'green' Member States hold sufficient votes to block QMV decisions. Although no doubt important in specific cases, for instance where a lowering of standards is at stake, the impact of this should not be overstated. In the first place, actual voting seldom takes place. Even under the QMV rule, negotiations in the Council are usually carried on until the moment consensus is reached, or is at least very close, so that voting is no longer relevant. Second, it must be realized that a 'green' blocking minority is not, so to speak, very 'shockproof'. If either Germany or two of the other countries defect, for instance, the coalition loses all formal impact. And even if an alliance holds together, in the third place, the power of the six under QMV is only negative. They can in principle block legislation that does not satisfy them, but they cannot force the adoption of environmentally progressive proposals without the support of a considerable number of other members. Finally, as discussed in further detail below, Member States may have reasons of a more general strategic kind to be reluctant about constructing something like a 'green bloc'.

Nevertheless, the opinion was widely shared among policy-makers in the six Member States that the last enlargement had caused a certain strengthening of the 'green' input in the Council. Allegedly, 'green' standpoints are being taken more seriously and some noted a refining of consensus-seeking processes under QMV. This phenomenon has been described as the 'shadow of the vote'. According to Weiler (1991), the mere possibility of voting in case of a deadlock enhances the pressure to make concessions for the sake of reaching a compromise. Besides, parties that have *the potential* to form a blocking minority, as the six indeed do, may take advantage of this effect. The circumstance that it seldom comes to an actual vote may in fact even heighten this effect, as Member States do not have to lay all their cards on the table (for an illuminating game-theoretical analysis of decision-making under QMV underpinning several of these points, see Holzinger, 1997).

The Council's subordinate bodies

Apart from the work in the Council of Ministers itself, the lower levels of the Council apparatus are highly relevant for pushing issues and preferences. These levels include the Committee of Permanent Representatives (COREPER) and the Environment Group, consisting of the environmental attachés of the Member States' Permanent Representations in Brussels, usually assisted by experts from the capitals. In addition, in some cases permanent or ad hoc working groups at the expert level exist. It goes without saying that the vote casts a shadow in these bodies too, but at the same time discussions are far more detailed and substantive than in the Council meetings. In particular, the Environment Group, which meets more than once a week, operates at the crossroads of politics and technical expertise (Pellegrom, 1997).

Currently, the new Member States seem to focus on the technical aspect of the work in the Group. Especially in Sweden and Austria, good substantive argumentation and a coherent, well-prepared input into the daily policy process are seen as a major way to exert influence in Brussels. Domestically, efforts are made to ensure the high quality of this input. The Swedish Environment Ministry and the Environmental Protection Agency *(Naturvårdsverket),* for instance, take their task in preparing for EU negotiations particularly seriously, and the environment was the first policy sector in Sweden boasting an official strategic memorandum about EU co-operation (Det svenska miljöarbetet i EU, 1994–5, published in March 1995). In the eyes of other countries, the input notably of Sweden is sometimes regarded as overly driven by arguments that do indeed have a firm basis but leave little room for political wheeling and dealing.

While Denmark can be characterized as putting more emphasis on the political side of the work in the Environment Group, Germany, The Netherlands and to some extent Finland generally show a more pragmatic approach. They acknowledge that expertise can be a major resource in the Environment Group, but in the end it is seen as part of the larger political game. Eventually, one might say, achieving a common solution is considered more important than to be fully in the right. Technical details thus become subject to a process of give-and-take in an earlier stage than they do for countries that strongly stress the technical and scientific basis of their positions. This 'conflation' of political and technical aspects already at the Group level makes it possible to respond more flexibly to political opportunities, but it also reduces domestic control of the behaviour of negotiators in Brussels. As long as there is agreement on the broad lines of the national position, this need not be a problem. If there are serious differences between the domestic parties involved, however, it may give rise to continuous conflicts. According to Pehle (1997), the latter situation exists to some extent in Germany, mainly owing to a protracted struggle about international competencies between the Ministry of the Environment and other sectoral ministries.

Co-ordination and alliances between Member States

Particularly for the formation of blocking minorities, but also in order to exert more positive pressure on the political process in Brussels, alliance-building between countries is important. Alliances between the 'green' Member States, however, are by no means given. They have to be formed on an issue-by-issue basis and remain liable to defection. Long-term inter-issue reciprocity does not play an important role, neither within nor outside the circle of 'green' Member States. The assessment of the merits of each individual case, rather than general loyalties, determines the process of seeking allies in Brussels, at least in the environmental field. With this in mind it is obvious that potential allies are not restricted to a small group but in principle include all Member States. France, for instance, was drawn into a group supporting a special declaration regarding the application of the 'best available technology' in the framework of the Directive on integrated pollution prevention and control (IPPC), a group which was not joined by Germany and Austria (cf *Europe Environment* No.457, pI–13). Belgium and Luxembourg participated in an informal meeting of eight Member States advocating more effective climate policies, held at the instigation of the Dutch government in The Hague in January 1996 (*Europe Environment* No.471, pI–1), in which Germany again appeared as the most reluctant partner. The need to have a broad basis in order to produce positive results under the QMV rule, and in the 'concurrent majority' system of the EU in general (cf Weale, 1996), of course reinforces the tendency to recruit partners from as broad a range as possible.

Alliance-building in the Council or Council working groups is to a large extent an implicit process. Like-minded countries tend to 'find' each other in the course of negotiating in Brussels. And if they do decide actively to co-ordinate their strategies, this largely happens at the daily work level, ie between environmental attachés at the Permanent Representations in Brussels. In addition, regarding issues of major importance, bilateral contacts between capitals may occur, particularly in order to win doubters for one side or the other. Sub-EU meetings, like the one on climate policy in The Hague in January 1996, are in fact an exception, but in this case it may be explained by the wish to give an unorthodox impulse to the exceptionally slow and cumbersome process in this field. There can, of course, be no doubt that governments are aware that some Member States are more likely to Join them than others. It is also probable that they anticipate this and, either implicitly or explicitly, adjust their strategies in the Council to take advantage of perceived opportunities in specific cases. Closer and regular co-ordination between a 'green core' of Member States, however, appears to be in contradiction with the open and case-by-case character of alliance-building in the Council. If the 'green' Member States wish or need the support of as many others as possible, every suggestion of 'cliquism' has to be avoided.

Seen in this light, it is not surprising that actual attempts made to establish more regular forms of co-ordination between a limited group of Member States were received with little enthusiasm by most countries, including those that were supposed to be part of the group. After the accession of Sweden and Finland, Denmark in particular made an effort to arrange informal meetings between the ministers of the Nordic Member States immediately before Council sessions. Although the meetings were neither secret nor closed, it was felt that they might be associated with the formation of a Nordic 'bloc'. Finland, which generally gives lower priority to environmental issues in the EU than Denmark and Sweden and has a particularly strong geo-political interest in not becoming isolated, was especially eager not to create this impression.

A case in point is the Nordic campaign concerning the review of the Basle Convention on hazardous waste shipment in September 1995 (cf *Europe Environment* Nos.451–457). Earlier that year, Denmark had proposed that in this review the EU should go for a total ban on the export of hazardous waste destined for disposal and for recycling or recovery. After the Danish proposal had been turned down by the Commission, Denmark, together with Sweden, Finland and Norway, submitted an amendment of similar purport directly to the Secretariat of the Convention. In March 1995, however, the Council agreed on a considerably more modest common standpoint. Formally, and under the threat of a Court case, the Nordic Member States should now have withdrawn their own amendment to the Convention, leaving it to the Norwegians to keep up the position unilaterally. Denmark refused to do so and managed to get Sweden and Finland on its side. A political and juridical fight evolved about the affair. Helped by some pressure from the EP and after a stiff internal debate, in late April the Commission changed its mind and adopted the Nordic amendment, which was endorsed in June by the Council. The Commission even succeeded in pushing through the export ban during the Convention meeting with many exemptions *(Europe Environment* No.462, pI–5). The eventual effectiveness of the action cannot be denied, in sum, but the Danish self-will was looked upon critically, not only by the Commission and the other Member States but also within the Nordic 'coalition'.

Episodes like the confrontation on the Basle Convention are therefore bound to remain the exception. Generally speaking, it must be concluded that the Nordic countries have insufficient critical mass to play a role in the environmental field comparable to that of the French–German co-operation on the integration process at large. Owing to its limited political weight, the risk of a Nordic 'green core' being isolated appears to be greater than its opportunity to function as a 'nucleus' for wider coalitions. When thinking of possibilities to broaden the basis of a 'green core group', the crucial role of Germany is evident. Being by far the largest of the environmentally progressive countries in the EU, Germany's participation in such a group would give substance to the threat of a blocking minority and thus make it a power to be reckoned with by all Member States. The construction of a standing environmental coalition led or at least joined by Germany seems very unlikely, however, not only in view of the many factors that would actually divide the members of such a coalition, but also because of the basically pragmatic and ad hoc character of alliance-building in the Council, for the reasons pointed out above.

The Commission

If new policies are to be initiated at the EU level, the Commission cannot be circumvented. The Commission has the exclusive right to submit proposals for new legislation to the Council. For that reason, good relations with the Commission are of crucial importance, particularly for Member States attempting to push forward a policy field. For the new Member States, the building up of such relations is among the highest priorities.

The part of the Commission most obvious in this regard is the Directorate General for Environment, Nuclear Safety and Civil Protection (DG XI), which is in charge of the majority of environmental policies in the EU. DG XI is generally quite receptive to new developments in the policy field and is regarded by the 'green' Member States primarily as an ally against 'unwilling' DGs and Member States. In this context it is an illustrative detail that some of our interviewees talked about 'supporting' rather than 'influencing' DG XI. Contacts at the expert level, (participation in) the formulation of various kinds of preliminary policy proposals and position papers, and what may be called the strategic employment of nationals in Brussels are the most common ways for Member States to exert influence on the Commission's policies, and we will now consider these ways in some detail.

Experts from the Member States meet in Brussels basically for two purposes. In the first place, meetings of civil servants specializing in the issue at stake, usually from the relevant ministries or related government agencies, are convened by the Commission in the preparatory phase of a proposal for new legislation. The experts comment on the technical aspects of the proposal but are also supposed to give a first idea of the political support to be expected later in the Council. Second, there are several kinds of committee composed of national civil servants controlling the implementation of EU legislation, a system often referred to as 'comitology'. Both the committees in the preparatory phase and the implementation committees obviously give room for influencing the Commission's policy choices. Apart from that, they also function as a breeding ground for new steps. An expert committee may identify the need for follow-up policies or it may be a suitable place for a Member State to first test a new idea. Because of its large proportions and its opaque character, Pellegrom (1997) qualifies 'comitology' as 'a limitation on the co-ordinated input from the capitals, after all'. This may be correct from the point of view of central co-ordination by the Permanent Representations and, behind them, the Ministries of Foreign Affairs. From the perspective of policy-makers at the ministries and agencies directly involved, however, the evaluation may turn out somewhat differently. In most cases, the expert taking part in the consultations for new legislation is from the same specialized unit in the ministry as the one delegated afterwards to the implementation committee regarding the directive in question, if it is not the same person. In addition to this, the same people are usually involved in preparing positions for the Council negotiations that take place in the meantime. This offers excellent opportunities for governmental actors at the professional level consistently to propagate certain views or priorities throughout the policy process. These opportunities are recognized by all 'green' Member States. The Environment Ministries, particularly in the new

Member States, attach great value to a well-prepared and competent input into the various EU expert committees.

A second way to influence Commission policy is through various types of written statement. These can range from suggestions or designs for specific policy measures to general strategic memoranda. Apart from informal discussions with the Commission and, if relevant, other Member States, such papers may be presented to the Environmental Policy Review Group (EPRG). This group was set up in the early 1990s in order to improve communication between the Member States and the Commission, and it brings together the Directors-General of the Environment from all Member States and the EU. A document that is well received by this forum can hardly be neglected by the Commission. A Dutch position paper on a new structure for environmental framework directives was launched this way in May 1995. Regarding proposals for a framework Directive on ecological water quality, a route via the Council was followed. Dissatisfied with the first draft Directive submitted by the Commission in late 1994, The Netherlands and a number of other Member States decided to prepare quite detailed position papers containing alternative proposals. These papers were first discussed in the Council's Environment Group. Via the EP and the Council itself, the issue was eventually referred back to the Commission, which came up with an encompassing communication on 'European Community water policy' in February 1996 (COM(96)59; cf *Europe Environment* Nos.457, 465; also Van As, 1995).

The third and probably the most effective method for a Member State seeking to have an impact at an early stage is to penetrate into the Commission directly, that is, to place personnel at strategic places in the Commission. For this purpose the system of so-called national experts is very helpful. In many DGs, including DG XI, personnel temporarily 'on loan' from the Member States play an important role. All Member States make use of this by sending specialists in prioritized fields to the Commission. In this way, for example, the preparation of the Fifth Environmental Action Plan was led by a Dutch national expert (cf Kronsell, 1997). Shortly after its accession, Sweden seconded an expert to Brussels to help revitalize the area of acidification. Influencing the employment of regular EU personnel is more complicated, as this depends more on vacancies and other factors beyond the control of Member State governments. Particularly for the lower ranks, one of the main things a Member State can do is to try to ensure that it has a proportional share of the total number of employees. Stimulating sufficiently high-quality people to apply for jobs in the Commission appears to be a problem especially in Sweden, the most Euro-sceptic of the three new Member States. Appointments at the level of Directors and Directors-General, and of course of Commissioners themselves, are strongly determined by political factors, thus leaving more room for strategic manoeuvres by Member States. Conspicuous examples are the stable presence of the French at the highest level of DG VI (Agriculture) and the succession of two Dutch Directors-General in DG XI, Laurens-Jan Brinkhorst (1986–1994) and Marius Enthoven (1994–1997). National networks in the Commission consisting of both permanent and temporary staff can be very important. In the first place, they can function as a basis for 'lobbying' for concrete issues inside the Commission. Depending on the issue at stake, like-minded Commission officials from other Member States can be relevant here as well. Second, such networks can help in diffusing a certain way of thinking about environmental problems and policies. New Member States obviously have to make up arrears in this field but, as they are all well aware of the potential impact of such networks, this is mainly a matter of time.

The European Parliament

As the EP has often in the past delivered relatively progressive amendments and resolutions with regard to the environment (cf for instance Judge, 1992; Arp, 1992), it may be seen as a partner, especially by the 'green' Member States. Some of our interviewees, however, pointed to a certain unpredictability in the EP's stances. This may have to do with the EP's permanent involvement in an inter-institutional struggle for more power, which sometimes tends to prevail over sub-stantive considerations. In the case of a further increase of the Parliament's formal powers, moreover, influence on its positions will be sought by a growing range of interested actors and it is doubtful whether the 'green' image will be maintained to the same extent as it has been so far.

Member States maintain contacts to the EP mainly through 'their own' con-tingent of parliament members (MEPs). The best and most well-structured rela-tions were reported to exist between the British MEPs and London, among other things in the form of briefings and regular meetings. Most 'green' Member States see the UK as an example in this respect and are in different stages of improving their relations with national MEPs. A number of countries, including Germany, already inform 'their' MEPs of their positions in Council negotiations on a rou-tine basis. Among the new Member States, only Finland appears to be more or less regularly sending briefing notes on environmental matters to its MEPs. Aus-tria as well as Denmark are currently working on this. In all six countries, direct meetings still take place largely ad hoc, with an obvious focus on major and controversial issues. Furthermore, contacts are not always initiated by the Member States themselves. MEPs often seek information or assistance from their respec-tive capitals or Permanent Representations. So this is one more way for Member States to propagate their viewpoints, to be sure, but it indicates that cultivating contacts with the EP is hardly regarded as a top priority.

It should be added that, in this context, the EP is a considerably more impor-tant partner for the Commission. In the co-operation and co-decision proce-dures, amendments by the EP supported by the Commission are difficult to resist by the Council. A certain amount of co-ordination between the EP and the Com-mission in this sense is no exception.

Conclusion and Outlook

It must be stressed that this discussion on the strategies of the six 'green' Member States in EU environmental policy was based on only one year, 1995. For the three new members, moreover, this was the first year of full membership. An eval-uation of their role in particular should take into account that they were still in the process of defining their positions on the rolling train of the EU. Even with this limitation, however, there can be little doubt that Denmark is currently the most articulate 'green' Member State in the EU. It is important to realize, however, that the Danish activism has a strong defensive tendency. In the 1980s, the predominant Danish strategy was that of a defensive forerunner. A focus on developing and maintaining strict national policies was combined with an uncompromising approach in Brussels. Furthermore, the central role of the 'environmental guarantee' in the domestic debate showed that the idea of opting out was always present. Denmark is currently placing more emphasis on the pusher potential of its forerunner position, or in the terminology of our scheme: its potential as a pusher-by-example. This may be associated, among other things, with the fact that the environment is one of the few fields where the Danish government may be able to convince the Euro-sceptical population of the assets of EU membership (see Andersen, 1997; Liefferink and Andersen, forthcoming). Some major disappointments in the environmental field or a further decrease of Danish confidence in the EU, for instance in relation to the most recent treaty revision, may change this situation. In that case, a retreat to more defensive strategies seems likely.

Considering its rhetoric in the accession debate, as noted above, Sweden could have been expected to assume a role close to that of Denmark. In the first year of membership, and perhaps partly owing to relative inexperience in EU work, Sweden did not immediately choose a confrontational strategy. Rather, it adopted a more constructive approach based on good arguments and expertise. The end of the four-year transition period, especially with regard to the important issue of chemicals and pesticides, however, may force Sweden to make a more explicit choice between meagre results at the negotiating table in Brussels and the preferences of the domestic constituency. Although ambitions in the accession debate had not been set as high as in Sweden, Austria appears to be in a somewhat similar situation. In daily policy-making, the country so far mainly acted in a constructive manner, but the explosive issue of road transport through the Alps may lead to a direct conflict between domestic and EU policies and trigger a greater emphasis on Austria's forerunner position. In both countries, moreover, increasing Euro-scepticism among the population may enhance these trends.

While in Sweden and Austria the tendency to develop explicit forerunner positions may thus, in the longer term, come to overhaul the constructive approach, Finland and The Netherlands seem to be more genuine constructive pushers. For Finland at this time, this can mainly be related to a wish to avoid any conflict that might endanger its crucial economic and security interests. How these factors will develop in the long run, as well as how they are perceived in the Finnish domestic context, remains difficult to predict. For The Netherlands, an open economy in the polluted core of the Continent, the constructive approach is based on the conviction that, in the end, both the domestic environment and the national economy benefit more from international compromises than from unilateralism.

The remaining character in the tableau is Germany, the most important but at the same time the most ambiguous of the 'green' Member States. Owing, among other things, to severe economic problems and an inability to catch up fully with the shift in EU environmental policy from a standard-oriented to a more processual approach (Pehle, 1997), Germany has gradually lost the position of pusher-by-example that it had built up during the 1980s. What is left is not always clear. In some cases, such as climate policy, Germany appeared as the most reluctant 'green' Member State. In other cases, including many of the more 'traditional' environmental issues, Germany is still among the forerunners, but the willingness to make active use of this in the EU context, for instance by (threatening) *Alleingang*, has diminished. This situation may lead Germany increasingly to behave as a defensive forerunner, concerned primarily with maintaining its own standards.

By moving from activist to more defensive strategies, Germany appears to have changed places with Denmark. Obviously, this has profound implications for the group of 'green' Member States. Germany's participation is crucial for the formation of a successful 'green' alliance. The remaining five, if they are at all able to hold together, lack both the formal voting power and the political and economic impact to maintain pressure on EU environmental policy-making.

The German case makes it very clear that having strict domestic policies is not sufficient to be a 'leader' in EU environmental policy. While general strategic considerations prevent the formation of a standing environmental coalition, as discussed above, differences in the ways in which 'green' positions are articulated in the EU context may seriously thwart the building of 'green' alliances on an issue-by-issue basis.

Acknowledgements

We are grateful to the EU for funding this research under the 'Environment and Climate' programme (contract no. EV5V-CT94-0385) and to the officials at various national ministries and in Brussels who agreed to be interviewed. We would also like to thank the editor of the JEPP and three anonymous reviewers for helpful comments on an earlier version of this article.

Notes

1   Greece, Spain, Portugal and Ireland are usually counted among the 'laggards'. In several studies, in fact, a middle category of 'neutrals' is also distinguished, consisting of the UK, France, Luxembourg and, in most cases, Belgium and Italy (Krämer, 1992; Sbragia, 1996; Johnson and Corcelle, 1995).

2   In each country either the Head of the Division for International Environmental Affairs or the EU Co-ordinator (or in some cases both) at the Ministry for the Environment was interviewed, with the exception of Denmark where the Environmental Protection Agency (Miljøstyrelsen) was visited instead. In Sweden, both the Ministry and the Agency (Naturvårdsverket) were covered. At the Ministries of Foreign Affairs, internal organization showed more variation. Interviews were therefore held with either heads or environment experts from the International Trade or Internal Market Divisions or with officials responsible for general European integration matters

(and in two cases with both). For five countries, moreover, environment attachés at the Permanent Representations to the EU in Brussels were interviewed. All interviews were carried out between October 1995 and January 1996.

3   Artide 100a was amended and clarified in the Amsterdam Treaty, concluded in June 1997. After ratification, Member States will be explicitly allowed not only to *apply* but also to *introduce* stricter national measures. The new Artide 100a(5) seems to suggest, furthermore, that this is possible regardless of whether the Member State originally voted against or in favour of the harmonization measure. These changes are not pertinent to the present discussion, however.

4   It is interesting to note that in February 1996 a Danish ban on PCP, which had in fact been in force already for some years, was authorized by the Commission (cf *Europe Environment*, No.472, pp1–10).

References

Aguilar Fernández, S. (1997) 'Abandoning a laggard role? New strategies in Spanish environmental policy', in Liefferink, D. and Andersen, M. S. (eds) *The Innovation of EU Environmental Policy*, Copenhagen: Scandinavian University Press, pp156–172.

Andersen, M. S. (1997) 'Denmark: The Shadow of the Green Majority', in Andersen, M. S. and Liefferink, D. (eds) *European Environmental Policy: The Pioneers*, Manchester: Manchester University Press, pp251–286.

Andersen, M. S. and Liefferink, D. (1996) *The New Member States and the Impact on Environmental Policy. Draft Final Report to the Commission*, Aarhus: Aarhus University, Department of Political Science.

Andersen, M. S. and Liefferink, D. (eds) (1997a) *European Environmental Policy: The Pioneers*, Manchester: Manchester University Press.

Andersen, M. S. and Liefferink, D. (1997b) 'Introduction: the impact of the pioneers on EU environmental policy', in Andersen, M. S. and Liefferink, D. (eds) *European Environmental Policy: The Pioneers*, Manchester: Manchester University Press, pp1–39.

Arp, H. A. (1992) *The European Parliament in European Community Environmental Policy*, Florence: European University Institute, EUI Working Paper EPU No.92/13.

Axelrod, R. (1997) 'Environmental Policy and Management in the European Union', in Vig, N. J. and Kraft, M. E. (eds) *Environmental Policy in the 1990s*, 3rd edn, Washington, DC: CQ Press, pp299–320.

Det svenska miljöarbetet i EU – inriktning och genomförande (1994–5) Stockholm: Riksdagen, Regeringens skrivelse 1994/95, p167.

EU, EES och miljön, betänkande av EG-konsekvensutredningen

Haas, P. M. (1993) 'Protecting the Baltic and North Seas', in Haas, P. M., Keohane R. O. and Levy, M. A. (eds) *Institutions for the Earth, Sources of Effective International Environmental Protection*, Cambridge, MA: MIT Press, pp133–181.

Héritier, A. (1994) '"Leaders" and "laggards" in European Policy-making: Clean Air Policy Changes in Britain and Germany', in van Waarden, F. and Unger, B.

(eds) *Convergence or Diversity. The Pressure of Internationalization on Economic Governance Institutions and Policy Outcomes,* Aldershot: Avebury, pp278–305.

Héritier, A. (1996) 'The Accommodation of Diversity in European Policy-making and its Outcomes: Regulatory Policy as a Patchwork', *Journal of European Public Policy,* Vol.3, No.2, pp149–167.

Héritier, A. et al (1994) *Die Veränderung von Staatlichkeit in Europa. Ein Regulativer Wettbewerb: Deutschland, Grossbritannien, Frankreich,* Opiaden: Leske & Budrich.

Holzinger, K. (1994) *Politik des Kleinsten Gemeinsamen Nenners? Umweltpolitische Entscheidungsprozesse in der EG am Beispiel der Einführung des Katalysatorautos,* Berlin: Edition Sigma.

Holzinger, K. (1997) 'The Influence of New Member States in EU Environmental Policy Making: a Game Theory Approach", in Liefferink, D. and Andersen, M. S. (eds) *The Innovation of EU Environmental Policy,* Copenhagen: Scandinavian University Press, pp59–82.

Johnson, S. P. and Corcelle, G. (1995) *The Environmental Policy of the European Communities,* 2nd edn, London: Kluwer Law International.

Judge, D. (1992) 'Predestined to Save the Earth: the Environment Committee of the European Parliament', *Environmental Politics,* Vol.1, No.4, pp186–212.

Koppen, I. J. (1993) 'The Role of the European Court of Justice', in Liefferink, J. D., Lowe, P. D. and Mol, A. P. J. (eds) *European Integration and Environmental Policy,* London and New York: Belhaven, pp126–149.

Krämer, L. (1992) *Focus on European Environmental Law,* London: Sweet & Maxwell.

Kronsell, A. (1997) 'Policy Innovation in the Garbage Can: the EU's Fifth Environmental Action Programme', in Liefferink, D. and Andersen, M. S. (eds) *The Innovation of EU Environmental Policy,* Copenhagen: Scandinavian University Press, pp111–132.

Liefferink, D. (1996) *Environment and the Nation-state: The Netherlands, the European Union and Acid Rain,* Manchester: Manchester University Press.

Liefferink, D. and Andersen, M. S. (forthcoming) 'Greening the EU: National Positions in the Run-up to the Amsterdam Treaty', *Environmental Politics.*

Naturvårdsverket (1993) *Sverige och den Europeiska Miljöpolitiken,* Solna: Naturvårdsverket.

Nielsen, K. (1994) *Gröna stjörnor eller blå Dunster. Om EU och Miljön,* Göteborg: Miljöförbundet/Bokskogen.

Pehle, H. (1997) 'Germany: National Obstacles to an International Forerunner', in Andersen, M. S. and Liefferink, D. (eds) *European Environmental Policy: The Pioneers,* Manchester: Manchester University Press, pp161–209.

Pellegrom, S. (1997) 'The Constraints of Daily Work in Brussels: How Relevant is the Input from the National Capitals?', in Liefferink, D. and Andersen, M. S. (eds) *The Innovation of EU Environmental Policy,* Copenhagen: Scandinavian University Press, pp36–58.

Putnam, R. (1988) 'Diplomacy and Domestic Politics: the Logic of Two-level Games', *International Organization,* Vol.42, No.3, pp427–460.

Sbragia, A. (1996) 'Environmental Policy: the "Push-pull" of Policy-making', in Wallace, H. and Wallace, W. (eds) *Policy-making in the European Union,* Oxford: Oxford University Press, pp235–255.

Van As, C. (1995) *EU-Waterrichtlijnen in Beweging – een Tussenstand,* Wageningen: Wageningen Agricultural University, Department of Sociology, unpublished paper.

Weale, A. (1996) 'Environmental Rules and Rule-making in the European Union', *Journal of European Public Policy,* Vol.3, No.4, pp594–611.

Weiler, J. H. H. (1991) 'The Transformation of Europe', *The Yale Law Journal* Vol.100, pp2401–2483.

Wurzel, R. K. W. (1996) 'The Role of the EU Presidency in the Environmental Field: Does it Make a Difference Which Member State Runs the Presidency?', *Journal of European Public Policy,* Vol.3, No.2, pp272–91.

5

The Role of the European Court of Justice

Ida J. Koppen

Introduction

The decisions of the European Court of Justice (hereinafter 'the Court') have had a significant impact on the development of environmental policy in the European Community. The Court has consistently supported the view that the Community should have a broad legislative competence in this domain, notwithstanding the fact that such a competence originally did not appear in the Treaty of Rome, the source of all Community powers. It might seem rather exceptional for a court to take such an activist stance. The European Court, however, is known for its judicial activism in this and other areas of Community policy. In the field of human rights, for instance. Community policy developed entirely on the basis of a judicial inference of powers not mentioned in the Treaty. Similarly, in the field of external relations, the case law of the Court has been decisive in determining the scope of Community powers.

The active role of the Court in interpreting Community law and promoting Community policies is generally recognized as a driving force behind the process of European integration. Although most authors have been appreciative of the Court's attitude (Dauses, 1985, p418; Kapteyn and Verloren van Themaat, 1989, p169 and authors cited therein), some have criticized it, arguing that the Courts decisions trespass the boundary of judicial powers and run the risk of losing authority (especially Rasmussen, 1986).

The nature of the environmental issues addressed by the Court has changed through time. Two phases can be distinguished, with a potential third phase in prospect. The first phase lasted until 1987, when the Single European Act came into force, giving environmental policy a legal basis in the Treaty of Rome (hereinafter 'the Treaty'). Until then, the Court's role was largely confined to arguments about the legitimacy of Community environmental measures in view of the lack of attributed powers in the Treaty. The second phase concerns the situation that has arisen after the coming into force of the Single Act. The new provisions about environmental policy have created numerous legal uncertainties which the Court still has to resolve.

In this chapter the historical development of the Court's environmental case law is discussed as well as some general aspects of the functioning of the Court. We will start by looking at the different procedures before the Court and the Court's judicial activism in the field of human rights and with respect to external relations. This short excursion serves to put the discussion of the Court's case law concerning environmental issues in perspective. First, an overview is presented of the early case law of the Court, specifically addressing the legitimacy of Community environmental measures. Then, the important changes that were introduced by the Single European Act are described, followed by a discussion of the Danish bottle case and the Cassis de Dijon doctrine. The last Court case we will discuss concerns the different decision-making procedures to adopt environmental measures. The final section draws some conclusions and speculates about the future role of the Court in promoting European integration vis-à-vis European environmental policy.

The Different Court Procedures

The task of the European Court of Justice is to ensure the uniform interpretation and application of the Treaty. Proceedings in front of the Court are contentious or non-contentious. Contentious procedures can be initiated by a Community institution, by one of the Member States and, to a lesser degree, by private persons, ie individuals and legal persons. The non-contentious procedure is a matter of co-operation between the European Court of Justice and the national courts in the Member States.

The non-contentious court procedure

One non-contentious procedure exists, the so-called *preliminary ruling* or *preliminary judgment* (Article 177 of the Treaty), in which the Court interprets a specific rule of Community law (Kapteyn and Verloren van Themaat, 1989, p311ff; Hartley, 1988, p64). National courts can ask for a preliminary ruling whenever they have to apply a Community rule; if deciding in last instance, national courts are required to do so. A preliminary ruling is binding on the national court hearing the case and is intended to secure the uniform interpretation and application of Community law in all the Member States. No formal hierarchy exists, either between the European Court and national courts or between Community law and national law. The priority of Community law over national law stems from the fact that the transfer of certain powers from the Member States to the Community has created a new legal order in which sovereign national competences are restricted (Kapteyn and Verloren van Themaat, 1989, p36ff).[1] Thus, a preliminary judgment is recognized by the national legal order of each Member State as if it were issued by a national court (Articles 187 and 192 of the Treaty).

The contentious court procedures

Contentious proceedings before the Court can be divided into four categories: proceedings between Member States, proceedings between Community institutions, proceedings between the Commission and a Member State and proceedings between private persons and Community institutions (Kapteyn and Verloren van Themaat, 1989, p152ff). Other procedures exist that are of little relevance to our subject (see Articles 178–181 of the Treaty). A schematic overview of the different contentious proceedings is given in Table 5.1.

The Court procedure that is applied most frequently to environmental cases is the *infringement procedure,* initiated by the Commission against a Member State that fails to fulfil its obligations under the Treaty (Article 169 of the Treaty). An infringement procedure is brought before the Court after a mandatory round of consultation with the incriminated Member State. During the phase of consultation, a Member State is given the opportunity to voluntarily adjust the alleged infraction. It is the discretionary power of the Commission to decide whether or not to file suit if a Member State persists in its non-compliance. The Court hears

Table 5.1 *Plaintiffs and Defendants before the European Court of Justice*

	Defendant		
Plaintiff	*Member State*	*Commission*	*Council*
Member State	Inter-state infringement procedure (Art.170)	Action for annulment (Art.173) Action against failure to act (Art.175)	Action for annulment (Art.173) Action against failure to act (Art.175)
Commission	Infringement procedure (Art.169)		Action for annulment (Art.173) Action against failure to act (Art.175)
Council		Action for annulment (Art.173) Action against failure to act (Art.175)	
European Parliament		Action against failure to act (Art.175)	Action against failure to act (Art.175)
Private parties		Action for annulment (Art.173) Action against failure to act (Art.175)	Action for annulment (Art.173) Action against failure to act (Art.175)

Note: AU Articles refer to the Treaty of Rome

the parties before it delivers its judgment, often accompanied by an opinion of the Advocate General. If a Member State is convicted, its punishment is mostly restricted to political embarrassment, since the executive enforcement powers of the Court and the Commission are very limited.

With respect to environmental measures, infringement procedures are typically directed at the failure of a Member State to adopt national legislation implementing EC directives. In most cases, directives must be implemented within two years after the date of their issuance, but sometimes another time period is indicated in the directive itself. The number of infringement procedures in the area of environmental policy has recently increased dramatically: in 1990, 362 cases were pending (EC Commission Directorate General XI, 1991). We must keep in mind, however, that the effect of a preliminary ruling, addressed to the judiciary of the Member State in question, although limited in scope, since it only affects the outcome of the instant case, might be more direct than the impact of an infringement procedure directed at the legislature. It often takes a Member State years to adjust its legislation to the changes required by a condemnation in an infringement procedure.

Member States can initiate infringement procedures in the so-called *inter-State complaint* (Article 170 Treaty). In that case the Commission gives a reasoned opinion about the case. Member States, however, are usually hesitant to file a complaint against other Member States, in implicit recognition of the principle that those who live in glass houses should not throw stones.

The other two procedures mentioned in Table 5.1 are the *action for annulment of Community acts* and the *action against the failure to act in violation of the Treaty*. The first is a typical judicial review procedure in which the Court tests the legitimacy of decisions of the Council and the Commission (Article 173 Treaty) and annuls decisions that violate the Treaty (Article 174 Treaty). Although the Treaty does not mention decisions of the European Parliament, the Court has accepted on several occasions to review decisions of the Parliament.[2] Each Member State, the Council and the Commission can ask for the annulment of a Community act. Private parties have a limited right of action, confined to decisions with an individual character which directly affects them. The same restriction applies to private parties in the case of an action against a failure to act by Community organs (Article 175 Treaty). In the latter procedure, the European Parliament is granted an equal position to the Member States, the Council and the Commission; each of them can resort to the Court to ascertain the failure of the Council or the Commission to fulfil their obligations under the Treaty and to adopt the necessary measures (Article 175 Treaty).[3]

The Role of the Court in Other Policy Fields

The Court's role in the field of environmental policy must be assessed against the background of its contribution to other Community policies. Indeed, a brief review of the origins of the Court's judicial activism is indispensable to frame the role of the Court's jurisprudence in the shaping of the Community's environmental policy.

The Community's human rights policy

The lacuna in the Treaty of Rome with respect to human rights protection has been the subject of much academic and political debate. The suggestion that the Community joins the European Convention on Human Rights was given serious attention (Clapham, 1991, p84ff) and the Commission formally proposed accession in 1979 (Dauses, 1985, p414). The proposal, however, failed and the Treaty was never amended on this point. Thus, the Court did not seem competent to apply human rights.

After an initial period of 'judicial reticence' (Weiler, 1986, p1114), beginning in 1969 a series of decisions were issued in which the Court progressively established its power to apply fundamental human rights notwithstanding the constitutional omission in the Treaty. In its first judgment, the Court decided that human rights were enshrined in the general principles of Community law which the Court has to apply (Case 29/69, *Stauder v. City of Ulm*, ECR, 1969). Respect for human rights forms an integral part of the general principles of law protected by the Court, and has to be ensured within the framework of the structure and objectives of the Community (Case 11/70, *Internationale Handelsgesellschaft GmbH v. Einfuhr- und Vorratsstelle fur Getreide und Futtermittel*, ECR, 1970). In protecting human rights, the Court, moreover, draws inspiration from the constitutional traditions common to the Member States as well as from the international treaties for the protection of human rights of which the Member States are signatories (Case 4/73, *Nold v. Commission*, ECR, 1974 and Case 44/79, *Hazier v. Rheinland-Pfalz*, ECR, 1979).

The Court, in other words, applies human rights as if they were incorporated in the Treaty. The absence of a written bill of rights has been offset by the Court's judicial activism creating additional guarantees for the individual citizen (Weiler, 1986, p1117). The question whether this activism is driven by concern for human rights or by the interest of market integration recently surfaced again in two decisions reported by Clapham (1991, pp48–49). Contrary to other legal systems, the Court does not grant human rights the sense of absoluteness normally associated with rules that enjoy the highest rank within the legal order. The Court stated explicitly that restrictions may be imposed on the exercise of fundamental rights 'in the context of the common organization of the market' (ibid). Thus, we may conclude that the activist role of the Court in the field of human rights protection must be seen in the light of the Court's continuous contribution to European integration.

The external relations competences of the Community

Clear Community competences regarding external relations exist only in the area of foreign commercial policy (Articles 110–116 of the Treaty). In most other fields, competences are derived from the general provisions in the Treaty concerning the legal personality of the Community and its competence to conclude international agreements with third countries and international bodies (Articles 210, 228–231, 238). Besides the case law of the Court, the process of European political co-operation and the activities of the Commission have had a significant role in this development.[4]

The first important decision of the Court in the famous ERTA case (Case 22/70, *Commission v. Council*, ECR, 1971) was to abolish the principle of enumerated powers, *compétences d'attribution*, with respect to external relations, and to adopt the doctrine of implied powers. Contrary to the prevailing doctrine and contrary to the opinion of the Advocate General, the Court ruled that Community treaty-making powers concerning transport were to be inferred from its internal powers in this field. The Court determined that the Community had the power to enter into external relations in all the fields for which it held internal competence. No separation must be created, according to the Court, between the system of internal Community measures and external relations (ECR, 1971, p274). The adoption of certain internal measures necessarily confers on the Community the authority to enter into international agreements relating to the subject matter governed by that measure, to the exclusion of concurrent powers on the part of the Member States (ibid, pp275, 276). Implied powers exist, in other words, for external relations with respect to all fields in which the Community has internal competences. This is referred to as the doctrine of 'parallel powers'. The implied power doctrine was upheld in the *Kramer* case concerning agricultural policy (Joint cases 3,4 and 6/76, *Cornelis Kramer and others*, ECR, 1976). Here, the competence to enter into an agreement on the conservation of ocean fishing was derived from the power to adopt a common agricultural policy and from an internal Council regulation on fisheries conservation in the Member States (ECR, 1976, pp1309, 1310).

An issue not clarified in these decisions was to what degree external competences could only be derived from the existence of a specific internal measure, or could also be based on a general competence to adopt internal measures in a certain field. This question was addressed in a subsequent case which the Court heard in 1976. In Opinion 1/76 (*Draft Agreement establishing a European laying-up fund for inland water vessels*, ECR, 1977), the Court stated that treaty-making powers do not necessarily depend on a prior internal measure but may flow from the general provision creating the internal competence if the participation of the Community in the international agreement 'is necessary for the attainment of one of the objectives of the Community' (ECR, 1977, p755).

The Court's interpretation of the limited Treaty provisions concerning external relations has expanded the overall competences in this field considerably. In principle, the implied power doctrine applies equally to the Community's external environmental policy that has recently become an increasingly important aspect of Community foreign affairs (Nollkaemper, 1987).

The First Environmental Cases and the Single European Act

The beginning of the Community environmental policy can be traced back to 1972. In 1973, the Commission published its first Environmental Action Programme and issued proposals for several environmental directives (Koppen, 1988). Some Member States were slow in implementing the Community measures and by the end of the 1970s the Commission had started infringement procedures against several countries. In the cases against Italy and Belgium that are discussed below, the Court addressed the issue of the legitimacy of environmental measures in the absence of an explicit reference in the Treaty. By interpreting the general provisions in the Treaty, the Court determined that environmental policy fell within the sphere of competence of the Community as an implied power. In a preliminary ruling a few years later, the Court went even further, by stating that environmental protection was one of the Community's essential objectives. Considering the fact that environmental protection was not yet included in the Treaty, this was a bold statement, reminiscent of the Courts judgments in the fields of human rights and external relations.

Infringement procedures against Belgium and Italy

The Commission filed suit against Italy for not implementing a Council Directive on the approximation of the laws of the Member States relating to detergents as well as a Directive on the approximation of the laws of the Member States relating to the sulphur content of certain liquid fuels.[5] The first provided for an 18 months' implementation period, which expired on 27 May 1975, the second gave the Member States until 26 August 1976 to adopt the necessary internal measures. The Commission started the infringement procedures in May 1979 and the Court issued its judgments in March of the following year (Cases 91 and 92/79, *Commission v. Italy,* ECR, 1980, p1099 and p1115). Against the claim of the Commission that it had failed to fulfil its obligations under the Treaty, Italy stated that it would not raise the question whether the Directives were 'valid in the light of the fact that combating pollution was not one of the tasks entrusted to the Community by the Treaty' (ECR, 1980, p1103 and p1119). However, Italy did maintain that the matter lay 'on the fringe' of Community powers and that the contested measures were actually an international convention drawn up in the form of a directive (ibid). The argument Italy was trying to make was weak. First of all, as was pointed out by the Advocate General, if Italy really wanted to challenge the validity of the Directives it should have brought an action for annulment under Article 173 of the Treaty (ECR, 1980, pp1110–11). Moreover, the Directives were not only adopted as part of the Environmental Action Programme but also under the General Programme for the elimination of technical barriers to trade, adopted by the Council in 1969. The Court ruled that the Directives in question were both validly based on Article 100 of the Treaty, which authorizes the Community to adopt all measures necessary to eliminate trade barriers resulting from disparities between provisions in the national legislation of the Member States. Article 100, in other words, was recognized as the legal basis for environmental measures which were adopted in order to harmonize national provisions. 'If there is no harmonization of national provisions on the matter', according to the Court, 'competition may be appreciably distorted' (ECR, 1980, p1106 and p1122). Thus, the legitimacy of Community environmental measures was recognised to the extent that the harmonization of national measures was necessary to eliminate trade barriers.

A few years later, in a series of six cases against Belgium, the Court broadened the legal basis of environmental directives by interpreting Article 235 of the Treaty which authorizes all Community action which is not explicitly included in the Treaty, but proves to be 'necessary to attain, in the course of the operation of the common market, one of the objectives of the Community' (Cases 68–73/81, *Commission v. Belgium,* ECR, 1982, pp153, 163, 169, 175, 183 and 189). The cases were similar to those against Italy. Belgium had failed to implement a number of environmental directives and the Commission brought an action against it for failure to comply with its obligations under the Treaty.[6] All six Directives were based on Articles 100 and 235 of the Treaty. The Court accepted this dual basis, repeating that environmental measures may on the one hand be required to 'eliminate disparities between the laws of the Member States likely to have a direct effect upon the functioning of the common market' (ECR, 1982, p171) and, on the other hand, may be necessary 'to achieve one of the aims of the Community in the sphere of protection of the environment and improvement of the quality of life' (ECR, 1982, p191). By adding the second phrase, the Court established environmental measures as one of the implied powers of the Community, similar to the case law regarding external relations competences. As far as the relevant objectives of the Community are concerned, they were to be found in the Preamble and in Article 2 of the Treaty. Inter alia, such objectives include the constant improvement of living and working conditions and an accelerated raising of the standard of living.

Preliminary judgments about the Directive on the disposal of waste oils

The French association of waste oil incinerators contested the validity of some provisions in the EC Directive of 16 June 1975 on the disposal of waste oils (OJ No.L194/23) in a national case before the Tribunal de Grande Instance de Creteil. Since the matter regarded the interpretation of Community law, the Tribunal asked the Court for a preliminary judgment (Case 240/83, *Procureur de la Republique v. l'Association de Défense des Bruleurs d'Huiles Usagées,* ECR, 1985, p531). The question put before the Court was whether the Directive, by empowering Member States to create restrictive systems of waste oil collection and treatment, violated the principles of freedom of trade, free movement of goods and freedom of competition (ECR, 1985, p548). Articles 5 and 6 in particular, concerning the assignment of exclusive zones to waste oil collectors and the prior approval and licensing of disposal undertakings, were under scrutiny.

In an earlier judgment about the same Directive, the Court had ruled that the Directive did not authorize Member States to prohibit the export of waste oils to other Member States since this would constitute a barrier to intra-Community trade. France had adopted national legislation to implement the Directive which had this effect (Case 172/82, *Fabricants raffineurs d'huile de graissage v. 'Interhuiles',* ECR, 1983, p555).

In its 1985 judgment, the Court referred to the earlier decision, adding that the legitimacy of the restrictions to the freedom of trade, adopted by France on the basis of the Directive, had to be interpreted in the light of its aim 'to ensure that the disposal of waste oils is carried out in a way which avoids harm to the environment' (ECR, 1985, p549). 'The principle of freedom of trade,' according to the Court:

*is not to be viewed in absolute terms but is subject to certain limits justified by the
objectives of general interest pursued by the Community … The Directive must
be seen in the perspective of environmental protection, which is one of the Community's essential objectives* (ibid).

Restrictions posed by environmental measures may be justified, according to the
Court, as long as they are not discriminatory nor disproportionate. The Court
concluded that the Directive had not exceeded these limits (ibid).

Two aspects of the judgment deserve particular attention. First of all, we
observe that the Court digressed to state that environmental protection was one
of the Community's essential objectives. The phrase was added to strengthen the
line of reasoning of the Court, but it was not indispensable. It was, moreover, not
true. Environmental protection was not yet mentioned in the Treaty as a Community policy, let alone as a Community objective. Why then did the Court
choose such a strong formulation? Undoubtedly, the judgment had an impact at
the time on the discussions that were being held about the proposed treaty
changes. The Court took a position in these discussions, by showing its support
for the proposal to include environmental protection among the objectives of the
Community. This is indeed a typical instance of judicial activism of the Court.
The Court ruled according to what it thought the law ought to be and not
according to what the law was (Hartley, 1988, pp77–78).

Having put environmental protection on an equal footing with other Community objectives, the Court was then able to make a relative assessment of the
different interests at stake. It was the first time that the Court undertook to balance the interests of environmental protection against the interests of the internal
market, applying the principles of non-discrimination and proportionality. A few
years later, the Court applied this method again and developed it further (see the
discussion of the Danish bottle case, below). It must be kept in mind, however,
that this was after environmental protection had been included in the Treaty. In
1985, the Court's reasoning was certainly beyond the limits of legal interpretation. With its activism, the Court made up for some of the political and legislative inertia of the Community, just as it had done in other policy areas (Rasmussen, 1986, p416; Weiler, 1986, pp1116–1117).

The Amendments Introduced by the Single European Act

With the coming into force of the Single European Act on 1 July 1987, environmental protection was included in the Treaty as one of the Community policies
(Articles 130r, 130s and 130t). Environmental protection is also mentioned in
Article 100a, a provision inserted in the Treaty by the Single Act, which authorizes
the adoption of all harmonization measures necessary for the establishment of the
internal market. Thus, a dichotomy is created between environmental measures that
are part of the internal market programme and action that is not related to the functioning of the internal market. The distinction has several important consequences.

First of all. Article 100a establishes that all harmonization measures adopted
in the context of the internal market are adopted by qualified majority, whereas

measures based on Article 130s require a unanimous vote in the Council. The difference in the voting procedure is furthermore reflected in different roles for the European Parliament. This particular aspect will be discussed separately, in the light of recent case law of the Court.

Another difference that needs to be considered regards the margin of discretion of Member States to enact national legislation after the adoption of a Community measure. If a measure is adopted on the basis of Article 130s, this 'shall not prevent Member States from *maintaining or introducing* more stringent protective measures compatible with this Treaty' (Article 130t, italics added). Measures adopted on the basis of Article 100a, however, allow a Member State to *apply* a national provision after notifying the Commission who must verify that the national provision is not 'a means of arbitrary discrimination or a disguised restriction on trade between the Member States' (Article 100a, para. 4). The different wording of the two articles – 'maintaining or introducing' as opposed to 'applying' – is generally interpreted as follows. If a measure is adopted on the basis of Article 100a, Member States can continue to apply already existing national provisions, to the extent that they have been approved by the Commission. In the case of measures based on Article 130s, Member States are free to adopt new national legislation on the same topic as long as it contains more stringent standards. The requirement that the national provisions must be compatible with the Treaty means that they have to fulfil the same general requirements that apply to national environmental legislation in the absence of Community rules. Therefore, the choice of the legal basis of a proposed environmental measure has significant ramifications and it is one of the issues addressed by the Court in its case law after the Single Act (see below).

Among the principles that underlie Community environmental policy, enumerated in Article 130r, one deserves special attention. The 'integration principle' requires that environmental considerations be an integral part of all other Community policies. This principle gives environmental policy a unique status in the Community since it is the only policy field for which such a requirement is formulated. Although many were sceptical at the time about the implementation of the new principle, five years later we must acknowledge that some results have been attained. Recent initiatives in the transport sector might serve as an example (EC Commission Directorate General VII, 1992). Moreover, the principle has served the Court as a guidance in interpreting other aspects of Community environmental law.

With respect to Community external relations in the field of environmental protection, the Single Act has created an ambiguous situation. Article 130r, para. 5, determines that the conclusion of international agreements by the Community 'shall be without prejudice to Member States' competence to negotiate in international bodies and to conclude international agreements'. The provision seems to imply that Community competence in this field never excludes concurrent powers on the part of the Member States. This interpretation, however, would be contrary to the general case law of the Court on external relations. It would especially come into conflict with the Court's decision in the ERTA case. A partial solution to the dilemma can be found in a Declaration that was added to the Final Act of the Intergovernmental Conference where the Single Act was adopted, which states that the provisions of Article 130r, para. 5, 'do not affect the principles resulting from the judgment handed down by the Court of Justice in the ERTA case'. From this we can deduce that the ERTA doctrine of implied external competence is applicable to environmental policy. Obversely, this would mean that the other relevant decisions of the Court in this matter, most notably the *Kramer* case and Opinion 1/76, do not apply to environmental policy. External powers could then be legitimately based on an existing internal measure, excluding concurrent powers of the Member States. They could not, however, be deduced from the existence of the general competence to adopt internal measures concerning a certain subject matter. The Court of Justice has not yet had occasion to clarify the situation. It is doubtful that the Court would limit itself to applying the ERTA doctrine to international environmental agreements without reference to the other aspects of the jurisprudence it developed about external relations competences. For the moment, we can observe that in practice the Community assumes exclusive powers only concerning matters for which internal rules have been adopted. For all other issues the Community participates in international negotiations alongside the Member States. Most international environmental agreements are so-called mixed agreements, signed by the Community and by the Member States (Nollkaemper, 1987, p70ff; Haigh, 1991, p173).

Towards 'Diversified Integration': The Freedom to be Cleaner than the Rest

The judgment of the Court in the Danish bottle case (Case 302/86, *Commission v. Denmark*, ECR, 1988, p4627) is one in a series of decisions about the scope of admissible exceptions to the general prohibition of quantitative import restrictions and all measures having equivalent effect in the Community (Article 30 of the Treaty). The Treaty itself lists a number of acceptable reasons, including public morality, public security, public health and the protection of national monuments (Article 36). Member States have extensively tried to exploit these categories of exceptions to try and convince the Court of the necessity to apply a national rule that created an obstacle to free trade. The argument of consumer protection, for instance, was used on a number of occasions, and the case law thus developed served as a precedent for the first decision about environmental protection as a legitimate exception.

French liqueur, Belgian margarine and German beer

The first relevant case law of the Court dates back to 1979, when the Court issued its Cassis de Dijon decision (Case 120/78, *Rewe-Zentral AG v. Bundesmonopolverwaltung fur Branntwein*, ECR, 1979, p649). Germany had banned the import of the French liqueur Cassis de Dijon on the grounds that its alcohol content, 15 to 20 per cent, did not satisfy the German requirements for the import of spirits contained in the Law on the Monopoly in Spirits of 1922, which required a minimum wine-spirit content of 32 per cent. The Court observed dryly that the fixing of a minimum wine-spirit content for potable spirit could certainly not be justified by reasons related to human health, as the German government had maintained, and obliged Germany to adjust its national legislation in order to allow for the marketing of the French liqueur. A similar decision was issued in 1982, when the Court ruled that Belgian legislation concerning the shape of the packaging of margarine constituted an obstacle to free trade unwarranted by the need to protect or inform the consumer (Case 261/81, *Walter Rau Lebensmittel-werke v. De Smedt PvbA*, ECR, 1982, p3961).

Two years later, the Commission brought an action against Germany for its restrictive legislation on the quality of imported beer. German legislation prohibited any additives in beer. The Commission observed that this resulted in limited imports of beer into Germany while favouring the export of German beer. The German government emphasized that its legislation, referred to as the 'Reinheitsgebot', the purity requirement, dating back to 1516, was a measure to protect public health, and was thus acceptable as a legitimate exemption from the prohibition of Article 30. The Commission maintained that this was merely a pretext, since additives were allowed in Germany in other products. In its judgment (Case 178/84, *Commission v. Germany*, ECR, 1987, p1227), the Court repeated the arguments it had put forward in the two cases mentioned above, also referred to as the 'Cassis de Dijon formula':

> *In the absence of common rules relating to the marketing of the products concerned, obstacles to free movement within the Community resulting from disparities between the national laws must be accepted in so far as such rules, applicable to domestic and to imported products without distinction, may be recognized as being necessary in order to satisfy mandatory requirements relating inter alia to consumer protection. It is also necessary for such rules to be proportionate to the aim in view. If a Member State has a choice between various measures to attain the same objective it should choose the means which least restricts the free movement of goods.* (ECR, 1987, p1270)

It was with respect to the last requirement that the Court deemed the German legislation excessive. An absolute prohibition on additives was not necessary, according to the Court, since it was 'contrary to the principle of proportionality' (ibid, p1276).

Recapitulating, we can say that the Court has been reluctant in recognizing consumer protection as a legitimate argument to justify the application of national rules that create obstacles to intra-Community trade.

The Danish bottle case

In view of the Court's restrictive interpretation of consumer protection as a ground to justify quantitative import restrictions, the Commission must have been quite certain of its case when it filed suit against Denmark for the packaging requirements it had issued for beer and soft drinks. It was certainly a test case, and the Commission made it clear that it was of great importance to establish:

> *whether and to what extent the concern to protect the environment has precedence over the principle of a common market without frontiers since there is a risk*

that Member States may in future take refuge behind ecological arguments to avoid opening their markets to beer as they are required to do by the case law of the Court (ECR, 1988, p4611).

In Denmark, legislation had been enacted requiring that beer and soft drinks be marketed in reusable containers approved by the National Agency for the Protection of the Environment. A limited number of 23 containers had so far been admitted. The number was kept small since that was the only way to make sure that each container would be taken back by every retailer of beverages, irrespective of the place where the product had been purchased. This, in turn, greatly enhanced the effectiveness of the mandatory system, ensuring a return rate of 99 per cent, a figure that could never be reached with any other deposit-and-return system. Beverages in non-approved containers were allowed up to a yearly quantity of 3000 hectolitres per producer, provided that a deposit-and-return system was established by the producer. Non-approved containers would only be taken back by the retailer who sold the beverages. No form of metal container was allowed. The rationale behind the system, according to the Danish government, was to protect the environment and to conserve resources and energy as well as to reduce the amount of waste.

Allegedly, the Danish requirements made it very difficult to import beer and soft drinks into Denmark and the Commission questioned whether this trade barrier was justified on the grounds put forward by the defendant. The Commission did not question the general principle that environmental protection was one of the Community's essential objectives and, as such, one of the *mandatory requirements recognized by Community law* that could justify certain import restrictions. The Commission questioned the sincerity of Denmark's ecological concerns, just as it had challenged Germany's concern for consumer protection in the case concerning beer additives, noting that the severe packaging requirements only applied to beer and soft drinks and not to other products like milk and wine which were not subject to competition between foreign and domestic producers. If Germany was not allowed to invoke its 'Reinheitsgebot' to justify import restrictions on beer, then Denmark could not hide behind mandatory recycling requirements that had a similar effect. The Advocate General supported the Commission's claim and expressed the opinion that the judgment of the Court had to be similar to the judgment in Case 178/84: the Danish requirements were disproportionate in view of their aim (ECR, 1988, pp4619–4926). But the Court took a more subtle stance. First of all, the Court referred to the Cassis de Dijon formula: obstacles to the free movement of goods within the Community must be accepted in so far as 1) no common rules relating to the marketing of the products in question exist, 2) the national rule in question applies equally to domestic and imported products and 3) the rule is necessary to satisfy mandatory requirements of Community law. The national rules must, moreover, be proportionate to the aim in view. Then the Court repeated its decision in Case 240/83: environmental protection is one of the Community's essential objectives which may as such justify certain limitations of the principle of the free movement of goods. Thus the Court recognized that environmental protection is one of the mandatory requirements which may limit the application of Article 30 of the

Treaty and extended the Cassis de Dijon doctrine to include environmental protection. This was the first important pronouncement in the case.

The Court then went on to interpret the proportionality of the Danish measures in view of the alleged aim of environmental protection. In full support of the Danish arguments, the Court stated simply that the establishment of an obligatory deposit-and-return system with a limited number of containers was indispensable to ensure the reuse of containers and therefore necessary to achieve the aim. Only one aspect of the rules was disproportionate, according to the Court, namely the fact that a maximum marketing quota of 3000 hectolitres was established for beverages sold in non-approved containers in addition to the requirement that the producer set up a deposit-and-return system for the containers. This aspect of the Danish rules was considered in violation of Article 30 of the Treaty.

Determining where to draw the line between disproportionate and proportionate measures is hardly a matter of juridical interpretation. It is a subjective assessment of advantages and disadvantages and an allocation of responsibilities. In this case, the Court tried to strike a balance between the economic interests of the Community and the increasing concern for environmental values. The decision shows that the internal market does not preclude differences between environmental standards in the Member States. From an environmental point of view this is an important achievement. The situation is still more complex if Community measures on the same topic exist. In that case the freedom of the Member State to adopt divergent national standards depends on the legal basis that was chosen for the Community rule (see above). This is one of the topics that will certainly be brought before the Court in the near future.

Different Procedures to Adopt Environmental Measures

As we have seen, since the coming into force of the Single European Act, two different procedures exist to adopt environmental measures. The Single Act introduced the so-called *co-operation* procedure which grants the Parliament the power to put forward amendments to proposed measures. This procedure applies to all measures related to the internal market that are adopted by the Council with qualified majority. Instead, if a measure is based on Article 130s, the Council must decide unanimously, after *consultation* of the Parliament. In the consultation procedure, the opinion of the Parliament does not have any binding effect. In both cases proposals must come from the Commission since in the legislative system of the Community, the Commission has the exclusive right of initiative.

The ambiguous system thus created left a major question unanswered: how to determine when an environmental measure has to be adopted on the basis of Article 100a as part of the internal market programme and when a measure should be based on Article 130s. The Court addressed this question in a case in which the Commission, the Parliament and the Council disagreed about the legal basis of an environmental directive. Before looking at the Court decision itself, we will briefly examine the role of the Parliament in the different procedures. A final section describes the situation that will arise when the Maastricht Treaty on European Union comes into force.

The role of the European Parliament

The co-operation procedure introduced by the Single European Act enlarged the role of the Parliament in the Community legislative process. Although Parliaments powers are still limited and the democratic content of Community decision's remains questionable, a slight increase in influence was achieved. The co-operation procedure basically adds a phase to the procedure followed in the case of consultation. When the Commission issues a proposal, the proposal is first sent to the Parliament for its opinion. The Commission is free to adjust the proposal to the changes suggested by the Parliament. The proposal and the Parliament's opinion are then forwarded to the Council. If the procedure of Article 130 is followed, the Council at this point takes a final decision and the proposal is adopted if the Council reaches unanimity. In the case of the co-operation procedure, however, the Council adopts a common position about the proposal. The common position is returned to the Parliament. If the Parliament agrees with the common position, the Council can adopt the proposed action by qualified majority. If the Parliament rejects the common position, the Council can adopt the action only by unanimity. If the Parliament proposes amendments, these are reviewed by the Commission who sends a revised proposal to the Council. At this stage the Council can adopt the second Commission proposal by qualified majority. If the Council wants to make any further changes these have to be adopted by unanimity. The main effect of the second phase is that the Parliament's opinion can force the Council to decide unanimously which sometimes means that a decision actually gets blocked. Another effect of the enlarged procedure is that Parliament is kept better informed of the considerations and arguments of the Council. Communication between the institutions is, therefore, intensified.

Commission and Parliament versus Council: majority versus unanimity voting

A little more than a year after the coming into force of the Single European Act, the first dispute arose between the Council and the Commission about the different procedures envisaged to adopt environmental measures. In June 1991, the Court passed its first judgment about the issue (Case 300/89, *Commission v. Council,* ECR, 1991, pI-2867).[7] The Commission, supported by the European Parliament, asked for the annulment of Directive 89/428/EEC of 21 June 1989 about the harmonization of programmes to reduce waste from the titanium dioxide industry (OJ No.L201/56). Contrary to the Commission's proposal, the Directive had been adopted unanimously by the Council on the basis of Article 130s. The Commission had suggested Article 100a as the basis for the Directive since its principal objective, its 'centre of gravity', according to the Commission, was to improve the conditions of competition in the titanium dioxide industry, which made it clearly an internal market measure.

In its judgment, the Court stressed that the legal basis of a proposed measure has to be chosen according to objective criteria like the aim and the content of the measure (ECR, 1991, pI-2898). The aim and the content of the Directive under scrutiny, however, did not result in a clear answer since the Directive is as much related to environmental protection as it is related to the internal market (ibid, pI-2898/2899). A dual legal basis was excluded by the Court, arguing that the two Articles in question require different and incompatible decision-making procedures. If Articles 100a and 130s were to be applied simultaneously, this would force the Council to decide unanimously. This, in turn, would exclude the co-operation procedure and limit the role of the European Parliament. In that context the Court recalled the importance of the stronger role of the Parliament emphasizing that the co-operation procedure was added to the Treaty:

> to strengthen the participation of the European Parliament in the legislative proc- ess of the Community... This participation is the reflection, at the Community level, of a fundamental democratic principle, by which the people participate in the exercise of power through the intermediary of a representative assembly (ibid, pI-2900).

Besides the emphasis placed on the role of the European Parliament, three ele- ments can be discerned in the Court's decision to annul the Directive. First of all, the Court argued that the integration principle implies that measures to protect the environment do not always have to be adopted on the basis of Article 130s (ibid, pI-2901). Second, the Court referred to its early judgments in the cases against Italy, to recall that the harmonization of national environmental measures is often necessary to prevent the distortion of competition. This type of harmo- nization measure thus contributes to the establishment of the internal market and falls within the scope of Article 100a. Finally, the Court pointed to the fact that Article 100a itself requires that harmonization measures concerning environmen- tal protection take as a base a high level of protection. This provision is a guaran- tee, according to the Court, that environmental objectives can be effectively pur- sued on the basis of Article 100a.

The consequences of the decision are rather complex. From now on, most environmental measures are likely to be based on Article 100a, which makes envi- ronmental protection more closely related to the internal market policy of the Community. This is a realistic solution in view of the fact that the two policy fields need to be integrated. The Court's favourable attitude towards the co-operation procedure and the role played by the European Parliament is certainly positive in view of the democratic content of Community legislation. The potential danger of the decision concerns the fact that majority decisions have been shown to facil- itate the adoption of low standards. Member States are, moreover, prohibited from adopting more stringent national standards, an option they have if a Com- munity rule is adopted on the basis of Article 130s. Until now there is little reason to have much confidence in the requirement that proposed harmonization meas- ures take as a base a high level of protection. The conclusion, then, must be that the Court's judgment was primarily inspired by considerations of integration; not the integration of environmental requirements into other Community policies, but the integration of the European market, a Community objective that contin- ues to have priority over environmental protection.

Conclusions

It would be too simple to characterize the case law of the European Court of Justice concerning Community environmental policy as merely pro-integrationist. The cases described above show a more complex picture/a line of reasoning in which a twofold orientation can be discerned. Besides elements of traditional judicial activism in favour of market integration, we also notice an increasing concern for the protection of the environment in Europe.

A strong element of market integration was present in the first environmental cases (Cases 91 and 92/79, *Commission v. Italy*, ECR, 1980, p1099 and p1115) in which the Court recognized environmental measures to the extent that they harmonized national provisions which would otherwise create trade barriers and distort competition. Two years later, the Court slightly adjusted this reasoning by adding that environmental measures may also be necessary to achieve one of the aims of the Community (Cases 68–73/81, *Commission v. Belgium*, ECR, p153ff), thus establishing a broader legal basis for Community action. In the preliminary judgment issued in 1985 (Case 240/83, *Procureur de la Republique v. l'Association de Défense des Bruleurs d'Huiles Usagées*, ECR, 1985, p531), the Court started to challenge its own concern for market integration by first of all stating that environmental protection was in itself one of the Community's essential objectives and secondly upholding the contested French measures even though they created obstacles to trade in the field of the treatment and disposal of used oils. The argument is a matter of simple deduction: environmental protection is a Community objective, all Community objectives are equal and may pose limits to each other's application, environmental protection may therefore pose limits to the application of other Community objectives. The same construction was applied again in the Danish bottle case with respect to intra-Community trade. The Court upheld Danish packaging requirements even though they did, in fact, create an obstacle to the import of beer and soft drinks into Denmark. The Court accepted the Danish argument that the requirements were justified by reasons of environmental protection and ruled that, as one of the Community's essential objectives, environmental protection was one of the mandatory requirements of Community law which may limit the scope of the general prohibition of quantitative import restrictions of Article 30 of the Treaty.

It is beyond doubt that the objectives of market integration and environmental protection are at times hard to reconcile. In this respect it is important to note that the Court in its most recent case law seems to have given priority to the imperative of market integration. Faced with the question of which legal basis must be chosen for environmental measures, the Court insisted on linking environmental protection closely to the internal market programme (Case 300/89, *Commission v. Council*, ECR, 1991). Although the Court stressed in its judgment that the provision contained in Article 100a para. 3 – that all Commission proposals must take as a base a high level of protection – should function as a guarantee, the fear remains that the harmonization measures adopted by the Community will force several Member States to lower their national standards.

It seems to us, however, that the best guarantee for a high level of environmental protection, is the freedom for Member States to adopt their own national measures, a freedom that does not exist if a Community measure is adopted on the basis of Article 100a. If most environmental measures are based on Article 100a, this may indeed hamper the progressive development of environmental protection in Europe.

So far, the Court has not passed any judgments about the extent to which national measures may diverge from Community rules. This is likely to be one of the first issues which the Court will address in its future case law. Once the Court discovers that the guarantee contained within Article 100a does not always lead to the desired effect, the Court might very well review its decision in Case 300/89 and rule that more environmental measures must be based on Article 130s, thus leaving Member States the freedom to adopt more stringent national rules. Such a revirement in the jurisprudence of the Court is all the more needed when one realizes that the different realities existing in Member States require decentralized environmental action. If the Court wants to continue to support environmental protection it will then have to elaborate the doctrine of 'diversified integration', the basic tenets of which were set forth in the Danish bottle case.

Notes

1   The special features of Community law vis-à-vis national law were established by the Court in a series of cases, the most important of which are: Case 26/62, *Van Gend en Loos v. Nederlandse Administratie der Belastingen*, ECR, 1963; Case 6/64, *Costa v. ENEL*, ECR, 1964; Case 106/77, *Amministrazione delle Finanze dello Stato v. Simmenthal SpA*, ECR, 1978. Other relevant case law is cited in Kapteyn and Verloren van Themaat, 1989, p38ff. See also Hartley, 1988, p219ff.

2   The most important cases are: Case 230/81, *Luxembourg v. European Parliament*, ECR, 1983; Case 108/83, *Luxembourg v. European Parliament*, ECR, 1984; Case 294/83, *Parti Ecologiste Les Verts v. European Parliament*, ECR, 1986; 34/86, *Council v. European Parliament*, ECR, 1986.

3   The Parliament did so once, in a famous case regarding the (lack of a) Community transport policy: Case 13/83, *European Parliament v. Council*, ECR, 1985. For a detailed discussion of the peculiar position of the Parliament in both procedures, see Barnard, 1987; Hartley, 1988, pp77–78, 374–375; Kapteyn and Verloren van Themaat, 1989, pp143–145, 281–290.

4   It is not possible here to analyse these complex processes in any detail; I refer to the overview article by Stein (1991) and the literature cited there for further reading. See also Kapteyn and Verloren van Themaat, 1989, pp21–28 and Hartley, 1988, pp153–176.

5   Council Directive No 73/404/EEC of 22 November 1973 on the approximation of the laws of the Member States relating to detergents (OJ No.L347/51) and Directive No 75/716/EEC of 24 November 1975 on the approximation of the laws of the member states relating to the sulphur content of certain liquid fuels (OJ No.L307/22).

6   The following Directives had not been implemented: Directive No.75/439/ EEC of 16 June 1975 on the disposal of waste oils (OJ No.L194/23); Directive

No.75/440/EEC of 16 June 1975 concerning the quality required of surface water intended for the abstraction of drinking water in the Member States (OJ No.L194/26); Directive No.75/442/EEC of 15 July 1975 on waste (OJ No.L194/39); Directive No.76/160/EEC of 8 December 1975 concerning the quality of bathing water (OJ No.L31/1); Directive No.76/403/EEC of 6 April 1976 on the disposal of polychlorinated biphenyls and polychlorinated terphenyls (OJ No.L108/41); Directive No.78/176/EEC of 20 February 1978 on waste from the titanium dioxide industry (OJ No.L54/19). See the Opinion of the Advocate General (ECR, 1982, pp159) and Koppen (1988) for a description of the cases.

7   References to the titanium dioxide case apply to the French documents, because the English versions had not been published at the time of writing.

References

Barnard, J. (1987) 'The European Parliament and Article 173 of the EEC Treaty', EUI Working Paper No.87/290, Florence: European University Institute.

Cappelletti, M. 1987, 'Is the European Court of Justice "Running Wild"?', *European Law Review*, Vol.12, pp3–17.

Clapham, A. (1991) *Human Rights and the European Community: A Critical Overview*, Baden-Baden: Nomos Verlag.

Dauses, M. A. (1985) 'The Protection of Fundamental Rights in the Community Legal Order', *European Law Review*, Vol.10, pp398–419.

EC Commission Directorate General VII, (1992) *Green Paper on Transport and Environment*, COM (92) final.

EC Commission Directorate General XI, (1991) *Implementation. of Community Law in the Field of Environmental Protection*, COM (91) 321 final.

Haigh, N. (1991) 'The European Community and International Environmental Policy'. *International Environmental Affairs*, Vol.3, pp163–180.

Hartley, T. C. (1988) *The Foundations of European Community Law* (second edn), Oxford: Clarendon Press.

Kapteyn, P. J. G. and Verloren van Themaat, P. (1989) *Introduction to the Law of the European Communities: After the Coming into Force of the Single European Act* (second edn by L. W. Gormley (ed)), Deventer: Kluwer Law and Taxation Publishers.

Koppen, I. J. (1988) *The European Community's Environment Policy: From the Summit in Paris, 1972, to the Single European Act, 1937*, EUI Working Paper 88/328, Florence: European University Institute.

Krämer, L. (1987) 'The Single European Act and Environmental Protection: Reflections on Several New Provisions in Community Law', *Common Market Law Review*, Vol.4, pp659–688.

Nollkaemper, A. (1987) 'The European Community and International Environmental Cooperation: Legal Aspects of External Community Powers'. *Legal Issues of European Integration*, Vol.2, pp55–91.

Rasmussen, H. (1986) *On Law and Policy in the European Court of Justice: A Comparative Study in the Judicial Policymaking*, Dordrecht: Martinus Nijhoff Publishers.

Stein, E. (1991) 'External Relations of the European Community: Structure and Process'. *Collected Courses of the Academy of European Law*, Vol.1, pp115–168.

Weiler, Joseph H. H. (1986) 'Eurocracy and Distrust: Some Questions Concerning the Role of the European Court of Justice in the Protection of Fundamental Human Rights within the Legal Order of the European Communities', *Washington Law Review*, Vol.61, pp1103–1142.

Weiler, J. H. H. (1987) 'The Court of Justice on Trial', *Common Market Law Review*, Vol.24, pp555–589.

6

The European Parliament: The European Union's Environmental Champion?

Charlotte Burns

Introduction

The European Parliament (EP) is the only directly elected European Union (EU) institution. Since the introduction of direct elections in 1979, it has used its democratic status to push for general increases in its own powers and to expand and improve EU environmental legislation. Indeed, due to the activities of its Environment Committee, the EP has been identified as an environmental champion (Judge, 1992; Weale et al, 2000, p92). Once derided as a powerless talking shop, today the Parliament is recognized as an equal legislative partner with the Council under the co-decision procedure, which is used for the adoption of most environmental legislation (see Chapter 3). Hence, the EP can no longer be ignored during the legislative process as in earlier days, as it now enjoys the opportunity to initiate and shape EU environmental legislation. The aim of this chapter is to explain the Parliament's structure and powers, how and why it has come to be regarded as an environmental champion and to explore the future challenges that the institution faces. It is argued that the EP's Environment Committee has played a key role in advancing the EU's environmental agenda, and in exploiting and further developing the Parliament's formal and informal influence. However, there are still some important gaps in the EP's powers. Furthermore, the 2004 enlargement may disrupt the continuity of purpose and dedication to higher environmental standards that have characterized its behaviour since 1979.

Composition

Political groupings

There are currently 732 members of the European Parliament (MEPs), who sit in seven transnational political groups, with 29 members remaining unaffiliated (see Table 6.1). The work of the Parliament is carried out through its 20 standing committees, the composition of which reflects the political balance of the EP as a whole. Within the committees, each group is allocated a certain number of points, which they can use to bid for the right to draft legislative reports. The group that is able and prepared to pay the most points gets the report. This system ensures that even the smaller groups, such as the Greens, have the opportunity to prepare reports on important and sensitive subjects. The group that wins the bidding process appoints one of its members, (known as a rapporteur), to draft the committee's opinion on a legislative proposal, which the committee as a whole then amends and approves (or not) before submitting the report to a vote before the whole Parliament at its plenary session. As Table 6.1 shows, no single political group in the Parliament has an overall majority. Therefore, for amendments and legislation to be adopted by the plenary, the two largest political groups must form coalitions, particularly for the adoption of legislative amendments under the co-decision procedure, which require absolute majority support (367 votes).

This need to co-operate and form coalitions has both positive and negative effects. On the negative side it means that the Parliament rarely takes a radical position on legislation. For example, although the EP has been prepared to propose environmental amendments that impose costs upon the Member States and industries, broadly speaking it has adopted the ecological modernization agenda

Table 6.1 *Political Groups in the European Parliament*

Political Group	No of Members
European People's Party	268
Party of European Socialists	200
European Liberal Democratic and Reformist Group	88
Group of the Greens and European Free Alliance	42
Confederal Group of European United Left/Nordic Green Left	41
Independence and Democracy Group	37
Union for Europe of the Nations Group	27
Non-Affiliated Members	29
TOTAL	732

Note: As of 20 July 2004
Source: www.europarl.eu.int

of the Commission, based upon 'greening' capitalism and furthering growth in the EU. While this trend towards consensus affects all the political groups, from an environmental perspective its most obvious impact is upon the Greens, who find it difficult to secure the adoption of radical amendments. Indeed, the Greens find themselves in a dilemma:

> *[G]oing along with the larger groups means that [their] ... ideas are swallowed up and become indistinguishable from those of the mainstream parties. Yet to hold out often leaves [them] ... isolated, marginalized, and no nearer achieving their goals* (Bomberg, 1998, p141).

Realistically, the Greens cannot afford to be purist on a regular basis; they need to form coalitions to have any chance of seeing their amendments adopted. Hence the consensus politics of the Parliament has a de-radicalizing effect upon what both the Greens and the Parliament as a whole can achieve.

However, this effect is not wholly negative, as it cuts both ways. For example, after the 1999 elections, when the right-of-centre European People's Party (EPP) was, for the first time in the Parliament's history, the largest political group, there were fears that the EP would cease to be a progressive environmental force. These fears were prompted by the Parliament's failure, following the EPP's refusal to support key amendments, to offer an opinion on a key piece of legislation on lorry emissions (Friedrich et al, 2000, p605). However, the EPP realized that it could not afford regularly to ignore the position of the Party of European Socialists (PES) and other groups in the Parliament, as it needed their support to secure the adoption of its own preferred amendments. So after a little initial uneasiness, the Parliament appeared to settle back into business as usual, based upon compromise, consensus and middle-of-the-road politics.

Committee structures

Within the EP, the Committee for the Environment, Public Health and Food Safety is responsible for drafting reports on environmental legislation. With 63 members, it is the second largest committee in the Parliament, and, because it deals with more co-decision legislation than any other committee, it is also one of the most powerful (see below). The Committee's leadership is provided by its bureau, which comprises a chair and three deputies who are responsible for running meetings and representing the Committee in intra- and inter-institutional negotiations. Although the policy areas that the Environment Committee has dealt with over the years have changed, expanding in 1994 to include public health and consumer protection, and changing again in 1999 to cover food safety, overall the Committee has been characterized by a remarkable continuity in the focus of its work and in its leadership and direction. The same person, Ken Collins, was the Committee chair for 15 years (1979–1984, 1989–1999) and sat as a deputy in the bureau between 1984 and 1989. A long-standing member of the Committee, Caroline Jackson, succeeded him after his retirement in 1999. While Jackson comes from a different political group (she is a member of the EPP, whereas Collins was PES), the Committee has continued to promote an environmental agenda within the Parliament. The new chair from 2004, Karl Heinz-Florenz, is a German EPP member, but like Jackson, he is a long-standing member of the Committee. Hence, while there may be some difference in leadership style, it is highly likely that the Committee's traditions of entrepreneurship and commitment to environmental goals will continue. This continuity of leadership, particularly from 1979 to 1999, goes some way towards explaining the distinctive approach that the Committee adopted in seeking to enhance its own ability to initiate and shape environmental legislation (Judge, 1992; Bomberg and Burns, 1999). It also explains the reputation that the Committee developed from 1979 onwards. This period saw an enormous increase in the EP's legislative influence and formal powers, as it was transformed from little more than a consultative assembly into a genuine co-legislator. The following section traces the EP's transformation and the activities of the Environment Committee during that period, demonstrating the ways in which the Parliament has been able to secure its reputation as an environmental champion.

The Evolving Parliament

Following the first direct elections of 1979, the EP's legislative powers were very limited. The EP had a right to be consulted on Commission proposals, but the Council could effectively ignore the Parliament's opinion until the landmark isoglucose rulings of 1980. In its judgment on these cases, the European Court of Justice (ECJ) upheld the claims of two isoglucose producers (who were supported by the Parliament), that a Council regulation should be declared invalid on the grounds that the Council had failed to obtain the Parliament's opinion prior to adopting the regulation (Kirchner and Williams, 1983, p173). The Court's ruling 'gave Parliament a de facto delaying power' (Corbett et al, 2000, p4), which the EP exploited to the full by introducing a new rule of procedure that allowed it to postpone the final vote on a Commission proposal until the Commission had taken a position on EP amendments. If the Commission did not accept the Parliament's amendments, the matter could be referred back to committee for reconsideration, thereby delaying the Parliament's opinion and holding up the whole procedure (Corbett, 1998, p119). Thus, as Corbett (ibid, p120) notes, the EP had 'a strong bargaining position to fall back on' in any cases where the legislation was urgent, and as a result was able to exert more legislative influence in such situations.

This strategy of using its own internal rules of procedure as a vehicle for improving its legislative position is one that the Parliament has used very effectively, particularly in the 1979 to 1986 period when the EP's power was so circumscribed. For example, the EP was forced to be a very reactive institution; it had to wait until legislation was proposed before offering an opinion. The Parliament's response to this constraint was to develop an informal right of legislative initiative by introducing (in its rules of procedure), the right to adopt own initiative (OI) reports and resolutions. In 1980, this move led to more OI reports being adopted by the Parliament than legislation under the consultation procedure (Bourguignon-Wittke et al, 1985, p45). The Environment Committee has been particularly adept at using OI resolutions as a means of setting the Commission's agenda. For example, in 1982, the committee drafted an OI resolution calling for the banning of imports of baby-seal skins, which was supported by a public petition and eventually led to legislation. Over the years several other directives on major industrial hazards, ozone-depleting substances, lead content in petrol, tobacco advertising, transfrontier shipments of waste and zoo standards have been introduced as a result of Environment Committee resolutions (Judge, 1992, pp190–191; Judge and Earnshaw, 2003, p211). The Committee has also become skilled at using other means of agenda-setting such as conferences and hearings to which experts and representatives from other institutions are invited. Such events are used to highlight the need for policy in certain areas, and have prompted and shaped Commission proposals on, inter alia, urban policy, water legislation and eco-labelling (Judge, 1992, pp191–192).

In addition to these informal means of exercising influence, the formal powers of the EP and, by extension, the Environment Committee, were widened in the Treaty reforms of 1986 (the Single European Act (SEA)), 1992 (the Maastricht Treaty), and 1997 (the Treaty of Amsterdam).[1] With each formal increase in power came the prospect of new avenues of informal influence. The first major amendment to the Treaties in 1986 introduced several important changes that have shaped the later development of the Parliament in a profound way. For the first time, the environment was recognized as an area of EU policy competence, giving the Commission scope to introduce a range of environmental measures (see Chapters 2 and 5). Moreover, the Treaty introduced a deadline for the completion of the Single European Market (1992) and decision-making was made easier in the Council with the introduction of qualified majority voting (QMV), thereby ending the log jam of proposals that had been stuck in the Commission due to the prospect of their veto by a single state. Finally, the SEA introduced the co-operation procedure, which gives the European Parliament a second reading of legislation and, most importantly, a conditional right of veto, ie the EP can reject legislation, but a unanimous Council can overturn that rejection (see Chapter 2). Under this procedure, the Parliament is also able to act as a conditional agenda-setter (Tsebelis, 1994), which means that it has the power, under certain conditions, to make proposals that the Council will find easier to accept than to reject. This agenda-setting power stems from the inclusion of the rule under co-operation that when the Commission supports the EP's amendments, the Council requires unanimity to reject those amendments but can accept them by a qualified majority. Consequently, when the EP can satisfy the condition of Commission support, it can make proposals that the Council will find easier to accept than to reject (ibid, p131).

The introduction of the co-operation procedure had important ramifications for inter-institutional relations. If the EP wanted to exercise influence it needed to secure the goodwill and support of relevant personnel in the European Commission, especially in the field of environmental policy. The co-operation procedure was used for the adoption of harmonization measures necessary to complete the Single European Market (SEM) under Article 100a of the SEA. Consequently, proposals seeking to harmonize national environmental standards in order to facilitate the completion of the SEM were adopted under co-operation. However, all other environmental measures were adopted under Article 130s of the SEA, which carried the consultation procedure (Judge, 1992, p195). The EP therefore had a double interest in improving relations with the Commission: first, in order to persuade the Commission to propose legislation under Article 100a so that the co-operation procedure would be used; and second, when co-operation was used, to secure the Commission's support for its amendments.

Consequently, a series of measures was taken at both the institutional and personal levels to improve co-ordination and communication between the two institutions. For example, the Commission decided to encourage:

> *consultation préalable with the Parliament whereby the Commission would sound out MEPs before formalizing the Commission's initial legislative proposals. This would be done informally by contacts with the responsible parliamentary committees, rapporteurs, spokespersons of political groups and their staff* (Corbett, 1998, p270).

For its part, the EP took advantage of the Commission's new willingness to engage in informal dialogue throughout the policy-making process, and, by doing so, was by all accounts able to exercise more legislative influence (Corbett, 1989, p366; Earnshaw and Judge, 1997, pp549–550). For example, in their study of the co-operation procedure Earnshaw and Judge (1997, p561), found that 'in interview MEPs and officials alike pointed to the importance of informal negotiations between Parliament and the Commission in determining the eventual legislative impact of the EP'.

More specifically, in the field of environmental policy, the Commission's fledgling Directorate General for the Environment (DG Environment) saw the EP's Environment Committee as a natural ally against both the Council and colleagues in the Commission who were unsympathetic to environmental policy (Judge, 1992, pp199–200). Hence, there is some evidence to suggest that the DG Environment was prepared, where possible, to bring forward proposals under Article 100a. For example, between 1989 and 1992, 15 out of the 29 environmental proposals brought forward by the Commission were based on Article 100a (ibid, p195). Moreover, the Commission would use the EP as a conduit for inserting its own preferences into legislative proposals, leading officials in the Council to suspect that there was 'an incestuous relationship' between the EP's Environment Committee and DG Environment (DG Environment official, quoted in Judge (1992, p199)). Indeed, Committee Chair Collins established regular meetings between himself and the Commissioner as a key means of keeping dialogue between the Commission and Parliament open. Consequently, the period after the entry into force of the SEA was a critical one for the development and consolidation of close ties between the EU's two natural environmental champions: DG Environment and the EP's Environment Committee.

Quantitative analyses of the rate at which the EP's amendments are accepted, demonstrate the legislative influence that it is able to wield under the co-operation procedure. For example, Tsebelis et al (2001, p580) find that the Parliament was successful in seeing approximately 48 per cent of its co-operation amendments adopted by the Commission and 31 per cent adopted by the Council. More significantly, in a separate study of 24 proposals adopted under co-operation,

Kreppel (2003, p797) finds that 73 per cent of the EP's amendments adopted by the Commission made substantive and important changes to the legislative proposals. In short, the co-operation procedure allowed the Parliament successfully to amend legislative proposals in a significant and substantive way. Moreover, Tsebelis and Kalandrakis (1999) find that the new procedure offered the EP new ways in which to set the Commission's environmental policy agenda indirectly. They argue that the EP adopted the practice of deliberately proposing amendments that the Commission could or would not accept, in order to place certain policy items on the Commission's legislative agenda (Tsebelis and Kalandrakis, 1999, pp142–143).

What of the other key power that co-operation offered the Parliament, namely the right to reject legislation? Interestingly the EP has rarely used its veto under co-operation, deploying it successfully on only seven occasions (for details, see Judge and Earnshaw, 2003, pp255–256). There are two main reasons for the Parliament's reluctance. First, the Parliament always regarded the co-operation procedure as a stepping stone to its preferred power of co-decision. Consequently, the EP felt it had to demonstrate to the Council and Commission that it could be trusted as a legislative partner (Westlake, 1997, p245). Second, as a general rule the EP prefers having some – albeit inadequate – legislation, to no legislation at all (Earnshaw and Judge, 1997, p560). Consequently, it is in the Parliament's interest to seek to amend proposals, reserving its right of rejection for all but the most extreme cases. Moreover, the threat of rejection can be invoked without the veto actually having to be used. For example, in the landmark and oft-cited case of small car emissions, the EP, with the support of DG Environment, was able to force the Council and other members of the Commission to adopt more stringent US emission standards for small cars by threatening to reject the proposal. If the EP had rejected the proposal there was a strong likelihood that the EU's common market in cars would collapse, as states in favour of the tighter emission limits, such as Denmark, Germany and The Netherlands, would adopt the more stringent US standards (Hubschmid and Moser, 1997, pp238–240). Moreover, these states would not face a legal challenge for adopting national laws that imposed restrictions on trade, as the ECJ had ruled in the famous Danish bottle case that such restrictions are acceptable, if they aim to protect the environment (see Chapter 5). Under these circumstances, the mere threat of an EP rejection, with its wide-ranging implications for the Community trade in cars, was enough to shift the Council and Commission position on this important piece of environmental legislation. The case also demonstrates the way in which close co-operation between DG Environment and the EP can result in the adoption of higher environmental standards by the Council.

Today, the co-operation procedure applies to only four Treaty articles on Economic and Monetary Union.[2] Nevertheless, as the above discussion demonstrates, its introduction paved the way for an increase in the EP's formal and informal power. Moreover, by using its new rights under co-operation responsibly, the EP was able to strengthen its claim for further increases in power, which it was eventually awarded in 1992 in the Maastricht Treaty. Under the terms of the Treaty, the EP's powers of scrutiny were improved by a new right to establish committees of inquiry to investigate alleged contraventions or misadministration in the implementation of Community law (Shackleton, 1998). In addition, the EP gained new powers of appointment and its ability to control the Commission was enhanced by the terms of office of the two institutions being brought into line with one another, and the EP being awarded the right to a vote of confidence on the incoming Commission, and the right to a consultative vote on the nominee for Commission President (Westlake, 1998).

From a legislative perspective, there were two key innovations. First, the EP's right to initiate legislation was formally recognized under Article 192. Following this move the Environment Committee took the opportunity in May 1994 to request that the Commission bring forward legislation establishing a liability regime for environmental damage. Although it took eight years and a threat to reject another piece of legislation (on the deliberate release of genetically modified organisms) if a liability regime was not established, the Commission did eventually bring forward a proposal in 2002, thereby demonstrating that the EP had carved out for itself an important right to set the Commission's legislative agenda (Judge and Earnshaw, 2003, p212). Second, the Treaty introduced the EP's long-preferred power of co-decision (see Table 6.2).

Initially the co-decision procedure applied to only 15 Treaty articles, but its scope was extended in the Treaty reforms of 1997 and 1999, so that it now covers 43 policy areas, including many areas of environmental policy. Co-decision makes the Parliament a genuine co-legislator with the Council: the agreement of both institutions is necessary for legislation to be adopted. The procedure introduces a third reading; an unconditional right of rejection for the EP, ie the Council can no longer overturn an EP veto; and a conciliation procedure, which is triggered after the EP's second reading if the Council cannot accept the Parliament's amendments (see Table 6.2). The conciliation process involves a committee composed of delegations of equal size from both the Council and EP, who negotiate a compromise that both sides are prepared to accept. The Commission is also present and acts as a facilitator to agreement. If either institution fails to adopt the compromise text negotiated by the conciliation committee, then the proposal falls.

In addition, under the terms of the Maastricht Treaty, in the event that the conciliation committee could not reach agreement, the Council had the power to reimpose the position it had adopted after the EP's first reading, the so-called 'common position'. The Parliament was then faced with the choice of adopting the common position as it stood, or rejecting the whole law and taking the responsibility for doing so. This rule puts the Council in a potentially powerful position, as representatives could gamble that the EP would be unlikely to reject legislation and they could therefore adopt an intransigent bargaining position in conciliation, knowing full well that they could simply revert to their common position if agreement could not be reached. The Council could then present the EP with a 'take-it-or-leave-it' offer. However, to counter this threat, the EP introduced a new rule (78) into its own rules of procedure, which allowed it to request the Commission to withdraw legislation upon which a conciliation committee could not find agreement. If the Commission refused, and the Council tried to reaffirm its common position, the EP could automatically table a motion to reject the Council text at the next plenary session (Hix, 1999, p94). The one

Table 6.2 *The Co-decision Procedure since 1999*

Stage of decision-making	Options
Commission Proposal	
EP First-Reading Opinion	Accept or amend Commission proposal.
Commission Opinion	Accept, amend or reject EP first-reading amendments.
Council Common Position	Accept or reject EP amendments. If all EP first-reading amendments are accepted, or if no amendments have been proposed then the legislation is adopted.
EP Second-Reading Opinion	Accept, amend or reject common position. If the common position is accepted the legislation is adopted. If the common position is rejected the proposal falls.
Commission Opinion	Accept, amend or reject EP second-reading amendments.
	Council needs QMV for EP amendments with Commission support, and unanimity for amendments rejected by Commission.
Council Position	Accept or reject EP second-reading amendments.
	If EP amendments are accepted, legislation is adopted.
	If EP amendments are rejected, a conciliation committee is convened.
Conciliation Committee in order to negotiate a compromise on those EP amendments that the Council cannot accept.	If co-legislators (EP and Council) cannot reach agreement, the proposal falls.
	If co-legislators do reach agreement, the legislation is adopted.

Source: author

time in 1994 that the Council tried to reaffirm its common position after a failed conciliation, the Parliament rejected the legislation as a matter of principle (Earnshaw and Judge, 1995, pp643–645).[3] Subsequently, the Council never tried to use this particular power again. So, for example, when a conciliation committee failed to reach agreement on the issue of transferable securities in 1998, the Council chose not to reaffirm its common position in the certain knowledge that if it tried to do so the Parliament would simply reject the legislation (European Parliament, 1999, p6). The co-decision procedure was reformed in the Amsterdam Treaty (which entered into force in 1999), in order to remove the Council's right to reaffirm its common position, thus making conciliation the final stage of the legislative process (see Table 6.2). Hence, the EP had successfully used its own rules of procedure to establish an informal norm that was subsequently formally recognized in the Treaty.

There is no doubt that since its introduction in November 1993, co-decison has had a profound effect upon inter-institutional relations. Its main impact has been to facilitate the development of direct informal relations between the Council and Parliament, largely at the expense of the Commission. These informal relations emerged as a response to the difficulties of negotiating an agreement with thirty or more people present in a full-blown conciliation meeting. They were initiated under the German presidency in 1994, when Environment Committee Chair, Ken Collins, met his counterpart from the Council, Jochen Grünhage, privately to discuss amendments to the Packaging Waste Directive (Garman and Hilditch, 1998, pp274–275). The success of these meetings, along with others held between Grünhage and representatives from the Culture Committee, led over time to the regular use of the slightly more formal meetings known as trialogues (European Parliament, 1995, pp20–21; Shackleton, 2000), which are typically attended by the rapporteur, the competent committee chair, the delegation chairs from the Council and EP, and a representative of the Commission. As trialogues are easier to arrange and manage than full conciliation meetings, they are now widely used, with conciliation meetings reserved for all but the most intractable issues.

However, the trend of arranging informal meetings with Council officials in his office is one that Collins continued to use successfully, as for example during the long and complex negotiations on the Auto-oil Programme (see above). This programme sought to regulate car emissions via legislation aimed at both the oil and car industries. It represented a departure from the traditional approach to car emission policy in the EU, as previously, for example, in the small car emissions case, emission limits had been tightened incrementally in line with the development of the best available technology (BAT) (Friedrich et al, 2000, p593). By contrast, when drawing up the auto-oil proposals, the Commission sought to develop environmental quality objectives through the adoption of cost-effective regulation. The Commission also adopted a new approach to policy-making by consulting closely with the automobile and oil industries when drawing up the legislation, while excluding Member State governments, non-governmental organizations (NGOs) and the EP (ibid, pp593–594). Unsurprisingly, none of these excluded actors was content with the Commission proposals, and a huge lobbying campaign followed, which eventually resulted in the European Parliament adopting 36 amendments at its second reading. Those amendments principally aimed to tighten the emission standards and to introduce strict deadlines, both of which would be mandatory (ibid, pp600–602). Given the enormous complexity of the dossiers and the large number of amendments, Collins, with the co-operation of officials from the UK presidency, arranged a series of informal meetings in his own office to allow the rapporteurs and Council officials to start negotiating with one another. It was only through these important and small-scale encounters that agreement became possible (Warleigh, 1999, pp10–12).

Significantly, the Commission appears to have played a limited role in these informal meetings. Criticized for excluding key stakeholders from the policy-making process, producing unambitious proposals and favouring the oil industry, the Commission found itself under attack from all sides (Friedrich et al, 2000, pp599–602). In addition, competence for the proposal was shared between DGs Environment and Enterprise who were divided in their approach. The Commission was only able to offer policy leadership belatedly when DG Environment was given the lead role during the conciliation process (Warleigh, 1999, pp8–9), however that only happened after the Commission had been excluded from one conciliation meeting by Collins because representatives from DGs Enterprise and Environment were advancing contradictory positions (Friedrich et al, 2000, p604). By the time DG Environment took the lead in negotiations, representatives from the Council and Parliament had already forged a close relationship in their efforts to reach agreement, and the Commission remained a peripheral actor (Warleigh, 1999, pp8–9). Hence, auto-oil illustrates the dangers that DG Environment faces when it ignores its key allies such as the EP's Environment Committee and environmental NGOs, and it provides an example of one of the key challenges that the Commission faces under co-decision: the potential to be sidelined by the Council and Parliament (Shackleton, 2000; Burns, 2004).

Traditionally, the EP and the Commission have been portrayed as partners and rivals (Westlake, 1997). Certainly the relationship between DG Environment and the EP's Environment Committee was characterized by close partnership, particularly in the all-important 'initiative phase' of the EU's evolving environmental policy regime between 1986 and 1992 (see Chapter 2). Nevertheless, this partnership was unequal, as the Commission always enjoyed an informational advantage over the Parliament due to its closer relationship with the Council (for example, Commission officials sit in on all key Council meetings). However, with the introduction of co-decision, the Parliament has been placed on a more equal footing, as MEPs can now communicate directly with the Council. This fact, coupled with the increased assertiveness of the EP in its dealings with the Commission (for example, by holding hearings in order to quiz the Commissioner designates on their suitability for posts, and even forcing the entire Commission to resign in 1999), has shifted the balance of power between the Commission and EP. The EP is now a more equal partner, less reliant upon the goodwill of the Commission, which as the auto-oil case shows, the EP is now prepared to sideline. Consequently, DG Environment has to work harder to maintain its traditional alliance with the EP, which it can no longer take for granted. Nevertheless, it still remains in the interests of both institutions to co-operate whenever they can, in order to strengthen and improve the EU's environmental policy regime.

The auto-oil case also provides a good example of another key impact of co-decision: the way it has increased the EP's legislative power. In the auto-oil case, the EP adopted 36 amendments at second reading, of which the Council accepted 27 (European Parliament, 1999, p40), a significant achievement given that auto-oil was one of the most important policy initiatives launched by the Commission in the environmental field in the 1990s (Friedrich et al, 2000, p593). Friedrich et al (ibid, p604) argue that the EP emerged as the clear winner from the conciliation process and former Committee Chair Collins claimed that the auto-oil negotiations were the 'biggest success story' of his time in office (Wurzel, 1999, p22). However, the amount of time and energy that went into the negotiations – in the end there were four trialogues, five technical meetings and four meetings of the EP delegation (European Parliament, 1999, p40) – is indicative of another key impact of the co-decision procedure: it has massively increased the workload of the Parliament and its Environment Committee. With the extension of the application of co-decision from 15 to 38 policy areas in 1999,[4] there was a 144 per cent increase in the number of co-decision dossiers concluded by the EP in its fifth parliamentary term (1999 to 2004). Moreover, the Environment Committee has dealt with more co-decision legislation than any of the other EP committees. Between 1993 and 1999, it dealt with 36 per cent of all co-decision dossiers and with 29 per cent between 1999 and 2004 (European Parliament, 1999, p52; 2004a, p55). Hence the Environment Committee has assumed a disproportionate share of the workload since the introduction of the co-decision procedure.

This active legislative involvement has both positive and negative effects. On the positive side, as under co-operation, the Environment Committee has been in the vanguard of efforts to strengthen the EU's environmental standards. Since the procedure's introduction, the Parliament has forced the Council to conciliation on 34 environmental proposals covering a wide range of issues including air quality, car emissions, waste management, water quality, implementation and environmental liability (European Parliament, 1999; 2004a). In all these cases, the EP has been able to tighten limits and timetables. For example, in negotiations in 2000 on the regulation of substances that deplete the ozone layer, the Parliament was able to persuade a Council that was not prepared to countenance any deadlines for the phasing out of hydrochlorofluorocarbons (HCFCs), to agree to set dates of 2010 for virgin HCFCs and 2015 for recycled HCFCs (European Parliament, 2004a, p15). In negotiations on the deliberate release of genetically modified organisms (GMOs), the Parliament forced the Commission to agree to bring forward proposals on environmental liability, and a new labelling and traceability scheme for products containing GMOs (European Parliament, 2001). In the 2002 negotiations on the Directive on waste from electrical and electronic equipment (WEEE), the EP forced the Council to include binding collection rates of waste per inhabitant per year, with the Council agreeing to a 4 kg average weight. The EP also persuaded the Council to agree that individual producers should be liable for the recovery of WEEE from private users (European Parliament, 2002). So although Judge (1992, p207) notes the EP cannot always be successful in its attempts to strengthen legislation (see also Weale et al, 2000, pp425–426), the advent of co-decision and its application to most environmental policy means that neither the Commission nor the Council can now afford to ignore the EP, which is consequently in a much more powerful position to tighten the EU's environmental legislation.

The increase in the European Parliament's powers has also opened up access to the legislative process to actors (eg environmental NGOs) that might otherwise be excluded, or that the Commission neglects to consult when drawing up proposals. While the increase in the EP's powers has also resulted in an expansion in the lobbying of MEPs by business interests (which are often better resourced than smaller NGOs), the success of European Green parties in seeing their members elected to the EP has allowed an informal network to develop encompassing Green MEPs and key third-sector lobbyists. The two groups try to co-operate closely, exchanging information and advice in order to maximize their legislative impact. Hence while the environmental NGOs seek to build relations with many of the political groups in the Parliament, they enjoy particularly close relations with the Greens.

The Green group has also benefited from the expansion of the EP's power and the rules designed to guarantee a fair distribution of work. For example, the allocation of reports in the Environment Committee via the bidding process, guarantees that the Greens can take responsibility for high-profile reports and therefore shape their content in a fundamental way, as Finnish Green MEP, Heidi Hautala was able to do as one of the rapporteurs on the Auto-oil Programme. On balance, therefore, the increase in the EP's powers has presented a range of opportunities for environmental activists that they otherwise would not enjoy. They have gained access to the decision-making process and to the Parliament in which their natural allies – the Greens – are increasingly well represented. For example, in the 2004 election the Greens were, for the second time, able to form the fourth largest group in the EP (see Table 6.1).

The Environment Committee has also been able to play an important institutional role by shaping the development of the co-decision procedure. As shown above, Committee Chair Ken Collins was actively involved in the development of the use of bilateral informal contacts between the Council and Parliament. He also established a reputation for forcing the Council to negotiate in conciliation on amendments that the EP had not formally adopted at second reading. This habit resulted in the new co-decision rules introduced in 1999 explicitly stipulating that only those amendments that the EP *had* adopted at second reading could be discussed in conciliation (Hix, 2002, p276). Hence the Environment Committee has had a profound effect upon inter-institutional relations and treaty reform, as well as upon the quality of EU environmental legislation.

However, having to be involved with so much, often highly technical legislation, inevitably places a strain upon the Committee and its personnel. Although the rapporteurs in the auto-oil case were well able to cope with the complexity of that legislation, such a high level of technical knowledge cannot necessarily be guaranteed. A key drawback facing the Environment Committee and the Parliament more generally is the lack of in-house expertise upon which MEPs can draw when preparing their reports. Instead, members have traditionally relied upon the Commission and the briefings of lobbyists as a source of information and expertise. Yet, as the auto-oil case shows, the Commission cannot always be relied upon to be an independent source of help as officials have their own agenda, as do lobbyists whether they are from the environmental or industrial sectors. One way in which the Committee has dealt with this problem has been to invite key experts to parliamentary hearings and conferences. The European Environment Agency (EEA) has also been a useful source of independent reports. Moreover, since 2003, the Committee has addressed this issue directly by concluding framework contracts with two independent research institutes, the Institute for European Environmental Policy and the European Academies' Science Advisory Council. The MEPs call upon these bodies to offer expert advice on emerging issues falling within the Environment Committee's competence (European Parliament, 2004b). Hence, despite the drawbacks that increased legislative power may pose, the Environment Committee is seeking new ways in which to deal with its responsibilities. Nevertheless, the Parliament and Committee will face a series of key challenges in the coming years and it is to these that the next section turns.

Future challenges

The story of the Parliament and environmental policy seems to be one of success up to the Treaty of Amsterdam in 1997, but the Treaty of Nice was a disappointment (see Chapter 3). It made few substantive increases in the Parliament's power, only extending co-decision to a further five policy areas and making no substantive revisions to the procedure's operation. Consequently, there are still a number of key gaps in the EP's power in areas of critical importance for the EU's environmental policy regime. For example, the EP has no power of co-decision in relation to environmental measures with fiscal and energy supply implications, land use, town and country planning and the quantitative management of water resources (Article 175(2)), which also require unanimity in the Council. Nor does it have rights of co-decision over agricultural policy. Therefore in some key policy sectors, which make major contributions to environmental problems such as climate change, the EP has its hands tied.

The Parliament also still plays an incredibly limited role in common foreign, security and trade policies; these areas remain dominated by the Council and Commission. Therefore, it is difficult for the EP to exert any impact upon the positions adopted by the EU in important international environmental and trade negotiations such as those on ozone, climate change and tariff reductions (see Chapter 12). The Parliament's role is limited to assenting to agreements reached by the Council and Commission and offering its opinion on their implementation, rather than being able to shape their content in any meaningful way. The EP also has a limited role in justice and home affairs and the implementation of environmental legislation, which largely remain the preserve of the Member States. The Commission *has*, however, brought forward legislation on environmental liability, and the Treaty of Nice has given the EP the right to bring Court actions directly without having to demonstrate a specific concern, an important recognition of the EP's role as a co-legislator (Judge and Earnshaw, 2003, p241). On implementation, the EP has concentrated upon persuading the Commission to bring forward measures such as the Liability Directive and has sought to strengthen the powers and resources of bodies such as the EEA and the Network for the Implementation and Enforcement of Environmental Law (IMPEL). The Parliament also plays an awareness-raising role in cases of severe transgressions of Community law.

However, the EP cannot intervene directly in the affairs of Member States with poor implementation records. Moreover, many of the problems of implementation stem in part from the difficulties that states face in shaping the content of EU environmental legislation so that it is suitable for their local environmental conditions. For example, states may find that they do not have the appropriate administrative infrastructure or expertise to implement EU environmental policies: a phenomenon often described as 'policy misfit' (Börzel, 2003, pp36–38). Consequently, the implementation problem is one that needs to be addressed at the initiative stage of legislation, when states can consider and draw attention to the implementation problems that they may encounter, rather than when transgressions have happened and irreversible damage has been caused (Jordan, 2002).

But again, the Parliament is not well placed to intervene in the negotiations that take place between states and the Commission when legislation is developed.

In addition, the Parliament has little scope to shape the launch and development of European Council initiatives, ie strategic policy programmes launched by the EU's heads of government and State when they have their biannual meetings. For example, the Parliament had no input into the Cardiff process launched in 1998, which committed the EU to better integration of the environment into all policy sectors (see Chapter 16). Nor does the EP have any input in the Lisbon agenda, which was launched in 2000 with the aim of further liberalizing European markets. Hence in two key areas of strategic environmental importance the EP again finds itself in a classically reactive position, ie waiting for the Commission to issue policy proposals rather than being able to shape the broad direction of the EU.

However, perhaps the key challenge facing the Parliament in its sixth term is the EU's enlargement to take in ten new states, many of which have little or no experience of environmental policy (see Chapter 15). The entry of these states seems likely, at least in the short term, to exacerbate the implementation deficit. Moreover, the entry of 162 MEPs from the new states raises concerns about the Parliament's internal cohesion. Will the EP's increasingly heterogeneous political groups be able to achieve internal agreement, as well as being able to form broad coalitions in order to get amendments adopted? Will the entry of MEPs from new states change the priorities of the Parliament, shifting away from its traditional concerns such as the environment and social policy towards other issues? The fact that in the 2004 European election no Green Party MEPs were elected in the new member states of the EU suggests that the environment will be of limited concern to this new cohort of European Parliamentarians. Indeed, given the number of new states represented in the EU and their comparatively lower level of economic development, it is likely that this enlargement will, at least in the short term, have a significant impact upon the policy priorities and operation of the EP.

At the broader institutional level, the 2004 enlargement also raises questions about the EU's capacity to operate effectively as a legislative system. The entry of 15 new states has brought more veto players (actors capable of stalling the legislative process (see Chapter 8)) into the EU's complex decision-making system, raising the spectre of institutional deadlock and policy stasis, or, alternatively, the increased use of side-payments to guarantee agreement from reluctant/difficult states. Given the high costs associated with implementing environmental legislation, the EU's environmental policy regime may suffer. Add into this complex brew the Commission's difficulties in achieving the goals of the fifth Environmental Action Programme (EAP), entitled 'Towards Sustainability', and the proposal of a much less ambitious EAP, one cannot help but conclude that the EU's environmental policy is heading for uncertain times: particularly when one takes into account the appointment of Stavros Dimas, a former employee of the World Bank who has no experience of environmental policy, as the new Commissioner for the Environment. Dimas's appointment has been greeted with dismay in environmental circles as a sign of the downgrading of the environment as an EU policy priority. It remains to be seen whether he and his staff can maintain the still-healthy working relationship that was developed between DG Environment and the EP's Environment Committee in the 1980s. Hopefully, he will recognize, as his predecessors have, that the European Parliament can be a useful ally.

Finally, it is worth observing that, regrettably, none of these gaps in the EP's environmental powers are really addressed in the proposed EU constitution (see Chapter 1). For example, the proposed constitution includes provisions to apply co-decision with QMV to all policy areas. However, there are some notable exceptions, including those environmental measures currently subject to consultation, which are to be adopted by co-decision, but with unanimity in the Council. Hence, the EP's bargaining position in those areas will remain weak. The draft treaty seeks to simplify decision-making and introduces new rules for the adoption of legislation in the Council, which effectively vest power in the hands of the larger members, which may or may not be good from an environmental perspective. Moreover, as the Treaty has yet to be ratified by the Member States and with the additional hurdle of referenda in France, the UK and several other states, there are serious uncertainties about whether it will ever be adopted.

Conclusion

There is no doubt that the European Parliament has played a critical role in developing the EU's environmental agenda. The Environment Committee has skilfully expanded its influence over the years through developing an intricate web of informal contacts with the other key EU environmental champion, DG Environment in the Commission, as well as with Council officials, policy experts and NGOs. The Committee has also helped to develop and shape the EP's formal policy role through the judicious use of its powers. The successive increases in the EP's influence have opened up the policy process to a wide range of actors who might otherwise be excluded from decision-making, and have also offered the opportunity of shaping legislation to an increasingly successful Green group. While the need to form coalitions tends to have a de-radicalizing effect upon the EP's opinions, the Parliament has nevertheless managed to strengthen the EU's environmental policy in a number of significant ways. However, at the start of its sixth term of office, the EP faces some major challenges. The entry of MEPs from ten new states, eight of which are still relatively new democracies with little experience of environmental policy, is likely, at least in the short term, to disrupt the cohesive modus operandi that has evolved within the Parliament since 1979. In addition, the EP still has some important gaps in its powers. The immediate challenge for the Parliament then, is to find ways of dealing with its new cohort of MEPs without being distracted from its wider mission to be an environmental champion within the EU.

Notes

1   The SEA was agreed in 1986, but came into force in 1987; the Maastricht Treaty came into force in 1993, and Amsterdam in 1999.
2   Articles 99(5), 102(2), 103(2) and 106(2).

3 As under co-operation, the Parliament has only rarely used its veto under co-decision, namely in relation to: voice telephony in 1994; biotechnology patenting in 1995; takeovers in 2000; and market access to port services in 2003 (European Parliament, 2004a).

4 The number of co-decision dossiers increased from 165 completed between 1993 and 30 April 1999, to 403 completed between 1 May 1999 and 30 April 2004 (European Parliament, 1999, p52; 2004a, p10).

References

Bomberg, E. (1998) *Green Parties and Politics in the European Union*, London: Routledge.

Bomberg, E. and Burns, C. (1999) 'The Environment Committee of the European Parliament: New Powers, Old Problems', *Environmental Politics*, Vol.8, No.4, pp173–179.

Börzel, T. A. (2003) *Environmental Leaders and Laggards in Europe. Why There is (Not) a 'Southern Problem'*, Aldershot: Ashgate.

Bourguignon-Wittke R., Grabitz, E., Schmuck, O., Steppat, S. and Wessels, W. (1985) 'Five Years of the Directly Elected European Parliament: Performance and Prospects', *Journal of Common Market Studies*, Vol.24, No.1, pp39–59.

Burns, C. (2004) 'The European Commission and Co-decision: A Study of Declining Influence?', *Journal of European Public Policy*, Vol.11, No.1, pp1–18.

Corbett, R. (1989) 'Testing the New Procedures: The European Parliament's First Experiences with its New Single Act Powers', *Journal of Common Market Studies*, Vol.27, No.4, pp359–372.

Corbett, R. (1998) *The European Parliament's Role in Closer Integration*, London: Macmillan.

Corbett, R., Jacobs, F. and Shackleton, M. (2000) *The European Parliament*, Fourth Edition, London: John Harper Publishing.

Earnshaw, D. and Judge, D. (1995) 'Early Days: the European Parliament, Co-decision and the European Union Legislative Process Post-Maastricht', *Journal of European Public Policy*, Vol.2, No.4, pp624–649.

Earnshaw, D. and Judge, D. (1997) 'The Life and Times of the European Union's Co-operation Procedure', *Journal of Common Market Studies*, Vol.35, No.4, pp543–564.

European Parliament (1995) *European Parliament Delegations to the Conciliation Committee Progress Report for the Second Half of 1994*, Brussels: European Parliament.

European Parliament (1999) *Activity Report 1 November 1993–30 April 1999, From Entry into Force of the Treaty of Maastricht to Entry into Force of the Treaty of Amsterdam, of the Delegations to the Conciliation Committee*, Brussels: European Parliament.

European Parliament (2001) *Report on the Joint Text Approved by the Conciliation Committee for a European Parliament and Council Directive on the Deliberate Release into the Environment of Genetically Modified Organisms and Repealing Directive 90/220/EEC*, Brussels: European Parliament.

European Parliament (2002) *Report on the Joint Text Approved by the Conciliation Committee for a European Parliament and Council Directive on Waste Electrical and Electronic Equipment (WEEE)*, Brussels: European Parliament.

European Parliament (2004a) *Activity Report 1 May 1999 to 30 April 2004 (5th Parliamentary Term) of the Delegations to the Conciliation Committee*, Brussels: European Parliament.

European Parliament (2004b) 'Experts: Background', European Parliament Environment Committee website, 20 July 2004, www.europarl.eu.int/comparl/envi/externalexpertise/default_en.htm, accessed January 2005.

Friedrich, A., Tappe, M. and Wurzel, R. K. W. (2000) 'A New Approach to EU Environmental Policy-Making? The Auto-Oil I Programme', *Journal of European Public Policy*, Vol.7, No.4, pp593–612.

Garman, J. and Hilditch, L. (1998) 'Behind the Scenes: An Examination of the Importance of the Informal Processes at Work in Conciliation', *Journal of European Public Policy*, Vol.5, No.2, pp271–284.

Hix, S. (1999) *The Political System of the European Union*, Basingstoke: Macmillan.

Hix, S. (2002) 'Constitutional Agenda-setting Through Discretion Rule Interpretation: Why the European Parliament Won at Amsterdam', *British Journal of Political Science*, Vol.32, pp259–280.

Hubschmid, C. and Moser, P. (1997) 'The Co-operation Procedure in the EU: Why was the European Parliament Influential in the Decision on Car Emission Standards?', *Journal of Common Market Studies*, Vol.35, No.2, pp225–242.

Jordan, A. (2002) 'The Implementation of EU Environmental Policy: A Policy Problem Without a Political Solution?', in Jordan, A. (ed) *Environmental Policy in the European Union* (1e), London: Earthscan.

Judge, D. (1992) 'Predestined to Save the Earth: The Environment Committee of the European Parliament', *Environmental Politics*, Vol.1, No.4, pp186–212.

Judge, D. and Earnshaw, D. (2003) *The European Parliament*, Basingstoke: Palgrave Macmillan.

Kirchner, E. and Williams, K. (1983) 'The Legal, Political and Institutional Implications of the Isoglucose Judgments 1980', *Journal of Common Market Studies*, Vol.22, No.2, pp173–190.

Kreppel, A. (2003) 'Moving Beyond Procedure, An Empirical Analysis of European Parliament Legislative Influence', *Comparative Political Studies*, Vol.35, No.7, pp784–813.

Shackleton, M. (1998) 'The European Parliament's New Committees of Inquiry: Tiger or Paper Tiger?', *Journal of Common Market Studies*, Vol.36, No.1, pp115–130.

Shackleton, M. (2000) 'The Politics of Co-decision', *Journal of Common Market Studies*, Vol.38, No.2, pp325–342.

Tsebelis, G. (1994) 'The Power of the European Parliament as a Conditional Agenda Setter', *American Political Science Review*, Vol.88, No.1, pp128–142.

Tsebelis, G. and Kalandrakis, A. (1999) 'The European Parliament and Environmental Legislation: The Case of Chemicals', *European Journal of Political Research*, Vol.36, pp119–154.

Tsebelis, G., Jensen, C., Kalandrakis, A. and Kreppel, A. (2001) 'Legislative Procedures in the European Union: An Empirical Analysis', *British Journal of Political Science*, Vol.31, pp573–599.

Warleigh, A. (1999) 'Multi-dimensional Chess: The Influence of Co-decision on EU Policy-making – The Case of Auto-Oil', Conference Paper, Sheffield: UACES, September.

Weale, A., Pridham, G., Cini, M., Konstadakopoulos, D., Porter, M. and Flynn, B. (2000) *Environmental Governance in Europe*, Oxford: Oxford University Press.

Westlake, M. (1997) 'The Commission and the Parliament', in Edwards, G. and Spence, D. (eds) *The European Commission*, London: Cartermill International Limited.

Westlake, M. (1998) 'The European Parliament's Emerging Powers of Appointment', *Journal of Common Market Studies*, Vol.36, No.3, pp431–444.

Wurzel, R, K, W (1999) 'The Role of the European Parliament: Interview with Ken Collins', *Journal of Legislative Studies*, Vol.5, No.2, pp1–23.

7

Environmental Groups and the European Community: Challenges and Opportunities

Sonia Mazey and Jeremy Richardson

Lobbying and Policy-making in the European Community: Some Special Characteristics

While the environmental sector exhibits some special characteristics – not least of which is the currently very high political salience of environmental and 'green' issues and the almost unique cross-sectoral nature of the environmental issue – groups lobbying in this sector face the same range of opportunity structures as other groups in the European Community (EC). Indeed, we argue elsewhere (Mazey and Richardson, 1993a, 1993b) that the fundamental rules of the game for lobbyists at the European level are much the same as at the national level. Although politics in Brussels is not yet akin to the 'village life' which is thought to exist, say, in Whitehall in Britain, there are nevertheless some basic cultural norms that are not so dissimilar to those of more tightly integrated and unified national bureaucracies.

Thus, the successful groups are those that exhibit the usual professional characteristics – namely resources, advance intelligence, good contacts with bureaucrats and politicians, and above all an ability to provide policy-makers with sound information and advice. Reputations for expertise, reliability, and trust are key resources in lobbying in Brussels as elsewhere. A respondent from the Directorate General for the Environment (DG XI), for example, stressed the need for groups to be 'responsible' – by which was meant a willingness to be involved in the policy-making process without publicity. This means that lobbying *styles* may be as important as the content and objectives of the lobbying itself. The way that business is conducted will affect policy outcomes, as it plays a significant part in shaping the perceptions of participants and, therefore, their willingness to listen to each other, and to make concessions during the processing of issues. As another respondent remarked to us, there was a marked difference in the degree of professionalism of groups that approached the Commission and hence in the weight that was attached to their views. As we will suggest in the next section, perceptions may be especially relevant to a consideration of the politics of the environment in the EC, as the three main groups of interests – bureaucrats, environmentalists, and industrialists – have particular perceptions of each other which may affect their effectiveness in the policy-making process.

Even though the 'basic rules of the game' may be familiar, however, the EC policy process is in many ways unique. Its multi-national, neo-federal nature, the openness of decision-making to lobbying, and the considerable weight of national politico-administrative elites within the process, create a rather unstable and multi-dimensional environment to which all pressure groups must adapt if they are to achieve their objectives.

A major problem for all groups in the EC policy process is the comparative instability and unpredictability of the agenda-setting process. In the UK, to take what may be an extreme example, significant policy change is usually preceded by a rather slow and well-known process, in which the 'affected interests' are given early warning of the possibility of policy change. Moreover, once the policy process is under way, it is unusual for there to be abrupt changes once basic agreement within the 'policy community' has been achieved (Richardson and Jordan, 1979; Jordan and Richardson, 1987). The existence of these well-defined policy communities at the national level (especially in the northern European democracies) is possibly the greatest contrast between national and EC policy-making at present. The European Commission is not yet sufficiently mature as an organization for it to have developed widespread 'standard operating procedures' for processing policy issues. Of particular relevance to the lobbying strategies of groups trying to influence the EC is the fact that the Commission is still in the process of developing its consultation and co-ordination procedures. (For a discussion of the early development of the Commission see Mazey (1992).)

As two DG XI officers described the process to us, it can still appear 'far too haphazard' and something of a 'free for all ... [leaving] the door open for any groups wishing to contact Commission officers, rather than a selective grouping'. Yet there is an apparent contradiction in this characterization of the consultation process, possibly explained by the fact that the Commission is an 'adolescent' bureaucracy'. Thus a mixed style of consultation appears to exist. For example, there is some evidence that something like standard operating procedures are emerging in some sectors. Thus, in social policy there is a quite developed framework for negotiation and consultation, and in the environmental sector itself there are now plans to set up an official environmental forum (see conclusion below). There may now be sufficient examples of institutionalized and regularized consultation to suggest at least the existence of a 'procedural ambition' on the part of Commission officials to achieve a more stable (though possibly informal) set of policy actor relationships. Arp (1991, p14) cites the example of car emission regulations which are translated into the language of engineers and discussed as technical questions. These discussions are chanelled through the Motor Vehicle Emissions Group composed of Commission officials, national experts, the car industry, and consumer and environmental organizations. Similarly, the issue of how to respond in practice to the EC's international treaty obligations regarding the depletion of the ozone layer was processed with the advice and participation of a group of industry representatives which the Commission convened.

In contrast to most national policy-making systems, policy-making power in the EC is dispersed and there are several informal policy initiators. Though the Commission announces its own legislative programme at the beginning of each year, other more pressing items may be added as a result of European Summit decisions. In addition, every national government uses its six-month presidency of the Council of Ministers (during which period it also chairs and sets the agenda of all Council working groups) to push favoured projects to the front of the agenda (for example, the promotion of the 'social dimension' of the internal market by the French government) while MEPs, individual commissioners, ambitious ministers and interest groups all seek to push the Commission in certain directions. The multiplicity of 'opportunity structures' for groups is often perceived to be an advantage by all groups, but particularly by those denied access to national policy-makers. Yet this permeability of the system is also a disadvantage to groups. With few exceptions (agriculture may be the only one) no one set of groups – and certainly no individual group – can rely on *exclusive* access.

Thus, the process is best described as policy-making through loose, open, and extended issue networks, rather than through well-defined, stable, and exclusive policy communities. Participation in the policy process is unpredictable, and policy ideas may appear suddenly and from little-known sources. In practice, therefore, keeping track of EC policy initiatives is a major undertaking for groups, many of which lack sufficient resources to perform this task on their own. Our own research to date suggests that the need to monitor EC policy developments is now widely acknowledged by national lobbies and is often cited as an important factor in their decision to form and join Euro-groups, however ineffective those groups might be. For example, one British company told us that it joined virtually every relevant trade association, at both the national and European level, as part of its information-gathering system and in order to demonstrate to its peers that it was a good corporate citizen within the various industrial sectors in which it operated. In practice it often did not rely on the relevant Euro-group and preferred to lobby Brussels directly itself.

A second reason for the uncertain agenda is the existence of different national political agendas, which in turn leads to a degree of competitive agenda-setting within the EC itself. Again, our industrial contacts have suggested to us that this is their main weakness – an inability to influence, let alone control, the agenda-setting process within Brussels and Strasbourg. This produces a *reactive* style of lobbying. More often than not, firms and industries are conducting rearguard or fire-brigade campaigns in response to agendas set by others – often by the environmentalists. While many Community issues are common across national boundaries, others are country-specific; in other cases there are cross-national variations in the position of common issues or differing ideological stances, or both. Environmental policy is an example of the differing emphases found in EC states and of the EC's own agenda being pushed along by certain enthusiastic actors. For example, domestic 'green' pressure in West Germany played a part in encouraging its government to take the initiative in pressing for limits on car exhaust emissions, as did the interests of the German car industry. In the event, the issue soon became more complicated than a simple conflict between environmentalists and polluters (Jordan and McLaughlin, 1992). The controversy in 1991/1992 over possible EC controls on packaging is also a case of a national agenda impinging on the EC's agenda. The German 'Packaging Decree', implemented in January 1992, placed responsibility upon manufacturers and distributors to the German market for the collection and disposal of all packaging materials, with further restrictions coming into force in April 1992 and January 1993. The German interest in the issue had a knock-on effect at the EC level, where a draft Directive on packaging was being prepared. Fear that something like the German legislation would be introduced at the EC level caused consternation in the European packaging industry. For example, a representative of the Euro-federation – the Industry Council for Packaging and the Environment (INCPEN) – commented on the German proposals as follows: 'Never mind the Nimby factor (Not in My Back Yard), they seem to be suffering from the Banana syndrome – Build Absolutely Nothing Anywhere Near Anyone' (*The Independent*, 10 September 1991). Significantly perhaps, INCPEN is a relatively new and predominately British actor at EC Level.

This particular example is illustrative of another general phenomenon of relevance to any discussion of environmental politics in the EC – namely that national action in the environmental field can soon be caught up in broader questions relating to the single market. There is an increasing fear that environmental action at the national level can be used as back-door trade restrictions or to give special market advantages to firms that are launching new products or that have perfected a particular innovation (Sargent, 1993) The environmental field may be especially rich in cases of a close link between innovation and regulation and we must, therefore, be cautious in portraying the politics of the environment as a straightforward conflict between two blocks of interests groups – polluters and environmentalists. We suspect that, as the sector becomes more stable (in the sense that competing interests, and interested bureaucrats, may all tend to seek stability of processes and structures) we may see the emergence of rather unusual and complex coalitions of interests around particular policy problems. For example, the exhaust emissions issue was not a simple case of polluters versus environmentalists because of the different anti-emission technologies being developed by different car manufacturers, who soon came into conflict with each other over the preferred solution to the problem.

As suggested above, stability and predictability have certainly not yet arrived – if only because the basic formal processes of EC policy-making (and *implementation* mechanisms) are still in a state of flux. Also in the environmental sector, the legal competence of the Commission is relatively new. In that sense, all players are involved in a game in which the goal posts are bound to move. Yet, as Majone suggests, in the 20 years from 1967 to 1987 almost 200 directives, regulations and decisions were introduced by the Commission. This is despite the fact that environmental protection is not even mentioned in the Treaty of Rome and that the Commission's authority in this area was not recognized until the passage of the Single European Act (SEA). Moreover, as he notes, the rate of growth of environmental regulation appears to have been largely unaffected by 'the political vicissitudes, political crises, and recurrent waves of Euro-pessimism of the 1970s and early 1980s' (Majone, 1989, p165). Thus, environmental policy-making is now relatively well developed and in some cases the appropriate 'constituencies' of interests have been organized and mobilized and to some degree integrated into the policy process. More recently, the possibility of a 'partnership' between the interested parties has been emerging as an important concept presenting the opportunity to produce a greater degree of stability and predictability than described by the officers cited above (see conclusion below).

In fact, very little detailed research has been done on the subject of how groups generally have responded to the shift in policy-making power away from national capitals to Brussels, although much research is now under way. It is very clear, however, that the nature of the interface between the EC and interest groups generally is in a state of flux and is recognized by the Commission and the Parliament as a problem to be addressed. It is also clear that the constant shift in power to Brussels has resulted in increased pressures upon national groups to co-ordinate their lobbying activities through the European Federations. This trend has been encouraged by European Commission officials who are currently trying to rationalize the growing problem of group consultation and who have an official preference for dealing with Euro-groups. Preliminary findings suggest, however, that many European Federations (especially industrial sectoral federations) are beset by internal cleavages along national, ideological, organizational and policy lines (Collie, 1993).

Moreover, the European community, despite its growing importance, is not a sovereign state. Legislative power is shared between national member states and the Community. In consequence, groups must maintain existing national lobbying strategies while developing new strategies in response to the growing legislative competence of the EC. They must do this in a way which does not undermine existing relationships at the national level. Thus, 'playing the Brussels card' against a national administration may work on any given issue, but it may have serious long-term consequences in undermining relationships at the national level which have taken a very long time to build. This is especially relevant to environmental groups, many of which have worked hard over many years to achieve the respectability and consultative status at the national level which industrial associations have traditionally enjoyed.

A further problem for groups is that they have to contend with the fact that within the European Commission, policy-making is highly compartmentalized with little horizontal co-ordination between different Directorates General (DGs) which have a shared interest in an issue. Despite the fact that the Commission is a collegiate body, there is nevertheless a risk that once a legislative proposal has become the property of a particular DG and the particular constellation of interests surrounding it, other groups may find it difficult to be consulted effectively. Conflicting policy proposals relating to the same issue can emerge from different parts of the Commission. In order to avoid being taken by surprise, groups must be able to monitor and respond to policy developments in more than one DG. For environmental groups, for example, this task is rendered more difficult by the high turnover of people employed by the Commission on temporary contracts and the considerable variation in the internal organization, culture and working methods (including consultation procedures) of different DGs, and different divisions within the same DG.

Another important feature of the Commission is its small size. Despite the popular image (especially in Britain!) of the Commission as a bloated bureaucracy, it is in fact very small when compared with national administrations. If we take an environmental example, there are approximately 15 staff in DG XI concerned with the control of chemicals yet in the US the Environmental Protection Agency has over 500 staff. The small size of the Commission has two important consequences for lobbying – it leaves the Commission very dependent upon outside sources (both pressure groups and national administrations) for expertise and information and it leaves the Commission very weak in terms of the oversight of EC directives once they have been incorporated into national legislation. (The European Court is, of course, also involved in the oversight of implementation and the Commission is involved in cases which come before the Court).

The Commission's aspiration is to be able to deal with Euro-groups which are at the same time *representative* and *expert*. In practice Commission officials regularly depart from this procedural ambition and consult not only national groups but individual firms. There is also a tendency to bypass representative structures altogether, as for example in the establishment of the Industrial Round Table in 1983. This horizontal Euro-grouping brings together the heads of the leading European companies and multinationals. Significantly, membership of the European Round Table of Industrialists is by invitation only. (It currently consists of approximately 44 members drawn from individual companies and is chaired by Wisse Dekker from Philips, with Vice-Chairmen from Siemens and La Compagnie Lyonnaise des Eaux-Dumez.) Similar groupings include the European Information Technology Round Table created in the late 1970s at the initiative of the Commission and the Association for the Monetary Union of Europe, established in 1987. Those companies denied access to these groupings are under further pressure to join forces with their EC counterparts in the various Euro-groupings. Commission attempts to 'rationalize' the process of interest intermediation may mean that the EC policy-making process becomes corporatist in nature in those areas which have hitherto been more pluralist. The corporatist ambitions of the Commission are widely acknowledged. The key issue, however, is the extent to which the deregulatory thrust of the Single Market Programme, the internal characteristics of key interest groupings and the EC decision-making structures will permit such a development (Gorges, 1991; Rhodes, 1990). In the case of the environment, there are very specific problems with the SEA. As Huelshoff and Pfeiffer (1991, p145) argue, 'the ambiguity of the SEA and the opposition of some Member States to higher environmental standards have led to market goals being put before environmental goals in the EC'.

Since all legislative proposals are drafted by the Commission, it tends to be the focus of EC lobbying. Of particular importance in this respect are the 1000 or so advisory groups and consultative committees some of which can play an important role in the initial drafting of EC proposals as well as being involved in the implementation of policy. Not surprisingly, membership of these groups is highly valued by groups. Since the adoption of the SEA, the European Parliament has also become a more important focus of lobbying activities and if the Maastricht Treaty is adopted, it looks set to increase further its role in environmental policy. However, within the EC the final decision on all policies is taken by *national* officials and politicians in the Council of Ministers. Groups at this stage must rely principally upon the negotiating skills and support of national civil servants and government ministers. Thus, somewhat paradoxically, the growing importance of EC legislation may sometimes reinforce the dependency which exists at the national level between groups and 'their' ministers. The degree of co-operation between groups and national administrations in this respect varies considerably, both between countries and between groups – not all of which enjoy the same degree of political legitimacy. In the environmental sector, groups at the national level are often in conflict with their own national administrations and hence see the EC as an alternative arena in which to excercise influence.

Finally, any assessment of the techniques of Euro-lobbying must examine the use of the courts by groups. The European Court of Justice, which is responsible for interpreting and enforcing EC law, is of crucial and increasing importance for EC lobbyists concerned with *implementation* of EC law. Since the 1970s, environmental organizations and women's groups especially, have used the Court (whose appellate powers resemble those of the US Supreme Court) as a means of forcing recalcitrant national governments to implement EC legislation concerning, for example, the quality of drinking water and equal treatment between working men and women (on the latter see Mazey (1988)). Under Articles 169 and 170 of the EEC Treaty, the Court rules on whether Member States have failed to uphold their Treaty obligations. Actions may be brought by the European Commission or by other Member States. More generally, the principle of direct effect means that individuals and groups can rely upon EC law in national courts.

Environmental Groups in the EC: A Preliminary Analysis

If we set the ambitions and activities of environmental groups in the context of the characteristics of EC policy-making, as described in the first section, how might the groups be rated in terms of their likely efficacy as lobbyists? What are their strengths and weaknesses?

It appears that environmental groups have at least three fundamental strengths in the context of the EC at present[1] (although, as we shall argue, these advantages may be eroded over time). They are (in no particular order of priority):

* a capacity to build European-level coalitions in the form of Euro-groups, umbrella organizations, or through the creation of cross-national Euro-level networks;
* through these coalitions, an ability to contribute to European integration in the manner predicted by neofunctionalist theory and hence, in a manner likely to be attractive to the Commission;
* an ability to set the political agenda in the environmental sector and to structure the content of issues in ways which place other interests at a disadvantage.

In contrast, environmental groups may have certain fundamental weaknesses:

* these groups may be too dependent upon good relations with one part of the Commission, namely DG XI, and upon the European Parliament;

- they may lack the resources or will to participate within the policy process *intensively* from the initiation phase right through to policy decision and beyond, up to implementation;
- other interests are becoming more effective in their mobilisation around the environmental issue, presenting much more competition for the attention and consideration of policy-makers;
- notwithstanding (1) above, the environmentalists may be subjected to some of the competitive and entrepreneurial tendencies to which all pressure groups are subject, and this may ultimately limit the effectiveness of their coalition-building capacities;
- their lobbying style may limit their capacity to influence policy-making, yet if it changes, they may face problems in maintaining support within their own constituencies.

We shall deal with these strengths and weaknesses in turn, although it should be emphasized that they are, of course, interrelated.

All researchers have emphasized the weakness of Euro-groups, essentially because these groups are usually composed of very diverse interests, often in fierce competition with each other in the marketplace. The Euro-federation representing the chemical manufacturers (the European Chemical Industry Council, CEFIC) is usually cited as one of the few really successful Euro-federations. This alleged success has much to do with the fact that CEFIC is dominated by a few large manufacturers within European and worldwide interests and that the structure of the European Chemical Industry does not vary as much as, say, the financial services sector in Europe (Knight et al, 1993). The most common criticism of Euro-federations representing industry is that they are understaffed (Collie, 1993) and that in so far as they have anything to say, it is characterized by the label 'lowest common denominator' – that is, the internal divisions are such that their policy statements are more like peace treaties designed to keep the federations together, than well-argued technical proposals on which EC officials can act. Thus many, if not most, peak and sectoral associations representing industry are not highly regarded, are under-resourced with small (but increasing) staffing, and subject to unwitting undermining by the actions of the Commission itself – namely by the Commission regularly consulting individual firms and national organizations. Moreover, it is often the case that these federations are often not staffed by people who have a long-term future in their own industries, in that it is relatively common for them to be staffed by personnel who are nearing retirement. Thus, it appears that few companies see sending their young or middle managers to Euro-federations as part of a programme of long-term career development.

Following the EC's increasing involvement in international affairs (the EC is currently involved in the negotiation of over 20 international treaties), environmental groups and other non-governmental organizations (NGOs) are present in large numbers whenever and wherever international negotiations take place and are of increasing influence in these negotiations, albeit that they are not *directly* involved in them. There is also, of course, a widespread and genuine recognition within the environmental movement that problems are cross-national and worldwide and that there is little point in trying to redistribute environmental costs between one country and another through the lobbying process. Few *industries* are capable of taking a co-ordinated industry-wide European – let alone a world-wide view – of their long-term interests (for example, in such industries as tele-communications, the concept of national champions dies hard). The big conflicts of interest which arise within European industry (and between European indus-try and the Americans and Japanese) generally do not arise between environmen-tal groups. They have different interests and emphasize different issues, but they are essentially on the same side fighting the same cause and have a common inter-est in better environmental regulations. There is not the kind of competition to use regulatory regimes to gain comparative advantage in which industrial and commercial interests are engaged.

This relative lack of conflict of interest enables environmental groups – and other NGOs (Harvey, 1992) – to construct large networks of interests which link Euro-level organizations and national-level organizations. These are *potentially* powerful if they can be managed successfully. The European Environmental Bureau (EEB) is one example of such a network, consisting of over 120 NGOs in the environmental field. It was founded 16 years ago, in part because the Com-mission (particularly DG XI) needed an NGO movement as a counterweight to the industrial lobby. Consequently, the EEB receives significant amounts of the EC funding to hold seminars (for example, on eco-labelling) and round tables on specific issues, although opinions on EEB's actual policy impact differ considera-bly. The mobilization and management of these networks (there is a proliferation of them) is a problematic task, but they represent a considerable resource – both in political and expertise terms – if they can be made to work, and there are few if any permanent equivalents on the industrial and commercial side.

The networks do also possess the potential predicted for groups by the neo-functional theorists such as Haas (1958), who suggested that groups would play a central role in European integration. They would turn to supranational means when this course appears profitable to their members. He argued that this process of group formation would be purely *tactical* as organized employer interests in a pluralistic setting outgrew the nation state (Haas, 1958, p354). This lack of 'ideo-logical cohesion' which he saw in industrial and commercial interests is not, how-ever, as we have argued, really a problem within the environmental movement, which is much more often able to express a genuinely European view. This is, of course, attractive to the Commission which is particularly anxious to see all lob-bying presented in European terms. (All commercial lobbying firms advise their commercial clients to present arguments in European and not national terms, for example.) In this sense, the environmentalists have reached a much more advanced stage in the Europeanization of lobbying and have already adopted the ideals of European integration. They are much more integrated in their behav-iour than are the groups with whom they normally compete, and do not find the adoption of a European perspective nearly as problematic as industrial and com-mercial groups (for an example see Knight et al (1993)).

The ability of environmental groups to set the political agenda is perceived by the industrialists to whom we have spoken as perhaps the greatest current asset of the environmentalists. Indeed, one leading European environmental campaigner told us that he saw his organization as very much at the 'ideas level' and rather less involved in the very specific technical details of policies. Indeed, he argued that his organization has eschewed the 'expertise' approach. It saw itself as dealing in the currency of ideas and in creating the conditions under which the level of detail could then be decided. The strategy appeared to be to place issues on the agenda and to define the issues sufficiently clearly so that technical detail could safely be left to others. We might qualify this view by suggesting that the environmentalists are in fact rather effective in translating scientific findings of a complex kind into more generally comprehensible political issues (for example, global warming, or heavy metal pollution) to which policy-makers and other interests have to respond. Indeed, environmental groups might be said to be one of the key links in modern society between science and politics, often being responsible for some kind of 'megaphone' effect transmitting scientific ideas from the private world of professional science into the world of public policy. The fact that many of the groups have especially good links with the European Parliament also lends support to the thesis that agenda-setting is their forte; in so far as the Parliament has influence, it is better at raising issues than in processing them. The downside of this power on the part of groups is that it may be heavily dependent on what Gregory (1971) termed the 'halo effect' of the environmental issue. Currently (as in the 1970s) the environment is high on the political agenda and all interests are inclined to take it seriously. But if the environment were again to enter the downward sector of the Downsian issue attention cycle (Downs, 1972), the environmentalists might find greater difficulty in exercising what Schattschneider terms the supreme exercise of political power – determining what politics is actually about (Schattschneider, 1960).

Turning now to the possible weaknesses of the environmental movement at the EC level, perhaps the most obvious is their relative dependence on DG XI. Indeed, one Commission official suggested to us that the task force which preceded the formation of DG XI was originally so weak that it sought the support of the NGOs and mobilized and supported them in order to defend itself. He believed that without NGO support DG XI might have died in its early years. This suggests that the Directorate is possibly an example of a phenomenon described by Downs as being common to all bureaucracies – namely that in the early stages of their life, they deliberately cultivate external clients who then come to depend upon them and will defend them in times of crisis faced by the agency (Downs, 1967). It is certainly the case that the NGO movement generally (including environmental groups) receives financial support from the Commission (directly or via various contracts) and it can be argued that as a result, there is an unhealthy degree of dependency (indeed one Commission official described some of the environmental groups as having been 'tamed'; however, groups like Greenpeace deliberately avoid Commission funding, and WWF has set a limit of between 10 and 15 per cent on funding from public agencies). Gradually, the environmentalists are gaining more access to other Directorates General – quite successfully on some specific issues – but most environmental respondents reported what we would see as 'skewed' access to the Commission, with much better access to DG XI than elsewhere. Some (rival) interests see this ready access as 'agency capture' by the environmentalists and argue that it is extremely difficult to represent an alternative (industrial) view to most of DG XI. They therefore seek representation at levels higher than the service level and attempt to mobilize other Directorates General to fight their corner on environmental issues. Of much more importance to the environmentalists is the fact that so many other Directorates General are responsible for policies which have major environmental implications. This means that the task of lobbying the Commission is that much more difficult (say compared with that for interests in the IT field) and demands vast resources if the 'environmental waterfront' (in lobbying terms) is to be covered properly. Even in those areas where the environmentalists have especially good contacts. Commission officials have the ability to 'close' the issue without much difficulty, unless the group can mobilize pressure in the European Parliament. There is no doubt, however, that there is a degree of 'greening' of the Commission as a whole, reflecting European-wide pressure on all national governments and parliaments to pay greater attention to environmental issues.

The question *of resources* and its impact on the efficacy of environmental groups is quite difficult to assess. The European-level environmental groups may seem quite well resourced when compared with sectoral business associations at the European level. For example, Greenpeace has 12 full-time staff in its European office compared with a typical sectoral federation such as the European Association for Textile Polyolefins (EATP) which has only four staff yet represents 60 members drawn from 15 European countries (Peckstadt et al, 1992), or indeed with a peak business association such as UNICE (Collie, 1993). Moreover, Greenpeace claims to have access to over 1200 environmental and scientific experts worldwide and feels able to compete with industrial groups in terms of specialist advice, as well as in the more political arena for which it is best known through its publicity-seeking activities. Our own interviews with officials within DG XI also suggest that environmental groups (and indeed the NGO movement generally in other fields such as poverty, housing and health) are rather well regarded by many (though not all) officials for their groups' expertise in environmental matters. Groups like World Wide Fund for Nature (WWF) can also claim considerable field expertise and have a degree of legitimacy from their direct involvement in the *implementation* process. Thus, WWF spends a large amount of money each year on conservation work in Europe. By no means all of the work is in Western Europe, as WWF has recognized the growing importance of environmental problems in Eastern Europe, for example, and is involved at a very practical level in developing schemes for better environmental management of resources (WWF, 1991). It is not simply an advisory group, raising issues and helping to define the agenda, but it also has the resources (a limited proportion of which, unlike Greenpeace, came from the EC) both to devise and implement practical solutions. This is particularly important in certain areas of the EC where local administrations may not be the best agents for service delivery – for example, in Spain. In these contexts, WWF can actively devise and deliver field projects.

Groups such as WWF, Greenpeace, and Friends of the Earth (FoE) can also mobilize the resources of their *national* organizations to lobby individual national administrations, thus influencing deliberations in the Council of Ministers. Yet, there still remains a doubt concerning the group's ability to stay with an issue from A to Z of the EC policy process. Two important rules of lobbying in Brussels are that groups need to get in *early* – when the issue is but a gleam in an official's eye (Hull, 1992) and to *stay* with the issue at every stage throughout the whole process. Our interviewees suggest that the environmentalists do not really have the capacity to stay with the detail of an issue through its life cycle in the policy process. (Thus, the view cited above, to the effect that agenda-setting may be sufficient, is a high-risk strategy; the devil may be in the details!) Alternatively, they may not have the deep-seated *interest* that, say, a company whose very survival is threatened by EC legislation would have. Sargent's (1993) study of trade associations points out that firms are often reluctant to commit resources to a trade association (at either the national or the European level) but are more willing to set up specific, ad hoc, well-resourced organizations, on issues that are of special significance to them. It is, therefore, misleading to compare the resourcing of environmental groups with equivalent Euro- and national trade associations. Firms both devote resources to ad hoc, one issue, organizations and do a lot of direct lobbying with Commission officials and MEPs. Our evidence suggests that in those areas of environmental policy where industry has a really keen and vital interest, the resources mobilized are very considerable indeed and usually far outweigh those of any of the environmental groups. This is because, although industrial Euro-associations have very small staffs, they are able to call upon both the personnel and the expertise of their member firms.

In fact, key firms are probably the first port of call for some EC officials wanting particular types of data and information. The firm's national and Euro-association will be 'consulted' but often only after prior 'testing' of problems and ideas at the level of the firm. A related weakness for environmental groups, in terms of resources, is that – as one environmental group official put it to us – 'we can't follow *every* issue of relevance to the environment – they are too many – and we have to choose on which of the many issues we can concentrate our resources'. One consequence of this is that there appears to be a degree of 'product specialization' (itself an advantage in terms of expertise) by the main Euro-level environmental groups, which may be leaving significant tracts of 'environmental policy space' to the lobbying activities of industrial and commercial groups (IT policy and R&D policy may be examples). Thus, Greenpeace has a strategy of concentrating in four areas of campaigning – ocean ecology; toxics; nuclear; and atmosphere and energy, and WWF is especially interested in the EC Structural Fund's relationship between trade and the environment, and in the Common Agricultural Policy.

Perhaps the greatest long-term threat to the influence of environmental groups is that other interests are becoming much more active in this sector. Essentially, industrial interests are now taking the environmental issue much more seriously and are beginning to devote the lobbying resources needed if their voice is to become more effective and if they are to become less 'reactive' in their lobbying styles. There is increasing pressure on DG XI, for example, to talk to industrial interests. Also, the industrial interests can be expected to defend their existing relationships with other DGs as the environmentalists try to expand their sphere of influence. Moreover, we should not underestimate the capacity of industry to take on board the environmental issue at the company level, partly in response to their perception of public pressure and in part out of purely commercial self-interest. As one participant put it to us, he had not come across very many environmental issues that really were life and death to a particular company or industry. He was surprised how often legislation was originally opposed because it would be 'the end of the industry', only for the industry to absorb the extra costs (or pass them on to its consumers) with relative ease once the legislation was in place.

Thus, 'delay' rather than 'stop' may well be the slogan more appropriate to industrial lobbying in the environmental sector, with the more sophisticated industrial actors being aware that being proactive (pre-emptive strikes) may be the best lobbying stategy of all. Whether or not this is true, there is little doubt that industrial interests are becoming much more active in presenting technical and well-researched arguments when faced with challenges, and in actually *anticipating* possible challenges. Nor should it be assumed that industrial interests necessarily seek to obstruct the introduction of EC environmental legislation. Within the internal market, a competitive advantage accrues to environmentally progressive companies. This may gradually improve the bad public image of industrialists and enable them to engage in political dialogue more effectively. Also, they may be more willing to enter into a direct dialogue with the environmental interests, forcing the latter to rethink their own lobbying strategies, too.

Finally, we may speculate that, in practice, the environmental sector is not quite as 'uncompetitive' as we have earlier suggested. There is broad ideological agreement and generally an absence of conflicts over policy – yet in one sense there is a degree of competition within the environmental sector. True, there is much collaboration and co-ordination at the European level – for example the main Euro-level organizations have regular meetings every four to six weeks in order to exchange information and ideas. Similarly, as we have suggested, there is a degree of 'product specialization' or 'niche marketing' – to use two commercial analogies. Yet it is also possible to characterize the leaders of environmental groups – and of other NGOs – simply as essentially entrepreneurs who wish to expand the influence of their organizations just as firms wish to expand their markets – and whose own success to some degree depends on their organization's achieving some special status in the policy process. They may also be in competition for members and financial support and need to demonstrate 'action' and 'success' (not always synonymous) to their members as well as to the broader policy network as a whole. This is especially true at the national level, where the organizational representation of the environmental issue may well be beyond saturation point in some of the northern democracies. However, it is not at all certain that there is a total absence of competition at the European level or that some organizations might not be squeezed by a degree of over-representation of interests at the European level.

Conclusion: Lobbying Styles and Long-term Success

By way of brief conclusion we now turn to the difficult concept of 'lobbying styles', as this does still present a problem to the environmentalists. The sometimes confrontational styles of environmental groups – and the increased use of legal actions (see below) – may be perpetuating an image which at least some of the groups might wish to shed. For example, one environmental respondent told us that his organization was working hard to create a rather different image because some EC officials saw environmentalists as obstructionist, anti-growth and heavily reliant on the use of the media to attack both decision-makers and companies alike. His ambition was to emphasize a new perspective, which was to engage in a political and economic discussion in those policy areas 'hitherto regarded as more centrally economic than environmental'. (Significantly one official, dealing with this group, commented to us that he had indeed found the group considerably more useful and better informed of late.)

If our underlying assumption is correct – namely that the Commission will gradually seek to establish a more regularized and structured form of group participation in the policy process (whether by the establishment of policy communities or even corporatist structures, or by structures that are peculiarly European, remains to be seen) – then this will present a serious challenge to the environmentalists. This is because confrontational and challenging styles of lobbying may well be incompatible with the unwritten rules of the game implied by the policy community model or its variants. Essentially, policy communities are about the private management of public business (Richardson and Jordan, 1979). However, the nature of the EC policy process, with increased use of the Court and an increased role for the Parliament, may mean that it will be difficult to confine the processing of issues within the bounds of well-defined policy communities. Whether resort to more public and openly conflictual arenas of decision-making is conducive to the development of stable long-term relationships between decision-makers and groups is, however, open to doubt.

A particular problem may arise because of the increase in 'whistle-blowing' by environmental groups who now play an important role in warning the Commission of implementation failure at the national level. Thus the number of complaints by individual citizens (often encouraged by pressure groups) and the number of legal actions by groups themselves is showing a rapid increase. For example a number of British groups, including the UK branch of FoE, have been involved in complaining to the Commission about the British government's handling of various road schemes – notably the M11 link road and the East London river crossing – resulting in Carlo Ripa di Meana's challenging the UK government in October 1991.

In the short run, national groups are gaining considerable benefit from this type of activity and the Commission seems anxious to maintain this unofficial monitoring function by groups, as it is increasingly conscious of the 'implementation gap'. Yet it does risk placing the groups in what at the national level would be regarded as the 'outsider group' category and this process may be counterproductive in terms of their developing a more co-operative dialogue with national governments (still of central importance in the implementation of environmental policy, despite the growth of EC influence). It may also affect the perception that Commission officials have of the Euro-level environmental groups. The temptations of demonstrable success now – of considerable importance in maintaining membership support and media coverage – may be at the price of a more fundamental influence in the policy process in the long run. The trade-off may be between maintaining a high public profile through an action-oriented approach to lobbying, and sacrificing a chance of long-term influence in the *processing* of issues.

Acknowledgements

This study is part of a project on lobbying in the EC funded by the Economic and Social Research Council (ESRC). The authors wish to thank David Judge and Laura Cram for their comments on an earlier draft, and the many Commission officials and environmental groups and firms who agreed to be interviewed.

Note

For the purposes of this study the term 'environmentalists' is used to describe individuals or groups whose primary objective is the introduction of policies beneficial to the environment. In contrast to firms and industrial federations which may promote environmentally friendly products, environmentalists have no direct material interest in EC environmental policy.

References

Arp, H. (1991) 'European Community Envppironmental Policy: What to Learn From the Case of Car Emission Regulation?', paper presented to Conference on European Integration and Environmental Policy, Woudschoten, Netherlands, 29–30 Nov 1991.

Collie, L. (1993) 'Business Lobbying in the EC: The Union of Industrial Employers' Confederations of Europe', in Mazey and Richardson (1993b).

Downs, A. (1967) *Inside Bureaucracy,* Boston, MA: Little, Brown.

Downs, A. (1972) 'Up and Down with Ecology: the "Issue Attention Cycle"', *The Public Interest,* Vol.28, pp38–50.

Gorges, M. J. (1991) 'Euro-Capitalism? The System of Interest Intermediation in the European Community', paper delivered to the Annual Meeting of the American Political Science Association, Washington, DC, 29 Aug–1 Sept 1991.

Gregory, R. (1971) *The Price of Amenity,* London: Macmillan.

Harvey, B. (1992) 'European Lobbying: The Experience of Voluntary Organisations', in Mazey and Richardson (1993b).

Hass, E. B. (1958) *The Uniting of Europe: Political, Social and Economic Forces* Stanford, CA: Stanford University Press.

Huelshoff, M. G. and Pfeiffer, T. (1991). 'Environmental Policy in the EC: Neo-functionalist Sovereignty Transfer or Neo-realist Gatekeeping', *International Journal,* Vol.47, No.1, pp136–58.

Hull, R. (1992) 'Lobbying in Brussels: A View from Within', in Mazey and Richardson (1993b).

Jordan, A. G. and Richardson, J. J. (1987) *British Politics and the Policy Process,* London: Allen & Unwin.

Jordan, A. G. and McLaughlin, A. M. (1992) 'The Rationality of Lobbying in Europe: Why are Euro-Groups So Numerous And So Weak: Some Evidence from the Car Industry', in Mazey and Richardson (1993b).

Knight, J., Mazey, S. and Richardson, J. (1993) 'Groups and the Process of European Integration: The Work of the Federation of Stock Exchanges in the European Community', in Mazey and Richardson (1993b).

Majone, G. (1989) 'Regulating Europe: Problems and Prospects', in Ellwein, T., Hesse, J. J., Mayntz, R. and Scharpf, F. W. (eds), *Jahrbuch zur Staats- und Verwaltungswissenschaft*, Baden-Baden: Nomos, pp159–178.

Mazey, S. (1988) 'European Community Action on Behalf of Women: The Limits of Legislation', *Journal of Common Market Studies*, Vol.27,' No.1, pp63–84.

Mazey, S. (1992) 'The Administration of the High Authority 1955–56: Development of a Supranatural Bureaucracy?', in Morgan, R. and Wright, V. *The Early Principles and Practice of the EC (European Yearbook of the History of Administration)*.

Mazey, S. P. and Richardson, J. J. R. (1993a) 'Interest Groups in the European Community', in Richardson, J. J. R. (ed.) *Pressure Groups,* Oxford: Oxford University Press.

Mazey, S. P. and Richardson, J. J. R. (eds) (1993b) *Lobbying in the EC,* Oxford: Oxford University Press.

Peckstadt, J. P., Mazey, S. P. and Richardson, J. J. R. (1992) 'Defending and Promoting a Sectoral Interest Within the European Community: The Case of the Textile Polyolefins Industry', in Mazey and Richardson (1993b).

Rhodes, M. (1990) 'The Social Dimension of the Single European Market: National vs. Transnational Regulation', *European Journal of Political Research,* Dec.

Richardson, J. J. and Jordan, A. G. (1979) *Governing Under Pressure.* Oxford: Martin Robertson.

Sargent, J. (1993) 'The Corporate Benefits of Lobbying: The British Case and its Relevance to the EC', in Mazey and Richardson (1993b).

Schattschneider, E. E. (1960) *The Semi-Sovereign People: A Realist's View of Democracy in America,* New York: Holt, Reinhart & Winston.

WWF (1991) *Focus in WWF in Europe,* Brussels: WWF.

Part 3
POLICY DYNAMICS

PART 3
POLICY DYNAMICS

8

Environmental Rules and Rule-making in the European Union

Albert Weale

Introduction

What does the case of environmental policy tell us about the evolution of rules in the European Union (EU) and what are the implications of the development of European environmental policy more generally for our understanding of EU rule-making institutions? This chapter advances the argument that environmental policy displays the policy-making process of the EU as a decision system characterized by the principle of concurrent majorities. A system of concurrent majorities exists when agreement is needed by a high proportion of participants in a set of decision-making institutions before a policy is adopted. Thus, in the case of environmental policy, agreement needs to be secured both within and between key institutional actors (the Commission, the Council, the Parliament and the Court), as well as with the functional constituencies of important interest groups. The result is a 'joint-decision trap' (Scharpf, 1988) in which the status quo is given privileged place and policy *lourdeur* (Wallace, 1994, p80): important policy measures are not adopted, or adopted only in sub-optimal form.

Such institutional arrangements mean that we cannot account for environmental policy in either purely neofunctionalist terms (in which EU rule-making is seen as a consequence of spillover) or in purely intergovernmental terms (in which EU rule-making is seen as a co-ordination device among nations). Thus, contrary to realist views, there is a European governance structure (Bulmer, 1994) that cannot be understood as the operation in the international arena of purely national policy preferences, but has to be understood in terms of its own institutional characteristics. Equally, there is no smooth transition from the single market to the development of European policy-making as a supranational set of institutions possessing or demanding jurisdiction over pre-existing national states, as there would be on a neofunctionalist analysis.

If this is true of environmental policy, is there any reason for supposing that it has lessons for European policy-making more generally? Three reasons come to mind for thinking that environmental policy is an important test case in the broader context of European integration. First, many environmental problems are intrinsically cross-boundary or international. Pollution knows no boundaries, and problems such as acidification or global climate change require international action for their solution. Since, on virtually all accounts, the EU exists to solve problems that cannot be solved at the level of the nation state, environmental policy provides a prime example of policy-making in the circumstances of complex international interdependence in which transnational regimes are said to arise (Keohane and Nye, 1989). Since European environmental policy-makers often conceive of their role as dealing with problems that transcend the boundaries of the nation state, the field of environmental policy seems a good case to take to see how far European integration is being driven by a functional logic of international problem-solving.

Second, there are – in purely technical terms to do with spillovers arising from interdependent effects – close links between the outcomes and effects of the internal market and the concerns of environmental policy. These interdependent effects were identified by the Task Force set up to look at the environment and the single market (Task Force Report on the Environment and the Internal Market, 1989; cf Haigh and Baldock, 1989), and they included increased pollution as a consequence of higher levels of production and increased traffic, as well as opportunities for less intensive resource use once national barriers to trade were removed.

Third, at various times, depending on fluctuations in the issue attention cycle, environmental problems and policies have been a highly salient issue in the politics of the EU. If we are looking for one area of policy that highlights the conflicts between the strong sectoral interests of producers and the more diffuse interests of citizens in general, it is likely to be found in the field of the environment. Looking at the policy area, then, tells us something intrinsically important about what Bulmer (1994, pp370–5) has called the European 'governance regime' of particular policy sectors and the policy networks to which they give rise.

The overall argument will proceed by elimination. In the next section, the evolution of EU environmental policy is laid out together with a brief account of the policy-making culture and belief system that has accompanied this development. In the subsequent section, it will be argued that neither neofunctionalist nor realist logic can account for some central features of this process of policy development, so that we have to think of the environmental rule-making process itself as a set of institutional rules with its own form and logic that requires measures to secure agreement from a wide range of actors. The resulting joint-decision trap, it will be argued, suffers from certain pathologies.

European Environmental Policy: From Silence to Salience

The 1957 Treaty of Rome did not contain any reference to environmental protection and, until the Single European Act (SEA) came into force, environmental legislation had to be passed either under the single market provisions of Article 100 or under the general 'catch-all' provisions of Article 235. Under the SEA, environmental policy was formally recognized as a proper competence to be exercised at European level (subject to the principle of subsidiarity) and, under the 1992 Treaty on European Union (the Maastricht Treaty), it became possible to pass most environmental measures through the Council of Ministers by qualified majority.

Despite this anonymity, EU environmental policy led a tangible, if somewhat marginal, existence from the early 1970s. A Directorate General emerged, which could be traced back to the Environment and Consumer Protection Unit that had been set up in the Commission in 1971. There was also an Environment Council, representing the ministries of the national governments. Moreover, in successive environmental action programmes the EU began increasingly to elaborate its ambitions for the development of environmental policy.

Behind this growth in activity, it is possible to detect the influence of various political pressures, both in the form of public opinion and in the form of international negotiation. Thus, the beginnings of European environmental policy as a distinct sector of policy are normally traced back to the European Council meeting in Paris in 1972, which reflected the surge of public concern about environmental protection that had swept through the developed world in the late 1960s and early 1970s (see Haigh, 1989, p9; Rehbinder and Stewart, 1985, p17; and Würzel, 1993). The inclusion of environmental competences in the SEA, by contrast, can perhaps best be understood as the result of a tacit bargain between northern and southern states over the terms of their future co-operation. The north wanted high consumer and environmental standards along with the single market and the south wanted greater structural funds without the single market. The bargain that was eventually struck involved both a commitment to high standards of environmental protection and the use of the structural funds to aid southern countries.

Moreover, the growth of policy at the European level has been fostered by the European Court of Justice (ECJ). Arguably, the ECJ is at the 'federal' end of a federalist/intergovernmentalist spectrum of EU institutions (Shapiro, 1992; Wallace, 1994, p38–9), developing early in its life the doctrine of direct effect and the precedence of EU over domestic law. In the environmental field it has passed down a series of landmark judgments that have affected the character and scope of environmental policy. Thus, in the case of Danish restrictions on bottle imports, it allowed that the protection of the environment is a legitimate ground for restraint of international trade, provided that the means employed are not disproportionate to the purpose in hand (Case C-302/86). It also sided with the Commission against the Council of Ministers in a case concerned with the regulation of titanium dioxide emissions, deciding that a measure should have been taken under Article 100, rather than Article 130s, when there was still a distinction in terms of the use of qualified majority voting between single market and environmental protection measures (Case C-155/91). The ECJ has therefore both supported strong environmental measures and made their passage easier.

Judged in legislative terms, the development of environmental policy has been striking. In the 1970s, a number of directives and regulations were passed, beginning in 1975 with a Directive on the control of the ambient quality of surface drinking waters. Other early measures, like the Directive on vehicle emissions and the common classification, packaging and labelling of dangerous substances, had an obvious rationale in the attempt to create a single European market. After the 'conversion' of the German government to a pro-environment stance in 1982 on the question of acidification, the pace of developments speeded up considerably, notably with the 1984 framework Directive on the control of air pollution from large stationary sources and the passing of the Environmental Impact Assessment Directive of 1985. 1988 saw the passing of the Large Combustion Plant Directive and 1990 saw Directives on the control of genetically modified organisms, the establishment of a European Environment Agency and public access to environmental information. All in all, between 1959 and 1992 there were well over two hundred measures passed at European level, leaving aside amendments, covering a wide range of environmental problems.

The legislative measures not only increased in number, they also increased in scope. Habitat and species protection came on to the agenda in the 1980s following the Wild Birds Protection Directive of 1979. During the 1980s, measures to protect whales, seals and environmentally sensitive areas subject to pressure from farming were passed. Similarly, air quality standards were specified and important procedural measures, like environmental impact statements and public access to environmental information, were adopted. These measures go beyond any conceivable standards that would be strictly necessitated by a concern to ensure a single functioning market.

Moreover, the number and scope of the measures were accompanied by an increasing stringency. The example of vehicle emissions illustrates this trend well. The standards of the 1970s lagged behind those of the US and Japan. During the mid-1980s it looked as though the countries of Europe would divide in their willingness to pursue higher standards, with some countries like Germany threatening to go it alone. However, after a complex series of negotiations and procedural wrangles involving the European Parliament, the 1989 Directive introduced stricter second-stage emission limits for smaller cars, effectively requiring the use of three-way catalytic converters, and thereby brought European standards up to US and Japanese standards (Arp, 1993). It also made the implementation dates mandatory rather than optional, as had been the previous practice. Similar stories could be told of bathing waters, urban waste water treatment, stationary air pollution sources and a range of other measures.

One obvious and visible sign of the growing European importance of environmental policy is the substantial growth of organizational resources, notably but not exclusively related to the Directorate General for the Environment (DG XI). In 1987, for example, the full-time permanent professional staff in DG XI numbered between 50 and 60. By the beginning of 1993, their number had grown to some 450. This growth was accompanied by a move to new and improved offices and owed much to the administrative and diplomatic skills of the Director-General throughout the period, Laurens-Jan Brinkhorst. It is true that a significant portion of this growth occurred in temporary, rather than permanent, staff, and to this extent the interpretation has to be qualified. Still, the growth is striking.

Administrative capacity in relation to European environmental protection has also been increased by the establishment of the European Environmental

Agency. Although the long-running dispute about the location of various important institutions, including the European Monetary Institute, held up the establishment of the agency, it is now housed in Copenhagen and staff have been appointed and programmes developed. Although its formal remit is primarily concerned with the collection and standardization of data, one could argue that it has the potential to be a powerful force for the Europeanization of environmental policy, not least given the concerns often expressed about poor implementation of international agreements being disguised by the practice of countries collecting the data on their own performance (House of Lords, 1992, p84).

These European developments have implications for Member States and in some cases it is possible to identify clear instances where the environmental policy of the EU has altered the policy position, institutions or practices of Member States. The UK provides a number of examples, despite (or perhaps because of) its reputation as an 'awkward partner'. Much of the UK's 1990 Environmental Protection Act was necessary in order to implement the requirements of the 1984 Air Pollution Framework Directive, and it was this Directive that led to the creation of air quality standards in the UK for the first time. Similarly, the retrofitting of flue-gas desulphurization equipment to power stations was necessary in order to conform with the 1988 Large Combustion Plant Directive. Directives on water pollution have also led to expensive investments in waste water treatment facilities that otherwise would have occurred later.

The UK is not alone in this regard, however. It is possible to point to instances in all Member States where practices have had to be changed in order to conform to EU legislation. Perhaps the most striking example among the new Member States of the 1980s is provided by Spain. Its dependence on Brussels has been notably marked in the environmental field, with the whole corpus of EU legislation being adopted after entry in 1986. The decision was taken in the atmosphere of high politics in which entry to the EU was seen as confirming Spain's transition to democracy. Despite the strong emphasis in Spain on economic development, no attention was paid in 1986 to the economic implications of the environmental measures it took over, with the result that the whole process took two years and caused considerable administrative blockage (Pridham, 1994, p91).

As well as these developments in terms of substantive policy, there has also been the development of a well-articulated environmental policy discourse among EU policy-makers. This discourse has a number of distinct elements. First, there emerged in the 1980s the perception that new problems of pollution had to be dealt with and innovative approaches were needed to cope with such problems. The issue that came to symbolize this problem for the early part of the 1980s was acidification (Hajer, 1995). Unlike previous examples of pollution, the science of acidification was poorly understood and gave rise to contested hypotheses about cause-and-effect relationships. Moreover, everyone agreed that if acidification did have significant effects they were long range, cumulative and difficult to remedy once they had occurred. This in turn led policy-makers in the Community to stress the importance of precaution in the development of policies, and in particular to stress that positive action could not always wait for a complete understanding of the pollution problem at hand without risking the neglect of problems until the environmental damage had been done.

A second theme started from the observation that pollution typically had its source in a variety of otherwise legitimate activities, in particular transport, agriculture and industry. The conclusion to be drawn was that environmental protection could not be the responsibility of a separate administrative section but had to be integrated into a wide range of public policies if harmful effects from those policies were to be anticipated and counteracted. This view found expression in the clause of the SEA stating that 'environmental protection requirements shall be a component of the Community's other policies' (Article 132r(2)). At the national level, this theme has been most vigorously pursued by The Netherlands in its National Environmental Policy Plan of 1989 (see Second Chamber of the States General, 1989; and for commentary Weale, 1992, Chapter 5). It is clear that the Community *Fifth Environmental Action Programme* (Commission of the European Communities, 1992) bears a strong resemblance to the Dutch approach, with its proposals for collaborative working relations between DG XI and other sections of the Commission's administration, and the formalizing of contacts with interested parties outside the Commission through consultation groups.

Along with the observation that pollution problems had their origin in otherwise legitimate activities, policy-makers began to stress that a wider range of policy instruments was needed than the hitherto conventional use of regulation. The most important thinking has concerned the use of voluntary agreements and the growing interest in economic instruments. The greater use of voluntary instruments might be said to be implicit in the *Fifth Environmental Action* Programme building as it did on its Dutch precedent and therefore drawing on a system in which voluntary agreements have come to play an important part in the repertoire of policy instruments. Thus, in 1993, the Commission inaugurated the auto-oil research programme in conjunction with the motor and oil industries to find ways of cutting exhaust emissions. Although its success is mixed (Plaskett, 1996), it represents an important precedent. Moreover, there is continuing general discussion about the conditions and circumstances under which voluntary agreements are suitable policy instruments, and DG III (Directorate General III, now known as Enterprise) has also commissioned studies of their use (*ENDS Report*, 1995, No.246, p34).

In terms of economic instruments, two claims may be distinguished. One is that there are existing subsidies and tax advantages that encourage a wasteful use of resources (for example, exemption from Value Added Tax (VAT) of pesticides or subsidies to car use), which need to be phased out. Second, it is argued that only a greater use of economic instruments will be adequate to meet the goals that have been set in the environmental field, a case that DG XI has sought to articulate particularly in relation to the control of greenhouse gas emissions, and which found detailed expression in proposals for a carbon/energy tax.

The final element in the new policy discourse has been to expand the interest in economic instruments to a concern with the ecologizing of the economy. During the 1980s it became common for policy-makers within the EU (though not exclusively within the EU) to argue for the role of environmental policy in promoting a new sort of economic competitiveness. The argument ran that, with the advent of global markets, the standard of product acceptability for international consumers would be increasingly set by the country with the most stringent pollution control standards, so that the future of the post-industrial economy will depend on its ability to produce high-value, high-quality products meeting high environmental standards. Thus, on this argument, Europe would only be able to take full advantage of economies of scale in globally competitive markets provided that it legislated for high environmental standards on a par with those to be found in Japan and the US (Weale, 1992, Chapter 3; Weale, 1993).

This argument thus sought to turn on its head the most familiar objection to stringent environmental policy, namely that there was always a trade-off between the imposition of environmental standards and the protection of economic interests, most notably the protection of employment. In the case of environmental policy, it became almost an article of faith that environmental protection was a precondition of the economic success that was associated with the European project. (In conducting interviews in DG XI, one often finds oneself listening to anecdotes about how firms that had reluctantly taken up environmental measures found after a short while that they had profited thereby.)

It is clear that these arguments were developed extensively within DG XI and the Commission at large, and they surfaced in relation to the Commission's White Paper on growth, competitiveness and employment (Commission of the European Communities, 1993). The background to the document is well known. Amid the growing public and political anxiety about recession and rising unemployment in Europe, the Copenhagen European Council in June 1993 invited the Commission to prepare a document on the subject outlining a diagnosis and discussing possible policy solutions. In terms of environmental policy, there is a clear formal recognition within the White Paper of the role of environmental projects and concerns in promoting enhanced growth and competitiveness. It appears that this acknowledgement of the fundamental tenets of ecological modernization was mediated through the work of Dolors' *cabinet* which became convinced during 1992 of the potential of environmental measures in stimulating economic activity. The last section of the Commission's document is entitled 'Towards a new development model', and it advocates fiscal and other policy instruments as devices for moving costs away from the employment of labour and towards the use of resources. Existing policy instruments, the chapter argues, will have to be reorientated to encourage the more efficient use of resources (thus leaving open the possibility of eco-taxes) and priority should be given to environmentally friendly innovation both by mean of subsidies for technical improvement and by funds for research and development.

In summary, then, we can see that there has been both a significant growth in environmental policy activity and the development of an elaborated set of policy principles for European environmental policy. In this way we have a governance regime in Bulmer's sense, involving not just a set of actors and institutions at the European level, but also a collection of norms and procedures for pursuing environmental objectives.

Rule-making Processes and the Limits of Europeanization

Told in the above way, the Europeanization of environmental policy might seem to follow an elegant political logic. Political decision-makers respond to the public's concerns by adapting procedures and institutions that previously did not include an environmental competence, and when the scope of that competence grows, they adapt the institutions and procedures themselves both to cope with an expanded range of problems and to foster the development of policy learning and development. This is a view that would be consistent with neofunctionalist accounts of European integration, according to which the dynamic effects of spillovers from one aspect of European integration create conditions for integration in others. Just as the internal market has a logic leading to a single currency (Cameron, 1992, pp25–27), so it also has a logic leading to environmental policy at European level to counteract market failures. However, this simple interpretation needs to be qualified in certain important respects.

Although EU rule-making institutions can be said to have a life of their own in the field of environmental policy, they still need to be connected to the life-support machine of the nation states if they are to function at all. Indeed, there are strong constraints at the European level limiting the range of measures that can be adopted as well as the scope and character of European environment policy. These stem most notably from a range of factors including:

1   the ability of the Member States to exercise their veto power in areas of special concern;
2   the role of national economic interests in the conduct of environmental policy;
3   the pattern of agenda-setting at European level which still owes much to national preferences; and the persistence of national norm-setting and policy-making.

In terms of national veto power, the clearest effects on environmental policy occur in relation to questions of taxation. The EU is limited in the amount of taxation that it can collect and its principal source of revenue is from VAT proceeds. This means that it cannot impose pollution taxes as an instrument of policy, and under the Treaty on European Union, any environmental measures that involve fiscal considerations have to be agreed by all Member States before they can be passed. By comparison with fully federal systems of governance, like Germany or the US, it is clear that there is a significant limitation built into the development of environmental policy at the European level.

These constraints were manifested most clearly over the issue of the carbon/energy tax proposals emanating from the Commission in 1992. In the run-up to the United Nations Conference on Environment and Development in that year, the Commission was anxious to secure agreement from Member States on the imposition of a carbon/energy tax that would contribute to the reduction of greenhouse gas emissions. The original proposal would have required a tax on fossil fuels and most sources of electricity, building up to a value equivalent to US$10 per barrel by the year 2000. The measure was opposed by a number of Member States, with France objecting to the taxation of nuclear power, Spain, Portugal, Greece and Ireland claiming exemptions on the grounds of their low contribution to overall levels and their need for economic development, and the UK arguing it was opposed to the extension of tax-making powers to the EU (*ENDS Report*, 1995, No.244, p39). Current projections by the Commission suggest that the EU as a whole will fall short of its announced target of stabilizing greenhouse gas emissions at 1990 levels by the year 2000, despite the intervening recession (*ENDS Report*, 1996, No.255, p38). The failure of the measure also shows the political limits of proposals to ecologize the economy by shifting taxes from labour to resources.

Just as the case of the carbon/energy tax shows the constraints imposed by national vetoes, so there are some clear examples where it is difficult to account for developments in European environmental policy without seeing the economic interest of particular countries at stake behind the proposal of an environmental measure. The original draft of the Large Combustion Plant Directive is the most well-known example. Here, the relevant official in DG XI, who was German, was simply given the recently agreed German large combustion ordinance and told to translate it into Euro-speak. The most recent example would be the pressure from Germany to agree a Directive on packaging. Similarly, the UK's reluctance to move as quickly as some other countries have wished in terms of higher pollution-control standards has sometimes been ascribed to the view that the UK wishes to use its geographical comparative advantage (westerly winds, short fast-running rivers and clay soils) to maintain low-cost production (Haigh, 1989, p22).

Another feature of the European rule-making process is the way in which the agenda is often set by national concerns and perspectives, with individual countries seeking to ensure that their priorities are generalized within the EU. For example, it is the UK – usually regarded as a European environmental policy laggard – that has taken the lead on such matters as environmentally sensitive farming, integrated pollution control and eco-audits, while Germany has certainly resisted the last of these. On this basis Héritier and her colleagues (Héritier et al, 1994) have spoken of a regulatory competition in which Member States struggle to secure their own regulatory styles in European legislation.

On this account, what we are seeing in the formation of EU environmental standards is *not* a European agenda, but a process by which national concerns are displaced on to a higher level. If this intergovernmentalist account is correct, it would also make sense of the complaints of the Mediterranean countries that their environmental priorities (for example, water supply and forest fires) were regularly ignored in the making of EU policy, as representatives sometimes allege (Pridham, 1994, p93). However, the story is not quite as straightforward as this argument would suggest, as can be illustrated from the development of the Directive on integrated pollution prevention and control. Integrated pollution control has been a cause close to the heart of UK environmental policy-makers and advisers for a number of years (Weale et al, 1991). Although it originally sought to put the issue on to the EU agenda, the UK found that its scope and significance were expanded in the course of the Directive's passage through the process of decision-making, in particular to include a wider range of industries, especially intensive livestock plants and food and drink plants. In other words, the development of the Directive took a more stringent direction than had originally been intended and the original initiative was thereby transformed.

The amount, scope and stringency of EU environmental regulation has certainly grown in the 1980s, but this is quite consistent with a great deal of important norm- and standard-setting going on at national level. One clear indication of this is to be found in the fields of product norms and packaging. As developments have been stalled at the European level, so individual Member States have been developing their own schemes. In the case of eco-labelling, for example, national organizations have set different standards for products and, just as importantly, have identified different products as priorities. Moreover, even in sectors that are regulated at the European level, like air and water pollution, there are many pollutants where it is still left to individual Member States to set standards.

It is also worth noting that there is an open question about the extent to which there is a genuine convergence of interpretation around measures that have been formally agreed at an international level. Consider, for example, the principle of 'best available technology not entailing excessive cost', which is to be found in the 1984 Air Pollution Framework Directive. This provision is also found in the national legislation that followed in the implementation of the measure, but as Faure and Ruegg (1994, p52) have pointed out, there can be considerable differences of national interpretation as to what the principle means in particular cases.

Behind these varying responses to EU policy developments and principles, there are persistent differences of national environmental policy preference and principles. To some extent, national differences in policy-making style and priorities are not simply a lagged response by countries at different levels of economic development to a common set of environmental problems, but reflect the fact that national environments differ and so their policy needs differ. The most marked contrast here, of course, is between the relatively undeveloped countries of the south (Portugal, Spain and Greece, as well as the Mezzogiorno) and the industrialized densely populated countries of the north (notably Germany and The Netherlands). Here the argument is that there are simply objective differences in the nature of the problems faced by these different countries, and some of these differences will not be eroded over time. Germany, post-unification, is not going to acquire a longer coastline and Spain is not going to acquire a river Rhine. Hence, so the argument goes, it is unrealistic to expect a high degree of policy convergence and we should be surprised if issues dealt with at the European level did not reflect the priorities of different countries.

Moreover, there is a fallacy, so it could be argued, in inferring the Europeanization of environmental policy from observations of the policy-making process in Brussels. Such evidence is bound to distort our perceptions since we are only looking at the cases that countries think are worth arguing about at an international level. What about the times that they are happy to pursue their own priorities or simply do not bother to kick up a fuss because their own standards are higher than the Commission is proposing anyway? Liefferink (1996, pp121–123) provides an interesting example in connection with the development of policy on the 1980 Directive on air quality limit values and guide values for sulphur dioxide and suspended particulates. Dutch policy had already developed on this issue and there was little interest in seeking to influence the Commission in its drafting process, since it was clear that any standard that was set at the European level would be less strict than had already been agreed in The Netherlands. For this reason, there was no lobbying by Dutch industry at European level. Similar considerations apply, Liefferink argues, in connection with the air quality standards on lead and nitrogen oxides.

Finally, there is not much evidence of convergence in formal structures of environmental policy-making among the Member States (Weale et al, 1996). If we simply measure the degree of concentration of environmental functions within a single ministry, for example, it is clear that there is more variance between countries than there is over time. These organizational differences reflect different environmental priorities and different priorities given to the environment. In other words, despite the growing common recognition across Europe of the increasing importance of environmental issues, there is little evidence of convergence in the institutional arrangements that different countries use to formulate and implement policy.

Thus, in summary, the functional links between the single market and environmental policy are not sufficient to explain the form and character that the policy has taken, and there is no simple transfer of jurisdiction from the level of the nation state to the European level. Indeed, there remain what look like ineliminable features of national policy-making and interest in the environmental field. What are the implications for the environmental governance regime of the EU?

Concurrent Decision-making among Institutional and Functional Actors

Scharpf (1988, p242) has argued that the EU is one of a class of political systems in which decision-making authority is not allocated in a zero-sum fashion between different levels of government but is instead shared. Thus, just as the German federal government shares authority with the *Länder* through the need to secure a majority in the Bundesrat, so the EU shares authority with national governments through the pivotal role in decision-making of the Council of Ministers. In such systems, decision-making must necessarily take the form of requiring concurrent majorities of actors, and may in practice – whatever the formal rules say – tend to the rule of unanimity.

Some of the implications of this decision-making structure were spelt out in the previous section, where national actors could block certain measures and where there was a constant tendency to wish to displace national agendas on to the European level. National champions are often needed for measures to succeed, and even under qualified majority voting in the Council of Ministers proposed measures need widespread agreement, or at least acquiescence, if they are to be adopted.

However, the principle of shared authority applies not simply to the relations between the EU and the Member States, but also to the relations between different elements of the EU decision-making process itself: the Commission, the Court, the Parliament and the Council of Ministers. The involvement of all these actors in the decision-making process increases the number of 'veto players', that is actors whose agreement is required for a change in policy (Tsebelis, 1995, p301). The principle of concurrent majorities thus operates both vertically, in respect of the EU and the Member States, and horizontally, in respect of policy actors at the European level itself.

But the complexity of the story does not stop here. In addition to the formal involvement of various actors in the decision-making process, the Commission has also been called a 'promiscuous bureaucracy' (Mazey and Richardson, 1993), because of its tendency to involve interest groups in the making of policy. Moreover, given diminishing marginal returns in the imposition of environmental standards, many apparently small 'technical' changes in the rules can turn out to have major cost or environmental implications, so that the involvement of interest groups in the processes of standard-setting and rule-making should not be regarded as trivial or simply as a matter of courtesy. Instead, we should think of it as involving the concurrence of functional groups, in which sectional interests can often have something close to veto power.

What, then, might be the implications of this institutional and functional sharing of rule-making authority? The first consequence is that in a system in which the agreement of so many actors is necessary in order to have any chance of policy change, policy-makers within the Commission have a strong incentive to be opportunistic in their agenda-setting, taking proposals from Member States, safe in the knowledge that there is at least some support at the beginning for a measure. Add to this incentive the organizational disadvantage of having little by way of resources to conduct policy analysis and development, and the stage is set for opportunistic decision-making relying on the initiative of Member States. This is the most obvious way of accounting for the regulatory competition identified by Héritier and her colleagues.

However, once inside the process of decision-making, any issue is subject to capture by other actors, so that what eventually emerges at the other end may contain elements uncongenial to its original proponents. Again, given the impact of apparently small 'technical' features of rules on costs and compliance, there is a great deal of scope for a transformation of proposals during the course of their passage: timetables for implementation can be changed, emission limit values altered, new processes brought under control, administrative requirements changed, and so on. Moreover, the need to secure a concurrent majority in the process of decision-making means that the there is little incentive for policy participants to point out the full implications of measures to Member States even if they know them. It is much more attractive to secure agreement in principle and then argue later about the extent to which Member States are implementing what they have already signed up to.

European environmental standards, then, are neither a reflection of a dominant coalition of countries pushing their own national style of regulation (as is sometimes suggested by those who see the UK as subject to an alien form of environmental regulation via uniform emission limits imposed from Germany), nor a merry-go-round in which different countries have a go at imposing their own national style in a sector that is of particular importance to them. Instead, they are the aggregated and transformed standards of their original champions modified under the need to secure political accommodation from powerful veto players.

In addition, in a system like that of environmental policy-making in the EU where not only are the rules being made quickly but also the rules for making rules are changing quite rapidly, there are plenty of opportunities for procedural wrangling, as happened between the Commission and the Council over the Directive on titanium dioxide, and as also happened over various attempts to repatriate certain environmental competences (Wallace, 1994, p78). Concurrent majority systems are well known to have high transaction costs attached to them, most notably as the decision rule tends to unanimity, but the procedural wrangling adds to such transaction costs by creating disputes not just about the substance of the measure, but also about the terms and conditions under which the measure is to be taken.

The theory of social choice suggests that as actors with diverse policy positions obtain a share of decision-making power, so the chances of policy change go down (Tsebelis, 1995, pp308–313). A clear recent example of this effect is provided by the European Parliament's rejection of the proposed Landfill Directive (*ENDS Report*, 1996, No.256, pp38–39). The Parliament has the general reputation of having a policy position that is more pro-environment than the Council of Ministers. In the case of the proposed landfill Directive, the crucial issue was a provision that enabled Member States to exempt smaller landfills with a low density of inhabitants (an exemption favoured by Portugal and Ireland). Thus, requiring simultaneous agreement between the Council and the Parliament results in a situation in which it is difficult to move from the status quo.

When we turn to the functional component of the concurrent majority one feature in particular is evident, namely that environmental policy involves co-ordination with other policy sectors, most notably industry, transport and agriculture. Thus, an environmental policy taken on its own may secure the reduction in harmful emissions from individual vehicles, but if transport policy is leading to more vehicles being put on the road, the gain at the individual level is offset by the increase in total emissions arising from the volume increase, a phenomenon that has been observed in respect of nitrous oxide emissions from cars, for example. Since, at the European level, DGs are the guardians of their sectoral interests, it is hardly surprising that sectoral complexity makes for difficult decision-making in institutional terms.

By contrast, environmental policy-makers will also want to be seen to be supporting their own functional constituency, a trend reinforced in the case of DG XI by the fact that a number of the officials clearly have a commitment to environmental protection that is personal as well as professional. It may be this tendency which creates the impression among some other officials that DG XI has a limited perspective, as the interviewee quoted by Peterson illustrates:

> *These DG XI people are like the Trappist monks who make Chimay Bleu [a strong Belgian beer]. They don't consult with anyone besides their religious patrons and they cook up very strong stuff, which will always appeal to a certain segment of the 'beer-drinking public'. They don't ever think about what a ferocious hangover is induced by the stuff they cook up* (Peterson, 1995, p482).

Similarly, there are officials in DG XI who will volunteer the thought that no one in Agriculture is willing to talk to anyone about the environmental problems that the Common Agricultural Policy causes.

Can we characterize the decision-making style that emerges from this institutional process? One important feature of it is that it is difficult for policy actors to adopt what Scharpf terms a 'problem-solving' mentality as distinct from a 'bargaining' mentality. In this sense the attempt to create a discourse of ecological modernization, around which policy could be organized and discussed, has failed. There is simply too much heterogeneity of interest (especially arising from different stages of economic development) for there to be a consensus on the priority to be given to environmental measures. Moreover, even if it is true in the aggregate that environmental protection and economic development pull in the same direction, there is too much conflict in the particular case for the tension to be easily eliminated.

One consequence is that over time the development of environmental policy tends to follow a pattern of *immobilisme* punctuated by activism. Between 1982 and 1992 there was an upsurge of activism in which many environmental measures were passed, partly as a consequence of the need to harmonize environmental measures in the context of the internal market and partly because of the high salience that the environment had as an issue among European publics and governments. Despite some consolidation and advance since 1992, the scale and pace of development have slowed down considerably, and some high-profile measures have been stalled.

How well overall is the environmental system of governance performing? In particular, how far is it producing high-quality decisions that are well adapted to solve the problems at which they are directed? It is difficult to come to a judgement on these questions, not least because the criteria of evaluation will vary according to one's own policy position. But some things are clear. There *is* environmental spillover from the single market. It was *not* anticipated in the creation of the internal market. Moreover, in so far as EU environmental policy has transcended the logic of the single market, it is not easy to see how rule-making activity has pursued an effective problem-solving strategy. Decision processes operating on the principle of concurrent majorities and sharing authority between nation and Community as well as both functionally and institutionally are not perhaps best adapted to deal with environmental issues.

Acknowledgements

This chapter draws on the research project 'Environmental Standards and the Politics of Expertise' conducted under the Economic and Social Research Council's (ESRC's) Single European Market Research Programme (award No. W 113 251 025). I should like to thank my co-researchers in the project (Michelle Cini, Dimitrios Konstadakopoulos, Geoffrey Pridham, Martin Porter and Andrea Williams) for discussions and material. In addition, I am grateful to Iain Begg, Maarten Hajer, Duncan Liefferink and Geoffrey Pridham for detailed comments and suggestions on earlier versions. Remaining errors are my responsibility.

References

Arp, H. (1993) 'Technical Regulation and Politics: the Interplay between Economic Interests and Environmental Policy Goals in EC Car Emission Legislation', in Liefferink, J. D., Lowe, P. D. and Mol, A. P. J. (eds) *European Integration and Environmental Policy*, London and New York: Belhaven Press, pp150–171.

Bulmer, S. J. (1994) 'The Governance of the European Union: A New Institutionalist Approach'. *Journal of Public Policy*, Vol.13, No.4, pp351–380.

Cameron, D. R. (1992) 'The 1992 Initiative: Causes and Consequences', in Sbragia, A. M. (ed) *Euro-Politics. Institutions and Policymaking in the 'New' European Community*, Washington DC: The Brookings Institution.

Commission of the European Communities (1992) *Fifth Environmental Action Programme,* COM (92) 23 final, Luxembourg: Commission of the European Communities.

Commission of the European Communities (1993) *Growth, Competitiveness, Employment, The Challenges and Ways Forward into the 21st Century,* Luxembourg: Commission of the European Communities (two volumes).

ENDS Report, various numbers, see www.ends.co.uk.

Faure, M. and Ruegg, M. (1994) 'Environmental Standard Setting through General Environmental Law', in Faure, M., Vervaele, J. and. Weale, A (eds) *Environmental Standards in the European Union in an Interdisciplinary Framework,* Antwerpen and Apeldoorn: MAKLU.

Haigh, N. (1989) *EEC Environmental Policy and Britain,* 2nd edn, Harlow: Longman.

Haigh, N. and Baldock, D. (1989) *Environmental Policy and 1992,* London: Institute for European Environmental Policy.

Hajer, M. (1995) *The Politics of Environmental Discourse,* Oxford: Clarendon Press.

Héritier, A. et al (1994) *Die Veränderung von Staatlichkeit in Europa,* Opladen: Leske and Budrich.

House of Lords, Select Committee on the European Communities (1992) *Implementation and Enforcement of Environmental Legislation, Volume II – Evidence,* HL Paper 53–11, London: HMSO.

Keohane, R. O. and Nye, J. Y. (1989) *Power and Interdependence,* London: HarperCollins.

Liefferink, J. D. (1996) *The Making of European Environmental Policy,* Manchester: Manchester University Press.

Mazey, S. and Richardson, J. J. (eds) (1993) *Lobbying in the European Community,* Oxford and New York: Oxford University Press.

Peterson, J. (1995) 'Playing the Transparency Game: Consultation and Policy-making in the European Commission', *Public Administration,* Vol.73, No.3, pp473–492.

Plaskett, L. (1996) 'Airing the Differences', *Financial Times,* Wednesday, 26 June, p20.

Pridham, G. (1994) 'National Environmental Policy-making in the European Framework: Spain, Greece and Italy in Comparison', *Regional Politics and Policy,* Vol.4, No.1, pp80–101.

Rehbinder, E. and Stewart, R. (1985) *Environmental Protection Policy,* Berlin and New York: Walter de Gruyter.

Scharpf, F. W. (1988) 'The Joint-decision Trap: Lessons from German Federalism and European Institutions', *Public Administration,* Vol.66, No.3, pp239–278.

Second Chamber of the States General (1989) *National Environmental Policy Plan. To Choose or Lose,* 's-Gravenhage: SDU Uitgeverij.

Shapiro, M. (1992) 'The European Court of Justice', in Sbragia, A. M. (ed) *Euro-Politics. Institutions and Policymaking in the 'New' European Community,* Washington DC: The Brookings Institution.

Task Force Report on the Environment and the Internal Market (1989) *1992; The Environmental Dimension,* Luxembourg: Commission of the European Communities.

Tsebelis, G. (1995) 'Decision Making in Political Systems: Veto Players in Presidentialism, Parliamentarianism, Multicameralism and Multipartyism', *British Journal of Political Science*, Vol.25, No.3, pp289–325.

Wallace, W. (1994) *Regional Integration: The West European Experience,* Washington DC: The Brookings Institution.

Weale, A. (1992) *The New Politics of Pollution,* Manchester: Manchester University Press.

Weale, A. (1993) 'Ecological Modernisation and the Integration of European Environmental Policy', in Liefferink, J. D., Lowe, P. D. and Mol, A. J. P. (eds) *European Integration and Environmental Policy,* London and New York: Belhaven Press, pp196–216.

Weale, A., O'Riordan, T. and Kramme, L. (1991) *Controlling Pollution in the Round,* London: Anglo-German Foundation for the Study of Industrial Society.

Weale, A., Pridham, G., Williams, A. and Porter, M. (1996) 'Administrative Organisation and Environmental Policy: Structural Convergence or National Distinctiveness in Six European States?', *Public Administration*, Vol.74, No.2, pp255–274.

Würzel, R. (1993) 'Environmental policy', in J. Lodge (ed) *The European Community and the Challenge of the Future,* 2nd edn, London: Pinter, pp178–199.

9

Task Expansion: A Theoretical Overview

Anthony R. Zito

Introduction

Despite the initial lack of an explicit treaty basis, the European Union (EU) nevertheless has constructed a very wide-ranging set of regulations that cover the critical environmental media (water, air, and soil) and a range of products and industrial processes. From Table 9.1 the tremendous expansion of environmental policies between 1957 and 1994 is evident, although the 1995 Figures raise interesting questions about the future trajectory of EU environmental policy.

In this chapter, I investigate how well current theories explain 'task expansion' in the sphere of EU environmental policy over the past 40 years. Pollack (1994, p96) defines 'task expansion' as 'the initial expansion of the Community agenda to include new policy areas' and the subsequent growth of substantive policies in these new areas. A study of task expansion is primarily focused on the outputs – the laws, regulations, and policy documents – of the EU policy process rather than on measuring the relative influence of national and supranational authorities in bringing that process about, which is the primary concern of European integration theory. This chapter is a stocktaking exercise. I will be asking two basic questions: (1) How well do five popular theories explain the scope and level of policy outputs in the EU environmental arena?; and (2) What are the critical empirical issues that might allow us to adjudicate between the different perspectives?

The analytical perspectives included here frequently appear in EU studies: namely, neofunctionalism, intergovernmentalism, 'new' institutionalism, ideational-epistemic approaches, and policy networks. Peterson (1995) provides a useful framework for ordering these theories, distinguishing between macrotheories (for, example, traditional integration theories such as neofunctionalism that examine the international state system in which the EU operates), systemic analysis (theories explaining political behaviour in the context of the EU), and meso-level perspectives (showing the linkage between the EU macro-structure and micro-interests within the larger European society). Peterson notes that the macrotheories

Table 9.1 *The Expansion of European Union Environmental Policy*

	Period				
	1958–72	*1973–86*	*1987–92*	*1993–95*	*1995 alone*
Number of laws adopted[a]	5	118	82	60	5
Average number of laws adopted per annum	0.3	8.4	13.7	20	5
Total number of laws adopted[b]	9	195	192	144	28
Average number of new and amended laws adopted per annum	0.6	13.9	32	48	28

Notes: a Regulations, directives, and decisions only.
       b Including amendments and elaborations.
Source: McCormick, 1998, p195.

are better equipped to explain the broad historical trends in integration, but that these perspectives are less well equipped to explain the choices made by specific actors operating within the EU structure. Nevertheless, although such perspectives are more oriented towards the broader question of EU integration in a larger context, neofunctionalism and intergovernmentalism do provide insights into task expansion in particular sectors (for example, Cram, 1993; Golub, 1997). At the same time, scholars are increasingly studying the EU as a comparable polity, using traditional political approaches to study factors such as institutions that shape policy outcomes (Hix, 1994). 'New' institutional and ideational perspectives provide important systemic insights into how the EU operates, whereas policy network analysis reveals what occurs in policy sectors within the EU structure.

   One cannot simply fuse the theories described above together because they operate at different levels. Some are macrotheories whereas others operate at a meso-level. However, they all contain interesting explanations of task expansion. In this chapter I explore these different perspectives in the context of four time periods defined by the following four key events: (1) the creation of the common market in 1957; (2) the Paris Summit of 1972; (3) the enactment in 1987 of the Single European Act (SEA); and (4) the adoption in 1993 of the Maastricht Treaty (Hildebrand, 1993, pp17–28).

Theoretical Approaches

Neofunctionalism

In this chapter I examine only the basic neofunctional programme (Haas, 1958), recognizing that later versions either addressed many of the deficiencies noted here (for example, Lindberg and Scheingold, 1970) or adopted slightly different perspectives yet borrowed key assumptions (for example Marks et al, 1996). Original versions of neofunctionalism hypothesize that successful supranational policy-making can induce people to learn to reorient their national identities towards European institutional structures. The key agents of change are held to be actors in the European institutions and external socio-economic interests who seek to expand the scope of supranational policy. When national populations witness the benefits of integration occurring in one policy sector, they will embrace the extension of supranational control into other sectors. This 'spillover' process gradually embraces an ever-increasing set of issue areas (Haas, 1958, pp514–518).

The neofunctional perspective contains a clear and parsimonious explanation of why change occurs. It focuses not only on the independent role of entrepreneurial institutions, particularly supranational bodies such as the Commission and the European Court of Justice (ECJ) (Burley and Mattli, 1993), but also on national interests such as the business sector. This entrepreneurial activity tends to be technocratic. The more entrepreneurial EU organizations such as the Commission and the European Parliament exert influence by helping to define agendas and initiating policy proposals. Such powers fit more in the realm of influencing the interests of other actors than of having the ultimate power to pass and veto legislation (Golub, 1996a, p332). Neofunctionalism explains task expansion by asserting that EU institutions and societal actors seize opportunities to promote common environmental policies.

Despite these insights, a number of analytical problems dissuade most researchers working in EU environmental studies from relying solely on a neofunctionalist framework. Neofunctionalism implies a unidirectional progression for task expansion when empirical evidence from the environmental sector, notably the recent emergence of the subsidiarity principle, emphasizes the likelihood of policy reversals (or what neofunctionalists might term policy 'spillback') (Corbey, 1995). This deterministic outlook reflects the inadequate theorizing of national governments and popular loyalty (Pentland, 1973, pp85–86) and of the often significant internal politics within the supranational institutions (Peters, 1992, p115–121). National governments may fear that regulatory task expansion erodes national interests, and non-environmental Commission Directorate Generals (DGs) may resist the intrusion of environment regulation into their policy sector. Consequently, the neofunctional expectation that achievements in more technical environmental policy will 'spill over' into more politically contested environmental issues is questionable. The assumption that environmental areas are easily separable from the political realm is itself debatable. Last, neofunctionalism suffers from a tendency to presume the naturalness of outcomes when reality is far more contingent on varying choices of conscious actors (Tsebelis, 1990, p102).

Intergovernmentalism

Like neofunctionalist approaches, recent versions of intergovernmentalist theory also contain more sophisticated accounts of the domestic political process shaping national preferences and other factors (for example, Moravcsik, 1993, pp486–487, 514–515). A realist-intergovernmental approach highlights national governments and interests seeking integration on certain issues and pushing the process forward yet also notes the importance of external pressures, particularly interdependence, and the national governments' ability to learn to co-operate to protect national interests (Taylor, 1975, pp338–347).

Intergovernmentalism remains a powerful, relatively parsimonious explanation of EU environmental task expansion because it recognizes the importance of external pressures such as economic interdependence; the critical influence exerted by Member States in the EU process (especially in the Council of Ministers); and the linking of the national political process to the EU system. For intergovernmentalists, task expansion occurs because the Member States agree that co-operative environmental policies are mutually beneficial, based on an assessment of their own domestic political concerns and transnational environmental pressures. Consequently, task expansion is tightly constrained to reflect those domestic concerns.

Few EU environmental policy studies rely solely on intergovernmentalism for their explanation. Current versions of intergovernmentalism emphasize the policy impact of treaty renegotiations (for example, Moravcsik, 1993, pp496–499), although they have been applied to the day-to-day process of environmental policy-making (Golub, 1997, p4). However, intergovernmentalism underestimates the role of actors in defining problems and shaping agendas. It also plays down the influence of non-state actors and small EU states in furthering task expansion (Peters, 1994). Although one should not ignore the ultimate Council veto, many key moments in the policy-making process occur before the decision to act has been taken, which constrains national actors later in the process. Even when the Member State governments make a determined effort to control the process, they may not be able to manage the future implications of these decisions, because of such factors as the restricted time horizons of actors and because of unintended consequences (Pierson, 1996, pp131–143). Moreover, autonomous EU institutions (for example, the European Parliament, under the co-operation and co-decision procedures) constrain the Member States' ability to control the processing of specific items of legislation (Garrett and Tsebelis, 1996, pp285–294; Golub, 1996a, pp330–335).

'New' institutionalism

A common criticism of integration theories derived from international relations is that they cannot anticipate the EU outcomes shaped by the independent, unique EU institutional structures. EU scholars, such as Pierson (1996) and Pollack (1996), have returned to institutional analysis to interpret European integration. 'New' institutionalism is a mid-range theory that can explain specific policy outcomes and task expansion. Accordingly, EU institutions provide structures that shape how EU actors define their roles, interests, and relations to other actors, and that frame the general context for acting and making choices. The EU structures consist of rules and norms that embody certain identities, interests and values, and therefore define appropriate actions for policy-makers (March and Olsen, 1989, pp159–161). Weale (1996, pp606–609) argues in favour of an institutionalist approach to studying EU environmental policy.

A 'new' institutional approach clarifies the complex relationships between EU actors at the supranational, national, and subnational levels and how those relations shape environmental policy. Such an approach accepts the importance of agenda-setting as well as the ability to veto actions. The perspective explains task expansion in terms of organizations enhancing their institutional mandates, which define their worldviews (Peters, 1992, pp115–121). Therefore, a 'new' institutionalist explanation of EU environmental task expansion suggests that institutional actors in the European Parliament and other organizations seek to fulfil their mandates and carve out a larger role for themselves by expanding the quantity of environmental regulation (Judge, 1993). Another institutionally based explanation of the EU policy process, principal-agent analysis, suggests that these motivations will lead to complex relationships between the institutions (Pollack, 1997). In creating the EU treaties the Member States delegate power to the Commission to perform certain regulatory tasks, such as protecting the environment, that are better performed at the EU level than within the individual Member States. These institutional interpretations differ from neofunctionalism in that they do not presume an integrationist motivation on the part of EU actors; it may be that institutions work against task expansion in several key respects.

Although institutionalist perspectives provide necessary insights into the EU political system their ability to explain EU task expansion remains limited. Although institutional structures shape many of the important opportunities that policy actors face they do not determine those interests. Institutional analysis also emphasizes the role of formal institutional bodies as opposed to equally significant informal networks. Last, although institutional approaches are good at explaining why certain decisions recur over time, they are less able to explain non-incremental policy change (Pollack, 1996, pp453–454). The institutional explanation focuses on how EU institutions channel external pressures for change and how new decisions will tend to follow the course set by previous decisions.

Ideational-epistemic accounts

The need to understand why policies change has led scholars to turn increasingly to the realm of ideas. Ideational perspectives contend that ideas and knowledge influence actors into redefining their interests and seeking policy change. Ideas serve as a road map for determining actor interests, prescribing the choices and values of actors (Goldstein and Keohane, 1993, pp12–13). In order to infuse some agency into the ideas argument, scholars have suggested that epistemic communities, a policy network organized around shared causal beliefs, shape policy-making, especially in areas involving a high degree of policy complexity and uncertainty (Haas, 1992, p3). Ideas, and the communities that wield them, gain influence when proponents secure positions of authority within decision-making processes (Haas, 1990, pp226–231).

Because they focus on the formulation of actor interests in times of uncertainty, ideas or epistemic approaches better explicate the EU problem-definition and agenda-setting stages of the EU policy process as opposed to the subsequent institutional bargaining (Raustiala, 1997, pp507–508). Nevertheless, ideational approaches clarify how substantial policy change occurs and how interests evolve over time. Important scientific knowledge about pollution and new ideas such as sustainable development may alter actor interests, convincing them to incorporate more EU regulation which in turn sparks further task expansion.

The role of ideas is beginning to gain some prominence in European environmental studies (for example, Lenschow and Zito, 1998; Weale, 1992). Nevertheless, the perspective faces difficulties, particularly the ambiguous distinction between ideas and interests: do interests follow ideas or vice versa? The receptivity of policy actors to ideas may remain a function of their perceived interests (Litfin, 1994, pp186–188). Policy uncertainty may lead policy-makers to interpret the knowledge in different ways, as opposed to following one approach – again raising the question of actor agency and individual interest. The epistemic community approach is one attempt to explore the question of agency in policy analysis. It also recognizes the potentially international scope of ideas. However, the narrow criteria of what constitutes an epistemic community suggests that other vehicles also translate ideas into the EU policy process (Zito, 1998).

Policy networks

Institutional and ideational-epistemic perspectives present a difficult challenge in that their frameworks emphasize abstract concepts that are difficult to link to actual actor behaviour and policy outcomes. Policy network analysis is attractive because of its inherent focus on the actors operating in the network. These actors make calculations of interest in the context of the policy network, which in turn shapes their worldview.

The policy network approach provides a meso-level analysis because it links specific actors to the larger EU institutions and structures (Peterson, 1997). This linkage between societal groups and public organizations mirrors neofunctionalism. The internal characteristics of the network, namely the resource dependencies between individual actors, is said to shape the political outcome of this interaction (Rhodes, 1988, pp77–78). An epistemic community is a very cohesive knowledge-driven policy network in which the independent impact of ideas is crucial.

Policy networks are a popular means of understanding the day-to-day process of deciding and implementing EU environmental policies (for example, Héritier et al, 1996; Richardson, 1994). Their advantages include the ability to recognize the importance of less formal relationships and multilayered processes operating in the EU. Networks also fit the fluid structure of environmental policy structure brought about by actors attempting to expand the competence of the EU (Bomberg, 1994, pp47–48). It is especially concerned with the alliances that develop between pro-environment actors in different organizations (for example, the Commission Directorate General for the Environment (DG XI) and the European Parliament's Environment committee) as they battle to set the EU-wide agenda and introduce new EU environmental policies (Mazey and Richardson, 1993, pp120–125). To achieve such changes, this environmental network must overcome other actor coalitions with less 'green' sectoral and/or organizational interests (for example, agricultural interests that seek to control issues within their respective network).

Network analysis faces the difficulty of cleanly differentiating actor interests from ideas and institutions. Moreover, the approach focuses on EU policy-making in specific sectors; it was not intended to explain the broader EU process of integration. Networks form only one part of the structure that determines task expansion. The approach illuminates the agenda-setting phase before the Member States make their final decision in the Council of Ministers, but the intergovernmental decision-making remains (Rhodes et al, 1996, p382). Policy network explanations also have difficulty explaining why substantial EU policy change occurs (Richardson, 1996, pp34–37).

The Founding Period: 1957–1972

Having set out the theories, let us turn to reconsider the history of task expansion. The slow rate of adoption during the period 1957–1972 (see Table 9.1) suggests the intermittent nature of EU environmental regulation-building during this first period. Nevertheless, this era raises several theoretical issues. As the founding Treaty made no explicit reference to environmental priorities, a wide range of legal justification, particularly Articles 235 and 100, provided the basis for the infrequent regulations with environmental implications (also, see Hildebrand, 1993, pp17–20). A pattern of embedding environmental issues in the building of the European common market emerged: policy-makers used Article 100 to give the European Economic Community (EEC) institutions the power to protect the construction and operation of the common market, thereby fulfilling indirectly some of the broad objectives contained in Articles 2 and 3 of the Treaty of Rome (Rehbinder and Stewart, 1985, pp16–28). Article 100 provided the basis for regulations of dangerous substances and noise and exhaust emissions – the foundation for future legislation in these areas.

Given the rather creative interpretation of an environmental mandate, this period appears to bear all the hallmarks of functional spillover, or what Weale (1999) describes as 'integration by stealth'. Commission officials had the opportunity to link the functioning of the common market, protected by Article 100, to other policy issues when national legislation impinged on the market (Pollack, 1994, pp123–125). The Commission's ability to harmonize national legislation in different economically related areas suggests it seized the opportunity to extend the Community's scope and protect the objectives of the market.

Although the case for neofunctionalism during the agenda-setting stage of the EU policy process is highly suggestive, individual Member States continued to hold a veto in the Council of Environment Ministers. An intergovernmental interpretation argues that this arrangement allowed Member States and national interests to retain control over the overall direction of task expansion. Certain national governments took the initiative by creating legislation. The Member States responded by permitting the Community process to harmonize environmental legislation as long as it was mutually beneficial. However, the Commission's exclusive right of initiative grants it a gate-keeping role, enabling it to define problems in particular ways. More research is needed into the motives of the Community institutions during the foundational period to judge whether the neofunctional or the intergovernmental perspectives best explain the spillover process.

The application of the mid-range approaches is more clear-cut. The influence of institutions is particularly salient: ideas, centred around the economic goals of the common market which are embedded in the EU institutional structure, played an indirect role. After all, developing a common market is the Community institutions' raison d'être. Even without the drive to extend supranational control over environmental policy, other, more powerful, parts of the Commission such as DG III (at the time covering the internal market and industry) would have watched for issues that threatened the common market and diluted them. An alternative interpretation based on principal-agent theory is also plausible: the technical nature of regulations, such as the classification and handling of hazardous substances, and the uncertainty of what is happening in all of the Member States, creates incentives for the Member State governments to delegate regulatory functions to the Commission. Thus institutionalist analysis, which focuses on how organizations seek to fulfil their tasks and protect their mandate, can reinforce either the neofunctional or the intergovernmental interpretations.

In terms of the ideas and policy network approaches, the intermittent appearance of environment-related regulation underlines the absence of powerful clearly focused political groups capable of defining the environment as a distinct political issue. More often than not, 'environmental' measures often were ushered through under the guise of 'health' or 'safety' matters (Vogel, 1993, pp244–250). In these circumstances, the historical record prior to 1972 offers little evidence either of a united coalition of environmental interests or of an influential set of environmental ideas capable of progressing task expansion.

The regulatory record for the era suggests that the key question is to define whether the Commission or the Member States set the EEC agenda and spurred spillover. The degree to which the policy issue is technical is an important angle to this question. The more technical and less salient the issue is to the general public, the more tenuous the linkage between the regulation and distinct national interests (and the less the pressure on national politicians to intervene). There is also a dimension that gives intergovernmentalism an analytical edge over neofunctionalism and the mid-range theories: intergovernmentalism acknowledges that external factors can have an impact on the EU. For example, the Community institutions based Directive 70/157 (noise emissions from cars, buses, and lorries) on a United Nations Economic Commission for Europe regulation (Haigh, 1997). Policy emulation such as this emphasizes the importance of international factors in EU policy-making.

The Institutionalization of Environmental Concern: 1972–1987

The impact of rising levels of environmental awareness during the 1970s is reflected in the upsurge of environmental legislation adopted by the EEC in the period following the adoption of the first action programme (see Table 9.1). Nevertheless, task expansion followed the paths laid down during the foundational era because of the continuing lack of an explicit treaty basis.

The speed and scale of expansion, and the increasingly prominent role of supranational institutions, would appear to confirm early neofunctional predictions: namely that institutions such as the Commission and European Parliament expanded the presence of the EEC in national affairs. The creation of dedicated environmental organizations such as the European Consumer Protection Service was significant in reinforcing task expansion. The European Parliament created a dedicated Environmental Committee in 1972 (Judge, 1993, p189). The establishment of Commission Directorate General for the Environment (DG XI) in 1981 created both an institution dedicated to promoting environmental priorities in the larger EEC arena and a focus for environmental coalition building (Mazey and Richardson, 1993; Sbragia, 1993, pp345–348). Pro-environment actors in the Commission used their mandate to propose a battery of new regulations.

On the surface, these developments seemed to follow neofunctionalist predictions. Nevertheless, the empirical question remains of how much problem-definition and agenda-setting influence is attributable to the Commission when it comes to the actual *output* of new regulations. Supranational actors cannot claim the entire role in agenda-setting, as the presence of intergovernmental actors is also discernible. The Commission's attempts to harmonize national legislation induced a large portion of the expansion in legislation in this era. But national policy priorities and interests of certain pro-environment states were also critical in pushing task expansion forward (Sbragia, 1996). The enormous impetus given to EEC environmental policy by West Germany's conversion to 'green' thinking was mentioned by Jordan (1999a) in his introductory paper. The German government's primary objective was to define the EU legislation in such a way as to minimize its own legal adjustment costs and reduce the economic burden on its industry (Héritier et al, 1996, pp175–176).

Germany's role in the adoption of the landmark Directive on large combustion plants (Sbragia, 1996; Weale, 1996) broadly confirms an intergovernmental perspective. Nevertheless, the sequence of events which culminated in the adoption of the Directive also contains some special features: acid rain was an issue at the top of political agendas in a number of key Member States because of the visibility of its effects and the potentially very high economic cost of remedial measures. The issue was not completely dominated by scientific or technical argumentation. In other words, the circumstances were precisely those in which one would expect intergovernmental forces to be strong. Low-visibility issues are more likely to engage officials in the lower echelons of the Commission and national ministries, and those interests directly affected by control measures. In this scenario, the Commission's agenda-setting role and ability to act as a mediator may have given officials the leeway to guide the agenda.

Although the large combustion plant outcome broadly fits an intergovernmental view of European environmental policy, institutions helped shape the precise pathway of task expansion. Significantly, the German government used its Council presidencies and the Commission's agenda-setting and brokering roles to make headway on the Directive (Héritier et al, 1996, pp200–202; Sbragia, 1996, pp238–239). The UK found itself in a minority of one. This gave DG XI, which at the time was headed by a German official, room to mediate between national positions. The influence of institutions is likely to be even stronger in other less salient issues. Acting not as a neofunctional body seeking to expand the EU role but rather as an organization seeking to enhance its own position, the European Parliament helped define the agenda in such areas as the trade in hazardous waste (Zito, 1995).

Idea-based explanations also present a rather equivocal picture during this era. At a basic level, the knowledge about the impact of human processes placed tremendous pressure on EEC policy-makers to respond with concrete policies. Unprecedented levels of environmental awareness pushed EEC leaders to give the Commission an institutional mandate to propose large quantities of regulation. However, this was a general, region-wide movement shaping EEC actions rather than a specific set of ideas spurring task expansion. However, the presence of specific new ideas capable of reshaping EEC interests and expanding the EEC role are noticeable in the three environmental action programmes (EAPs). For instance, the Third EAP contained the new policy idea of focusing environmental policy on prevention and of integrating environmental factors into other sectors (Johnson and Corcelle, 1989, pp17–19). Nevertheless, despite the requirement that the Council adopt these programmes, the actual regulatory influence of EAPs is fairly indirect; they raise issues for discussion rather than promulgate specific legislative actions.

It is more difficult to assert that policy networks played a consistently important role in EU task expansion during this period. Although networks of interested parties do surround the environmental policy process they are more likely to be fluid because of the novelty and openness of the EEC environmental policy structure (Mazey and Richardson, 1993, p112). There was no solid 'green' coalition pushing for task expansion across the entire environmental policy sector. The Commission looked to producer groups to help on technical details on relevant legislation, but these interests would concentrate their efforts there. Although organizations such as Greenpeace focus on highly visible issues such as nuclear power, climate change and acid rain, they do not have sufficient resources to mount a sustained campaign across a range of issues. There does not seem to have been an organized coalition pushing the EEC into new environmental areas. It is only when the EEC expanded into new areas that policy networks became prominent, supporting a particular aspect of task expansion such as a legislation on emissions of a particular type of chemical.

The analysis above suggests that supranational (neofunctional or 'new' institutionalism) and intergovernmental theories provide the most convincing account of task expansion in the period 1972–1987. In order to determine more decisively the relative influence of institutions versus Member States a comprehensive overview of EEC policy output during this time period is necessary. The difficulty of penetrating actor motivations across such a huge spectrum of cases can be overcome by examining how far Community policy has moved beyond pre-existing Member State laws (Golub, 1997). If Community policies move significantly beyond those found at the national level, this might imply that external ideas or institutions have pushed the majority of Member States beyond the lowest common denominator of state preferences (as predicted by intergovernmentalism).

A study of particular types or cases of regulation in the 1972–1987 period may provide a more rapid resolution of these questions. A regulatory typology indicates the cases that present a strong challenge to the intergovernmental thesis. First, technical issues of low political salience provide a stiff test for intergovernmentalism. Second, process-oriented legislation seems a more difficult test for intergovernmentalism than does product regulation. Both Pollack (1994, pp125–126) and Gehring (1997, pp342–345) argue that the EU's efforts to reconcile the tension between protecting environment policy and promoting an internal market led to two distinct categories of intervention: process-related regulation and product-related regulation. Product-related regulation creates relatively high minimum standards across all Member States, whereas process-related regulations, which typically rely on more indirect incentives, have had greater difficulty gaining Member State acceptance.

A substantial portion of EU regulation in the 1972–1987 period falls under the product harmonization rubric (for example, vehicle emissions regulations). The Commission proposed the basic Waste Framework Directives to deal with the consequences of national legislation. Although this case highlights Commission entrepreneurship and activity by the European Parliament, the legislation that was finally adopted amounted to a basic compromise between the legal characteristics of the Member State legislation (Zito, 1995). Product standards suggest a stronger presence of national interests in pushing task expansion and setting the agenda.

Process standards regulation provides a clearer test of the intergovernmental thesis because the linkages between industrial competitiveness (often a national priority) and environmental protection may be less clear-cut. Although many of the air pollution Directives were strongly influenced by pre-existing national legislation in some of the most environmentally concerned northern states (Golub, 1997), EU water policy presents a slightly different picture (Sbragia, 1993, pp342–343). Water legislation, such as the bathing and drinking water Directives, offers a case where a less 'green' UK government went along with Community proposals without realizing some of the long-term regulatory costs (Golub, 1996b, pp708–709; Jordan, 1999b). Nevertheless, the presence of national governments shaping the details of Community legislation is evident in many of the water Directives in this process-oriented environmental sector (Haigh, 1997).

A third likely area for investigation is wildlife conservation (Pollack, 1994). Popular interest in protecting endangered species often outweighs the concerns of economic actors dependent on the species. Both the European Parliament and the Commission achieved Council acceptance for the Wild Birds Directive (EEC/79/409) despite Member State haggling. The process forced concessions from certain Member States, and protecting certain aviary categories has caused particular states unanticipated problems and costs (Haigh, 1997, Section 9.2, pp5–7). The need to find regulatory characteristics that favour environmental priorities is important given that the economic logic found in the typical EU environmental regulation often reflects (and therefore is difficult to distinguish from) national economic priorities.

Comparing the prior Member State positions with actual EU regulation enables one to extrapolate from limited research material, but it has some drawbacks. It is difficult to isolate what shapes state preferences. Non-state actors may have convinced Member States that a Community approach was important to their national interests and minimized the perception of negative costs. Furthermore, decision-makers may not realize the long-term consequence of supranational control; unforeseen circumstances may make the legislation more important in the future (Pierson, 1996, pp135–144).

1987–1992: the High-water Mark?

Although the second phase created the regulatory foundation for EU environmental policy, one can see from Table 9.1 the enormous rate of task expansion in the third period as the EU created new directives and amended old legislation. The period before the ratification of the Maastricht Treaty reveals the increase in pressures towards constraining new environmental proposals. The long, conflictual discussions about subsidiarity, enshrined in Article 3b of the Maastricht Treaty indicate the challenge to continued policy task expansion. The UK used its presidency of the EU in 1992 to push the subsidiarity principle in the environmental arena (Maddox, 1992).

Neofunctionalism provides a general explanation for the sheer number of new policies and the effort to link environmental priorities to other EEC policies during this period. The goal of completing the common market by 1992 presented a huge challenge to pro-environment actors (TFEIM, 1990). This policy linkage strongly suggests the neofunctionalist notion of spillover between issue areas. However, neofunctionalism suffers from a teleological view of continued supranational expansion and integration. Both Jordan (1999a) and Lenschow (1999) show that, by 1992, task expansion had become more focused on consolidating the *acquis communautaire* (that is, better implementation, more policy consultation and co-ordination, and greater integration) rather than expanding it into new areas. Furthermore, neofunctionalism does not explain why some Member States eagerly endorsed the subsidiarity principle. Nor does it specify the directions that the EU took (that is, developing new environmental instruments such as voluntary agreements and eco-taxes). To answer these questions we need to turn to the mid-range theories.

The increasing level of rhetoric about subsidiarity perfectly fits intergovernmentalist expectations. This interpretation emphasizes the ability of Member States to control and shape the EU according to their preferences. Countries such as the UK have used subsidiarity as a means of shifting the Commission's organizational direction and of constraining task expansion. This action occurred despite the greater institutional recognition of environmental priorities and the extension of qualified majority voting in the SEA and Maastricht Treaties (Golub, 1996b). National business interests have been extremely effective at pushing the theme of competitiveness and deregulation (Collier, 1997). Two prominent examples of relatively strict EU legislation, the Packaging Waste Directive and the Automobile Emissions Directive, are product-oriented regulations and are Commission responses to externalities triggered by national regulations.

Although intergovernmentalism explains the general shift in direction, it is less successful in explaining the nature and specific impetus of this change. The evolution of regulatory policy seen from 1992 onwards has not necessarily reduced regulatory costs for national businesses. A 'new' institutionalist perspective suggests that the policy leadership did not consist merely of national interests. The Commission recognized the need to create environmental policy which was more effective and to enhance implementation to fulfil its organizational aims; this motivation is not the supranational expansionism suggested by neofunctionalism.

To some extent one must credit this change of thinking to Member State pressure to accept the subsidiarity principle and to economic hardship. The Maastricht Treaty negotiations and the critical reaction from the public to the final agreement appear to have changed the Commission's outlook.

'New' institutional analysis also provides a slightly different explanation for the task expansion witnessed before 1992. It highlights the changing dynamics between the various EU actors in this time period. Specifically, the explicit Treaty references strengthened the organizational mandate of 'pro-environment' actors such as DG XI. By using the explicit organizational mandate of the Member States, DG XI then developed a wide range of proposals and looked at new instruments, such as an energy/carbon tax, which gave Europe (and the Commission) a stronger international profile on global issues such as climate change (see Sbragia, 1999). Because the tax was a fiscal measure, certain states opposed it in principle. Nevertheless, the Member States have had to adapt to protect their interests by sustaining a blocking coalition in other issue areas. Perhaps even more important, Member State governments were forced to pursue different strategies to protect their interests in this setting: they must seek to define the environmental problem and solution far in advance of the Council stage in areas where qualified majority voting applies (Héritier et al, 1996, pp160–161).

This behaviour argues strongly for the importance of an institutional approach, which also recognizes the increasing impact of the European Parliament and the ECJ in a way not fully captured by neofunctionalism (Arp, 1993). Jordan in his introductory paper (1999a) records how the Court supported informal integration against the wishes of individual states. The Court ruled in favour of the Parliament and the Commission in the titanium dioxide case (Koppen, 1993, pp126–149), and it has directly supported the environmental *acquis* by ruling against the Commission when it argued that a Wallonian law on wastes violated the free movement of goods (Lenschow and Zito, 1998).

In evaluating the direction the EU institutions have taken towards constructing new environmental regulations, the ideational-epistemic literature provides a different set of insights. However, the call for new ideas in this time period is as much a question of justifying political options as opposed to trying to understand complex issues within the context of a high degree of problem uncertainty (policy uncertainty being the favourable condition for epistemic communities). The subsidiarity principle is a good case in point.

During the rapid expansion of environmental regulation prior to 1992–1993 new ideas were prominent and arguably helped actors to promote EU task expansion. The Fourth and Fifth EAPs reflect the ideas that national and EU actors were considering. A key theme of the Fifth EAP was sustainable development. This has three critical elements: (1) integration of the environmental priorities into other societal activities; (2) greater participation of all relevant actors; and (3) greater internalization of external costs (Collier, 1997, p5). All three principles suggest a recalibration of EU environmental policy, leading to an expansion in the EU's role. Policy integration expands the scope of EU environmental policy actors to participate in the decision-making for other areas such as the Regional Development Fund (see Lenschow (1999); see also Lenschow (1997, pp111–113)).

Even if one accepts the intergovernmentalist premise, the ideas explanation illuminates how the discourse led to policies that did not always reduce regulatory burdens. For example, the shared-responsibility theme suggested the need for new kinds of legislation and policy instruments that would increase private actors' regulatory role as long as minimum EU standards were met. The importance of getting private actors to regulate themselves and the subsidiarity concept are all ideas tied to the emphasis of sustainable development on actor involvement and shared responsibility (Collier, 1997; Lenschow and Zito, 1998).

The policy networks approach also has a greater analytical utility in this period, although it is difficult to identify policy networks consistently pushing task expansion. Much of the important expansion into new regulatory areas occurred prior to 1986 – for example, the creation of the Waste and Water Framework Directives. Nevertheless, the elaboration and amendment of substantive policies within these areas is more likely to preoccupy the technical experts in DG XI, the national environmental ministries and interested private groups than involve substantial intergovernmental decision-making – unless the issue is of such vital national interest that it requires top-level political involvement (Peterson, 1997).

The greater prominence of pro-environment institutions also spurs the creation of policy networks. The European Parliament's Environment Committee has become part of an institutional alliance and network of interests promoting stronger environmental EU regulations (Judge, 1993). Economic interests are also devoting greater attention to DG XI's activities and are trying to exert more influence within these admittedly fluid networks (Mazey and Richardson, 1998). This greater attention partially explains the change in regulatory philosophy witnessed at the end of the period. Moreover, the Commission and national environmental ministries have changed their focus on what constitutes effective environmental regulation and are seeking to create conditions that favour the appearance of networks. The Commission has tried to use private organization and public awareness to prevent Member States violating EU standards (Héritier et al, 1996; Jordan, 1999a). Ward and Williams (1997, pp448–453) note how DG XI has pushed an innovative Green Paper to build networks with regional and local authorities in the area of urban environment. Although not binding on Member States, this document nevertheless constitutes task expansion.

Finally, the struggle to integrate environmental priorities into other EU sectoral areas suggests very strongly the utility of the policy network approach, which helps to gauge the opposition to pro-environment forces. Environmental interests are trying to insert themselves into comparatively stable policy sectors where stronger, more identifiable networks among Commission, national ministry, and interest-group officials are likely to exist. In sectors such as the Common Agricultural Policy there are more cohesive economic and producer networks seeking to resist the incursion of pro-environment interests (Lenschow, 1997; 1999).

Post-1993: Task Expansion or Retrenchment?

Although the data in Table 9.1 are suggestive of continued regulatory expansion, many of the important trends discernible in the early 1990s have carried over in the current era. The 1995 data show a considerable decline in task expansion; the expansion witnessed in the period 1993–1994 may be a function of a backlog of proposals that the EU process has since eliminated. Of course, one should not extrapolate too far on the basis of one year's results. In fact, the latest edition of Haigh's (1998, Section 2.2) handbook suggests that 1995 (only 22 items adopted) was an anomaly, with 43 and an unprecedented 51 items of environmental legislation adopted in 1996 and 1997, respectively (see McCormick, 1998; Mazey and Richardson, 1998). In his introductory paper, Jordan (1999a) identified the Santer Commission's preference for using Green and White Papers to stimulate environmental action, backed up by regulation when it is absolutely necessary (McCormick, 1998, p194; Mazey and Richardson, 1998). Nevertheless, a number of recent developments may yet spark further environmental task expansion, such as the Amsterdam Treaty provisions (Jordan, 1998). The increased Scandinavian presence in the Council of Environment Ministers may also encourage the EU to expand its environmental scope, particularly if important external 'shocks', such as international negotiations and high-profile environmental disasters, trigger a sudden demand for concerted action.

Neofunctionalism, as traditionally defined, struggles to account for the changing momentum, typified by the current decline in Commission proposals. With its supranational expectations the approach cannot capture fully the fact that Commission activity may not be decreasing but rather channelled into new areas. This reality of continued Commission activity geared towards new aims also presents difficulties for intergovernmentalism. Elements of this change do highlight the importance of national preferences. The perspective that Member States have taken on subsidiarity and the impact of environmental regulation on economic competitiveness has altered the strategy of environmental regulators.

Nevertheless, a 'new' institutional analysis presents a more complicated picture of this process, with institutions such as the Parliament having a more autonomous role. The new Council decision-making rules have forced actors to pay attention to how the agenda is shaped; the Commission has retained its ability to influence and even guide this agenda through discussion papers and new instruments. Environmentally progressive actors in the Commission can only hope that increased information about how well Member States are addressing environmental problems (see Jordan, 1999a) will induce the public and environmental organisations to seek change.

The shift in direction towards regulatory expansion is consistent with an ideational explanation. The Commission may still seek to promote its organizational objectives of protecting the EU environment, but the means of doing so have had to be adapted to fit the real politik. The Auto-oil Programme, which involves the Commission, fuel producers, and car manufacturers in a tripartite negotiation process shows how task expansion continues without recourse to command-and-control instruments. Policy networks, oriented towards individual sectors, do not capture the overall nature of this change although the discussions in the policy networks probably are shaping the utilization of the available ideas.

Conclusions

Under which conditions do the five analytical approaches work best? I suggest that their explanatory power varies across the different stages of the task expansion process. It is therefore worth differentiating between the two broad phases of task expansion: (1) the initial period when regulatory parameters and frameworks are being set out for the policy area; (2) a subsequent period during which the *acquis communautaire* is fleshed out and amended. Macro-level theories seem better suited to the period 1957–1972, whereas the ideational-epistemic and policy network approaches come into their own in the second period (1972–1987). However, even in this second phase one cannot abandon international explanations – much of EU environmental policy continues to be shaped by external international actors, forces, and problems, and by the preferences of particular states. Mid-range theories have difficulty encompassing these factors although ideational explanations, such as those concerning epistemic communities, recognize that the ideas may have an international origin.

If one takes the theoretical approaches in turn, neofunctionalism remains a plausible theory for the period of task expansion up to 1991–1992. However, it makes a key assumption, namely that the Member State governments are willing to let the Commission take the lead in setting the agenda and defining the scope of EU activity. It is more likely that the Commission will do so when the issues are very technical, have low saliency among the national publics, and involve wildlife conservation and process regulations. Nevertheless, it is unwise to rely solely on neofunctionalism because it cannot explain the slackening pace of task expansion, the change in regulatory philosophy in the 1990s, or highly politicized cases of policy-making.

The intergovernmentalist approach, especially when supported by principal-agent analysis, suggests that the Commission's agenda-setting role may be conforming to national preferences; it thus offers a plausible explanation of pre-1992 task expansion. This is most likely to be true in highly politicized issues and product regulations where Member State economic interests are clearly defined and forcefully. articulated. The more technocratic policy areas present the difficult cases. Intergovernmentalism does not allow for the independent impact of the European Parliament and the ECJ on legislative outputs, such as the Auto-oil Programme and the philosophical switch to less regulatory forms of intervention.

As Weale (1996) argues, the role of institutions is critical throughout the history of a policy area. Institutional structures have defined the way in which EU actors have expanded the EU policy scope. Nevertheless, a 'new' institutionalist approach seems most appropriate during periods of institutional stability. Institutionalist accounts can explain how actors reacted to the non-incremental change which was operative in the early 1970s and early 1990s, but they struggle to explain instances of sudden change.

On the whole the ideational-epistemic perspective seems to explain how many of the regulatory outputs were framed, but there is no one idea (or overarching epistemic community) that accounts for the ebb and flow of task expansion since 1957. Individual ideas, such as sustainable development and subsidiarity, explain some of the changes since the SEA. However, it is difficult to tell how much the change is the result of independent ideas, and much is related to actors seizing on ideas as rhetorical weapons to protect bureaucratic, national, or other pre-existing interests. Ideas are likely to be powerful when causal beliefs come under challenge – owing for example to the challenge of new, unknown problems – and when policy-makers have to choose between several different and contentious policy directions.

The policy network framework has similar limitations. It can explain the course of action taken in specific issue-areas, especially where policy networks are present, but no single policy network seems to have provided the momentum to drive EU task expansion over the four time periods. For this reason, we should not completely dismiss either the policy network or the ideational approaches. Given the inherent limitations of international relations theory, we should take our cue from Corbey (1995) and Peterson (1995) and explore *combinations* of theories. An explanation of EU task expansion requires the ability to explain the stability or instability of policy-making in the system and to explore specific outcomes. To illustrate some possibilities, when there is little pressure on the EU system to change the nature of its environmental policy, an institutionalist analysis of the EU system combined with policy networks may explain the task expansion periods. When Member States are strongly divided on key issues, an intergovernmentalist approach helps to explain the systemic constraints whereas ideational explanations explain the specific policy direction. This theoretical strategy lacks parsimony, but it does provide the means for explaining task expansion and the absence of a single theory of task expansion.

References

Arp, H. A. (1993) 'Technical Regulation and Politics: The Interplay between Economic Interests and Environmental Policy Goals in EC Car Emission Legislation', in Liefferink, J. D., Lowe P. D. and Mol, A. P. J. (eds) *European Integration and Environmental Policy*, London: Belhaven Press, pp150–171.

Bomberg, E. (1994) 'Policy Networks on the Periphery: EU Environmental Policy and Scotland' *Regional Politics and Policy*, Vol.4, pp45–61.

Burley, A. and Mattli, W. (1993) 'Europe before the Court: a Political Theory of Legal Integration' *International Organization*, Vol.47, pp41–76.

Collier, U. (1997) 'Sustainability Subsidiarity and Deregulation: New Directions in EU Environmental Policy' *Environmental Politics*, pp61–23.

Corbey, D. (1995) 'Dialectical Functionalism: Stagnation as a Booster of European Integration' *International Organization*, Vol.49, pp253–284.

Cram, L. (1993) 'Calling the Tune without Paying the Piper? The Role of the Commission in European Union Social Policy' *Policy and Politics*, Vol.21, pp135–146.

Garrett, G. and Tsebelis, G. (1996) 'An Institutionalist Critique of Intergovernmentalism' *International Organization*, Vol.50, pp269–299.

Gehring, T. (1997) 'Governing in Nested Institutions: Environmental Policy in the European Union and the Case of Packaging Waste' *Journal of European Public Policy*, Vol.4, pp337–354.

Goldstein, J. and Keohane, R. O. (1993) 'Ideas and Foreign Policy: An Analytical Framework', in Goldstein, J. and Keohane, R. O. (eds) *Ideas and Foreign Policy: Beliefs. Institutions, and Political Change*, Ithaca, NY: Cornell University Press, pp3–30.

Golub, J. (1996a) 'State Power and Institutional Influence in European Integration: Lessons From the Packaging Waste Directive' *Journal of Common Market Studies,* Vol.34, pp313–339.

Golub, J. (1996b) 'British Sovereignty and the Development of EC Environmental Policy' *Environmental Politics,* Vol.5, pp700–728.

Golub, J. (1997) 'The Path to EU Environmental Policy: Domestic Politics, Supranational Institutions, Global Competition', paper presented at the 5th Biennial ECSA Conference, Seattle, WA; copy available from the European Community Studies Association, Pittsburgh, PA.

Haas, E. (1958) *The Uniting of Europe: Political, Social, and Economic Forces 1950–1957,* Stanford, CA: Stanford University Press.

Haas, P. (1990) *Saving the Mediterranean,* NY: Columbia University Press.

Haas, P. (1992) 'Introduction: Epistemic Communities and International Policy Coordination' *International Organization,* Vol.46, pp1–35.

Haigh, N. (1997) *Manual of Environmental Policy: The EC and Britain,* Harlow, Essex: Longman.

Haigh N, (1998) *Manual of Environmental Policy: The EC and Britain,* Harlow, Essex: Longman.

Héritier, A., Knill, C. and Mingers, S. (1996) *Ringing the Changes in Europe,* Berlin: De Gruyter.

Hildebrand, P. (1993) 'The European Community's Environmental Policy, 1957 to "1992": From Incidental Measures to an Iinternational Regime', in Judge, D. (ed) *A Green Dimension for the European Community: Political Issues and Processes,* Portland, OR: Frank Cass, pp13–44.

Hix, S. (1994) 'The Study of the EC: The Challenge to Comparative Politics' *West European Politics,* Vol.17, pp1–30.

Johnson, S. P. and Corcelle, G. (1989) *The Environmental Policy of the European Communities,* London: Graham and Trotman.

Jordan, A. J. (1998) 'Step Change or Stasis? EC Environmental Policy after the Amsterdam Treaty' *Environmental Politics,* Vol.7, pp227–236.

Jordan, A. J. (1999a) 'The Construction of a Multilevel Environmental Governance System' *Environment and Planning C: Government and Policy,* Vol.17, pp1–17.

Jordan, A. J. (1999b) 'European Community Water Standards: Locked in or Watered Down?' *Journal of Common Market Studies,* Vol.37.

Judge, D. (1993) '"Predestined to Save the Earth": The Environment Committee of the European Parliament', in Judge, D. (ed) *A Green Dimension for the European Community: Political Issues and Processes,* Portland, OR: Frank Cass, pp186–212.

Koppen, I. (1993) 'The Role of the European Court of Justice', in Liefferink, J. D., Lowe, P. D. and Mol, A. P. J. (eds) *European Integration and Environmental Policy,* London: Belhaven Press, pp126–149.

Lenschow, A. (1997) 'Variation in EC Environmental Policy Integration: Agency Push within Complex Institutional Structures' *Journal of European Public Policy,* Vol.4, pp109–127.

Lenschow, A. (1999) 'The Greening of the EU: The CAP and the Structural Funds' *Environment and Planning C: Government and Policy*, Vol.17, pp91–108.

Lenschow, A. and Zito, A. R. (1998) 'Institutional Linkages Across EC Economic and Environmental Policy Realms' *Governance*, Vol.11, pp415–441.

Lindberg, L. and Scheingold, S. (1970) *Europe's Would be Polity: Patterns of Change in the European Community*, Englewood Cliffs, NJ: Prentice Hall.

Litfin, K. 1994, *Ozone Discourses*, NY: Columbia University Press.

McCormick, J. (1998) 'Environmental Policy: Deepen or Widen?' in Laurent, P. H. and Maresceau, M. (eds) *The State of the European Union Volume 4: Deepening and Widening*, Boulder, CO: Lynne Rienner, pp191–206.

Maddox, B. (1992) 'UK Threat to European Green Laws' *Financial Times*, 9 July, p8.

March, J. and Olsen, J. 1989 *Rediscovering Institutions: The Organizational Basis of Politics*, NY: The Free Press.

Marks, G., Hooghe, L. and Blank, K. (1996) 'European Integration from the 1980s' *Journal of Common Market Studies*, Vol.34, pp341–378.

Mazey, S. and Richardson, J. (1993) 'Environmental Groups and the EC: Challenges and Opportunities', in Judge, D. (ed) *A Green Dimension for the European Community: Political Issues and Processes*, OR: Frank Cass, Portland, pp109–128.

Mazey, S. and Richardson, J. (1998) 'Framing and Re-framing Public Policy in the EU: Ideas, Interests and Institutions in Sex Equality and Environmental Policies', paper presented at the annual ECPR Joint Sessions of Workshops, Warwick University; copy available from ECPR Central Services, University of Essex, Colchester, Essex.

Moravcsik, A. (1993) 'Preferences and Power in the European Community: A Liberal Intergovernmentalist Approach' *Journal of Common Market Studies*, Vol.31, pp473–522.

Pentland, C. (1973) *International Theory and European Integration*, NY: The Free Press.

Peters, B. G. (1992) 'Bureaucratic Politics and the Institutions of the European Community', in Sbragia, A. (ed) *Euro-politics*, DC: The Brookings Institution, Washington, pp75–122.

Peters, B. G. (1994) 'Agenda-setting in the European Community' *Journal of European Public Policy*, pp19–26.

Peterson, J. (1995) 'Decision-making in the European Union: Towards a Framework for Analysis' *Journal of European Public Policy*, Vol.2, pp69–93.

Peterson, J. (1997) 'States, Societies and the European Union' *West European Politics*, Vol.20, pp1–23.

Pierson, P. (1996) 'The Path to European Integration: A Historical Institutionalist Analysis' *Comparative Political Studies*, Vol.29, pp123–163.

Pollack, M. (1994) 'Creeping Competence: The Expanding Agenda of the European Community' *Journal of Public Policy*, Vol.14, pp95–145.

Pollack, M. (1996) 'The New Institutionalism and EC Governance' *Governance*, Vol.9, pp429–458.

Pollack, M. (1997) 'Delegation, Agency, and Agenda Setting in the European Community' *International Organization*, Vol.51, pp99–134.

Raustiala, K. (1997) 'Domestic Institutions and International Regulatory Co-operation: Comparative Responses to the Convention on Biological Diversity' *World Politics,* Vol.49, pp482–509.

Rehbinder, E. and Steward, R. (1985) *Environmental Protection Policy, Volume 2: Integration Through Law: Europe and the American Federal Experience*, Berlin: De Gruyter.

Rhodes, R.A.W. (1988) *Beyond Westminster and Whitehall: The Sub-central Governments of Britain,* London: Unwin Hyman.

Rhodes, R. A. W., Bache, I. and George, S. (1996) 'Policy Networks and Policy-making in the European Union: A Critical Appraisal', in Hooghe, L. (ed) *Cohesion Policy and European Integration: Building Multi-level Governance*, Oxford: Oxford University Press, pp367–387.

Richardson, J. (1994) 'EU Water Policy: Uncertain Agendas, Shifting Networks and Complex Coalitions' *Environmental Politics*, Vol.3, pp139–167.

Richardson, J. (1996) 'Actor-based Models of National and EU Policy Making', in Kassim, H. and Menon, A. (eds) *The European Union and National Industrial Policy,* London: Routledge, pp20–51.

Sbragia, A. (1993) 'EC Environmental Policy: Atypical Ambitions and Typical Problems?', in Cafruny, A. and Rosenthal, G.(eds) *The State of the European Community: Maastricht Debates and Beyond*, Boulder, CO: Lynne Rienner, pp337–352.

Sbragia, A. (1996) 'The Push-pull of Environmental Policy-making', in Wallace, H. and Wallace, W. (eds) *Policy-making in the European Union 3rd edition*, Oxford: Oxford University Press, pp235–255.

Sbragia, A. (1999) 'From Laggard to Leader: the EU, Institution Building and the Politics of Climate Change' *Environment and Planning C: Government and Policy,* Vol.17, pp53–68.

Taylor, P. (1975) 'The Politics of the European Communities: The Confederal Phase' *World Politics,* Vol.27, pp336–360.

TFEIM, 1990, 1992 *The Environmental Dimension: Task Force Report on the Environment and the Internal Market Task Force Environment and the Internal Market,* Berlin: Economica.

Tsebelis, G. (1990) *Nested Games: Rational Choice in Comparative Politics*, Berkeley, CA: University of California Press.

Vogel, D. (1993) 'Representing Diffuse Interests in Environmental Policy-making', in Weaver, R. K. and Rockman, B. A. (eds) *Do Institutions Matter? Government Capabilities in the United States and Abroad,* Washington, DQ: The Brookins Institution, pp238–271.

Ward, S. and Williams, R. (1997) 'From Hierarchy to Networks? Sub-central Government and EU Urban Environment Policy' *Journal of Common Market Studies,* Vol.35, pp439–464.

Weale, A. (1992) *The New Politics of Pollution*, Manchester: Manchester University Press.

Weale, A. 1996, 'Environmental Rules and Rule-making in the European Union' *Journal of European Public Policy,* Vol.3, pp594–611.

Weale, A. (1999) 'European Environmental Policy by Stealth: The Dysfunctionality of Functionalism?' *Environment and Planning C: Government and Policy,* Vol.17, pp37–51.

Zito, A. R. (1995) *European Union Environmental Policy-making: Contending Approaches to Institutional Decision-making*, unpublished PhD thesis, Department of Political Science, Pittsburgh, PA: University of Pittsburgh.

Zito, A. R. (1998) 'Epistemic Communities and European Integration', paper presented at the annual ECPR Joint Sessions of Workshops, Warwick; copy available from author.

10

Pace-setting, Foot-dragging and Fence-sitting: Member State Responses to Europeanization

Tanja A. Börzel

Introduction

Europeanization is a two-way process. It entails a 'bottom-up' and a 'top-down' dimension. The former emphasizes the evolution of European institutions as a set of new norms, rules and practices, whereas the latter refers to the impact of these new institutions on political structures and processes of the Member States. For a long time, European studies have been mostly concerned with the bottom-up dimension, exploring the underlying dynamics and potential outcomes of the European institution-building process (see Chapter 9). In recent years, however, a literature has emerged which analyses the impact of the evolving European system of governance on the domestic institutions of the Member States (Cowles et al, 2001; Goetz and Hix, 2000; Héritier et al, 2002). Without denying the two-way nature of Europeanization, most studies self-consciously concentrate on one side of the equation. They 'bracket' European-level processes to analyse their effects at the Member State level or vice versa.

This chapter develops one approach to link conceptually the two dimensions of Europeanization. It focuses on the ways in which Member State governments both shape European policy outcomes and adapt to them. It is argued that national executives strive to minimize the costs which the implementation of European norms and rules may impose on their home constituencies. Therefore, they have a general incentive to upload their domestic policies to the European level. The better the fit between European and domestic policies, the lower the implementation costs at the national level. Since Member States have distinct institutions, they compete at the European level for policies that conform to their own interest and approach (Héritier et al, 1996). But not only do national governments pursue competing policy preferences depending on the level of domestic regulation, they also diverge in their capacity to participate in the European policy contest. Given the heterogeneity of their preferences and action capacities, the strategies of Member States in responding to Europeanization may vary significantly.

In order to develop this argument, this chapter proceeds in two steps. The first part presents a conceptual framework, which strives to account for the different ways in which Member States have responded to Europeanization. Three strategies are distinguished: pace-setting, ie actively pushing policies at the European level, which reflect a Member State's policy preference and minimize implementation costs; foot-dragging, ie blocking or delaying costly policies in order to prevent them altogether or achieve at least some compensation for implementation costs; and fence-sitting, ie neither systematically pushing policies nor trying to block them at the European level but building tactical coalitions with both pace-setters and foot-draggers. What kind of strategy a Member State is likely to adopt depends mainly on its level of economic development, which largely influences the degree of domestic regulation and the action capacities of a Member State, particularly in the area of regulatory policy.

This chapter draws on evidence from the field of EU environmental policy-making to illustrate how Member States engage in different strategies when responding to Europeanization. It also looks at the southern Member States, which have been largely neglected by the literature.

Europeanization as Two-way Process: Policy Up- and Downloading

One way of linking the bottom-up and top-down dimensions of Europeanization is to focus on the role of the Member State governments in the ascending and descending stage of the European policy process. 'Member States seek to shape European policy-making according to their interests and institutional traditions. At the same time they have to adapt their institutions to European legislation once the latter has been enacted' (Héritier, 1994, p278; Héritier et al, 1996; see also Wallace, 1971). This is not to say that supranational actors, such as the European Commission or the European Parliament, are irrelevant to European policy-making. Nor do Member State governments necessarily gate-keep the access of domestic interests to the European policy arena (Moravcsik, 1994, 1998). Nevertheless, national executives hold a key position in both the decision-making and the implementation of European policies and thus influence the way in which Member States shape Europeanization and adapt to it.

Without entirely taking on the theoretical baggage of two-level game approaches (Putnam, 1988; Evans et al, 1993), the European policy process can be conceptualized as a 'reciprocal relationship' (Andersen and Liefferink, 1997a, p10; Liefferink and Andersen, 1998b) between political negotiations at the domestic and the European level. At the domestic level, actors pressure their national executives to pursue policies at the European level that are favourable to their interests. At the European level, the Member State governments push for

European policies that satisfy domestic pressures, while minimizing their adverse consequences at the domestic level (Putnam, 1988, p434). Two-level game approaches establish a systematic relationship between domestic and European politics, with the national governments functioning as the core intermediaries between the two. Furthermore, two-level game approaches provide a link between the ascending (decision-making) and the descending (implementation) stage of the European policy process. Except for treaty revisions, European decisions are legally binding for Member States, and hence do not require ratification at the domestic level. Yet, while regulations are directly applicable, national parliaments must transpose directives into national law. Moreover, both regulations and transposed directives have to be practically applied and enforced by national administrations. Compliance problems with respect to European policies often arise when public administrators, and economic and societal actors, are not willing to bear the implementation burden (Börzel, 2000). They usually blame their national governments for the costs which European policies impose on them. At the same time, the Member State governments are held responsible by the Commission and the European Court of Justice if European policies are not properly implemented and complied with. Consequently, Member State governments tend to be somewhat cost sensitive in European policy-making.

An effective strategy to maximize the benefits and minimize the costs of European policies is to upload national policy arrangements to the European level. Firstly, uploading reduces the need for legal and administrative adaptation in downloading, that is, incorporating European policies into national policy structures. The more a European policy fits the domestic context, the lower the adaptation costs in the implementation process. In the absence of an elaborate policy structure, 'misfitting' European policies may still inflict significant costs since these structures have to be built up in the first place. Secondly, uploading prevents competitive disadvantages for domestic industry. Imposing strict standards on lower-regulating Member States maintains the competitive situation of the industry in higher-regulating countries. Likewise, European liberalization and deregulation policies open new markets for industries from low-regulating countries that benefit from lower production costs. Finally, uploading may enable national governments to address problems which preoccupy their constituencies but can no longer be dealt with effectively at the domestic level (eg organized crime, environmental pollution, or immigration).

Member States share a general incentive to upload their policy arrangements to the European level. But since they have distinct social, political and economic institutions, they often compete for policies that conform to the preferences of their constituencies (Héritier, 1996; Héritier et al, 1996). Thus, the British government, which runs a country with a somewhat open economy, may push for liberalization and deregulation in a policy sector. The French government, by contrast, wishes to defend its traditional approach of protecting certain industries from external competition (Ambler and Reichert, 2001). Likewise, high-regulating countries strive to harmonize their strict social or environmental standards at the European level where they may meet the vigorous opposition of industrial latecomers who want to avoid competitive disadvantages for their industry. But not only do Member State governments pursue diverging and often competing policy preferences, they also differ in their capacity to engage successfully in the European policy contest.

Pace-setting, Foot-dragging and Fence-sitting

Member States' responses to Europeanization are shaped, firstly, by their policy preferences and, secondly, by their action capacity. Both factors appear to be closely linked to the level of economic development, particularly in the area of regulatory policies. Highly industrialized and urbanized states have developed strict regulations which they wish to harmonize at the European level, and they command the necessary resources to do so. Industrial latecomers, by contrast, have neither the regulations nor the capacity for uploading. They wish to maintain their lower level of regulation to catch up with the industrially more advanced countries. Depending on their preferences and capacities, Member State governments may pursue three different strategies in defending their interests in the European policy contest.

Pace-setting

Pace-setting involves the active shaping of European policies according to domestic preferences. Ideally, domestic policies are exported to the European level and subsequently adopted by other Member States. If the strategy is successful, the subsequent downloading of the European policy creates few problems for the pace-setter, who can easily incorporate it into existing arrangements. In environmental policy, the pace-setters are called 'leaders', 'pioneers', 'forerunners' or 'first-comers'. Germany, The Netherlands and Denmark, together with the three Member States Austria, Sweden and Finland, which joined in 1995, have repeatedly shaped European policies according to their domestic preferences and priorities. These six countries are industrial states that have strict, highly differentiated legal regulations of environmental pollution in all media accompanied by just as highly differentiated state implementation arrangements. They have a strong incentive, therefore, to harmonize their high standards at the European level. First, high-regulating states strive to co-ordinate their efforts in fighting environmental pollution where its cross-boundary nature renders unilateral measures less effective. European air pollution control, for instance, started as an attempt by some Member States to fight the killing off of massive forests caused by certain air emissions, such as sulphur dioxide (SO_2) and nitrogen oxides (NO_x) being carried long distances. Second, high-regulating states would like to obtain favourable competitive conditions for their domestic industries and avoid environmental dumping in low-regulating Member States. Thus, German companies have repeatedly complained that they must invest more in environmental measures than any of their European competitors. Chemical firms have pressed the German government to spread their higher costs of compliance with environmental standards by means of stricter European laws across the other Member States. Likewise, German car manufacturers strongly opposed the setting of speed limits to fight air pollution and supported the mandatory imposition of catalytic converters throughout Europe, in which they had invested in order to export to the American market (Aguilar Fernández, 1997, p105). Harmonizing strict standards is often also supported by pan-European multinational firms, since it is in their operational interest to have only one set of EU rules to comply with rather than 15 different sets of national regulations. Third, high-regulating states hope to reduce the costs of adaptation by implementing European environmental policies. Incorporating 'alien' elements into a dense, historically grown regulatory structure that is ingrained in a particular state tradition can impose considerable costs, both material and cognitive. Procedural regulations, like the Integrated Pollution Prevention and Control Directive, which prescribe the evaluation of potentially harmful activities, contradict highly sectorized administrative structures with the medium-specific approach that they have developed in many countries. The incorporation of such integrated policy measures requires comprehensive legal and administrative adaptation to preserve the consistency of the regulatory framework. Adaptation is often rendered even more difficult because administrators tend to be reluctant to give up traditional problem-solving approaches and policy instruments, which they consider have proved effective in fighting environmental pollution (Knill and Lenschow, 2001). Fourth, national governments are anxious to respond to the 'green' demands articulated within their political systems. In the face of substantial environmental degradation and dramatic accidents such as Seveso and Chernobyl, environmental awareness and societal activism tends to be high in industrial societies. Societies expect their governments to push for effective environmental regulations at the European and international levels. Finally, high-regulating states may have an interest in expanding technology markets for their own industry. Compliance with strict environmental standards provides industry with a powerful incentive to develop and improve 'green' technologies, which can then be exported as 'best available technology' to lower-regulating countries to help them adapt to more stringent European standards (cf Héritier et al, 1996, pp10–15, 23–28).

High-regulating countries share a common interest in harmonizing their environmental standards at the European level. However, they differ significantly with respect to the regulatory structures, as a result of which they often compete for environmental rules and regulations that conform to their own interests and regulatory principles (Héritier, 1996). Britain and Germany, for instance, have opposing problem-solving philosophies as to how best to protect the environment. The German precautionary approach is based on strict emission standards that can only be complied with by applying the best available technology. The British approach, by contrast, is more reactive. It relies on quality standards and allows for weighing the economic costs against the ecological benefits of a policy. These two problem-solving philosophies, which emphasize different policy instruments, are hard to reconcile. The European Large Combustion Plant Directive of 1988, for instance, follows the German approach and thus imposes significant costs for the UK (Boehmer-Christiansen and Skea, 1991). The British administration was forced to adapt its regulatory approach, which has traditionally been based on voluntary regulation and negotiation with industry. It was forced to give way to more formal regulation. While German industry gained a competitive advantage because it already applied best available technologies to reduce harmful emissions, the British had to invest in new abatement technologies whose major producers happened to be German. The situation was reversed when the British successfully pushed for procedural regulations which entail a cross-media approach and aim at increasing public participation in pollution prevention and control. The European Directives on environmental impact assessment, access to environmental information, and integrated pollution prevention and control put considerable pressure on the highly sectorized structure of the German environmental administration and its tradition of administrative secrecy. In order to implement these European Policies, German environmental legislation is to undergo comprehensive reform. After the project to integrate all sectoral legislation into one environmental act (*Umweltgesetzbuch*) failed as a result of fierce resistance by the specialized environmental administration, as well as parts of industry and environmental groups, the German government limited its ambitions and opted for a framework law (*Artikelgesetz*), which lays down general principles for the application of sectoral legislation (Börzel, 2003).

Pace-setting not only presupposes established domestic policies but also the capacity to push them through the European negotiation process, very often against the opposition of other Member States with diverging policy preferences, This is not merely a question of voting power in the Council of Ministers, particularly since qualified majority voting has become more prevalent.[1] Smaller countries have effectively shaped European policies. Denmark managed to transform its national plan for the aquatic environment into the Urban Waste Water and Nitrate Directives (Andersen and Liefferink, 1997a, p14), while The Netherlands convinced the other Member States to adopt its high standards for small car and truck emissions (Axelrod and Vig, 1998, p77). Offering expertise and information to the European Commission in the drafting of policy proposals is a very effective way of injecting national preferences into the European policy process (Zito, 2000; Jänicke, 1990). Another is the strategic employment of national environmental bureaucrats in Brussels for up to three years. The Commission often asks the Member States to second experts with specific knowledge to help prepare a directive (cf Héritier, 1994; Liefferink and Andersen, 1998b, pp264–266). Coalition-building and interest accommodation skills provide a third important source of influence in shaping European policies. The Dutch have a particular reputation for working out complicated, tailor-made compromises which are acceptable to all parties involved (Andersen and Liefferink, 1997, pp27–28). But being present in the various networks that prepare and accompany the European negotiation process demands considerable staff power, expertise and information, which the Member States do not have to the same degree. The German Ministry of the Environment, for instance, counts some 900 employees and the Federal Environmental Agency has another 850 experts working in the field. The Dutch core environmental administration employs about 1500 people (Hanf and Gronden, 1998, p171).[2] Not surprisingly, German and Dutch experts are omnipresent in the environmental committees and hearings of the various European institutions like the Commission, the Council, the European Parliament, the Economic and Social Committee or the Committee of the Regions. High-regulating countries can offer practical and technical expertise and information not only to European policy-makers: the Commission in particular is responsive to the policy demands of environmental forerunners since their stringent legislation could distort trade, thereby jeopardizing the functioning of the single market (Sbragia, 2000, p240). Thus the EU, which had already adopted a Directive on beverage containers in 1985, passed the Packaging and Packaging Waste Directive in 1994 to accommodate recycling of other materials. The Directive was a reaction to emerging Danish, Dutch and German legislation that could potentially develop into trade restrictions (Haverland, 1999). Likewise, Germany successfully brought about the setting of stringent car emission exhaust regulations at the European level by threatening to introduce US standards unilaterally (Andersen and Liefferink, 1997, p15).

Since EU decision-making entails a need for consensus and coalition-building, no single Member State is able ultimately to win the regulatory contest and systematically shape EU environmental policies according to its regulatory style and tradition. Even if a Member State manages to frame a policy proposal according to its domestic arrangements, it cannot entirely control the dynamics of the European negotiation process. Germany successfully uploaded its regulatory approach for drinking water, and the European Drinking Water Directive of 1980 was largely modelled on the German regulation. Yet, some of the European standards became more stringent than the German ones. As a result it took Germany over 12 years, and a conviction by the European Court of Justice, to comply with the Directive. Major proposals for environmental legislation are subject to substantial intergovernmental bargaining in the Council of Ministers. European policy decisions (eg the eco-tax) not only require the consent of a certain number, if not of all Member States, but also have to accommodate the position of the European Parliament, whose co-decision powers have become considerably strengthened over the last few years and which usually takes a 'green' position (cf Weale et al, 2000, pp123–130). Given the heterogeneity of domestic regulations and policy preferences, European environmental legislation does not provide a coherent regulatory framework, but resembles a 'patchwork' (Héritier, 1996) where different regulatory approaches are sometimes linked within one single policy. In the absence of a consistent regulatory framework, each Member State is likely to face costly policies, which it has to download from the European level. This is a major reason why Germany has an implementation record that has started to resemble that of a laggard rather than a leader (see Figure 10.1). In general, Germany appears to have lost some of its former enthusiasm for functioning as 'the motor behind EU environmental policy' as it did in the 1980s (Liefferink and Andersen, 1998a, p71). Unification imposed a considerable economic burden on Germany. Sluggish economic growth and high unemployment have led to a certain shift in German priorities and dampened public and government ambitions for increased environmental protection (Pehle, 1997). While Germany has become a more reluctant pace-setter, the UK has increasingly developed from an initial footdragger into an occasional leader. Whether Britain ever qualified as an environmental 'laggard' (Sbragia, 2000, p251) has been contested in the literature. Britain is an industrialized state that has one of the oldest systems of environmental protection. Some consider it even a 'pathfinder in many areas of legislation and regulation' (Carter and Lowe, 1998, p20). After its accession to the EC, Britain was able to implement most EC environmental directives under existing laws

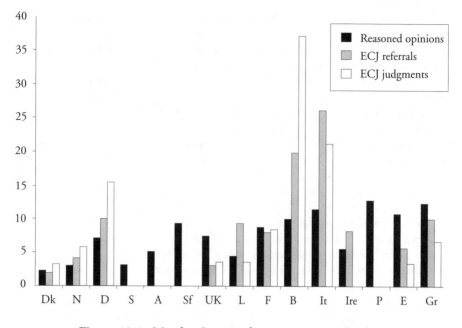

Figure 10.1 *Member State Performance in Downloading
EU Environmental Policies*

Source: Database on Member State compliance with Community law compiled on the basis of the infringement cases individually listed in the annexes of the Annual Reports on the Monitoring of Community Law, 1984–1999. The numbers of reasoned opinions for Finland, Austria and Sweden are likely to be skewed since the three countries joined only recently, and are still in the process of implementing the *acquis communautaire*. Neither have they therefore faced any proceedings before the European Court of Justice.[3]

Key: A = Austria, B = Belgium, D = Germany, Dk = Denmark, E = Spain, F = France, Gr = Greece, Ire = Ireland, It = Italy, L = Luxembourg, N = Netherlands, P= Portugal, S = Sweden. Sf = Finland, UK = United Kingdom.

with only minor administrative adjustments necessary. But with the gathering pace of European environmental policy in the 1980s, the British government found itself in repeated opposition to Commission drafts, which at that time were influenced by the German regulatory approach; the imposition of uniform air and water quality standards upset the British regulatory style with its emphasis on ad hoc, pragmatic and piecemeal regulation. Subsequently Britain earned itself the reputation of a 'laggard' and the 'dirty man of Europe'. At the beginning of the 1990s, however, the British position started to change. Having become aware of the considerable costs that European environmental policy may impose, the Department of the Environment adopted a more proactive role at both the national and European level (Jordan, 2001). The Environmental Protection Act of 1990 not only brought the UK into compliance with European legislation of the 1980s, but put it into the position of setting the pace in several areas of European environmental policy. British policy initiatives were facilitated because the

Commission had turned away from a German-influenced vertical 'command-and-control' approach of imposing strict substantive standards and instead moved towards horizontal measures with general cross-sectoral application. Procedural regulations which adopt an integrated approach, such as the Environmental Impact Assessment Directive, the Access to Information Directive and the eco-auditing regulation are prime examples of Britain's successful pace-setting strategy (cf. Héritier et al, 1996, pp207–265; Lowe and Ward, 1998).

Finally, environmental leaders may choose different ways of setting the pace in European policy-making. Liefferink and Andersen distinguish between *forerunners*, *pushers* and *pushers-by-example* (Liefferink and Andersen, 1998a, b; Andersen and Liefferink, 1997a) (see Chapter 4). Forerunners, like Denmark, focus on fighting pollution primarily at the national level. They wish to maintain the freedom to develop and implement their own national policies. European policies are welcome so long as they promote domestic policy goals. However, they must not constrain the autonomy of a Member State to set stricter standards. Pushers, like The Netherlands and Germany, by contrast, emphasize European cooperation to fight and prevent pollution since unilateral measures are considered as insufficient. High domestic standards are maintained but within the limits of European law. Pushers-by-example, like Sweden, finally, seek to combine the two approaches by using unilateral measures as a tool to encourage European initiatives. The domestic level serves as an experimental field to develop innovations in environmental policy which, if successful, are uploaded to the European level to be adopted by other Member States.

Irrespective of the way in which they strive to set the pace, the six environmental pace-setters are the makers of EU environmental policies and have shaped their Europeanization. They have consistently taken the initiative on environmental matters in the Council, and enact progressive national statutes. Consequently, their compliance with European environmental law is above average (see Figure 10.1)

Foot-dragging

Foot-dragging is exactly the opposite of pace-setting. It aims at stopping or at least containing the attempts of other Member States to upload their domestic policies to the European level. While foot-dragging is seldom able to prevent costly policies altogether, it aims at obtaining some compensation in the form of side-payments or package deals. Since such compensation is often insufficient to cover the costs, foot-draggers tend to show a poor level of compliance with Community law. In environmental policy, they are therefore often denounced as 'laggards'. Portugal, Greece, Spain, Italy and Ireland[4] are industrial latecomers whose regulatory structures are less developed than those of the firstcomers. They are reluctant to accept more stringent measures and hardly ever advance proposals of their own (Liefferink et al, 1993b, p7; La Spina and Sciortino, 1993, p228). First, less demanding regulations constitute a competitive advantage over high-regulating countries due to lower production costs, while complying with stringent protection requirements places a heavy financial burden on industry and hampers its efforts to catch up with the industrialized countries. Second, strict European standards provide no new sales opportunities. On the contrary, they may work as trade barriers until low-regulating countries have adapted. Moreover, in order to achieve compliance, companies often have to import environmental technology from firstcomers. Thirdly, latecomers are particularly averse to the costs of environmental policies since increasing the standard of living and generating employment are still the overriding priorities on their political agenda. Environmental protection is often viewed as having a sharp trade-off against economic development and employment creation (Yearley et al, 1994). Fourthly, since environmental awareness and ecological activism are only just emerging in these countries, policy-makers feel less pressure to take environmental measures and gain little support for enforcing costly policies. Green parties and environmental organizations have small constituencies. Social mobilization tends to centre around local environmental problems, suggesting a link between territory and environmental awareness (Pridham, 1994, p96; Kousis, 1994). While public concern for the environment is rising, people are still reluctant to accept protection measures that may impose significant costs. Finally, building up regulatory structures is often even more expensive than fitting European policies into historically grown and comprehensive domestic arrangements. New administrative units, procedures and technologies have to be established for the practical application and enforcement of European policies. In order to monitor compliance with the Drinking Water Directive effectively, Spain, for instance, envisioned an investment of US$52.9 million for the necessary extension and modernization of its national monitoring networks. Additional investments are necessary to build up staff power with the necessary technical and scientific knowledge to apply environmental regulations and assess compliance at the local level.

Latecomers face a double disadvantage in the European regulatory contest. Since their regulatory structures are less developed, they lack policies to upload to the European level. But even if they had such policies, they would lack sufficient staff power, money, expertise and technology actively to shape European policies. Latecomers have a limited number of administrators and scientific experts, who cannot draw on a lifetime's experience of fighting environmental pollution (Font and Morata, 1998; Spanou, 1998). Nor do they have the knowledge or information which they could contribute to the development of European solutions to cross-boundary problems, such as air pollution or toxic waste – problems which they only begin to experience as their industrialization gets up to full speed. Environmental latecomers have great problems in finding sufficiently qualified people to participate in the various networks preparing and accompanying the making of European environmental policies or to apply for jobs in the Commission. Their national networks in the European policy-making bodies, comprising both permanent and temporary staff, are small compared to those maintained by the environmental pace-setters. Instead of shaping environmental policies, environmental latecomers often emulate policy solutions from high-regulating countries, as the Catalans did when they modelled their waste management system on German legislation. Latecomers are policy-takers rather than policy-makers. Before Greece, Portugal and Spain joined the European Community in the 1980s, environmental policies had been only weakly developed. European policies became the determining factor in the development of their environmental regulatory structures through the downloading of EU directives (Pridham, 1996; Font and Morata, 1998; Spanou, 1998).

Since latecomers have neither the incentive nor the capacity to push or support strict European measures, they try to block or delay them, hoping at least to gain temporary exemptions (derogations), financial compensation (side-payments) or concessions in other issue areas (package deals). For example, the southern latecomers vigorously opposed the Large Combustion Plant Directive mentioned above, arguing that their particular economic circumstances would make it difficult to meet strict EU standards. Spain in particular emphasized its rapidly growing energy needs, which it met predominantly by coal-fired power stations. As the third largest SO_2 emitter in Europe (after Germany and the UK), its large combustion plants would either have to invest significantly in abatement technologies or to import better quality coal. Since coal mining is the main source of economic activity in the areas where Spain's two major power stations are located, the latter option appeared as costly as the former. Although in the end they did not block the Directive, Spain, Greece and Portugal traded their consent for exemptions from the reduction requirements.[5] In the negotiations on the Single European Act, the environmental latecomers linked their support for the single market, with its implied higher standard of environmental protection, to the issue of the structural funds (Weale et al, 2000, p45). And in exchange for the extension of qualified majority voting envisioned by the Maastricht Treaty, Spain and Ireland demanded financial compensation for Member States who could not easily bear the costs of environmental protection. Germany, in particular, rejected the idea of a European environmental fund. The conflict was ultimately resolved in a package deal. The latecomers' approval of extended qualified majority voting was literally bought by the establishment of the cohesion fund of which about 50 per cent were dedicated to financing the implementation of EU environmental policies in Spain, Portugal, Greece and Ireland. Spain alone received about US$7 billion from the fund during the period 1993–1999 (Font and Morata, 1998, p222).

Financial assistance granted by the cohesion fund and other EU environmental programmes could cover up to 50 per cent of the implementation costs. But this is often insufficient to compensate for the weak implementation capacities of environmental latecomers. The Urban Waste Water Treatment Directive of 1994 is a case in point. It obliges Member States to provide urban agglomerations with systems for collecting and treating waste water. Adequate facilities were largely missing in the low-regulating countries. In Spain, two-thirds of the treatment facilities did not comply with the requirements of the Directive. To finance the building of new facilities and the upgrading of existing ones, the Spanish water treatment plan of 1995 envisioned public investments of about US$9.5 billion, which is five times more than Spain had invested in waste water treatment between 1985 and 1993. The cohesion fund will cover less than half of the total costs.

The regulatory contest in European policy-making exacerbates the capacity problems of industrial and environmental latecomers. They would like their industrialization to catch up with other Member States. At the same time, however, they have to download European policies and build up regulatory structures to fight environmental pollution that most of the rich and high-regulating countries established only after they had completed their industrialization process.

High costs and low capacity often make it difficult, if not impossible, for latecomers to comply effectively with European environmental law. It is hardly surprising that foot-draggers and policy-takers, such as Greece, Spain and Portugal, have a worse compliance record than the pace-setters and policy-makers (see Figure 10.1).

Fence-sitting

Fence-sitting is a more ambivalent strategy, which consistently aims neither at initiating or promoting specific policies at the European level, nor at preventing the attempts of others to do so. Fence-sitters neither set the pace nor put the brake on EU policies. Rather, they tend to take an indifferent and neutral position, or they build changing coalitions with pace-setters and foot-draggers, depending on the issue involved. In environmental policy, Belgium, France, Ireland, Italy, Luxembourg, and to some extent the UK, sit on the fence between environmental first-comers and latecomers (Andersen and Liefferink, 1997a, p6; Holzinger, 1994). Fence-sitters do not share the strong incentive of pace-setters for uploading, nor would they always have the action capacity to do so. Their level of environmental regulation ranges between the first- and the latecomers. As a result, they anticipate fewer costs in downloading European policies. At the same time, their industry does not necessarily gain competitive advantage from strict, EU-wide standards, and neither does it suffer significant disadvantage. Governments may also face less pressure from their societies to push for 'green' standards because environmental protection ranks lower among the political priorities of the electorate. Finally, fence-sitters tend to lack the action capacity systematically to shape European policies according to their interests. With less pronounced policy preferences and/or constrained action capacities, Member States are likely to take a neutral or indifferent stance in the European policy-process, and to engage in changing coalitions, respectively.

Fence-sitting is likely if, first, Member States do not anticipate any significant costs resulting from the uploading attempts of others because they have similar policies in place which can be easily adapted. The French regulatory framework is less coherent and mixes elements of the German formalistic 'command-and-control' approach with the British style of using flexible standards which leave room for negotiations with the target groups (Larrue and Chabason, 1998; Héritier et al, 1996, pp203–207). Therefore, France feels more at ease with adapting to such diverse European policies as the Drinking Water and the Environmental Impact Assessment Directives. This does not mean, however, that France is not concerned with adaptational costs and competitive (dis)advantages for its industry. France has often taken a reluctant or indifferent position in the regulatory contest among the environmental pace-setters. However, in the 1990s, it occasionally started to act as a 'friendly onlooker' and 'hesitant pace-setter' (Héritier, 1996, pp262–276). In the fields of ambient air quality and SO_2 products for liquid fuel, for instance, France sought to influence the regulatory contest in its favour, being supported by the UK in the former case and by Germany, The Netherlands, and Denmark in the latter (Héritier, 1996, pp262–276).

Second, fence-sitters may miscalculate the costs involved in downloading a European policy or do not give much importance to the issue. When Britain joined the EC in 1973, it failed to take environmental directives very seriously since they could be easily incorporated into existing legislation. With the EC becoming more active, however, '[i]t was a shattering blow when it became apparent that we were going to have to spend a very considerable sum of money' as a British official put it (cited in Golub, 1994, p126). Thus, Britain had agreed to the Urban Waste Water Treatment Directive in 1991, but two years later asked the EU to delay the implementation deadline since the costs for Britain turned out to be five times greater than the original estimates (Sbragia, 2000, p252).

Third, fence-sitters may hope to achieve policy results which they have not been able to deliver at the domestic level due to their constrained action capacities. By shifting the blame on to Brussels, governments strive to overcome decisional paralysis by claiming that they were outvoted or did not want to be isolated at the European level. Scapegoating Brussels for inconvenient policy decisions works particularly well in Member States with low action capacity but high public support for European integration, like in Italy or Belgium (Lewanski, 1998).

Fence-sitters, finally, may prefer to avoid costly European policies simply by not implementing them rather than raising opposition in the decision-making process. Italy, Belgium and Luxembourg have consented to European policies although they know that they do not have sufficient action capacity to implement them effectively. Thus, these three countries have supported the pace-setters on the issue of climate policy despite the anticipated high costs (Skjærseth, 1994). They largely refrain from foot-dragging because blocking European policies is difficult to reconcile with the pro-integration stance they wish to convey (Giuliani and Piattoni, 2001; Beyers et al, 2001). Instead of pressing for compensation or exemptions, they tend to minimize costs at the implementation stage by circumventing inconvenient obligations. Not surprisingly, the implementation record of the fence-sitters is closer to the foot-draggers than the pace-setters, and in the case of Belgium and Italy is even worse (see Figure 10.1).

Conclusions

The literature has identified a wide range of factors, both country-specific and policy-specific, which may influence the strategy a Member State government is likely to pursue in trying to shape European policy outcomes (Héritier et al, 1996; Andersen and Liefferink, 1997b). While not denying the relevance of these various factors, this chapter argues that at least in the area of regulatory policy, there are two factors, which are particularly important for the ultimate strategy choice – policy preferences and action capacity. Both factors are largely influenced by the level of economic development of a Member State, broadly measured by gross domestic product (GDP) per capita. Economically advanced countries are more likely to act as pace-setters and policy-makers at the European level since they have strict regulations and a strong incentive as well as the necessary resources to upload them. Economically less advanced countries, by contrast, lack both the policies and the action capacity necessary for uploading. They are therefore more prone to engage in foot-dragging. Member States with a medium level of economic development, finally, tend to have a medium-high level of regulation and a medium-low action capacity and therefore often sit on the fence, neither systematically pushing policy initiatives nor consistently opposing those of others.

Note, however, that those are general propositions that only indicate which strategy a Member State is likely to pursue. The ultimate strategy choice may still vary from policy sector to policy sector and sometimes even from policy issue to policy issue. Moreover, the dominant strategies of a Member State can change over time. Some have only reluctantly realized that Europeanization increasingly may challenge long-standing political, ideological and cultural traditions. The UK is the most striking example. In some policy areas, such as the environment, telecommunications or transport, it developed from a foot-dragger and fence-sitter into an active pace-setter (Héritier et al, 1996, 2002). Germany, by contrast, seems to be moving in the opposite direction. Since the early 1990s, it has repeatedly played the role of an obstructer rather than a promoter of European policy initiatives.

If the level of economic development has a strong influence on the ways in which Member States respond to Europeanization, the question arises as to whether their diverging preferences and strategies give rise to interest coalitions, which pitch industrial firstcomers in the north against industrial latecomers in the south. European environmental policy-making has indeed been characterized by a leader–laggard dynamic where the leaders or pace-setters push the Community process along, drawing the laggards up to their levels of environmental protection (Haas, 1993; Héritier, 1994). This 'push-pull' process (Sbragia, 2000) has not only promoted environmental progress at the European level, but repeatedly given rise to substantial tensions between northern leaders and southern laggards, which can also be observed in other policy areas (structural policy, consumer protection, transport). The southern latecomers tend to view EU environmental legislation as imposing the standards of the 'rich north' on the 'poor south' (Aguilar Fernández, 1993, pp232–233; Yearley et al, 1994). This view is based on their perception that EU environmental policies are tailored to the economic interests and environmental concerns of the industrialized north. The regulatory contest among high-regulating countries produces policy outcomes that not only impose high implementation costs, but also do not necessarily address the most pressing environmental problems of the south. 'The environmental problems of the peripheral countries, which basically embrace soil erosion, desertification, and forest fires, have been traditionally put aside in comparison with the problems of countries at the centre; namely, air pollution, waste management, control of chemical substances, and so on' (Aguilar Fernández, 1994, p105). If environmental latecomers increasingly feel compelled to implement policies that are costly and do not take into account their economic and environmental concerns, the regulatory contest in EU policy-making may not only exacerbate their capacity problems but also undermine their willingness to comply. This is not to suggest that European environmental regulations should become less ambitious. Yet the EU has to come to terms with the dynamics of the regulatory contest, which threatens to undermine the effectiveness and legitimacy of its policies. While a high level of regulation is necessary and desirable, environmental latecomers need to be given more time and flexibility to adapt. Moreover, they have to be assisted in coping with the costs. Flexibility and capacity-building could be combined by making assistance conditional on progress in implementation. Financial instruments to support the implementation of EU legislation would also have to be stocked up considerably. This, however, has already met resistance in current Member States, both in the north and the south. Finally, European policies should also focus more on specific environmental problems of latecomers, helping these countries to develop and implement adequate solutions. If EU policies are not sensitive to the economic and environmental concerns of latecomers, eastern enlargement (see Chapter 15) may indeed split the EU into 'leaders' and 'laggards' camps, with the latter clearly outweighing the former.[6] Since the logic of regulatory contest is not confined to environmental policy, this could have serious implications for the prospects of Europeanization.

Acknowledgements

For comments and suggestions I am grateful to Simon Bulmer, Bridget Laffan, Helen Wallace, John Peterson and two anonymous reviewers.

Notes

1   The six pace-setters can, in case of mutual agreement, form a blocking minority. Although actual voting seldom takes place, the 'shadow of the vote' (Weiler, 1991) has increased the ability of the 'green' Member States to extract concessions from the others (Holzinger, 1997).

2   The Italian Environmental Ministry, on the other hand, employs about 400 people (Lewanski, 1998, p139) and the French 500 (Larrue and Chabason, 1998, p68).

3   In order to compare their non-compliance with EU environmental law, the scores of the Member States were 'standardized' since they differ in their years of EU membership. First, the number of reasoned opinions, referrals to the European Court of Justice (ECJ) and ECJ judgments of the individual Member States were divided by their years of membership. Second, these average scores were added and made to equal 100 per cent. Finally, the percentage of the average scores for each Member State was calculated.

4   Italy is an environmental and industrial latecomer, but has largely caught up with the firstcomers. Its environmental regulations are also more developed than those of the other latecomers, even though its implementation capacity is rather weak (Lewanski, 1998). As a result it has acted as a fence-sitter rather than a foot-dragger in European policy-making (see below). Ireland has leaned more towards the foot-draggers, but increasingly strives to promote a 'green' image (Coyle, 1994). These two Member States are therefore considered as fence-sitters rather than foot-draggers (see below).

5   Spain believes that postponing the introduction of emission reduction measures by five years saved it some US$3.5 billion (Aguilar Fernández, 1997, p108).

6   In an enlarged EU the six pace-setters will no longer be able to present the lowering of existing environmental standards, since they can no longer form a blocking minority.

References

Aguilar Fernández, S. (1993) 'Corporatist and Statist Design in Environmental Policy: The Contrasting Roles of Germany and Spain in the European Community Scenario', *Environmental Politics*, Vol.2, No.2, pp223–241.

Aguilar Fernandez, S. (1994) 'Spanish Pollution Control Policy and the Challenge of the European Union', *Regional Politics and Policy*, Vol.4, No.1 (special issue), pp102–117.

Aguilar Fernández, S. (1997) *El Reto Del Medio Ambiente. Conflictos e Intereses en la Politica Medioambiental Europea* Madrid: Alianza Universidad.

Ambler, J. S. and Reichert, M. S. (2001) 'France: Europeanism, Nationalism, and the Planned Economy', in Zeff and Pirro (2001), pp29–57.

Andersen, M.S. and Liefferink, D. (1997a) 'Introduction: The impact of the Pioneers on EU Environmental Policy' in Andersen, M. S. and Liefferink, D. (eds), pp1–39.

Andersen, M. S. and Liefferink, D. (eds) (1997b) *European Environmental Policy: The Pioneers* Manchester: Manchester University Press.

Axelrod, R. S. and Vig, N. J. (1998) 'The European Union as an Environmental Governance System', in Vig, N. J. and Axelrod, R. S. (eds), *The Global Environment: Institutions, Law, and Policy*, Washington DC: CQ Press pp72–97.

Beyers, J., Kerremans, B. and Bursens, P. (2001) 'Belgium, the Netherlands, and Luxembourg: Diversity Among the Benelux Countries' in Zeff and Pirro (2001), pp59–88.

Boehmer-Christiansen, S. and Skea, J. (1991) *Acid Politics: Environmental and Energy Policies in Britain and Germany*, London: Belhaven Press.

Börzel, T. A. (2000) 'Why there is no Southern Problem: On Environmental Leaders and Laggards in the EU', *Journal of European Public Policy*, Vol. 7, No.1, pp141–162.

Börzel, T. A. (2003) *On Environmental Leaders and Laggards in the European Union: Why There is (Not) a Southern Problem,* London: Ashgate.

Carter, N. and Lowe, P. (1998) 'Britain: Coming to Terms with Sustainable Development?', in Hanf and Jansen (1998), pp17–39.

Cowles, M. Green, Caporaso, J. A. and Risse, T. (eds) (2001) *Transforming Europe: Europeanization and Domestic Change,* Ithaca, NY: Cornell University Press.

Coyle, C. (1994) 'Administrative Capacity and the Implementation of EU Environmental Policy in Ireland' in Baker, S., Milton, K. and Yearley, S. (eds), *Protecting the Periphery*, London: Frank Cass, pp62–79.

Evans, P. B., Jacobson, H. K. and Putnam, R. D. (eds) (1993) *Double-Edged Diplomacy: International Bargaining and Domestic Politics*, Berkeley CA: University of California Press.

Font, N. and Morata, F. (1998) 'Spain: Environmental Policy and Public Administration: A Marriage of Convenience Officiated by the EU?' in Hanf and Jansen (1998), pp208–229.

Giuliani, M. and Piattoni, S. (2001) 'Italy: Both Leader and Laggard' in Zeff and Pirro (2001), pp115–144.

Goetz, K. H. and Hix, S. (eds) (2000) 'Europeanised Politics? European Integration and National Political Systems', *West European Politics*, Special Issue, Vol.23, No.4.

Golub, J. (1994) 'British Integration into the EEC: A Case Study in European Environmental Policy', DPhil thesis, Department of Political Science, University of Oxford.

Haas, P. M. (1993) 'Protecting the Baltic and the North Seas' in Haas, P.M., Keohane, R. O. and Levy, M. A. (eds) *Institutions for the Earth: Sources of Effective International Environmental Protection,* Cambridge, MA: MIT Press, pp133–182.

Hanf, K. and Gronden, E. V. D. (1998) The Netherlands: Joint Regulation and Sustainable Development' in Hanf and Jansen (1998), pp152–180.

Hanf, K. and Jansen, A-I. (eds) (1998) *Governance and Environment in Western Europe: Politics, Policy and Administration,* Harlow: Longman.

Haverland, M. (1999) *National Autonomy, European Integration and the Politics of Packaging Waste,* Amsterdam: Thela Thesis.

Héritier, A. (1994) '"Leaders" and "Laggards" in European Clean Air Policy' in Unger, B. and Waarden, F. V. (eds) *Convergence or Diversity? Internationalization and Economic Policy Response,* Aldershot: Avebury, pp278–305.

Héritier, A. (1996) 'The Accommodation of Diversity in European Policy-making and its Outcomes: Regulatory Policy as a Patchwork', *Journal of European Public Policy,* Vol.3, No.2, pp149–176.

Héritier, A., Knill, C. and Mingers, S. (1996) *Ringing the Changes in Europe Regulatory Competition and the Redefinition of the State: Britain, France, Germany,* Berlin/New York: De Gruyter.

Héritier, A., Kerwer, D., Knill, C., Lehmkuhl, D. and Teutsch, M. (2002) *Differential Europe – New Opportunities and Restrictions for Policy Making in Member States,* Lanham, MD: Rowman & Littlefield.

Holzinger, K. (1994) *Politik des Kleinsten Gemeinsamen Nenners? Umweltpolitische Entscheidungsprozesse in der EG am Beispiel der Einführung des Katalysatorautos,* Berlin: Sigma.

Holzinger, K. (1997) 'The Influence of the New Member States on EU Environmental Policy Making: A Game Theory Approach' in Liefferink, D. and Andersen, M. S. (eds) *The Innovation of EU Environmental Policy,* Copenhagen: Scandinavian University Press, pp59–82.

Jänicke, M. (1990) 'Erfolgsbedingungen von Umweltpolitik im International Vergleich'. *Zeitschrift für Umweltpolitik,* Vol.3, pp213–232.

Jordan, A. (2001) 'National Environmental Ministries: Managers or Ciphers of European Union Environmental Policy?' *Public Administration,* Vol.79, No. 3, pp643–663.

Knill, C. and Lenschow, A. (2001) 'Adjusting to EU Environmental Policy: Change and Persistence of Domestic Administrations', in Green Cowles, M., Caporaso, J. A. and Risse, T. (eds), pp116–136.

Kousis, M. (1994) 'Environment and the State in the EU Periphery: The Case of Greece', *Regional Politics and Policy,* Vol.4, No.1 (Special issue), pp118–135.

Larrue, C. and Chabason, L. (1998) 'France: Fragmented Policy and Consensual Implementation', in Hanf and Jansen (1998), pp60–81.

La Spina, A. and Sciortino, G. (1993) 'Common Agenda, Southern Rules: European Integration and Environmental Change in the Mediterranean States', in Liefferink, Lowe and Mol (1993b), pp217–236.

Lewanski, R. (1998) 'Italy: Environmental Policy in a Fragmented State', in Hanf and Jansen (1998), pp131–151.

Liefferink, D. and Andersen, M. S. (1998a) 'Greening the EU: National Positions in the Run-upto the Amsterdam Treaty', *Environmental Politics*, Vol.7, No.3, pp66–93.

Liefferink, D. and Andersen, M. S. (1998b) 'Strategies of the "Green" Member States in EU Environmental Policy-making', *Journal of European Public Policy*, Vol.5, No.2, pp254–270.

Liefferink, D., Lowe, P. and Mol, A. P. J. (1993a) 'The Environment and the European Community: The Analysis of Political Integration', in Liefferink, Lowe and Mol (1993b), pp1–13.

Liefferink, D., Lowe, P. D. and Mol, A.P. J. (eds) (1993b) *European Integration and Environmental Policy*, London/New York: Belhaven.

Lowe, P. and Ward, S. (eds) (1998) *British Environmental Policy and Europe,* London: Routledge.

Moravcsik, A. (1994) 'Why the European Community Strengthens the State: Domestic Politics and International Cooperation', Working Paper 52, Cambridge, MA: Harvard University Press.

Moravcsik, A. (1998) *The Choice for Europe: Social Purpose and State Power From Rome to Maastricht,* Ithaca, NY: Cornell University Press.

Pehle, H. (1997) 'Germany: Domestic Obstacles to an International Forerunner' in Andersen, M. S. and Liefferink, D. (eds) *European Environmental Policy: The Pioneers,* Manchester: Manchester University Press, pp161–209.

Pridham, G. (1994) 'National Environmental Policy-making in the European Framework: Spain, Greece and Italy in Comparison', *Regional Politics and Policy*, Vol.4, No.1 (special issue), pp80–101.

Pridham, G. (1996) 'Environmental Policies and Problems of European Legislation in Southern Europe', *South European Society and Politics*, Vol.1, No.1, pp47–73.

Putnam, R. (1988) 'Diplomacy and Domestic Politics. The Logic of Two-Level Games', *International Organization*, Vol.42, No.2, pp427–460.

Sbragia, A. (2000) 'Environmental Policy: The "Push-Pull" of Policy-Making' in Wallace, H. and Wallace. W. (eds), *Policy-Making in the European Union,* Oxford: Oxford University Press, pp293–316.

Skjærseth, J. B. (1994) 'The Climate Policy of the EC: Too Hot to Handle?' *Journal of Common Market Studies*, Vol.32, No.1, pp25–45.

Spanou, C. (1998) 'Greece: Administrative Symbols and Policy Realities', in Hanf and Jansen (1998), pp110–130.

Wallace, H. (1971) 'The Impact of the European Communities on National Policy-Making', *Government and Opposition*, Vol.6, No.4, pp520–538.

Weale, A., Pridham, G., Cini, M., Kostadakopulos, D., Porter, M. and Flynn, B. (2000) *Environmental Governance in Europe: An Ever Closer Ecological Union?* Oxford: Oxford University Press.

Weiler, J. H. H. (1991) 'The Transformation of Europe', *Yale Law Journal*, Vol.108, No.8, pp2403–2483.

Yearley, S., Baker, S. and Milton, K. (1994) 'Environmental Policy and Peripheral Regions of the European Union: An Introduction', *Regional Politics and Policy*, Vol.4, No.1 (special issue), pp1–21.

Zeff, E. E. and Pirro, E. B. (eds) (2001) *The European Union and the Member States. Cooperation, Coordination, and Compromise*, Boulder, CO: Lynne Rienner.

Zito, A. R. (2000) *Creating Environmental Policy in the European Union*, Basingstoke: Palgrave.

Part 4
MAKING EU
ENVIRONMENTAL POLICY

11

Regulating Biotechnology: Comparing EU and US Approaches

Lee Ann Patterson and Tim Josling[1]

The United States and the European Union share a common desire to provide a safe food supply and credible regulatory systems. However, they have adopted two very different regulatory approaches to deal with the increasing numbers of genetically modified (GM) food and feed products coming to market. Consequently, the transatlantic relationship has become fraught with conflict over this issue. In August 2003, this conflict resulted in the US, Argentina, Canada, and Egypt filing a World Trade Organization (WTO) case against the European Union for suspending the approval of biotechnology products. In addition, the case was brought against several individual EU Member States that maintain a number of national marketing and import bans on biotechnology products. The US claims they have lost exports equalling at least US$1.8 billion due to the EU's sanctions.

This chapter explores the roots of this conflict and the potential impact of these two regulatory systems on international trade. We distinguish between producer protectionism, a commonly recognized trade impediment, and overprotection of consumers that can also have trade implications. One possible solution to the inherent conflict lies in product labelling. Consequently, we distinguish between positive and negative labelling and positive and negative attributes. The chapter concludes that leaving the labelling to producers and retailers of food would allow the market to work effectively and could allow the EU and the US to reach consensus without resulting in major trade disruptions.

Background

The introduction of transgenic crops into the food supply has highlighted both the successes and the failures of the multilateral trade system. On the one hand, trade liberalization in the GATT (General Agreement on Tariffs and Trade) and the WTO has ensured that domestic and international markets have become ever more entwined through trade, thus allowing producers and consumers alike to benefit from competition and economies of scale. On the other hand, the rules of such institutions are not well designed to mediate political disputes between domestic players arising from the differences in domestic application of food trade law. The introduction of new technologies, such as biotechnology for food, illustrates this dilemma. The present open trade environment allows domestic political and regulatory differences to spill over into the international arena, with serious and detrimental effects on trade relations.

The US and the EU have taken very different approaches to the introduction of GM crops. Trade tensions have been brewing for some years. But these differences do not have to lead to conflicts if the parties can recognize common ground and can see the issue as an opportunity for transatlantic co-operation. Both the EU and the US face essentially the same challenges with respect to the health and safety of the food supply and the credibility of the regulatory system. The agricultural sectors on both sides of the Atlantic have similar incentives to make use of scientific advances that allow new characteristics to be inserted into plants and animals to improve productivity and enhance utility. The medical biotechnology industry has achieved widespread public support with no apparent negative publicity in the EU. Perhaps time will mellow the European reaction to transgenic crops and the market will take care of any residual concerns through the use of non-trade-distorting labelling. Or perhaps US consumers will acquire some of the same sensitivities as their EU cousins and demand an end to the use of such new varieties. Either would illustrate an important process of convergence. If public opinion and the regulatory approach in the US and the EU converge, then trade conflicts will fade away. Unfortunately, any actual convergence has been slow and the apparent regulatory divergence has resulted in a WTO dispute settlement case that could result in a serious disruption in transatlantic relations.

Despite the involvement of the WTO, the issue is inherently one about domestic regulation, not international trade, and it arises from consumer sensitivities, not producer protectionism. The implication of this distinction is that we should look closely at administrative and political structures and consumer attitudes. We therefore examine the differences in regulatory assumptions and procedures on either side of the Atlantic, the explanations for these differences, the various transatlantic and multilateral organizations that may be able to facilitate reconciliation of these differences, the consequences of these differences, especially for trade, and finally possible market-based solutions.

Transatlantic Differences in Regulation

Substantial regulatory differences between the US and the EU in the area of biotechnology have been apparent for some time. Vogel (Chapter 13) has described the US as moving from a strict regulatory stance in the early 1980s to one that is now more permissive, while the EU has changed over the same period to a more conservative and cautious approach (see also Vogel, 2001). This 'crossover' is

Table 11.1 *Alternative Models of Biotechnology Regulation*

	Precautionary approach	Preventive approach
Philosophy of regulation	Proactive regulatory approach anticipates environmental hazards that have not already been documented but which could conceivably occur.	Reactive regulatory approach attempts to minimize environmental harm whenever the existence of harm has been scientifically demonstrated.
Basis of regulation	Regulation based on process by which product is produced.	Regulation based on safety, quality, and efficacy of product regardless of method of production.
Type of regulation	Horizontal Regulation: Cross-cutting regulations need to be adopted to ensure a basic level of human and environmental safety.	Vertical Regulation: Existing sectoral regulations modified to ensure human and environmental safety of new biotechnology products.

Source: Adapted from Patterson (2000)

evidence of the dynamic nature of regulatory policy faced with a rapidly developing technology and growing political pressure. Incidentally, it also casts doubt on rigid cultural explanations for the current transatlantic differences. Whether the EU was ever more permissive than the US in its treatment of biotechnology depends on how one interprets the diverse regulations in the Member States before the Single Market Programme. It is clear, however, that the major split between the US and the EU happened in the mid-1980s. Further divergence and polarization characterized the 1990s.

Underlying this divergence are two different models of biotechnology regulation (Patterson, 2000), which are juxtaposed in Table 11.1. The first model represents a regulatory paradigm that is process-based, horizontal, and precautionary. The second represents a more traditional product-based, vertical and preventive approach to regulation. Most countries employ a combination of the two paradigms depending on the aspect that is being regulated and the political and other pressures on the regulators. The clash between the two different philosophies of regulation is often seen as being at the root of current transatlantic tensions on biotechnology issues. But aspects of both models have played a role in the development of biotechnology regulations in the US and the EU.

The precautionary philosophy of regulation is usually associated with the 'precautionary principle' of risk management, which puts a priority on anticipating and guarding against environmental damage (O'Riordan et al, 2001). This principle is derived from German socio-legal tradition and gained recognition in the 1980s with the rapid development of environmental laws. The purpose of the principle is to guide political and regulatory action. The principle is based on preventive action to safeguard ecological space (even in advance of scientific proof or need), and places the duty of care (or onus of proof) on those who propose change (see EC Committee of the American Chamber of Commerce (1994, p70) and O'Riordan et al (2001)). Levidow and Tait summarize the precautionary principle as a conservative approach to risk in which regulation anticipates the sort of environmental harm which has not already been documented for a given category of products, and which does not take into consideration the relative costs and benefits of regulation to industry and the public (Levidow and Tait, 1992; Tait and Levidow, 1992).

A precautionary approach tends to impose stricter regulations on researchers and producers. Those advocating a precautionary approach to biotechnology argue that this is necessary to protect the environment from potentially catastrophic events. The possibility of the occurrence of such an event is heightened by the complexity of ecosystems which preclude unambiguous identification of cause–effect relations. Lack of experience with genetically modified organisms (GMOs) increases the degree of uncertainty about what their impact on ecosystems will actually be (Tait and Levidow, 1992, p223). In addition, proponents argue that a precautionary approach is necessary to allay public fears about new technologies, and about the desire of industry to capitalize on these technologies.

Opponents of the precautionary approach argue on the other hand that while caution is certainly necessary, most experiments fall into the low-risk category. Majone has argued that the precautionary approach suffers from a number of shortcomings such as the lack of a sound logical foundation, the potential for it to distort regulatory priorities and the relative ease with which it might be used to justify protectionist measures (Majone, 2002). Furthermore, establishing a precautionary set of regulations could stifle important life-enhancing research and industrial competitiveness by creating unnecessary bureaucratic delays or even moratoria. In contrast to this, a preventive approach concentrates on identifying the damage and risk associated with particular products. As Tait and Levidow remark, the approach seeks to respond to:

> *Scientifically proven adverse impacts that have arisen in earlier generations of products. New products and processes are screened to ensure that they do not give rise to any similar hazards. The regulatory system is built up slowly... Decisions about the need for regulation and the level of regulation required are taken in relation to the relevant benefits and costs* (Tait and Levidow, 1992, p221).

Consequently, advocates of the preventive approach prefer a case-by-case and step-by-step approach to regulation, where rules are based on demonstrated harmfulness, different experiments are assessed on the basis of different risks, and different steps in the research and production process are examined according to the specific risks involved in each step. In this way, scientists can proceed and, in the process, accumulate knowledge that will help to clarify what the risks actually are. This approach still introduces bureaucratic delay as compared to an absence of regulations, but at least it guarantees some degree of flexibility.

To sum up, a product-based approach to regulation means that in the same way as food products are evaluated for product safety, quality, and efficacy and are regulated in a 'vertical' manner, all tomatoes, for instance, whether they were produced by genetic modification, cross-breeding, chemical or radiation mutagenesis, would be evaluated for human and environmental safety using the same criteria. On the other hand, process-based regulation would require a new 'horizontal' approach to regulation. Under this approach all recombinant DNA (rDNA) products including food products, livestock, drugs, pesticides, decontamination products and medical devices would be subject to the same set of safety regulations.

The EU followed the product-based model in the early 1980s. Prior to the widespread utilization of rDNA techniques in a variety of industries, most products were evaluated according to the safety, quality and efficacy of the final product, not according to the process by which the product was produced. The widespread use of rDNA, however, led some policy-makers to advocate regulations based on the process by which products were produced. The Directorate General for the Environment (DG Environment) gave the following justification for this new regulatory approach in a widely distributed pamphlet:

> *The new techniques of genetic engineering allow the identification of many useful genes and their transfer to other organisms that didn't possess them before. Biological barriers are bypassed and new organisms are created with novel properties not previously existing in nature. Micro-organisms with novel properties could cause adverse effects in the environment if they survive and establish themselves, out-competing existing species or transferring their novel traits to other organisms* (European Commission, DG XI/A/2, n.d.).

In the US, by contrast, the precautionary approach reigned at least until 1984. In case after case, regulatory decisions emphasized precaution and minimal risk to consumers and the environment. It reached its peak in the Delaney Clause to the Food, Drug and Cosmetic Act, which banned the use of any food additive if tests revealed that it caused cancer in either laboratory animals or humans (Chapter 13; see also Vogel, 2001). Air quality standards, pesticide restrictions, drug safety tests and ground water contamination rules all focused on the 'potential' rather than the 'probable' findings of hazards. Consistent use of scientific risk assessment was not a hallmark of US regulation. Yet by the mid-1980s, the positions were reversed: the US adopted a product-based, vertical, preventive approach, while the EC adopted a process-based, horizontal, precautionary approach to biotechnology regulation. This set the stage for the trade tensions that emerged at the end of the 1990s.

Reasons for the Transatlantic Differences in Regulation

Observers such as Vogel (Chapter 13) have suggested many reasons for the differences in regulatory approach and policy between the US and the EU. Some stress social and philosophical differences that have arisen from different historical experiences, along with differences in culture. Underlying cultural explanations are hard to quantify or even describe, if they exist at all. However, current policies may well reflect the (cultural) reaction to different pivotal events in recent history, as well as such factors as the different mix of political parties involved in policy-making, different rates of institutional capacity-building, and different institutional structures.

Some consumers in the EU seem to have a greater mistrust of technology, science, scientists, and policy-makers than consumers in the US. This has been exacerbated by several significant policy failures over the last few years. These include, among others, the failed promise that nuclear energy would be safe and clean. The meltdown of Chernobyl and the persistent problem of disposing of nuclear waste have led to a certain scepticism regarding scientific 'promises'. The more recent British policy debacle over bovine spongiform encephalopathy (BSE or 'mad cow disease') raised questions about policy-makers' allegiance to agribusiness over consumers, and the ability of EU institutions to protect EU consumers has come under question as health scandals continue in individual Member States (see Bomberg (1998); Echols (1998), pp525–543; Nelson (2001) and Vogel (Chapter 13)). Such scares cross product lines and include the scandal of AIDS-contaminated blood in France (which led to the death of 300 haemophiliacs), the cancer-causing dioxin contamination of feed in Belgium, and adulterated wine and olive oil. All of these have contributed to an overall feeling of distrust which has spilled over to genetically modified agricultural products.

The US has escaped the worst of these 'technological' crises. Having failed to embrace nuclear power to the same extent as several European countries, the US did not experience an equally strong public reaction against nuclear energy (the meltdown of the radioactive core at Three Mile Island notwithstanding). And there have been no large-scale threats to the food supply equivalent to mad cow disease, although the recent discovery of one case of BSE in the US cattle industry has resulted in a certain degree of caution among American consumers and America's trade partners. Perhaps as a result, the media portrayal of biotechnology in the EU has differed significantly from that in the US. In the US, the focus has been primarily on the positive health and environmental benefits to be gained from specific rDNA products. In Europe, especially the UK and Germany, the focus has been on 'Frankenfoods' and the problematic relationship between technology, society, large corporations, the environment and the state.

Political differences may also be significant. In particular, environmental parties have been more active in European politics than in American politics. The Green Party is an important player in several Member States and in the European Parliament. The Green Party's influence was felt as early as 1983 when it won 5.3 per cent of the national vote in Germany and secured 27 seats in the German Parliament. A major component of the Green Party's platform has been to promote the idea that GM foods may have a deleterious impact on both the environment and human health. The Greens have successfully used their influence within the European Parliament to shape the biotechnology debate (see Chapter 6). While the Green Party in the US has gained some momentum over the last few years, its influence with respect to actual biotechnology policy has been minimal at most.

Another reason for the differences in GM regulatory policy in the US and the EU is the difference in the institutional capacity that was in place to deal with complex, horizontal policy areas in the late 1980s and early 1990s when GM technology became more readily available. The EU, having just passed the Single European Act (SEA) in 1986 was actively involved in institution building, whereas the US had already established a system of interagency co-operation and consultation.[2] Administration of the regulations was more dispersed in the US.

In the EU, the DG Environment took the lead and set the standards that had to be met for the release or use of biotechnology products. Regulations were difficult to revise in the EU, and exemptions were not possible. In spite of (or perhaps because of) the dominance of DG Environment in the EU regulatory process, interagency (or inter-DG) co-ordination was not as effective in the EU as in the US. For instance, the EU only established an internal policy co-ordination mechanism that would allow a variety of perspectives to be considered in policy-making after adopting Directives 90/219 and 90/220, which are the key pieces of biotechnology legislation in the EU (Patterson, 2000; Patterson and Josling, 2002). Both these Directives were based on the precautionary approach. In addition, the lack of a US-style Federal Register process limited the input of scientists, special interests, other agencies and the public in general in the EU policy-making process. Because the rule-making process in the US was more open, and input from the scientific community easier to obtain, the system allowed for a more flexible response to new knowledge. Since 1990, the EU has built substantial institutional capacity and some of the initial problems in the early years of policy-making have been addressed. However, the passage of Directives 90/220 and 90/219 created a certain path dependency which has made it publicly and institutionally difficult, if not impossible, to redirect current policy.

Between 1992 and 1998, the EU approved 18 GM plants/crops for commercial marketing. The issue of labelling was not addressed until January 1997, when the Novel Foods Regulation was passed. According to this Regulation, only foods containing live GMOs or GMO-derived products that were no longer substantially 'equivalent' to traditional products, required labelling. Since both imported soya and maize were judged to be equivalent to traditional products, neither was required to bear a label indicating that it had been genetically modified. This resulted in a huge public outcry and, in June 1997, a technical adaptation to Directive 90/220 was introduced that essentially overturned the labelling provisions of the Novel Foods Regulation and required mandatory labelling of all GMOs approved for market. In the case of products placed on the market with mixtures of non-GM products, the label would indicate the possibility that GMOs 'might' be present. The issues of labelling and traceability have been central features of the development of EU policy since that time.

Although the EU's institutional capacity continued to evolve throughout the 1990s, trade tensions between the EU and the US continued to escalate. The EU approval procedure for GM crops is complicated and comprises a complex series of steps involving both the Commission and the Council (for an in-depth analysis of this process see Bradley (1998); Patterson (2000) and Sheldon (2004)). But the key to recent delays was the passage, in June 1999, of Council Decision 99/468/EC, which changed the voting procedure applied to GM crop approval to one in which only a qualified majority (as opposed to unanimity) was required to reject a proposal from the Commission. Under this new voting rule, Denmark, France, Greece, Italy and Luxembourg were able to declare that they would block future GM approvals. This amounted to a de facto moratorium on the introduction of new GM varieties into the EU and ultimately precipitated the WTO case brought by the US.

Further revision to Directive 90/220 occurred in 2001. Directive 2001/18/EC finally replaced Directive 90/220/EEC in 2003. It called for a scientific risk assessment to be carried out by the European Food Safety Authority (EFSA), the results of which were to be made public. After this, the Commission would develop a proposal for authorization which must be approved by a qualified majority of EU Member States. Product authorizations would be granted for a (renewable) period of ten years. The concept of substantial equivalence was abandoned, and the new legislation calls for all GM products to be labelled. Accidental traces of up to 0.9 per cent of authorized GM materials are exempt from labelling. Furthermore, Directive 2001/18/EC requires a system of traceability to be adopted, in which operators must transmit information at all stages of the marketing system and retain that information for five years in case any unforeseen risk arises to human health and the environment. By contrast, the US Food and Drug Administration (FDA) still follows the principles of substantial equivalence: labelling is required only in cases where a GM product is substantially different from an existing product, the GM product contains different nutritional properties, or it contains an allergen that would not normally be present in that food.

Transatlantic and Multilateral Attempts at Co-operation

The potential for trade conflicts between the EU and the US over GM foods, and the serious consequences that such conflicts could have for both the transatlantic relationship and the multilateral system of commercial rules, have spurred attempts to co-ordinate regulatory policies and reconcile differences. These attempts have been made at both the bilateral and the multilateral levels. However, to date, any successes have been overshadowed by the opportunity that such attempts offer for continued confrontation.

Bilateral attempts at co-operation

The Transatlantic Economic Partnership (TEP) of 1998, which grew out of the New Transatlantic Agenda of 1995, has made a limited impact in some areas of commerce. But one of the most elusive tasks for the TEP has been to improve commercial relationships in the area of agriculture and food trade between the US and the EU. The idea of the TEP was to encourage a spirit of co-operation rather than confrontation among regulatory agencies in the US and the EU. Several fora were created to bring together regulators from each side of the Atlantic, but to date there has not yet been the required political will to make such co-operation a natural way of defusing tensions.

In addition, several private sector or civil society structures were also set up including the Transatlantic Business Dialogue (TABD), the Transatlantic Consumer Dialogue (TACD) and, the Transatlantic Environmental Dialogue (TAED) (see Bignami and Charnovitz (2001), pp255–284, and Cowles (2001), pp213–233). The TABD has been successful in advocating and monitoring work on the mutual recognition of conformity assessments in a number of areas. The TACD has been concerned with public health issues including food safety. It has given particularly strong support to the mandatory labelling of genetically engineered food. The TAED was also originally intended to provide some balance to the business orientation of the TABD. However, it was not notably successful and suspended its activities in November 2000, due to lack of financial support from the US.

One concrete manifestation of the attempt to explore broad public consensus in biotechnology policy (as opposed to regulatory co-operation among government agencies) was the decision at the May 2000 US–EU Summit to create an EU–US Biotechnology Consultative Forum comprised of an 'independent group of experts representing diverse views on the two sides of the Atlantic' (EU–US Biotechnology Consultative Forum, 2000). The Forum provided a convenient opportunity for a review of the concerns and hopes for the new technology in the area of foods. The debate did not yield any surprises and the report covers most sides of the argument with some attempt at even-handedness. No action has followed the submission of the report. In short, despite minor successes here and there, transatlantic attempts at policy co-operation have generally failed, as clearly evidenced by the WTO case brought by the US against the EU in August 2003.

Multilateral attempts at co-operation

Biotechnology regulation appears on the agenda of a number of multilateral institutions. Consequently, tensions between the US and EU positions are often projected onto these bodies. Differences between the EU and the US can have a negative impact on these institutions. However, collaboration can strengthen them and make them more effective. The question is whether the institutions themselves offer the hope of avoiding trade conflicts across the Atlantic, or whether they provide just another platform for disagreements. The most important multilateral institutions dealing with issues of biotechnology are currently the Organisation for Economic Co-operation and Development (OECD), which has taken on a major role in the discussion, at least on a plurilateral level; the CODEX, which has responsibility for international standards on several aspects of food safety; and the WTO, which reluctantly finds itself in the hot seat on issues of trade impediments arising from national policies.

The OECD

The OECD has played an extremely important role in the formation of biotechnology policy since the early 1980s. Very early in the biotechnology policy debate, key policy-makers from several countries recognized that biotechnology was a policy area characterized by high levels of risk and uncertainty. In addition, biotechnology would have important implications for agricultural competitiveness and sustainability, and thus would benefit from a forum which would raise the debate above the realm of domestic politics. Consequently, the OECD has acted as a policy co-ordinator, information broker and forum for policy learning in the emerging field of biotechnology. An early and very influential attempt to agree some guidelines for biotechnology research was produced by the OECD's Group of National Experts (GNE) in 1986. The GNE was organized as part of the Committee for Scientific and Technology Policy and was composed of 80 experts from a wide variety of academic and professional backgrounds. In 1986, the GNE reached a consensus on guidelines to be used in biotechnology research based on the widely agreed rationale that there was no scientific basis for specific legislation to regulate the use of recombinant DNA organisms (OECD, 1986, pp7–8). In June 1999, the G8 heads of government invited the OECD Working Group on Harmonization of Regulatory Oversight of Biotechnology and the OECD Task Force for the Safety of Novel Foods and Feeds to undertake a study of the implications of biotechnology for food safety. These studies are still under way and the OECD continues to play an important advisory role. However, the OECD is limited in its ability to impose standards by its lack of enforcement powers.

CODEX and labelling

The Codex Alimentarius Commission (a joint FAO/WHO body) has played an important role in setting many international food standards. As a result of the widespread adoption of such standards, CODEX has become a widely recognized and highly respected organization. However, the problems of biotech foods have stretched its credibility and self-confidence. CODEX, on request from member countries, formed an Ad Hoc Intergovernmental Task Force on Foods Derived from Biotechnology which held its first meeting in March 2000. The meeting was attended by a wide variety of public officials from over 33 countries, five international governmental organizations, and about 14 international non-governmental organizations. The purpose of the meeting was to identify the work priorities and key concepts and definitions to be developed. At that meeting, the task force decided that it would proceed with the elaboration of two major texts. The first would address broad general principles for risk analysis of foods derived from biotechnology. This would include matters such as science-based decision-making, pre-market assessment, transparency and post-market monitoring. The second text would provide specific guidance on the risk assessment of foods such as food safety and nutrition, 'substantial equivalence', potential long-term health effects, and non-intentional effects. In addition, the task force agreed that a list of available analytical methods for the detection and identification of foods or food ingredients derived from biotechnology should be prepared. The task force continues to meet to discuss these issues. Without apparent agreement, transatlantic differences continue to be projected on to CODEX.

Another important CODEX committee that has become involved in the debate over biotechnology policy is the Committee on Food Labelling. This committee has established a set of proposed draft guidelines for labelling food and food ingredients obtained through genetic modification. In general, the committee advocates labelling when food and food ingredients are no longer equivalent to their conventional counterparts, and/or when they are composed of or contain a genetically modified organism or protein or DNA resulting from gene technology, and/or when they are produced from but do not contain genetically modified organisms, protein or DNA resulting from gene technology. But as a result of the wide variety of views on labelling and of domestic regulations in this area, no consensus has yet emerged.

The WTO

At the multilateral level, the issues of regulatory differences have posed problems for the GATT for many years. Under the 1947 GATT agreement, sanitary and phytosanitary measures that impinged on trade were covered by Article XX (b). This provision allows countries to employ trade barriers 'necessary to protect human, animal or plant life or health' which would otherwise be illegal so long as 'such measures are not applied in a manner which would constitute a means of arbitrary or unjustifiable discrimination between countries where the same conditions prevail, or as a disguised restriction on international trade' (Josling et al, 1996, p209). But Article XX had no teeth. Despite attempts in the Tokyo Round to improve Article XX, little was accomplished until the Uruguay Round (Patterson and Josling, 2002).

Intensive negotiations in the Uruguay Round led eventually to a new Sanitary and Phytosanitary (SPS) Agreement that tried to repair the faults of the existing code. This Agreement defined new criteria that had to be met when imposing regulations on imports more onerous than those agreed in international standards. These included scientific evidence that the measure was needed, assessment of the risks involved and recognition of the equivalence of different ways of testing and sampling. In addition, the dispute settlement mechanism was considerably strengthened under the WTO to make it easier to obtain an outcome that could not be avoided by the losing party.[3] Consequently, much was expected of the panel report in the beef hormone dispute between the EU on the one hand and Canada and the US on the other. This was widely seen as a test case for the new SPS Agreement. Though the panel and the subsequent appellate body reports did indeed clarify the scope and interpretation of the SPS Agreement, transatlantic trade tensions in this sector have not receded.

Although the new SPS Agreement represents a significant advance in rulemaking, it is difficult to say how effective it will be in curbing trade disputes arising from biotechnology. Many environmental and consumer groups fear that there will be an erosion of health and safety standards in the name of freer trade. The question of genetically modified foods poses a particularly difficult challenge to the SPS system.

In the focus on the SPS Agreement and its science test, the scope of the Technical Barriers to Trade (TBT) Agreement is often overlooked. This originated in the Tokyo Round but was modified somewhat in the Uruguay Round to ensure that it covered process-based regulations. This Agreement is, in fact, more likely to be the basis for a challenge to biotechnology food labelling regulations than the SPS Agreement. The SPS Agreement only covers regulations that are explicitly designed to protect plant, animal and human health. Any regulation that is not specified in these terms necessarily falls under the TBT Agreement (Heumeuller and Josling, 2001). Thus it is likely that a WTO action against a trade barrier arising from a technical regulation, standard or conformity assessment procedure will be judged by compliance with the TBT Agreement. This Agreement is not quite as strict in some respects as the SPS Agreement. It does not require a risk assessment and does not insist on scientific evidence as the main criterion for justification of a measure. But it is not by any means without constraints. It provides that technical regulations should be applied in a non-discriminatory way, should be used only in pursuit of legitimate objectives, and should be minimally trade-disruptive, taking into account the risks of not fulfilling the objective of the regulation. Risks should therefore be assessed, but in the broader context of a set of objectives that is not limited to health and safety issues. These legitimate objectives could include national security considerations and prevention of deceptive practices, as well as environmental protection. Indeed the list is open-ended, implying that countries might argue that such concerns as a consumer's right to know could be a legitimate objective for a technical regulation. Thus a TBT case involving GM labelling might hinge on whether there are less trade-disruptive alternative ways of informing consumers than a particular mandatory labelling regime.

Underlying the tensions between the US and the EU in the discussions about both the SPS and TBT Agreement are the different regulatory philosophies and practices described earlier in this chapter. The translation of these differences onto a multilateral stage mainly serves merely to emphasize them. Neither the SPS nor the TBT Agreement has caused a major change in domestic regulations in the US and the EU, though they could have made domestic regulators a little more circumspect.[4] But they have expanded the locus of discourse and provided a framework for disputes to be resolved.

The Consequences of Transatlantic Regulatory Differences

Differences in regulations can cause trade impediments, in areas of food law as in other sectors of commerce. Some of these impediments reflect different circumstances and different attitudes toward food safety. But many of the differences in food law are arbitrary, reflecting the action of separate legislatures writing regulations in various ways to the same end. Some of these differences are significant enough to generate strong vested interest in their perpetuation. Trade policy issues arise when regulatory differences both interfere with trade and are less-than-obviously justified by diverse circumstances (see Josling et al (2004)).

Under the rules of the multilateral trading system, domestic producers must not receive preferential treatment over foreign producers. The principle of 'national treatment' is enshrined in Article III of the GATT, now a part of the rules of the WTO. Most trade policy disputes that involve food safety regulations arise because this fundamental precept is thought to have been broken. However, biotechnology differs from other food issues in one crucial respect: its regulation is concerned more with consumers than with producers. Many GATT and WTO cases have involved an attempt by one party to provide protection to its domestic producers, often as a result of the 'capture' of the domestic regulatory process. The SPS Agreement negotiated in the Uruguay Round of GATT negotiations introduced the science test as a way to be able to distinguish such cases from genuine protection of animal, plant, and human health. Biotechnology regulatory policy, on the other hand, reflects a relatively new phenomenon, that of protecting domestic consumers from hazards, real or imagined. This has been referred to as 'consumer capture'. This form of capture has very different implications for trade compared to the more commonly discussed 'producer capture'.

The essence of consumer capture is that it is largely a domestic matter. Trade effects are of marginal importance to the protagonists. The debate on the adoption of the hormone that increases milk yields, Bovine Somatotropin (BST, also known as rBGH), has been largely about the effect on domestic milk markets, though some trading firms have been affected.[5] The irradiation of food is also a domestic issue, though some irradiated foods cross borders. The debate in the US has not been about whether to allow irradiated foreign food in, but rather about whether to allow the sale of such food on the domestic market regardless of its provenance. Seen in this light, the GMO conflict between the US and the EU is not primarily about trade, but about the adequacy of domestic food safety and environmental regulations themselves. The 'producer protection' problem is intrinsically a trade issue, as the producer is seeking protection from foreign suppliers. The 'consumer protection' problem affects all producers alike, and its influence on trade is less direct. Tight consumer regulations put up the cost of products on the domestic market but do not necessarily disadvantage the imported good relative to the domestic product.

Attempts by governments to discriminate against foreign suppliers can obviously be challenged under trade rules. But this has not happened in the GMO dispute, nor indeed was it a factor in the beef hormone case. Attempts to discriminate against domestic suppliers would be challenged immediately by domestic producer interests.[6] Thus the political economy of consumer capture is noticeably different from that of producer capture. This has been reflected in the transatlantic debate.

The Search for a Solution

Given the fundamental differences in approach between the EU and the US, is trade conflict inevitable? Do grounds for co-operation exist and can a trade war be averted? A total ban on GM products would result in consumer overprotection because consumers who might want to purchase GM products (which have not been scientifically proven to be harmful to humans or the environment) because they are either cheaper or because they have been positively enhanced would be unable to do so. In fact, because of the moratorium on approvals of agricultural biotechnology products, the US, supported by Canada and Argentina, requested the establishment of a WTO dispute settlement panel on 8 August 2003. The case was brought against both the EU as a whole and the Member States (Austria, France, Luxembourg, Germany, Italy, and Greece) that maintain a number of national marketing and import bans on biotech products. The US claimed US$1.8 billion in compensation for the loss of exports over the past six years. Given the firmly held beliefs of the European consumer that GMOs are undesirable and possibly dangerous, and the equally firmly held findings of numerous scientific bodies that GMOs are safe for human consumption, is any compromise position possible?

Labelling offers one possible solution. The international demand for some form of labelling of GM foods continues to grow stronger and in fact extends well beyond the EU (see Phillips (2000), Sheldon (2001) and Sheldon and Josling

Table 11.2 *Relationships between Attributes and Label Claims*

	Positive Attribute as seen by consumer (price premium)	Negative Attribute as seen by consumer (price discount)
Positive label ('does contain')	Likely to be provided by private sector: government mandate not necessary	Unlikely to be provided by the private sector: government mandate may be needed
Negative label ('does not contain')	Unlikely to be provided by the private sector: government mandate may be needed	Likely to be provided by private sector: government mandate not necessary

(2001)). In January 2000, 130 countries ratified the Cartagena Protocol on Biosafety which calls for bulk shipments of GMO commodities, such as corn or soybeans, that are intended to be used as food, feed or for processing, to be accompanied by documentation stating that such shipments 'may contain' living modified organisms and are 'not intended for intentional introduction into the environment'.

Although EU Directive 2001/18 already required traceability and labelling of some GM products, in September 2003, Regulation 1830/2003 was passed to amend 2001/18 and thus ensure a harmonized pan-EU framework for traceability and labelling (OJ L268/24, 18-10-03). Labelling, however, is no panacea. The extent to which it facilitates trade and avoids friction depends on the nature of the label and who provides or requires it. Two distinctions are important: whether the attribute that appears on the label is seen as positive by the consumer (such as a nutritional attribute) or negative (in effect, a warning label). The label itself can either contain a positive statement ('does contain') or a negative claim ('does not contain'). The incentives generated by the combinations of these factors are shown in Table 11.2.

Claims for positive attributes require no particular mandate: the role of government is to prevent fraud. Similarly, claims for negative attributes should be in the interest of the private sector, with the authorities merely making sure that the claims are true. The more contentious cases are the requirement of a positive label for a negative attribute and a negative label for a positive attribute. The private sector has no incentive to provide information that is contrary to its commercial interest.

This account conveniently summarizes the nature of the debate on labelling between the US and the EU. The EU has instituted positive labelling for what is perceived in Europe as a negative attribute (for example, 'This product has been genetically modified'). The US broadly recognizes (though it might regret) the demands of EU consumers for GMO labels, but argues that they should be of the negative kind and hence more likely to be introduced voluntarily (for example, 'This product has not been genetically modified'). When the biotechnology sector brings to market GM food products that are recognized as having a positive attribute, the private sector will wish to switch to positive labelling. Thus the issue is not so much whether to label, but whether to mandate positive labels in markets that treat GM ingredients in foods as a negative attribute (in the absence of any evidence of actual health consequences). In sum, leaving the labelling to producers and retailers of food may be a way in which to reach consensus between the US and the EU without resulting in huge trade disruptions. Precedent exists for this approach and it has been rather successful. Both Sainsbury and Marks and Spencer pledged that their stores were GMO-free. Gerber, Heinz, Unilever, Nestlé and McDonald's (for their French fries) have done the same thing. This allows the market to work and does not impose consumer overprotection.

Conclusions

Why do the differences among biotechnology regulations seem to be such a contentious transatlantic issue? One explanation seems to dominate others. The EU has yet to come to grips with the phenomenon of 'consumer protectionism', that is the capture by consumer and environmental groups in some European countries of the regulatory system in an attempt to avoid (or postpone) some of the perceived risks of modern food technology and society. The US at present reacts to this phenomenon as if it were a case of 'producer protectionism', such as has been evident in food and agricultural markets over the past 40 years. But whereas overprotection of producers harms trade, consumer overprotection can offer commercial opportunities.

The costs of producer protection in commodity markets are generally borne by exporters who have a clear incentive to ensure that importing countries base their regulations on 'science'. However, in the case of consumer protection the situation is not so clear. By voluntarily expressing strong feelings in the marketplace in favour of particular attributes of his or her food, the consumer is in a position to be targeted by retailers and food manufacturers. In the marketplace, consumers who value certain attributes (which exceed health standards) should be willing to pay a premium for these attributes, thus making market segregation worthwhile. Rather than cause a trade conflict, such market differentiation offers profitable openings. The US should encourage its exporters to exploit the regulations of the EU and only to challenge them when they discriminate against foreign supplies. But the US should also push the EU toward the type of labelling (negative claims on a perceived negative attribute) that it is in the interest of the private sector to introduce and that conforms to multilateral rules and standards.

Notes

1   An earlier draft of this chapter was published by the European Union Center, Center for West European Studies, European Policy Paper No. 8, May 2002.
2   For an in-depth analysis of institution building in the EU, see Cantley (1995), pp506–681
3   The new dispute settlement understanding now requires consensus to block the adoption of a Report from a Panel. Any party may appeal the ruling (on issues of law), but the Appellate Body Report is final unless overturned by consensus.

4   The SPS Agreement does, however, seem to have influenced the domestic regulation of smaller countries and in particular developing countries, which need to be seen to be following international rules with assiduity (Roberts et al, 2001).

5   It is perhaps not a coincidence that the firm that introduced BST was Monsanto, now the major player in the introduction of transgenic crops. Monsanto clearly did not learn the lesson of the problems with the acceptability of BST, but the opponents of the use of this product put their experience to good use in marshalling the opposition to GM foods.

6   Although it may be that some producers feel that they have a better chance to be competitive under the 'old' technology, and may resist the introduction of biotechnology if all competing producers are allowed to use it. Thus some link between consumer capture and producer protectionism could exist.

References

Bignami, F. and Charnovitz, S. (2001) 'Transatlantic Civil Society Dialogues,' in Pollack, M. and Shaffer, G. (eds) *Transatlantic Governance in the Global Economy*, Lanham, MD: Rowman and Littlefield, pp255–284.

Bomberg, E. (1998) *Green Parties and Politics in the European Union*, London: Routledge.

Bradley, K. St Clair (1998) 'The GMO Committee on Transgenic Maize: Alien Corn, or the Transgenic Procedural Maze' in van Schendelen, R. (ed) *EU Committees as Influential Policymakers*, Aldershot: Ashgate.

Cantley, M. (1995) 'The Regulation of Modern Biotechnology: A Historical and European Perspective. A Case Study in How Societies Cope with New Knowledge in the Last Quarter of the Twentieth Century' in Rehm, H. J. and Reed, G. in co-operation with Puhler, A. and Stadler, P. (eds) *Biotechnology*, 2nd edn, Vol.12 (Legal, Economic and Ethical Dimensions), Weinheim, Germany: VCH-Wiley, pp506–681.

CONSLEG 2001/L0018 (07/11/2003) Directive 2001/18/EC of the European Parliament and the Council of 12 March 2001 on the deliberate release into the environment of genetically modified organisms and repealing Council Directive 90/220/EC, Office for Official Publications of the European Communities, Brussels, available at http://europa.eu.int/eur-lex/en/consleg/pdf/2001/en_2001L0018_do_001.pdf

Cowles, M.G. (2001) 'The Transatlantic Business Dialogue: Transforming the New Transatlantic Dialogue' in Pollack, M. and Shaffer, G. (eds) *Transatlantic Governance in the Global Economy*, Lanham, MD: Rowman and Littlefield, pp213–233.

Echols, M. (1998) 'Food Safety Regulation in the European Union and the United States: Different Cultures, Different Laws', *Columbia Journal of European Law*, Vol.4, pp525–543.

European Commission, DG XI/A/2 Biotechnology (n.d.) 'The European Community and the Contained Use of Genetically Modified Micro-organisms', Brussels: CEC.

European Commission (November 1986) 'Communication from the Commission to the Council, A Community Framework for the Regulation of Biotechnology Com 86(573) final', Brussels: CEC.

European Community Committee of the American Chamber of Commerce (1994) *The EU Environment Guide*, Brussels: EC Committee of the American Chamber of Commerce.

EU–US Biotechnology Consultative Forum (2000) 'Final Report', available at http://europa.eu.int/comm/external_relations/us/biotech/report.pdf.

Heumeuller, D. (2001) 'Designing International Bodies on Risk Management in Evolving Science and Technology with Global Impact' (mimeo).

Heumeuller, D. and Josling, T. (2001) 'Trade Restrictions on Genetically Engineered Foods: The Application of the TBT Agreement', Paper presented to the Fifth International Conference on Biotechnology, Science and Modern Agriculture, Ravello.

Josling, T. (1996) 'Agriculture in a Transatlantic Economic Area' in Stokes, B. (ed) *Open for Business: Creating a Transatlantic Marketplace*, New York: Council on Foreign Relations.

Josling, T. and Roberts, D. and Orden, D. (2004) *Food Regulations and Trade: Toward a Safe and Open Global Food System*, Washington: Institute for International Economics.

Josling, T. and Tangermann, S. and Warley, T. K. (1996) *Agriculture in the GATT: Past, Present and Future*, London: Macmillan (Japanese translation published in 1999).

Levidow, L. (1992) 'A Precautionary Science for GEMs? Reflections on the Second International Conference on the Release of Genetically Engineered Microorganisms (REGEM 2)', *Microbial Releases*, pp55–60.

Levidow, L. and Tait, J. (1992) 'Release of Genetically Modified Organisms: Precautionary Legislation', *Project Appraisal*, Vol.7.

Majone, G. (2002) 'What Price Safety? The Precautionary Principle and its Policy Implications', *Journal of Common Market Studies*, Vol.40, No.1, pp89–109.

Mayer, O, and Eckart-Scharrer, H, (eds) *Transatlantic Relations in a Global Economy*, HWWA, Hamburg, Nomos Verlagsgesellschaft, Baden-Baden.

Nelson, G. (2001) *Genetically Modified Organisms in Agriculture: Economics and Politics*, London: Academic Press.

OECD (1986) *Recombinant DNA Safety Considerations*, Paris: OECD.

O'Riordan, T. and Cameron, J. and Jordan, A. (2001) *Reinterpreting the Precautionary Principle*, London: Cameron and May.

Patterson, L. (1998) *Regulating Competitiveness: the Development and Elaboration of Biotechnology Regulatory Policy in the European Union,* PhD Dissertation, Graduate School of Public and International Affairs, University of Pittsburgh.

Patterson, L. (2000): 'Biotechnology Policy: Regulating Risks or Risking Regulation', in Wallace, H. and Wallace, W. (eds) *Policy-Making in the European Union*, 4th edition, Oxford: Oxford University Press.

Patterson, L. and Josling, T. (2002) 'Regulating Biotechnology: Comparing EU and US Approaches', European Policy Paper No.8, European Union Center, Center for West European Studies, Pittsburgh: University of Pittsburgh.

Phillips, P. and Isaac, G. (1998) 'GMO Labelling: Threat or Opportunity?', *AgBioforum*, Vol.1, No.1, pp25–30, available at www.agbioforum.org.

Phillips, P. and McNeill, H. (2000) 'A Survey of National Labelling Policies for GM Foods', *AgBioForum*, Vol.3, No.4, pp219–224, available at www.agbio-forum.org.

Pollack, M. and Shaffer, G. (2001) 'The Challenge of Reconciling Regulatory Differences: Food Safety and GMOs in the Transatlantic Relationship', in Pollack, M. and Shaffer, G. (eds) *Transatlantic Governance in the Global Economy*, Lanham, MD: Rowman and Littlefield, pp153–178.

Roberts, D. et al (2001) 'The Role of Product Attributes in the Agricultural Negotiations', Commissioned Paper No.17, International Agricultural Trade Research Consortium, IATRC, University of Minnesota.

Sheldon, I. (2002) 'Regulation of Biotechnology: Will We Ever "Freely" Trade GMOs?', *European Review of Agricultural Economics*, Vol.29, pp155–176.

Sheldon, I. (2004) 'Europe's Regulation of Agricultural Biotechnology: Precaution or Trade Distortion?', *Journal of Agricultural and Food Industrial Organization*, Vol.2, pp1–26.

Sheldon, I. and Josling, T. (2001) 'Biotechnology Regulations and the WTO', paper presented to the IATRC Annual Meeting, Tucson, December.

Tait, J. and Levidow, L. (1992) 'Proactive and Reactive Approaches to Risk Regulation: The Case of Biotechnology', *Futures*, pp219–231.

Tangermann, S. (1999) 'The Common and Uncommon Agricultural Policies – An Internal Issue', in Mayer, O. and Eckart-Scharrer, H. (eds) *Transatlantic Relations in a Global Economy*, HWWA, Hamburg, Nomos Verlagsgesellschaft, Baden-Baden, pp134–162.

Vogel, D. (2001) *The Regulation of GMOs in Europe and the United States: A Case-Study of Contemporary European Regulatory Politics*, New York: Council on Foreign Relations.

World Trade Organization (2003) 'European Communities: Measures Affecting the Approval and Marketing of Biotech Products', request for the establishment of a panel by the United States, WT/DS291/23.

Young, C. (2004) *The Regulation of Genetically Modified Foods in the United States and the United Kingdom: The Intersection of Policy and Public Opinion*, BSc Honors Thesis, Stanford University, May.

12

Institution-building from Below and Above: The European Community in Global Environmental Politics

Alberta M. Sbragia

The European Community was created in a post-war world of proliferating regional and global institutions. Its unique characteristics did not insulate it from the international environment. How the Community was to relate to that environment was contested both within the Community and within its counterpart international institutions. What role should the Community play on the international stage?

The Member States that formed the Community retained their sovereign right to negotiate unilaterally in the myriad international organizations created after World War II. Their participation in the Community did not automatically pre-empt their right to negotiate and represent themselves at international bargaining tables. The one exception was clearly the General Agreement on Tariffs and Trade (GATT) as the Treaty of Rome gave the Community exclusive competence for commercial policy (although the Community itself did not become a signatory to the GATT). (See for example Woolcock and Hodges, 1996.) Given the retention of national sovereign rights in the international field outside of the GATT, the Community's role in external relations was problematic. Many of the Member States assumed that the international powers of the Community would be 'enumerated' powers and that they, the Member States, would control that process of institutionalization.

In 1997, as we examine the international role of the Community, we find it playing a major role in many international fora concerned with 'civilian' issues. While its negotiating cohesiveness is not as stellar as the proponents of a federal Europe would wish, its international presence is far more significant than the Treaty of Rome would predict. This is particularly true in the global environmental arena. How did the Community gain the power to be represented when the Treaty of Rome did not even mention the notion of environmental protection? How did this international presence emerge? What were the dynamics? For its part, how did the global system react to the Community's representation once it was legitimated within the Community itself?

The emergence of the European Community as a player on the stage of global environmental politics raises two questions: (1) how did the Community qua Community gain the powers to act and (2) how did the international system respond to the Community's demands for participation? The first question leads us to consider the process of institutionalization at the Community level while the second leads us to the process of institutionalization at the global level.

The European Union and External Relations

The power to negotiate and make treaties quickly emerged as one which the Commission wanted to institutionalize as a competence of the Community rather than resting primarily with the Member States. In the words of Eric Stein:

> *[I]n its earliest years the Community was understandably absorbed in the demanding internal task of building the common market; but because it was born into an interdependent world economy it was from the outset compelled to deal with third countries and the proliferating international organizations. By the nature of things, the treaty power was the principal instrument for the Community to replace bilateral relationships between its members and third countries and to create new relationships* (Stein, 1991, p141).

The Treaty of Rome specifically granted the Community the power to conduct external relations in the area of foreign commercial policy. The external role of the European Economic Community (EEC) in the trade arena was exercised without contestation. The EEC was not a signatory to the GATT, but given that it was the sole negotiator for the Community, its status was not challenged by the US (see, for example, Meunier, 1996). The European Community (EC) did, however, become a member of the World Trade Organization in its own right. (The EU's Member States also became contracting parties.) In fact, the EC's newly found status in the international trade arena 'gives formal international recognition to the role of the EC as laid down in the Treaty of Rome' (Scheuermans and Dodd, 1995, p35).

More recently, the European Court of Justice has given the Member States a much greater role in negotiations having to do with trade in services than they were given in trade in manufactured goods. Nonetheless, the capacity of the Community and the Commission in trade can be viewed as the most 'federal' of all external relations. The Community, represented by the Commission, is generally able to act as a unitary actor in trade negotiations.[1] It is important to note here that the European Parliament plays a minor role in the formulation of external trade policy. That is not surprising. National governments, when operating in the international arena, are executive-driven: foreign affairs are relatively insulated from legislative control in all democratic systems. The process of democratization (as well as judicial review) was held at bay when it came to foreign affairs.

In contrast to the Community's role in trade relations, its position in other global arenas has been viewed as weak. The external (as well as EU) dimension of internal security policy (pillar 3) is widely viewed as ineffective, and studies of common foreign and security policy (CFSP) often argue that it is embryonic. The Community's international environmental relations, however, have received very little scholarly attention in spite of the explosion of activity in that area and the high level of scholarly interest in global environmental politics generally.

The Community's international environmental relations are at first glance interesting because they reside in pillar 1 (typically viewed as the most effective pillar) but their subject matter is not economic in the strict sense of the word. The legal status of environmental policy as a Community policy was unusual until the Single European Act (SEA), in that the Community approved environmental directives and entered multilateral environmental agreements without having the environment mentioned in the Treaty of Rome. It is a policy area in which the Community and the Member States share competencies, rather than being in the same category as trade, agriculture, or fisheries. In environmental policy, the Community's powers are of a 'concurrent nature' and are characterized by 'the (only) partial delegation of power' (Hession and Macrory, 1994, p157). Therefore, international environmental agreements are known as 'mixed agreements' (O'Keeffe and Schermers, 1983; Groux and Manin, 1985, p61–69; Lang, 1986).

Looking at the question from the perspective of the Community's internal arrangements, how did the Community organize itself to deal at the international level? How were the relative competencies of the Commission and Member States sorted out? How did the balance between the Commission and the Member States manifest itself in this area of external relations?

Finally, the global (and often regional) dimension of environmental policy is addressed within the UN framework. The United Nations and its specialized agencies are perhaps the most prototypical of international organizations. The Community is merely an observer rather than a member.

The politics of global environmental politics highlight the barriers the international system qua system poses for the EU as an external actor outside the trade arena. Institution-building at the EU level does not merely involve sorting out the various competencies of the Commission, the Member States acting within the Community context, and the Member States acting unilaterally. It also involves the circumvention by the Member States of the structural barriers within the system to the EU's emergence as an international 'actor'. It is important to note here that the system is not only hostile to the juridical representation of an organization such as the Community but that it is not set up to even acknowledge the institutionalized 'pooling of sovereignty' at the global level. Thus, how did the Community come to have international status as a party to some treaties? Given that it is not a sovereign state, and that contracting parties to treaties are in fact typically sovereign states, how has the Community acquired that status?

The EU and the International Arena

The role of the EU in the international arena, the environmental arena included, has been nurtured by the implications of creating a common market on the one hand and by the European Court of Justice (ECJ) on the other. The institutionalization of the Community's international role occurred gradually, driven by the substantive aims of the Community, the ambitions of the Commission, and the decisions of the ECJ.

The common market

The attempt to create a common market led the Commission in 1968 to propose a programme to harmonize national regulations which threatened to create non-tariff barriers and distort competition. The national regulations which concerned the Commission included those in the field of environmental protection. The first environmental directives therefore were based on Article 100 of the EEC Treaty, for they involved ensuring the free movement of goods. In general, the Commission used the objective of ensuring free movement to enhance its own reach; environmental protection was one avenue to such enhancement (Dietrich, 1996; Pollack, 1996).

Although the Commission became more concerned with environmental protection as such, the implications of environmental regulations for the functioning of the common market were always a major concern. As Frank Boons has pointed out, 'environmental programmes that are adopted in one country can have substantial consequences for economic actors in other countries' (Boons, 1992, p85). Furthermore, environmental regulations often raise questions of economic competitiveness (Golub, forthcoming). The economic implications of environmental protection led the Community to focus on international environmental agreements.

As the Member States became active in negotiating and signing multilateral environmental agreements, the Commission began to fear that 'differences in national implementation measures would lead to disparities which, in turn, would hamper the proper functioning of the Common Market'. The Commission therefore included 'co-operation' with third parties as a component of the very first environment action programme (Leenen, 1984, p94). It subsequently became a party to a large number of multilateral conventions.

At a substantive level, therefore, the concern with the construction of the common market focused attention on international environmental agreements as these began to proliferate. National governments, acting unilaterally in negotiation and implementation, could well create non-tariff barriers under the rubric of environmental protection, barriers detrimental to the functioning of the market. Furthermore, the Commission saw environmental protection as giving it a policy reach which had not been included in the Treaty.

But while the substantive reasons might well have been compelling, the ability to be represented at the international level in the arena of environmental protection was not in the Treaty. In fact, environmental protection itself was not mentioned in the Treaty. The Member States had certainly not expected the Community to be represented in international environmental fora. How did the Community manage to become represented? Why was the international dimension able to be included in the very first action programme on the environment? Here we turn to a key Community institution – the European Court of Justice.

The ERTA decision by the Court coupled with the decision by the heads of government to include the environment in the Community's policy competence gave the Community the opening to participate in international environmental politics. The SEA and Maastricht reinforced the ability to participate. The Court, through its case law, institutionalized the power of the Community to exercise external powers once the Member States decided that environmental protection was an arena in which EC legislation could be adopted.

The European Court of Justice

The fact that the EU has emerged as an identifiable international actor in the field of environmental protection is rooted in the actions of the European Court of Justice. In Nollkaemper's words:

> *[T]he field of the external relations of the Community is, together with the problems of the direct application and priority of Community law, the field in which the Court of Justice has played its most innovative part. The extent to which the Community has become able to claim a place on the international plane over the years is mainly a consequence of the substantial body of case-law developed by the Court* (Nollkaemper, 1987, p61).

The ERTA (1971) case served as the keystone to the Community's emergence as an international actor because it created the 'link … between internal and external powers'. The Court ruled that if the Community had been given the power to legislate internally to the Community, it implicitly had been given powers to act externally as well. In its judgment it ruled that:

> *[E]ach time the Community, with a view to implementing a common policy envisaged by the Treaty, lays down common rules, whatever form these may take, the Member States no longer have the right, acting individually or even collectively, to contract obligations towards non-Member States affecting these rule.* (Mastellone, 1981, p104)

The ERTA case has emerged as the most significant benchmark for delineating the Community's role in international environmental politics. Typically, the Community first legislates and then exercises external jurisdiction. The Court's case law did not, however, clarify whether the Commission or the Council Presidency would represent the Community in international fora. There is no automatic assumption that in external relations the Commission is the Community; the Council Presidency can fulfil that role. Furthermore, the Court's decision did not change the international status of the Community's Member States. In Eric Stein's words:

> *[R]egardless of the scope of the horizontal and vertical transfer that distinguishes the Community from any other international organization, the Member States remain undisputed subjects of international law and retain their international personality. We thus have no less than 13 international persons, that is 12 sovereign states with a partially circumscribed sovereignty, as well as a new international person … endowed with a substantial international capacity and external relations powers* (Stein, 1991, p129).

Community and Member States entangled

International treaties highlight the entangled situation described by Stein. They cover areas not covered by the Community's directives – areas which therefore remain in the competence of the Member States. Because the implementation of international environmental treaties will involve the competencies of both the Community and the Member States, such agreements are signed by both the Community and the Member States. They are known as 'mixed agreements' and reflect the 'mixed competence' intrinsic to environmental policy.[2] Mixed agreements are legally very complex,[3] but for our purposes, it is enough to say that they involve ratification by both the Community and the individual Member States. They symbolize the complex intertwining of Member State governments and supranationality which characterizes the Community.

The importance of the link drawn between internal and external powers lies in the fact that:

> *the EC's external powers expand without the express approval of the Member States simply in the course of developing the EC's internal policies. An extra constraint has therefore been added to EC internal policy-making, since the Member States should now always consider whether the adoption of some desirable item of EC legislation might not result in the undesirable (to them) loss of external competence* (Haigh, 1992, p239).

For example, Member States refused to approve a Directive on the dumping of wastes at sea which the Commission 'had put forward at least partly to be able to accede to international dumping conventions (the Oslo and London Conventions)' (Haigh, 1992, p240).

The Member States have never recognized international environmental relations as belonging to the exclusive competence of the Community and have gone to some length to ensure that their role is safeguarded. In the case of the Basel Convention on the transport of hazardous waste, for example, the Member States used 'two marginal provisions ... on technical assistance and research to argue that the convention did not come into the sphere of exclusive competence of the Community, but that it was a mixed agreement, ie that it contained provisions for which the Community was responsible and others which were of the competence of Member States' (Kramer, 1995, pp85–86).

While the Member States have worked to ensure that they will not be excluded from the international arena, they have also ensured that the Community would be a presence in that same arena. The SEA and subsequently the Maastricht Treaty gave 'express competence to the Community to conclude international environmental agreements, which then are binding on the institutions of the Community and on the Member States' (Kramer, 1995, p84). Before the coming into force of the SEA, however, the Community became a party to a number of important conventions. In Ziegler's words, the Community's 'own competence to do so and the autonomous possibilities for its Member States were clarified only later by the jurisprudence of the Court of Justice' (Ziegler, n.d., p2). For example, in 1975 it became a party to the Paris Convention of 4 June 1974 for the prevention of marine pollution from land-based sources, in 1977 to the Barcelona Convention of 16 February 1976 for the protection of the Mediterranean Sea against pollution and to the Bonn Convention of 3 December 1976 for the protection of the Rhine against chemical pollution, in 1981 to the Bonn Convention of 23 June 1979 on the conservation of migratory species of wild animals, in 1982 to the Bern Convention of 19 September 1979 on the conservation of European wildlife and natural habitats, and in 1981 to the Geneva Convention of 13 November 1979 on long-range transboundary air pollution (ibid, pp2–3).

The link between the Community and other international bodies was explicitly recognized by the European Council held in Stuttgart in June 1983. The Council stated it saw 'the necessity to take co-ordinated and effective initiatives both within the Community and internationally, particularly within the ECE' in combating pollution (Johnson and Corcelle, 1995, p22). The Single European Act, for its part, in Article 130r (5) stated that 'within their respective spheres of competence, the Community and the Member States shall co-operate with third countries and with the relevant international organizations'. It gave the Community a legal basis for the negotiation of international environmental accords. In 1987, the heads of state and government at the Dublin Summit decided that the Community should play a key role in the area of international environmental activity.

The Maastricht Treaty reflected that commitment. Article 130r included a new objective for Community action: Community policy on the environment should contribute to 'promoting measures at international level to deal with regional or worldwide environmental problems'.[4] That new provision indicated how far-reaching the internationalization of environmental problems had become. It also strengthened the Community's prerogative in the international field. In Hession and Macrory's words, the new language in the Treaty:

> *confirms the independent nature of the Community's external power. This latter point is important as the Community previously had to rely on the existence of internal measures to justify external competence in application of the ERTA principle. [It] strengthens the argument that the Community's interest is general and is unrelated to any functional relationship with internal problems or measures* (Hession and Macrory, 1994, p158).

The Commission and International Organizations

The framers of the Treaty of Rome were well aware of the international organizations whose universe they were joining. The role of the EEC multilateral fora was explicitly dealt with in the Treaty of Rome. The Treaty in fact gave short shrift to external relations (other than foreign commercial policy) except in regard to international organizations. In particular, the UN, GATT, OEEC (later the Organisation for Economic Co-operation and Development, OECD) and the Council of Europe were given special mention. Article 229, for instance, specifically empowered the Commission to handle relations with international organizations, with specific reference to the UN, its specialized agencies, and GATT. In 1971, the EEC was only just about to upgrade the head of its Washington office to Director-General and yet it maintained 'permanent liaison, falling only just short of diplomatic missions with GATT in Geneva and OECD in Paris. When OEEC became OECD a special protocol gave to the EEC Commission the task and right to be involved in its work' (Henig, 1971, p10).[5]

Although the Community was only given observer status in those organizations, it is important that the Commission was explicitly given the role of representing the Community with regards to the international organizations mentioned. In what is known as pillar 1 in the post-Maastricht era, therefore, the Commission was given an international role although it was constrained by the very important fact that the Community was not a member of the organizations named. Furthermore, Article 229 does not authorize the Commission to engage in binding commitments (Macrory and Hession, 1996, p135). As the Community de facto became more important in the international arena and its competencies expanded, its official role within the international arena became more complicated.

In a report examining the relationships between the Community and global and regional intergovernmental organizations, the Commission wrote:

> *Not only does the Community have wide ranging relations with these intergovernmental organizations, but these have also undergone a certain evolution. New policies such as that relating to the environment, have involved it in new fields. Similarly, a larger place has increasingly been made for the Community by the international organizations such as the UN system, since in the exercise of its competence it has come to play a larger role* (CEC, 1989, p21).

The Community's participation in intergovernmental organizations, however, is often problematic. Given that the Community is now far more than an international organization but is not a state and that its unique structure is not recognized in international law, its role in international organizations is an awkward one. In the Commission's words:

> *The Community often shares observer status with intergovernmental organizations of the traditional type and is therefore in practice placed on the same footing as those organizations, at least for the present. The Community should be given a status higher than that of observer when the international organization in question is discussing matters falling within the jurisdiction of the Community, but in practice an approach along those lines often runs into difficulties. The basic problem is that traditional international law can accommodate only nation states, or groupings of nation states. Therefore, there has been some resistance to the implied change which is necessary in order for the traditional doctrine to accommodate the new legal entity constituted by the Community* (CEC, 1989, p19).

The key issue for the Commission has been to gain for the Community a separate 'right of access to, and participation in, the work of the deliberative organs of international organizations and conferences'. It was not sufficient for the Member States to agree to a common position among themselves and then have one of them state it within an international organization. The Community wanted to be recognized as a distinct entity with an international personality, and the acquisition of a separate status within international organizations symbolized that recognition. The recognition of such status was of 'great importance' (Groux and Manin, 1985, p43).

In fact, the right of the Community to 'have a seat' in the sense of taking part in meetings (but still officially as an observer and therefore without a vote) at international conferences or within international organizations did not come easily. In the case of the UN General Assembly, the Community did not receive the right to participate until 1974.[6] (While the Commission can speak at meetings of commissions of the UN General Assembly, it is not allowed to address the Plenary Assembly.) By the mid-1980s, 'this battle [could be] considered as almost over since the great majority of permanent international organizations have officially allowed ... the EEC to take part in their proceedings' (Groux and Manin, 1985, p43, 49). Nonetheless, the Community has no status with the Security Council, the Trusteeship Council, and the International Court of Justice (Brinkhorst, 1994, p610).

In the case of UN international conferences for specific negotiations, the Community must receive the right to participate in each case. The Community is represented at the UN by the Head of the Delegation of the Commission who, however, does not hold ambassadorial status and by the Permanent Representative of the country holding the Presidency of the Council (Brinkhorst, 1994, p610). Brinkhorst, the former Director-General of DG XI, the DG responsible for international environmental negotiations, argues that 'there is a growing disparity between this patchy legal situation of the Community and its political projection at the United Nations' (ibid, p611). The Community as such has less legal standing than its political profile would suggest.

In the case of the environment, the Commission has had contacts with the United Nations Environment Programme (UNEP) since the latter was founded in December 1972. The relationship was formalized in an exchange of letters between Dr Mostafa K. Tolba, Executive Director of UNEP, and Gaston E. Thorn, President of the Commission in June 1983. Those letters call for regular contacts between the two institutions, exchange of documentation, participation of the Community in UNEP meetings, and consultations on the Regional Seas Programme, activities pertaining to the assessment of the environment, and environment and development (CEC, 1989, pp85–86).

Up until the mid-1980s, however, the Community generally did not try to be recognized as an official member of an international conference organized under the auspices of the United Nations. The refusal of the Soviet Union and the East European countries to recognize the Community in any fashion was thought to bode ill for any such initiative (Groux and Manin, 1985, pp45–46). As we shall see, the Commission did make a strenuous effort at the negotiations leading to the Vienna Convention to become a contracting party to that Convention – that effort as well as its eventual success signalled a new era for the Community in the international arena.

In many cases, the Commission is a non-voting participant but the Member States are members of the international organization and field national delegations. Furthermore, the organization often deals with matters which fall under both Member State and Community jurisdiction. Those areas are known under the rubric of 'mixed competence'. Thus, Community representation is often that of 'dual representation'. In such cases, the Community is represented by both the Commission and the Member State holding the Presidency of the Council. The Commission typically speaks on those issues which fall under the Community's exclusive competence although it may also be asked to speak in areas of mixed competence. Such 'dual representation,' for example, is in place at the UN General Assembly, the Economic and Social Council, and the United Nations Conference on Trade and Development (UNCTAD) (CEC, 1989, p21).

It is important to note that 'dual representation' – which includes the Commission and the Presidency as representatives of the Community – incorporates both the 'supranational' and the 'intergovernmental' in the Community's external face. That type of representation in bodies such as the UN does not date from the going into force of the Maastricht Treaty with its provisions for CFSP. Rather, it has its institutional roots in the original mandate in the Treaty of Rome which gave the Commission the right to be involved with the United Nations and the ECJ's ERTA decision which coupled internal and external powers.[7] Institutionalization has been influenced by a wide variety of factors – not the least of which has been the new prominence of environmental regulations as challenges to cross-border trade – but clearly the Court has played a pivotal role in setting out the essential framework within which the Community's external representation would evolve. Over time, the Community has become a unitary actor more frequently, has worked out a working relationship between the Commission and the Council Presidency, and has secured international recognition. Each step in this process was hard-fought, but the Community is clearly more unitary, more 'balanced', and more recognized than it was in 1973 when environmental policy was added to its competencies.

Global Environmental Politics

The dynamics found in the field of global environmental politics reflect the tensions found in the international arena more generally. Although environmental protection is a relatively new field within global politics, the Community did not find it easy to be accepted by the global system. Although unique, the Community was not a state, and the system (the US in particular) had difficulty in accepting it as a negotiating counterpart. The legal complexities of 'mixed agreements', the shifting patterns of competencies over time, the evolution of power from the Member States acting unilaterally to their collective action on the international stage in partnership with the Commission, the general lack of precedents and benchmarks in understanding the Community's international role, and the problems for monitoring compliance of these ambiguities were instrumental in making it difficult for the diplomats to accept negotiating with the Community. From the point of view of third parties, it was difficult to know which authority – Brussels or the national governments – would be responsible for implementation and enforcement. That ambiguity made acceptance of the Community particularly problematic.

Internationalization of environmental issues

The Community has had to face the question of its international standing in the field of environmental protection because of the explosion of multilateral activities in this area. In Edith Brown Weiss's words:

> *In 1972 international environmental law was a fledgling field with less than three dozen multilateral agreements. Today international environmental law is arguably setting the pace for co-operation in the international community in the development of international law. There are nearly 900 international legal instruments that are either primarily directed to international environmental issues or contain important provisions on them. This proliferation of legal instruments is likely to continue* (Weiss, 1994, p30).

The density of environmental negotiations at the international level is striking. According to Weiss, 'between 1990 and 1992, there have been about a dozen highly important multilateral negotiations occurring more or less in parallel' (Weiss, 1994, p30). Not surprisingly, the implications of this much activity for traditional notions of sovereignty have not gone unnoticed.[8]

Scholars have increasingly paid attention to the creation of global institutions (regimes) in the environmental arena (Young, 1989, 1991, 1993; Hurrell and Kingsbury, 1992; Adler and Haas, 1993; Haas et al, 1993). The UN play an important role in such an effort. In particular, the establishment of the UN Environment Programme (UNEP) at the 1972 UN Conference on the Human Environment in Stockholm 'was probably the most important institutional consequence of increased concern with global environmental change in the Cold War era' (Adler and Haas, 1993, p15). UNEP's impact has been felt at the regional as well as at the global level. The Mediterranean Action Plan was an offshoot of UNEP, for example (Haas, 1990).

The most recent example of such global institution-building is the Framework Convention on Climate Change, signed at the UN Conference on Environment and Development (UNCED) in Rio de Janeiro in June 1992, the Conference on Environment and Development with its resulting Rio Declaration, Agenda 21, and Commission on Sustainable Development, and the Convention on Biodiversity also signed at Rio.

International negotiation

EU participation in international negotiations is complex. Its participation in binding commitments is rooted in Article 220. Typically, in areas characterized by mixed competence, the Commission will be the negotiator acting under a mandate unanimously agreed to by the Council. The Commission, while it is negotiating, 'continuously consults with a special committee composed of Member States' representatives. In practice, Member States also participate in the negotiation of the environmental agreements' (Kramer, 1995, p84). In areas where the Member States retain jurisdiction, they will negotiate on their own. Given the institutional evolution of the Community, each treaty negotiation has had a different dynamic. The actual representation of the Community is more flexible than the legal scholars might predict. At times the Commission may be asked by the Council to speak for the Community in areas which do not fall within the exclusive competence of the Community while at other times the Presidency may speak even in such areas. When the Presidency speaks for the Community, it will do so using the formula 'on behalf of the Community and its Member States' (Macrory and Hession, 1996, p136).

The following cases give a brief sketch of the key elements of the institution-building process – and its interaction with what can be seen as 'the' key third party, the US – which has characterized the Community's involvement in international environmental negotiations.

Global treaties and institution-building

CITES

In the case of the 1973 Convention on International Trade in Endangered Species (CITES), the major global treaty on nature protection, the Community was not a signatory but did enact a regulation implementing the Treaty (EEC/3626/82) which protected more than 250 species of fauna and flora more stringently than did the CITES Convention itself (Johnson and Corcelle, 1995, p306). The fact that the Community was not a signatory was at least partly a question of timing – it did not have competence for environmental protection at the time the Treaty was negotiated. The Member States in 1977 agreed that it should become a signatory, but the Treaty did not allow for the accession of regional economic integration organizations (Johnson and Corcelle, 1995, p417; Weiss, 1996). In 1983, an amendment to the Treaty (the so-called Gaborone Amendment) was negotiated with the US acting as the principal negotiator. The Gaborone Amendment would have allowed the Community to accede to the Treaty, but the US, concerned that the institutional structure of the EC would not be able to effectively implement CITES restrictions, decided not to follow through and accept the amendment. The Community is therefore not yet a signatory, primarily because of American opposition.

The knotty question of whether the EC can actually ensure compliance with global treaties as effectively as can national governments operating at the national level has remained largely unresolved from the American point of view. It is the concern with whether the EC can comply on the ground that has undergirded a sustained American scepticism or opposition to the EC's being recognized as an actor in international environmental negotiations.

Although the Community was not a signatory, the Member States' participation in the Conference of the Parties held in 1985 in Buenos Aires was coordinated on a daily basis by the Italian presidency. It must be remembered that in 1985 no treaty basis for environmental protection existed and the Community had not been allowed to sign – yet a regulation implementing CITES had been approved at the Community level and the Member States were acting in the EC framework because of that regulation. In those areas where a common position had been formulated, those positions 'were presented to the Conference on behalf of the Community by the Presidency, the Commission, or by the delegation of the Member States having a special interest or specific knowledge on the matter' (CEC, 1985a, p729, final, 2).

Nonetheless, in the Commission's words, 'the Conference witnessed a number of Community incidents' (CEC 1985a, p729, final, 2). The Member States disagreed with the Commission on a variety of issues as well as disagreed with each other. In some contentious areas, no common position was arrived at.

Thus, both the Commission and the Presidency played an important role in the negotiations. While the Community did act in a unitary fashion on some issues, disagreements in both discussions and voting indicated that it was not yet ready to act in a unitary fashion. Clearly, the Community would have been more influential if it had been able to act more cohesively. Yet it is unprecedented for a non-signatory to have the kind of influence which it did have on some issues.[9]

Ozone

American (as well as Soviet) opposition to the Community's emergence as a signatory to global treaties persisted throughout the 1980s. The US originally opposed the EC signing both the Vienna Convention on the ozone layer and the Montreal Protocol, at least partially because treating the Community as one political unit had implications for how individual Member States might or might not comply with the Treaty (Haigh, 1992, p242; Hampson with Hart, 1995, p265). In those treaties, however, the Member States backed the Commission's insistence on the Community becoming a contracting party.

The politics of ozone, however, have one clear feature. The Commission's 'insistence on special statutory treatment' became a key negotiating point, one which, from the point of third parties, was typically shrouded in confusion over what the power of the Community in the area actually was. The question of whether and when the Community exercised exclusive competence was particularly difficult to answer from a legal standpoint. The political ramifications of an answer to that question were often too problematic. As the Community's legal adviser John Temple Lange put it, 'precisely because the limits of exclusive competence are politically important, they are particularly difficult and controversial to define' (cited in Benedick, 1991, p95). The confusion over the entanglement between Community and Member States fuels concern over compliance. Who is responsible for ensuring compliance with the final treaty – Brussels or national capitals? Given the importance for economic actors of the Montreal Protocol, it was particularly important for many countries, the US included, that the accountability for compliance be relatively straightforward.[10]

In spite of the irritations caused to third parties (and at times to the Member States themselves) by the Commission's relentless pursuit of ensuring its international status, the Community was so important it could not be ignored or dismissed. The cohesion of the Community in the area of ozone generally has been such that it has emerged as a key actor (Szell, 1993, p36; Litfin, 1995a, b). During the Vienna Convention negotiations, the European position was so cohesive in its opposition to binding commitments that a framework convention laying out general principles only was seen as the only feasible option. The Community was in fact a unitary actor, with the Member States and the Commission acting in unison (Jachtenfuchs, 1990, p264).

Leaving aside the content of the environmental restrictions adopted, the Commission strenuously negotiated to be allowed to become a contracting party without restrictions (Benedick, 1991, p95). Given the lack of explicit competence for environmental protection before the adoption of the SEA, the Commission viewed the negotiations as a way to 'obtain greater competence in environmental affairs within the Community. Had it succeeded, it could claim the right to propose Community legislation to implement the ozone convention and future protocols' (Jachtenfuchs, 1990, p263). The Council had agreed in January 1982 that the Community should become a contracting party, and in October 1984 had agreed that the Community should be allowed to become a contracting party without any conditions being attached. However, both the US and the USSR had proposed restrictions. The US wanted 'a prior participation by one Member State' and the USSR wanted prior participation by a majority of the Member States (CEC, 1985b, p8, explanatory memorandum). A compromise was finally reached which was acceptable to the Commission.

Negotiations over the Montreal Protocol to the Vienna Convention had some of the same features. The status of the Community – which had both symbolic and substantive implications – was the subject of heated debate and only a last-minute compromise put forth by New Zealand's Environment Minister allowed the negotiations to conclude (Hampson with Hart, 1995, p265). Richard Benedick, the American negotiator, gives a sense of how important the dispute became:

> *After a nerve-racking midnight stand-off over this issue, during which the fate of the protocol hung in the balance, a compromise was reached at the last possible moment... this concession would obtain only if all member countries plus the EC Commission became parties to the protocol and formally notified the secretariat of their manner of implementation* (Benedick, 1991, pp96–7).

However, the issue of competence was highlighted when the issue under discussion was a fund to help developing countries obtain advanced technology. The Community could not be involved, and 'on this point the Member States acted on their own' (Haigh, 1992, p241).

During the Protocol negotiations, the Community again kept the agreement from being as stringent as the US and the Scandinavians wanted. After a political change at the Community level which transformed the politics of ozone, the Community emerged as a policy leader during the negotiations for the London and Copenhagen amendments. Regardless of whether the Community was a 'leader' or a 'laggard', however, the Community was cohesive enough to emerge as a key negotiating partner.

Climate change

By the time the climate change negotiations began officially in February 1991, the EC had become a recognized power in the area of international environmental politics. The UN General Assembly had created the Intergovernmental Negotiating Committee (INC) for a Framework Climate Convention under whose auspices the negotiations were conducted. Within that framework, 'the EC assumed a lead role in the negotiations by virtue of its commitment to returning its joint carbon dioxide emissions to 1990 levels by the year 2000' (Porter and Brown, 1996, p95).

While the Community's commitment did indeed provide a benchmark, the Commission's role in the actual negotiation of the Framework Convention was rather limited. The Member States, however, were involved.

Given the role of the US in international politics, environmental politics especially, it was essential for the success of the Rio Conference (at which the UN Framework Convention on Climate Change was to be signed) that President Bush personally attend. The American position, however, was opposed to binding commitments to reduce carbon dioxide emissions to a specific level by a specific date. The European Community was viewed by the US as a key adversary, and President Bush demanded the Europeans change their position. Bush 'personally called German Prime Minister Helmut Kohl to ask him to drop his government's demands for the stabilization commitment in return for Bush's participation in the Earth Summit' (Porter and Brown, 1996, p96). Whether that call was to Kohl as a German or whether it was to Kohl as a key player in the ECs politics of climate change is impossible to say, but it may be irrelevant. By that point, the European Community and its Member States were so entangled in a way which does not easily fit the legal language of 'competencies'.

Member States used their bilateral contacts with Washington to lobby the Bush administration to support the EU's position (unsuccessfully of course). The Member States and the Community were intertwined in such a way that the EC could be seen as a unitary actor using multilateral diplomatic channels to convince the USA to change its position (Porter and Brown 1996, p95). In the context of transatlantic negotiations, the Member States have been in a much stronger position than has the Commission (a situation which began to change under the Clinton administration).[11] The Member States clearly dominated that exchange – but acted in a unitary fashion. From the American point of view, it was the EC/Germans/Dutch/British who were lobbying rather than the Member States acting unilaterally.[12]

The entanglement of the Community and the Member States when dealing in transatlantic negotiations is evident in the negotiation of Article 4 (2) of the Convention. In Nigel Haigh's words,

> *[T]he UK Secretary of State for the Environment, Michael Howard, allegedly with the encouragement of some other Environment Ministers from EC Member States, travelled to the United States and agreed a form of words with US officials which forms the basis of Article 4(2) of the Convention. Whether this can be regarded as an EC contribution to the framing of the Convention is a matter of opinion. Formally it was not since no formal Council decisions were taken on the subject, but without the machinery provided by the EC for discussion between ministers it may not have happened* (Haigh, 1996, pp181–2).

The US is such an important actor that it is difficult to analyze the EU's role without taking into account the impact of American policy. Given that climate change policy is essentially an issue of international political economy because of the wide-ranging impacts on industrial activity and structure of carbon dioxide emission reductions,[13] the economic interdependence within the industrialized world cannot be ignored by the EU. It is for that reason that in 1992 EU Finance Ministers insisted that any EU carbon tax be implemented only on condition that the US and Japan acted in kind. Japan agreed on condition that the US enact some kind of carbon tax. The Clinton administration refused. Although there are significant Member State differences on the carbon tax issue (the UK opposes it in principle), there is no doubt that a change in the American position would transform the politics of the carbon tax debate within the EU as well as the international politics of climate change (Zito, 1995; Porter and Brown, 1996, p149).

The climate change negotiations once again highlighted the concern of third parties that implementation be transparent. Article 22 (2) specifies that regional economic integration organizations which accede to the Convention (ie the Community) must 'declare the extent of their competence with respect to matters governed by the Convention' (Macrory and Hession, 1996, p114). The entangled legal situation in areas of 'mixed competence' and 'mixed agreements', however, makes this difficult. Thus far the Community's statement is lacking specifics. That perhaps is not surprising, especially given the lack of specifics in the Framework Convention on Climate Change itself. As Macrory and Hession point out:

> [I]n the absence of a clearly defined area of exclusive Community competence for climate change and in the absence of a clear obligation detailing specific action it is extremely difficult to isolate Community and Member State obligations (ibid, 1996, p114).

UNCED

Once the General Assembly in December 1989 decided to convene a UN Conference on Environment and Development in 1992, the question of the European Community's participation arose. In March 1992, the Council of Ministers approved the full participation of the Community in the UNCED – 'on equal terms with the Member States' (Jupille and Caporaso, 1996, p20). However, as Jupille and Caporaso point out, when Portugal, in the exercise of the Community Presidency, asked during the New York PrepCom (IV) meeting that Commission President Delors be treated during the concluding ceremonies at Rio as if he were a head of state, a fierce dispute erupted with the US and the Member States themselves were unwilling to go that far (ibid, 1996, p21).[14]

A compromise position was put together which acknowledged the special position of the Community in the world of international affairs. The compromise allowed the Community to participate fully in the UNCED deliberations – the only international organization to be given that privilege. This privileged position was however not to be viewed as a precedent, and the Community would still not be allowed to vote. The following excerpt summarizing the compromise gives a sense of how the Community's actual participation was to take place:

The EEC will represent exclusively the Community's position to the Conference on issues falling within the EEC's exclusive competence. In cases of mixed competence, the EEC and its Member States will determine which, as between them will represent the positions of the Community and its Member States. The EEC shall inform the UNCED secretariat prior to consideration of an agenda item by the Conference if the EEC will be representing a position of the Community and its Member States with respect to specific matters within the scope of that agenda item (Jupille and Caporaso, 1996, p21).

On 13 April 1992, the General Assembly approved a special decision to grant the Community's request to be granted 'full participant status'. Brinkhorst, then the Director-General of DG XI, describes the content and significance of that decision in the following terms:

This status conferred on the EEC rights enjoyed by participating states, including representation in committees and working groups of the conference, the right to speak and to reply, and to submit proposals and substantive amendments. On two counts the position would be different from that of Member States: the EEC would not have the right to vote (including the right to block a consensus) nor to submit procedural motions. Although EC representatives made it clear from the beginning that the EC would not request a 13th vote, no new ground could be broken on this point in view of the clear language to the contrary of the UN Charter... the decision was considered as an important breakthrough of the general procedural rules prevailing at meetings of UN conferences (Brinkhorst, 1994, p612).

The Community had played what Brinkhorst characterizes as a 'certain mediating role' between developing countries on the one hand and the US and Japan on the other. The G77 (Group of 77 developing countries) therefore actively supported the granting of 'full participant status' to the Community (Brinkhorst, 1994, p613).

The Council Presidency played an active role during the negotiations. According to one negotiator from a non-Member State, at certain points the Presidency on behalf of the Community was negotiating with the G77 with the US and Russia sitting on the sidelines. In his words, 'the Community was a powerhouse'. Although the Commission's presence was weakened by the refusal of the Commissioner for the Environment to attend, the Community played an important role. The Commission's civil servants were involved and the Council Presidency was very visible. Third parties certainly interpreted the Presidency's actions as those of the Community. Given the codes of international negotiations, the fact that Ken Collins, the Chair of the important parliamentary committee on the environment, did not attend mattered much less than did the fact that the Council Presidency was active.

The relationship between the Commission and the Presidency seems to have been relatively smooth. The Council of Ministers had decided in March 1992 that the Presidency would typically represent and negotiate for the Community in areas of mixed competence but that the Commission could act in the same fashion if it were so agreed. In areas where important EC directives had been approved –

toxic chemicals, waste, and fisheries – 'the Commission representatives spoke exclusively on behalf of the Community' (Brinkhorst, 1994, p613).

The Community in fact was able to act in a unitary fashion more easily on environmental issues than on those dealing with development aid policy. No common EC position had been developed, and the Community in that area was unable to exert the kind of influence it did in the environmental arena (Brinkhorst, 1994, p614).

The Community did sign Agenda 21 even though it is not a legally binding document. From a legal perspective, such a signature was unusual. Martin Hession argues that 'the general powers of the Commission to maintain all appropriate relations with organs of the UNs (Article 229) cannot be considered sufficient for such general political declarations' (Hession, 1995, p156).

In fact, the Community has been active in its relations with the Commission on Sustainable Development (CSD), which was established by Chapter 38 of Agenda 21 as a Commission of the UN's Economic and Social Council. The General Assembly, in establishing the CSD in January 1993, explicitly called for the full participation of the Community. The Council of Ministers had on 23 November 1992 accepted a Commission recommendation that the Community should participate fully in CSD activities. The Member States which were elected to membership on the Commission (the Community itself would not seek election) would, on issues within the Community's exclusive competence:

> *exercise their votes on the basis of a Community position decided on in Community co-ordination. On issues of mixed competence, co-ordination would take place with a view to securing a common position of the basis of which the Community members of the CSD should vote* (Brinkhorst, 1994, p615).

The Council of Ministers in its meeting of 4 March 1996 laid out the guidelines to be used by the Union during the 4th Session of the Commission which met in New York from 18 April to 3 May 1996. These guidelines were also to be used in the preparation for the European Union's participation in the 1997 special session of the UN General Assembly which is to review the progress made in the implementation of the commitments made at Rio.

Conclusion

The European Community has over time developed the international standing and the capacity to become an important international actor in the area of international environmental relations. Third parties as well as the UN system have gradually acknowledged the Community's unique status vis-à-vis its Member States and are in the process of adapting international institutions to accommodate its unusual demands.

What is striking about the Community's role is that an institutionalized balance between the Commission and the Member States acting collectively within the framework of the Union is being constructed at the same time that the Community is emerging as an important actor in the global environmental context.

The Presidency is a key Community institution in the foreign environmental affairs of the Community. The Commission, for its part, is playing a role much more important than might have been expected given the importance of states in the international system. The Member States, although in constant conflict with the Commission over the internal allocation of responsibilities, are nonetheless consistently agreeing to have the Community play an important international role in the environmental arena.

The institutionalization of 'dual representation' represents an innovative way for the Community to be represented while maintaining a central role for the Member States. The Community has found a way to incorporate both inter-governmentalism (in the form of the Council Presidency) and the 'federal' (in the form of the Commission) in its external personality.

Significantly, the external role of the Commission was legitimized by the European Court of Justice. The Court, as it has so often, gave a powerful 'federal' impetus to the Community by recognizing the external dimension of what we now know as pillar 1. It, however, did not exclude the Member States. The entanglement between the Community and the Member States is packaged under the rubric of 'mixed competence' and 'mixed agreements'. The arcane and convoluted legal spiderwebs which make up the area of 'mixed competence' and 'concurrent powers' are in fact the foundation stones for the balance between Brussels and national capitals which makes the Community both so complex and so successful as an instrument of integration.

The environmental arena has proven to be a fruitful arena for institution-building. The Community has been able to increase its stature, its international reach, and its effectiveness within international organizations. Each global treaty has proven to be a step in a process of institution-building which is still ongoing. Its future role in the Commission for Sustainable Development and General Assembly activities in the post-Rio period is likely to continue on a similar trajectory – incremental steps which increase its status as well as its access to the decision-making centres within international fora (such as informal meetings), and therefore the likelihood that it will be able to act in a unitary fashion.

The Council Presidency, flanked by the Commission, and the Commission, flanked by the Council Presidency, are likely to force the international system to acknowledge an entity which does not require the constituent units to subordinate themselves to a 'federal' government or to a 'centre' as conventionally understood. The ever-more institutionalized coupling of the 'supranational' and the 'intergovernmental' in the conduct of international environmental politics represents a case of institution-building at both the Community – and the global – level.

Notes

1   Woolcock and Hodges (1996, p323), for example, conclude that in the Uruguay Round, 'in 14 of the 15 negotiating groups, the EC performed on a par with, for example, the US, if not better, in terms of presenting coherent consistent positions'.

2   Pillar 1 includes areas of exclusive competence – trade in manufactured goods – and areas of so-called 'mixed competence'. The latter is seen by many Commission officials as far from ideal. In the words of one, 'pillar 1 is being polluted by "mixicity" – the notion of mixed competencies'.

3   John Temple Lang defines a mixed agreement in the following fashion: 'International agreements are described as 'mixed' when both the European Community and some or all of its Member States become, or are intended to become, parties. In practice this is usually where the Community has exclusive competence over part of the subject matter of the agreement and non-exclusive or concurrent competence over the rest of the subject matter. However, the phrase 'mixed agreements' is also used to describe the much rarer situations in which either part of the subject matter of the agreement is outside the competence, even the concurrent competence, of the Community, or the Community becomes a party even though it has no exclusive competence over any part of the subject matter' (Lang, 1986, pp157–8).

4   The other three objectives are preserving, protecting, and improving the quality of the environment; protecting human health; and the prudent and rational utilization of natural resources.

5   With regards to the OECD, the Commission points out that 'although the Community is not a member of that organization, its status there is higher than that of an observer. Supplementary Protocol No. 1 to the Convention on the OECD stipulates that the Commission shall take part as of right in the work of the organization and that representation of the Communities shall be determined with the institutional provisions of the Treaties' (CEC, 1989, p19).

6   Much to its dismay, however, the Community has the same formal status vis-à-vis the UN General Assembly as the Commonwealth Secretariat, the International Committee of the Red Cross, the League of African Unity, and the Organization of the Islamic Conference. It is certainly true that such organizations have little similarity with the Community, representing 'both in law and in their factual position a totally different political reality' (Brinkhorst, 1994, p610).

7   The trade arena stands as a contrast. In the case of the Uruguay Round, Member States did not field national delegations. The Commission was the sole representative and the Presidency was not a partner nor was it included in the negotiating team. The Member States gave the Commission the right to negotiate for the Community even in those areas (such as services and intellectual property rights) characterized by 'mixed competence' (Woolcock and Hodges, 1996, p302).

8   See for example Hurrell and Kingsbury (1992); Conca (1994); Litfin (1995a,b).

9   For a more in-depth discussion of the EU's role in CITES, see Sbragia with Hildebrand (1998).

10 The politics of ozone depletion have been very much concerned with economics. As Jeffrey Berejikian argues, 'the central concern of the EC was the economic impact of ozone layer protection' (Berejikian, 1997, p790).

11 For a discussion of how the Clinton administration began to view the Community as a more important transatlantic partner, see Gardner (1997); Sbragia (1996).

12 The Member States, however, maintained control of the negotiations over the Global Environmental Facility. The Community is not a member of the GEF but is trying to become one. At least some of the Member States, however, are opposed to the Community's membership.

13 Michael Grubb has argued that the impact of reducing greenhouse gases will be significant. In his words 'No previous environmental problem has been at once so closely related to major sectors of economic activity'. Cited in Sell (1996, pp106–107).

14 I have drawn heavily from Jupille and Caporaso's excellent paper. Preparatory committees were very important in the UNCED process. In Stanley Johnson's words, 'Few international conferences can have been so thoroughly prepared as the UN Conference on Environment and Development. UNCED's Preparatory Committee (which became known as PrepCom) held four meetings, each of them four or five weeks in length, which were attended by most of the Member States of the UN, by the intergovernmental bodies both inside and outside the UN system, by a host of non-governmental organizations including the business, scientific, and academic communities, as well as the representatives of 'green' groups and charitable and other bodies interested in the environment and development. The task of these successive meetings of UNCED's PrepCom was to define the issues, to help shape the programmes and other proposals, to assess financial implications where this was possible and, finally to narrow down the areas of disagreement so that the Rio Conference might ultimately be confronted with a manageable agenda' (Johnson, 1993, p19).

References

Adler, H. R., and Haas, P. (1993) 'The rise of global ecopolitics' in Choucri, N. (ed) *Global Accord: Environmental Challenges and International Responses.* Cambridge, MA: MIT Press.

Benedick, R. E. (1991) *Ozone Diplomacy: New Directions in Safeguarding the Planet.* Cambridge, MA: Harvard University Press.

Berejikian, J. (1997) 'The Gains Debate: Framing State Choice'. *American Political Science Review,* Vol.91, pp789–806.

Boons, F. (1992) 'Product-oriented Environmental Policy and Networks: Ecological Aspects of Economic Internationalization'. *Environmental Politics*, Vol.4, pp84–105.

Brinkhorst, L. J. (1994) 'The European Community at UNCED: Lessons to be Drawn for the Future,' in Curtin, D. and Heukels, T. (eds) *Institutional Dynamics of European Integration.* Dordrecht: Martinus Nijhoff.

CEC (1985a) Commission of the European Communities (Serial) *Directory of the Commission of the European Community: On the Main Results of the Fifth Meeting of the Conference on the Parties to the Convention on International Trade in Endangered Species of Wild Fauna and Flora.* COM (85) 729, Luxembourg: Office for Official Publications of the European Community.

CEC (1985b) Commission of the European Communities (Serial) *Directory of the Commission of the European Community: Concerning the Negotiation for a Global*

Framework Convention on the Protection of the Ozone Layer, COM (85) 8, Luxembourg: Office for Official Publications of the European Community.

CEC (1989) Commission of the European Communities (Serial) *Directory of the Commission of the European Community: Relations between the European Community and International Organisations,* Luxembourg: Office for Official Publications of the European Communities.

Conca, K. (1994) 'Rethinking the Ecology Sovereignty Debate', *Millennium,* Vol.23, pp701–711.

Corbett, R. (1989) 'Testing the New Procedures: The European Parliament's First Experience with its New "Single Act" Powers', *Journal of Common Market Studies,* Vol.27, pp359–372.

Dietrich, W. F. (1996) 'Harmonization of Automobile Emission Standards under International Trade Agreements: Lessons from the European Union Applied to the WTO and NAFTA', *William and Mary Environmental Law and Policy Review,* Vol.20, pp175–221.

Gardner, A. L. (1997) *A New Era in US–EU Relations? The Clinton Administration and the New Transatlantic Agenda.* Brookfield, VT: Ashgate.

Golub, J. forthcoming, 'Global Competition and EU Environmental Policy: Introduction and Overview,' in Golub, J. (ed) *Global Competition and EU Environmental Policy.* London: Routledge.

Groux, J., and Manin, P. (1985) *The European Communities in the International Order.* Luxembourg: Office for Official Publications of the European Communities.

Haas, P. M. (1990) *Saving the Mediterranean: The Politics of International Environmental Co-operation,* New York: Columbia University Press.

Haas, P., Keohane, R. and Levy, M. (1993) *Institutions for the Earth.* Cambridge, MA: MIT Press.

Haigh, N. (1992) 'The European Community and International Environmental Policy,' in Hurrell, A. and Kingsbury, B. (eds) *The International politics of the Environment: Actors, Interests, and Institutions.* Oxford: Clarendon Press.

Haigh, N. (1996) 'Climate Change Policies and Politics in the European Community,' in O'Riordan, T. and Jager, J. (eds) *Politics of Climate Change: A European Perspective.* London: Routledge.

Hampson, F. O. with Hart, M. (1995) *Multilateral Negotiations: Lessons from Arms Control, Trade, and the Environment.* Baltimore: Johns Hopkins University Press.

Henig, S. (1971) *External Relations of the European Community: Associations and Trade Agreements.* London: Chatham House.

Hession, M. (1995) 'External Competence and the European Community', *Global Environmental Change: Human and Policy Dimensions,* Vol.5, pp155–156.

Hession, M. and Macrory, R. (1994) 'Maastricht and the Environmental Policy of the Community: Legal Issues of a New Environment Policy,' in O'Keeffe, D. and Twomey, P. M. (eds) *Legal Issues of the Maastricht Treaty.* London: Chancery Law Ltd.

Hurrell, A. and Kingsbury, B. (1992) 'The International Politics of the Environment: An Introduction,' in Hurrell, A. and Kingsbury, B. (eds) *The International Politics of the Environment.* Oxford: Clarendon Press.

Jachtenfuchs, M. (1990) 'The European Community and the Protection of the Ozone Layer'. *Journal of Common Market Studies,* Vol.28, pp261–277.

Johnson, S. P. (1993) *The Earth Summit: The United Nations Conference on Environ-ment and Development (UNCED).* London: Graham & Trotman/Martinus Nijhoff.

Johnson, S. P. and Corcelle, G. (1995) *The Environmental Policy of the European Communities,* 2nd edn. London: Kluwer Law International.

Jupille, J. H. and Caporaso, J. A. (1996) 'The European Community in Global Environmental Politics'. ECSA Workshop, The Role of the European Union in the World Community, Jackson Hole, Wyoming, 16–19 May.

Kramer, L. (1995) *E.C. Treaty and Environmental Law,* 2nd edn, London: Sweet & Maxwell.

Lang, J. T. (1986) 'The Ozone Layer Convention: A New Solution to the Ques-tion of Community Participation in "Mixed" International Agreements', *Com-mon Market Law Review,* Vol.23, pp157–176.

Leenen, A. T. S. (1984) 'Participation of the EEC in International Environmental Agreements'. *Legal Issues of European Integration,* 1984/1, pp93–111.

Litfin, K. T. (1995a) 'Rethinking Sovereignty and Environment: Beyond Either/ Or'. Presented at SSRC Workshop, Rethinking Sovereignty and Environment, University of Washington, 13–15 Oct.

Litfin, K. T. (1995b) 'Framing Science: Precautionary Discourse and the Ozone Treaties'. *Millennium: Journal of International Studies,* Vol.24, pp251–277.

Macrory, R. and Hession, M. (1996) 'The European Community and Climate Change: The Role of Law and Legal Competence,' in O'Riordan, T. and Jager, J. (eds) *Politics of Climate Change: A European Perspective,* London: Routledge.

Mastellone, C. (1981) 'The External Relations of the EEC in the Field of Envi-ronmental Protection'. *International and Comparative Law Quarterly,* Vol.30, pp104–117.

Meunier, S. (1996) 'Divided but United: European Trade Policy Integration and EC-US Agricultural negotiations in the Uruguay Round', presented at the ECSA Workshop, The Role of the European Union in the World Community, Jackson Hole, Wyoming, 16–19 May.

Nollkaemper, A. (1987) 'The European Community and International Environ-mental Co-operation – Legal Aspects of External Community Powers', *Legal Issues of European Integration,* 1987/2, pp55–91.

O'Keeffe, D. and Schermers, H. G. (eds) (1983) *Mixed Agreements,* Boston: Klu-wer Law and Taxation Publishers.

Pollack, M. A. (1996) 'Ignoring the Commons: International Trade, the Interna-tional Environment, and EC Environment Policy', paper presented at the Coun-cil for European Studies Conference of Europeanists, Chicago, 14–16 Mar.

Porter, G. and Brown, J. W. (1996) *Global Environmental Politics,* 2nd edn. Boul-der, CO: Westview.

Sbragia, A. (1996) 'Transatlantic Relations: An Evolving Mosaic. International Conference, Policy-Making and Decision-Making in Transatlantic Relations', Université Libre de Bruxelles, 3–4 May.

Sbragia, A. with Hildebrand, P. (1998) 'The European Union and Compliance: A Story in the Making,' in Weiss, E. B. and Jacobson, H. (eds) *Engaging Countries: Strengthening Compliance with International Environmental Accords.* Cambridge, MA: MIT.

Scheuermans, F. and Dodd, T. (1995) 'The World Trade Organization and the European Community', *Working Paper, External Economic Relations Series, E-1*. Brussels: European Parliament, Directorate-General for Research, External Economic Relations Division.

Sell, S. (1996) 'North-South Environmental Bargaining: Ozone, Climate Change, and Biodiversity'. *Global Governance*, Vol.2, pp97–118.

Stein, E. (1991) 'External Relations of the European Community: Structure and Process'. *Collected Courses of the Academy of European Law, 1, Book 1*. Deventer: Kluwer Law International.

Szell, P. (1993) 'Negotiations on the Ozone Layer', in Sjostedt, G. (ed) *International Environmental Negotiation*, Newbury Park, CA: Sage.

Weiss, E. B. (1994) 'International Environmental Law: Contemporary Issues and the Emergence of a New World Order', *Business and the Contemporary World*, Vol.6, pp30–44.

Weiss, E. B. (1996) 'The Natural Resource Agreements: The Living Histories', unpublished MS.

Woolcock, S. and Hodges, M. (1996) 'EU Policy and the Uruguay Round', in Wallace, H. and Wallace, W. (eds), *Policy-Making in the European Union*, Oxford: Oxford University Press.

Young, O. R. (1989) *International Co-operation: Building Regimes for Natural Resources and the Environment*, Ithaca, NY: Cornell University Press.

Young, O. R. (1991) 'Political Leadership and Regime Formation: On the Development of Institutions in International Society', *International Organization*, Vol.45, pp281–308.

Young, O. R. (1993) 'Negotiating an International Climate Regime: The Institutional Bargaining for Environmental Governance', in Choucri, N. (ed) *Global Accord: Environmental Challenges and International Responses*, Cambridge, MA: MIT Press.

Ziegler, A. R. (n.d.). 'International Co-operation for the Protection of the Environment in the European Community: Shared Tasks and Responsibilities of the Community and the Member States', unpublished MS.

Zito, A. (1995) 'Integrating the Environment into the European Union: The History of the Controversial Carbon Tax', in Rhodes, C. and Mazey, S. (eds) *The States of the European Community, III: Building a European Polity*. Boulder, CO: Lynne Rienner.

13

The Hare and the Tortoise Revisited: The New Politics of Consumer and Environmental Regulation in Europe

David Vogel

Since the 1960s, both the scope and stringency of environmental and consumer protection have significantly expanded in all industrialized countries. At the same time, regulatory politics and policies continue to exhibit substantial cross-national variation. For example, within Europe, Sweden, Austria, Finland, Germany, The Netherlands, Denmark and Norway are often regarded as environmental 'pioneers', while Greece, Italy, Spain and Portugal are considered environmental 'laggards' (Andersen and Liefferink, 1997). Over the last three decades, the former have typically been the first to enact new environmental regulations and their standards have tended to be relatively stringent, while 'laggard' countries have adopted regulations later and their standards tend to be weaker and less comprehensive. 'Although policy agendas, broadly speaking, have converged on a host of issues worldwide, specific national policies for managing health, safety and environmental risk continue to diverge, even when they are ostensibly based on the same bodies of scientific information (Jasanoff, 2000).

This chapter describes and explains an important shift in the pattern of divergence between consumer and environmental protection policies in Europe and the US. From the 1960s through the mid-1980s US regulatory standards tended to be more stringent, comprehensive and innovative than in either individual European countries or in the EU. The period between the mid-1980s and 1990 was a transitional period: some important regulations were more stringent and innovative in the EU, while others were more stringent and innovative in the US. The pattern since 1990 is the obverse of the quarter-century between 1960 and the mid-1980s: recent EU consumer and environmental regulations have typically been more stringent, comprehensive and innovative than those of the US.

To borrow Lennart Lundqvist's formulation, which he used to contrast US and Swedish air pollution control standards during the 1970s, since around 1990 the US 'hare' has been moving forward at a tortoise pace, while since the mid-1980s the pace of the European 'tortoise' resembles that of a hare (Lundqvist, 1980). To employ a different metaphor, in a number of significant respects European and US regulatory politics have 'traded places'. Regulatory issues were formerly more politically salient and civic interests more influential in the US than in most individual European countries or the EU. More recently, this pattern has been reversed. Consequently, over the last 15 years, the locus of policy innovation with respect to many areas of consumer and environmental regulation has passed from the US to Europe.

This historical shift in the pattern of divergence of European and US consumer and environmental regulations poses two questions. First, why has consumer and environmental regulation become more stringent, comprehensive and innovative in Europe since the mid-1980s? Secondly, why did it become less stringent, comprehensive and innovative in the US after 1990? This chapter addresses both these questions, but it focuses primarily on describing and explaining the shift in European regulatory politics and policies.

The first section of this chapter reviews comparative studies of European and US regulatory policies and politics prior to 1990. It then documents the subsequent changes in the relationship between US and European regulatory standards. The following section explores the changes in European public administration that have accompanied these shifts in European regulatory politics and policies. It then presents an explanation for the 'new' politics of consumer and environmental regulation in Europe. They are attributable to three inter-related factors: a series of regulatory failures within Europe, broader and stronger political support for more stringent and comprehensive regulatory standards within Europe, and the growth in the regulatory competence of the EU.

In a number of important respects, European regulatory politics and policies since the mid-1980s resemble those of the US from the early 1960s to 1990, a parallel which the chapter also explores. The final substantive section offers an explanation for the slowdown in the pace of US consumer and environmental regulation after 1990. The conclusion explores the contribution of this chapter to the literature on comparative government regulation. In brief, US regulatory politics and policies are no longer as distinctive as many scholars have portrayed them. Regulatory politics on both sides of the Atlantic can now be understood in terms of a similar political trajectory.

The Historical Context

From the 1960s through the mid-1980s, a number of important consumer and environmental protection standards were more stringent in the US than in Europe. According to a comprehensive study of chemical regulation published in 1985, the US, the UK, France and the Federal Republic of Germany 'have compiled similar records in controlling substances suspected of causing cancer in humans' (Brickman et al, 1985). Yet the study also points to a number of cases of relative US stringency. For example, 'British agencies generally require more definite evidence of carcinogenicity before initiating regulatory action than their US counterparts' (ibid, p203). More often than not, the US was the first country to take significant restrictive action on suspected or confirmed human carcinogens (ibid, p48). For example, the US Environmental Protection Agency (EPA) found the pesticides aldrin and dieldrin to be carcinogenic, while on the basis of the same studies UK authorities concluded that they did not present a risk of cancer (ibid, p203). The US subsequently banned most uses of these pesticides while the UK imposed no restrictions. Red Dye No. 2 was banned in the US, while its use was only restricted in Europe (ibid, p47). In 1971 EPA banned the insecticide DDT while its use was only restricted in the UK, Germany and France, and nearly a decade lapsed before it was banned by the EU. Similarly, the US imposed more extensive restrictions on 2,4,5-T/dioxin than did the UK, France or Germany.

Furthermore, US chemical regulations were also more stringent and comprehensive. The 1958 Delaney Clause to the Food, Drug and Cosmetic Act banned the use of any food additive if tests revealed that it caused cancer in either laboratory animals or humans on the grounds that such chemicals could cause irreversible harm. It had no counterpart in any European country. The 1976 US Toxic Substances Control Act (TSCA) established regulations for both new and existing chemicals while the EU's 1979 Sixth Amendment only established regulatory procedures for approving new chemicals. (French, UK and German national law did contain provisions for reviewing existing chemicals, but only in exceptional circumstances.) A similar pattern existed with respect to pesticide approval and renewals; US statutes enacted in 1972 and 1978 required more comprehensive reviews of existing pesticides than did either EU regulations or those of any Member State (ibid, p37).

During the 1970s the US adopted more stringent vehicle emission standards earlier than Sweden (Lundqvist, 1980, p170). A similar pattern held for US and EU vehicle emission standards: the US automobile emission standards enacted in 1970 and 1977 were consistently stricter than the five increasingly stringent standards enacted by the EU between 1970 and 1985 (Arp, 1993, pp150–172; Vogel, 1995, pp63–77). For example, while the US enacted legislation requiring all new cars to be equipped with catalytic converters and thus only use unleaded petrol in 1970, the EU did not adopt a similar requirement until 1989. During the 1980s, Sweden, Denmark and Germany, three of Europe's most consistent environmental innovators, phased in standards comparable to US standards only after the US (Lundqvist, 1980, pp170–171; Arp, 1993, p155). Likewise, the automotive standards established in the 1990 Clean Air Act Amendments were more stringent than EU standards.

Environmental impact assessments were adopted by the US in 1969; they were not required by the EU until 1985. The US Congress responded in 1971 to a sustained campaign by US environmentalists and voted to deny public funds to construct a supersonic aircraft after a coalition of US environmental groups argued 'the plane would create a dangerous sonic boom, increase upper atmosphere pollution and adversely affect the nation's weather patterns (Vogel, 1989, p78). In contrast, France and the UK continued to support the commercial development of this aircraft.

During the mid-1970s the issue of ozone layer depletion emerged as a major political issue in the US. Though there was considerable unscientific certainty about both the causes and magnitude of this environmental problem, the 1977 Clean Air Act Amendments authorized restrictions on chlorofluorocarbons (CFCs) on the grounds that a 'reasonable expectation' of harm was sufficient to generate regulatory action (Benedict, 1998, p25). However, even before this law was passed, EPA, acting under authority of TSCA moved to prohibit the use of CFCs as aerosol propellants in non-essential applications. This decision affected nearly US$3 billion worth of household products. Within three years nearly the entire US aerosol market had switched to non-CFC technologies. By contrast, in Europe, the issue of ozone depletion was less politically salient and the political influence of chemical producers was proportionally greater. Only Norway and Sweden, neither of which produced these chemicals, banned the use of CFCs as aerosol propellants. The EU initially refused to act, but in 1980, in response to US pressures, it agreed to a 30 per cent decrease from 1976 levels by 1981 – a reduction characterized by one European scholar as 'a minimum solution' (ibid, p25). According to UK environmental expert Nigel Haigh, 'There is reason to believe that the figure of 30 per cent was chosen because it was known that it could be achieved without causing too much difficulty for industry (ibid, p25).

Thompson's comparative study of the siting of liquefied energy gas (LEG) facilities in four countries provides a stark illustration of the differences between US and European standards regarding the management of environmental risks, in this case specifically those of the UK:

> *Recently California and the United Kingdom have approved sites for LEG termi-*
> *nals. In this, and perhaps this alone, they are the same. If the California siting*
> *criteria … were to be applied to the Scottish case, it would be impossible to*
> *approve [the site that was approved in Scotland], and if the United Kingdom cri-*
> *teria … were to be applied to the California case, any of the suggested sites could*
> *be approved, which means that the terminal would go to the first site to be sug-*
> *gested – Los Angeles harbor* (Thompson, 1983, pp232–262).

Nor is this comparison atypical. According to Vogel's 1986 comparative study of UK and US environmental policies, 'US regulations in the area of health and safety have frequently been significantly stricter than the UK's' (Vogel, 1986, p149).

In the area of consumer protection, the US established more rigorous stand- ards for the approval of prescription drugs than did any European country. After the scandal surrounding the near approval of thalidomide by the Food and Drug Administration (FDA), in 1962 Congress enacted the Kefauver Amendments to the Food, Drug and Cosmetic Act. This legislation significantly increased both the time and expense for securing approval for new prescription drugs in the US. The result was a substantial cross-Atlantic 'drug lag', with new drugs typically approved years earlier in Germany and the UK than in the US (Vogel, 1990, p458). Nearly four times as many new medicines were introduced in the UK as in the US during the 1960s. According to a US Government Accounting Office study which tracked the introduction of 14 significant new drugs, 13 were available in Europe years before they were approved for use in the US. A West German study reported that while the US remained, by a wide margin, the leading producer of new drugs, it ranked ninth out of twelve countries studied in being the first nation to make drugs available to its citizens.

During the 1960s and 1970s, 'no country ... so fully adopted the essence of the precautionary principle in domestic law as the United States' (Cameron, 1999, pp239–269). For example, a precautionary approach underlay US food safety regulation, requiring companies to establish the safety of a process or an additive prior to approval. Under the Endangered Species Act (1966), a finding of potential irreversible harm to a threatened species could lead to an order to desist all development activities. A precautionary approach also informed many US environmental statutes enacted during of the 1970s. The 1970 Clean Air Act Amendments required EPA to apply 'an adequate margin of safety' in setting emission limits for hazardous pollutants and authorized EPA to 'assess risk rather than wait for proof of actual harm' before establishing standards (ibid, p251). The Clean Water Act of 1972 adopted the precautionary and highly risk-averse goal of zero emissions. And, as noted above, US legislation enacted in 1977 providing for the regulation of CFCs was based on the precautionary principle.

A precautionary approach towards risk regulation was also reflected in and reinforced by a number of judicial decisions. In a 1976 Court of Appeals decision upholding EPA's ambient air standard for lead, the court reasoned:

> *A statute allowing for regulation in the face of danger is, necessarily, a precautionary statute. Regulatory action may be taken before the threatened harm occurs... the statutes and common sense demand regulatory action to prevent harm, even if the regulator is less than certain that harm is otherwise inevitable...* (quoted in Vogel, 1995).

In *Sierra Club* v. *Siegler* (1983), the Supreme Court interpreted the environmental impact requirement of the National Environmental Policy Act as requiring a worst-case analysis on the grounds that it was needed 'to assist decision-making in the face of scientific uncertainty' (Vogel, 1995). In *Reserve Mining* (1975), the Supreme Court permitted the EPA to regulate an effluent on the basis of a 'reasonable' or 'potential' showing of danger, rather than the more demanding 'probable' threshold requested by the industrial plaintiff. Thus, 'elements of the precautionary principle [are] firmly entrenched in US environmental law' (Applegate, 2000, pp438–439).

In sum, 'studies of public health, safety and environmental regulation published in the 1980s revealed striking differences between US and European practices for managing technological risks'. Moreover, 'these studies showed that US regulators were quicker to respond to new risks, more aggressive in pursuing old ones' (Jasanoff, 1993, pp61–82). These differences in risk management policies persist, but beginning in the mid-1980s, in a wide range of policy areas, it is now European regulators who have become 'quicker to respond to new risks, more aggressive in pursuing old ones'.

The New European Risk Regime

One important area in which EU policies have become more stringent than in the US is food safety. Europe and the US have historically had different food cultures, with European consumers and their governments more willing to accept the risks of traditional foods such as raw milk cheeses and cured meats than the US, while USs have been more open to new food technologies.[1] However, since the 1990s, differences between European and US food safety regulations have become more pronounced. The first significant EU consumer or environmental regulation more risk averse or stringent than its US counterpart was the Council of Ministers' 1985 Directive banning the use of all growth hormones for cattle. The Directive's approval followed a vigorous public campaign led by the Bureau of European Consumer Unions, a coalition of national consumer unions. The EU was strongly influenced by a widespread consumer boycott of meat inspired by reports of deformities in infants due to their parents' consumption of hormone-treated beef.

Although the EU's own scientific advisory bodies subsequently concluded that the five disputed hormones did not pose a threat to human health, and the European producers of the hormones vigorously opposed the ban, in the end public pressures won out. As Franz Andreissen, the EC's farm commissioner put it, 'Scientific advice is important, but it is not decisive. In public opinion, this is a very delicate issue that has to be dealt with in political terms'.[2] By contrast, in the US, the safety of any of the five growth hormones never entered the political agenda.

A related area in which the EU and the US adopted divergent policies involved BST, a hormone designed to boost milk production. The EU imposed a moratorium on its use in 1989, which was made permanent in 1999. According to an EU official, the Commission feared a 'consumer backlash... it's not easy to explain to consumers that everything is all right when you are injecting drugs into cows'.[3] By contrast, notwithstanding a determined effort by consumer groups, and some small milk producers, BST was approved for use in the US in 1993 (Libby, 1998, pp27–52). Similarly, in 1989 the EU banned the use of most antibiotics in animal feed and in 2001 announced plans to ban all use of antibiotics as growth-promoters by 2006. No comparable restrictions have been imposed in the US.

US regulations governing food irradiation are also more permissive than those adopted by the EU in 1997. While the UK banned the feeding of meat and bone-meal to cattle in 1988 – a decision adopted by the EU in 1994 – the US did not impose a comparable ban until 1997. And while the EU banned the use of mammal-based proteins (farines) for all animals in 2000, the US continues to permit their use in feed for farm animals other than cattle (Stecklow, 2001). The EU has also adopted a much more extensive array of animal protection measures than the US, including, for example, banning the use of leg-hold traps for capturing wild animals in 1991. In contrast, the US only adopted a partial ban following pressures from the EU in 1997 (Vogel, 1997, pp44–6). In 1988, the EU approved a Directive establishing minimum requirements for the protection of laying hens kept in intensive caged systems. These standards were further strengthened in 1999 and by 2012 the rearing of hens in intensive caged systems in the EU will be prohibited (Blanford et al, 2002, p86). Such rules remain non-existent in the US.

The regulation of genetically modified (GM) foods and seeds in Europe and the US provides a striking illustration of the pattern of recent European and US approaches to consumer and environmental regulation.[4] US regulatory officials have worked co-operatively with industry to facilitate the commercial development of this new technology.[5] There has been relatively little public participation in the regulatory process and only intermittent public scrutiny of regulatory decisions. By contrast, the European regulatory process has been highly politicized and contentious, with both the public and non-governmental organizations enjoying considerable access and influence. In marked contrast to the US, agricultural biotechnology firms in Europe have found themselves on the political defensive and have experienced a number of major political and economic defeats.

The US initially chose to regulate both GM foods and seeds under existing laws, while EU legislation established a distinctive and complex set of new regulatory requirements that apply only to this new agricultural technology. However, when EU standards for the commercial authorization of agricultural biotechnology were first issued in 1990 they did not differ substantially from those of the US. But after opposition to GM seeds and foods surfaced in Europe in the mid-1990s, European regulatory policies became increasingly restrictive. To date, while the EU has issued eighteen licences for biotechnology products, including nine GM crops (*The Economist*, 1999; Burros, 1999, pA16), the US Department of Agriculture has approved fifty and the EPA has approved eight (Tait, 1999, p6). Nearly three-quarters of the world's GM crop acreage is in the US; hardly any is in Europe. The EU and a number of Member States have enacted strict labelling requirements, while the US only requires that GM products be labelled if they differ from their non-GM counterparts. As of August 2002 the EU had not approved any new seed strains for nearly four years, while the marketing of new food products under the Novel Foods Regulation (1997) has been effectively halted. Moreover, four Member States continue to refuse to authorize the planting of GM crops that have been approved by Brussels. Foods grown from genetically modified seeds are found infrequently in European stores, largely because of EU labelling requirements, while their use is pervasive in the US.

Nor are recent cases of more stringent or innovative European consumer and environmental regulations confined to food safety or agriculture. While public or quasi-public eco-labelling schemes spread from Germany and Sweden to much of Europe during the second half of the 1980s and were adopted by the EU in 1992, they continue to play little part in the US.[6] In 1994, both inspired and pressured by policies previously adopted by Germany and Denmark, the EU established ambitious recycling targets for glass, paper, plastics and aluminium (Haverland, 1999). In the US there are no federal regulations governing packaging wastes; recycling requirements remain governed by local laws, which are typically less stringent and comprehensive than the 1994 EU Directive.

In 2000, the EU approved a vehicle recycling Directive, which, in addition to providing for the collection of vehicles at the end of their useful life, requires carmakers to recycle or reuse 80 per cent of car weight by 2006 and 85 per cent by 2015. It also bans the use of heavy metals such as lead, mercury and cadmium as of 2003 (Mann, 2002, p4). A 2002 Directive makes manufacturers responsible for the 'life-cycle' of all electronic products. This Directive requires collection standards for ten categories of products including all household appliances and telecommunications equipment. A related Directive will prohibit the use of heavy metals such as lead, mercury and cadmium in electronic products and batteries in order to promote recycling and reduce the toxicity of landfills. Neither regulation is on the national political agenda in the US, and there have only been a few modest policy initiatives at the state level.

In 1999, the European Commission banned the use of phthalate softeners in soft toys. It acted in part as a response to a determined Greenpeace campaign claiming that the chemical was both a carcinogen and a potential distorter of gender characteristics. This issue has been less salient in the US, where companies have only been advised to restrict their use (Durodie, 2000, pp140–174). The 1990 US Clean Air Act Amendments did continue the pattern of more stringent US automotive emission standards, though in the case of heavy duty vehicles, EU standards adopted in 1998 are now more stringent than those of the US (Vehicle Emission Reductions).

The EU has also replaced the leadership role of the US in addressing global environmental problems. Through the 1980s most major international environmental agreements – most notably the London Convention on Dumping at Sea (1972), the Conventional on International Trade in Endangered Fauna and Flora (1973) and the Montreal Protocol (1987), which phased out the use of CFCs to protect the ozone layer – were both initiated and strongly supported by the US, and subsequently ratified by either individual European countries or the EU. 'Since the early 1990s, however, effective US international environmental policy leadership has lapsed' (Paarlberg, 1999, pp236–255). By contrast, by 1994 the Basel Convention on Hazardous Wastes (1989) had been ratified by every EU Member State but has yet to be ratified by the US. Both the Convention on Biological Diversity (1992) and the Biosafety Protocol (2000) were signed by the EU, but not by the US.

The EU, as well as each of the Member States, has ratified the Kyoto Protocol, an international treaty to reduce emissions of greenhouse gases, and a number of European nations have established policies to reduce carbon emissions. The US refused to ratify the 1997 Kyoto Protocol, was not a party to the 2001 Bonn Agreement, and there are no federal controls on carbon emissions, only a set of voluntary guidelines.

The change in the relationship between European and US consumer and environmental standards can also be seen in the pattern of trade disputes between the EU and the US.[7] Earlier transatlantic trade disputes typically involved complaints by the EU or its Member States about the US use of regulatory standards as non-tariff barriers. Thus complaints were filed about US automotive fuel economy standards (adopted in 1975), Superfund taxes (adopted in 1986), and a ban on tuna imports to protect dolphins (adopted in 1990). But for complaints based on policies of more recent origin, it is the US which has challenged European regulations as non-tariff barriers. With the exception of the 1985 beef hormone ban, the European policies about which the US complained have been enacted since 1990. These include the EU's leg-trap ban (1991), eco-labelling standards (1992) and, most importantly, restrictions on the sale and labelling of foods grown from GM seeds (1990, 1997 onwards).

Another important indicator of the extent to which the US and Europe have 'traded places' has to do with the transatlantic direction of regulatory emulation. During the 1970s and 1980s, the European environmental agenda was strongly influenced by the US. Thus throughout the debates in Europe during this period over automotive emission standards, US standards often served as a benchmark, with environmentalists and their supporters pressuring the national governments and the EU to adopt them. Indeed, for both Sweden and the EU, the existence of more stringent US standards actually facilitated the strengthening of European standards; since global automobile manufacturers were now producing less-polluting cars for the US market, it made both economic and environmental sense to require these firms to market similar vehicles in Europe (Vogel, 1995, pp63–77). As a Swedish panel noted: 'the only realistic solution to the problem of strengthening the Swedish exhaust gas regulations seems, for the moment, to be an adaptation to the US regulations' (Lundqvist, 1980, p170). Similarly, in both tightening control over the introduction of new chemicals and phasing out the use of CFCs it was the US that influenced European policies. It is unlikely that the Sixth Amendment, which tightened EU controls over the approval of new chemicals, would have been enacted without the prior passage of TSCA, while the US clearly influenced European policies on CFC (Vogel, 1995, pp79–80).

More recently the transatlantic flow of influence has been in the opposite direction. US restrictions on leg-traps and its ban on animal feed for cattle have been influenced by developments in Europe.

Changes in European Regulatory Policies and Institutions

The emergence of the precautionary principle as a guide to regulatory decision-making represents an important dimension of the new European approach to risk regulation. This principle legitimates regulation when 'potentially dangerous effects deriving from a phenomenon, product or process have been identified, and ... scientific evaluation does not allow the risk to be determined with sufficient certainty [because] of the insufficiency of the data or their inconclusive or imprecise nature'.[8] Originally developed in Germany during the 1970s and 1980s, it was incorporated in the 1993 Treaty of the EU. Since 1994, it has been referenced in more than 30 reports and resolutions of the European Parliament.

While the precautionary principle cannot be divorced from science, since 'a scientific view of the risk is an essential component of the evaluation of the risk that the principle anticipates', its growing popularity in Europe reflects the perception that scientific knowledge is an insufficient guide to regulatory policy (Cameron, 1999, p244). It requires the extension of scientific knowledge while simultaneously acknowledging 'the possible intrinsic limitations of scientific knowledge in providing the appropriate information in good time' (Godard, 1997, p65). The principle thus both increases public expectations of science and reflects the public's scepticism of scientific knowledge. In effect, it reduces the scientific threshold for regulatory policy-making. By mandating or precluding regulatory action, in advance of scientifically confirmed cause–effect relationships, the principle, 'curtails the ability of politicians to invoke scientific uncertainty as a justification for avoiding or delaying the imposition of more stringent protection measures' (Jordan and O'Riordan, 1995, p71).

While its legal significance at both the EU and national level remains unclear, the practical effect of the precautionary principle has frequently been to permit, or even require, the adoption of more risk-averse policies. It explicitly acknowledges the inherently political nature of regulatory decision-making by enabling policy-makers to take into account a wide variety of non-scientific factors, including public opinion and social values. As Jordan and O'Riordan observe, 'The stringency with which the precautionary principle is applied depends upon and is also a useful barometer of deeper social and economic changes. Precautionary measures, for example, are most likely to be applied when public opinion is instinctively … risk averse' (ibid, 1995, p61).

The frequency with which the precautionary principle has been invoked in Europe among both activists and policy-makers also has an ideological dimension. It reflects not only a decline in the role of science as a guide to policymaking, but also a decrease in public confidence in the benefits of technological innovation. Frequently underlying its invocation is the assumption that modern technology poses dangers of which we are unaware and that to avoid future harm we need to introduce new technologies more cautiously. As Corrine Lepage, the former French environment minister, writes in her co-authored book on the precautionary principle, 'The precautionary principle precisely responds to the need for prudence when faced with the consequences of technological progress, whose repercussions are exponential and unknown' (Lepage and Guery, 2001, p144).[9] For many environmentalists, this is precisely one of its most important attractions.

Yet, somewhat paradoxically, European regulatory administration is also becoming more scientifically rigorous. At both the national and the EU levels, there is increased recognition of the need to strengthen the capacity of government agencies to conduct risk assessments and to improve the quality of scientific information available to decision-makers. An important factor underlying this development is an increase in judicial review of regulatory decisions at both the European and international levels (Breyer and Heyvaert, 2000, pp283–352; Scott and Vos, 2002, pp253–288). Just as US regulatory agencies engaged in more formal risk assessment in order to defend their decisions in federal court from challenges by both public interest groups and industry, so Europe's national authorities and the EU are undertaking similar steps in order to defend their decisions before the European Court of Justice (ECJ) and World Trade Organization dispute panels.

European regulatory institutions have also changed. In particular, to improve the quality of regulatory decision-making, risk assessment is increasingly being separated from risk management. The former is the advice and information scientists provide to policy-makers; the latter is what policy-makers decide. This separation has been institutionalized at the EU level by the establishment of regulatory agencies such as the new food safety agency that will perform risk assessments, with the decision being made by the Commission. Similar models have been adopted for food safety agencies in France, Germany and the UK. This separation has a number of purposes. Most obviously, it is designed to prevent 'regulatory capture' by making regulatory policy-making more transparent: when risk assessments are made public, the public can determine the extent to which political officials are accepting or ignoring the relevant scientific advice. Secondly, it enables policy-makers to take into account considerations beyond science in making regulatory decisions, such as public attitudes. Thirdly, it protects the integrity of the risk-assessors since their only role is to provide scientific information to policy-makers. But perhaps most importantly, it makes policy-makers more politically accountable for regulatory policy-making: if irreversible harm results from their decision or non-decision, it is now clearer whom to blame.

Explaining the New European Regulatory Regime

What accounts for these changes in European regulatory policies and institutions? Explaining a complex set of developments over a period of nearly two decades presents a difficult analytical challenge. However, three sets of interrelated factors appear to have contributed to these institutional and policy shifts. They are: a series of regulatory failures and crises; broader citizen support for more risk-averse regulatory policies within Europe; and the growth of the regulatory competence of the EU. The former two factors have affected policies at both the national and EU levels; the latter has affected regulatory policies at the European level.

Regulatory failures and crises

The most important factor contributing to the increased stringency of health, safety and environmental regulation in Europe has been a series of regulatory failures and crises that placed new regulatory issues on the political agenda and pressured policy-makers to adopt more risk-averse or precautionary policies. In 1986 both the nuclear accident at Chernobyl and the Sandoz chemical fire on the Rhine, had significant transborder impacts as well as important health and environmental consequences. The *Washington Post* observed in December 1988: 'Dead seals in the North Sea, a chemical fire on the Loire, killer algae off the coast of Sweden, contaminated drinking water in Cornwall. A drumbeat of emergencies has intensified the environmental debate this year in Europe, where public concern about pollution has never been higher' (Herman, 1988, p19). According to Elizabeth Bomberg:

> *These disasters made an impact. In 1992, the protection of the environment and the fight against pollution had become an 'immediate and urgent problem' in the view of 85 per cent of EU citizens… Eurobarometer surveys in 1989 and the early 1990s registered up to 91 per cent of EU citizens expressing support for a common European policy for protecting the environment… Questions on the environment evoked stronger and more positive support for unified EU action than did questions concerning any other area of policy* (Bomberg, 1998, p13).

During the latter half of the 1990s, Europeans experienced a second wave of crises, this time involving food safety. The most important of these was mad cow disease.[10] When BSE (bovine spongiform encephalopathy) was first detected in cattle in the UK in the mid-1980s the European Commission accepted assurances from the UK Ministry of Agriculture that it posed no danger to humans. Subsequently, the UK was forced to notify other EU Member States of a potential food safety problem, especially after scientific studies showed the disease was transmittable to mice. Following a massive outbreak of BSE in 1989–1990, the European Community banned human consumption of meat from the affected cattle. Although concern among the UK public over health effects of eating meat of cattle diagnosed with BSE continued to grow throughout the 1990s, the UK government denied the legitimacy of the public's concerns. Its position was accepted by the European Commission, which placed only limited restrictions on the sale of UK beef.

The crisis over BSE broke in 1996 in the UK, when the UK government announced that ten cases of Creutzfeldt-Jakob disease had been diagnosed in humans, and that these cases were likely to be related to exposure to the cattle disease, BSE. The Commission responded by issuing a global ban on the export of UK beef and the widespread slaughter of cattle in the UK and, to a lesser extent, in other Member States followed. While both the Commission and its scientific advisory body subsequently certified UK beef as safe for human consumption, the EU's failure to recognize its health hazards severely undermined public trust in EU food safety regulations and the scientific expertise on which they were based. It also led to the deaths of approximately 100 people, primarily in the UK.

The regulatory failure associated with BSE significantly affected the attitude of the European public towards GM foods (Jasanoff, 1997, pp221–232). This was especially true in the UK, where unfavourable press coverage of agro-biotechnology increased substantially following the BSE crisis: between 1996 and 1998 the per centage of those strongly opposing GM foods rose from 29 per cent to 40 per cent. But its ramifications were felt throughout the EU. The *Financial Times* noted, 'BSE has made people in Europe very sensitive to new technologies in the food supply industry, and very wary of scientists and government attempts to reassure them (Cookson and Houlder, 1999, p7). According to an official from Monsanto, 'That wound [about the UK government's long insistence that there were no human health risks from mad cow disease] still has not healed. You have this low burn level of anxiety about food safety, and in the midst of all this you have a product introduction of genetically modified soybeans' (Weiss, 1999, p19). A UK food sociologist observed, 'BSE was a watershed for the food industry in this country. For the first time people realized that merely attempting to ensure a culinary end product was safe to eat was not a good enough approach. We had to look at the entire process by which food is produced' (Williams, 1998, pp768–771).

As one UK scholar put it, 'the BSE scandal represents the biggest failure in UK public policy since the 1956 Suez Crisis' (Millstone, 2000, p19). It also emerged on the heels of a long line of food scares in the UK, including an outbreak of E. coli in Scotland, salmonella in eggs, and listeria. In 1999, a major public health scare emerged over dioxin contamination of food products produced in

Belgium, leading to both the fall of the Belgium government and the removal of all Belgian food products from stores throughout Europe, as well as a crisis involving the safety of Coca-Cola, though the latter turned out to have no scientific basis.[11] As a senior European official noted in 2000, 'the past years have seen a big dip in consumer confidence in the safety of the food supply and, as a consequence, in Member State authorities tasked with the job of overseeing the food industry. There seems to be an endless supply of [food scares]' (*Consumer Voice*, 2000).

The regulatory failure associated with mad cow disease also had important political consequences in Europe. It dramatically exposed the gap between the single market – which exposes all European consumers to goods produced anywhere within the EU – and the inability of European institutions to assure the safety of the products sold within that market. At the EU level it led to the decision in December 2000 to create a European food safety agency. It also called into question the functioning of the 'comitology' system, the EU's term for the structure of advisory bodies that it relies on for expert advice. For the European Commission had relied on the advice of the Scientific Veterinary Committee which was chaired by a UK scientist and which primarily reflected the thinking of the UK Ministry of Agriculture, Fisheries and Food – advice which subsequently proved flawed.[12] Many of the changes in European regulatory administration reflect the effort to establish institutional arrangements that will reduce the future likelihood of 'regulatory capture'.[13] The mad cow crisis also affected regulatory institutions and policy-making at the national level, leading, for example, to the creation of a consumer protection 'super ministry' in Germany and the establishment of national food safety agencies in both the UK and France.

There have also been regulatory failures in Europe in other policy areas. During the early 1990s, the French government was widely criticized for responding too slowly to the public health and workplace dangers associated with use of asbestos.[14] In spite of overwhelming evidence that asbestos constituted a serious health hazard, killing approximately 2000 people a year according to a French government study, its manufacturing, import and sale was not severely restricted until 1996, nearly two decades after the US began to take regulatory action and after it had been banned in seven other European countries. Another, far more important, scandal was the apparent failure of French government officials and doctors to protect haemophiliacs from blood contaminated with the AIDS (Acquired Immune Deficiency Syndrome) virus.[15] This issue, which became highly visible during the early 1990s, led to the resignation and criminal indictment of three senior government officials, including the Prime Minister. Three senior medical officials were convicted of criminal negligence and fraud and were sentenced to prison. Officials were accused of failing to screen blood donors adequately, delaying the approval of a US technology to test blood in order to benefit a French institute and knowingly allowing contaminated blood to be given to patients. The deaths of more than 300 haemophiliacs were linked to these decisions. While haemophiliacs were given contaminated blood in several countries, their rate of HIV (human immunodeficiency virus) infection was significantly higher in France. As in the case of asbestos, the French government's regulatory failure was widely attributed to its placing economic interests over public health.

'Le sang contaminé' (contaminated blood) scandal in France, like mad cow disease in the UK, had significant domestic repercussions. It shocked French public opinion, calling into question the public's historic high regard for the competence of the public sector in a highly paternalistic state. It also continues to haunt French politicians, making them highly risk averse, particularly with respect to potential threats to public health. Significantly, ministers have accepted nearly every recommendation of L'Agence Française de Securité Sanitaire des Aliments (AFSSA) France's recently established food safety agency, which has statutory responsibility for reviewing all government food safety policies – lest they be accused of (again) endangering public health and possibly face legal penalties. The French decision to maintain its ban on imports of UK beef, made in defiance of the EU and against the advice of the Ministry of Agriculture, was taken in response to the recommendations of the AFSSA. The haste with which the French government responded to an increase in the number of BSE cases among French cattle in November 2000 by banning the feeding of farines (bone-meal) to all animals – without even waiting for a scientific assessment by AFSSA – reflects the continuing impact of the contaminated blood scandal on French health and safety policies, as do French policies towards GMOs (genetically modified organisms).[16]

Regulatory failures or crises do not automatically lead to shifts in public attitudes or public policy. After all, Europe had experienced regulatory failures prior to the mid-1980s. But the policy impact of the regulatory failures and crises during the second half of the 1980s and the 1990s has been broader and deeper. Their cumulative impact has been to increase the public's sense of vulnerability to and anxiety about the risks associated with modern society and this in turn has affected the political context in which regulatory policies have been made. As the *Washington Post* observed in the spring of 2001:

> *Wealthy, well-educated Europe is regularly swept by frightening reports of new dangers said to be inherent in contemporary life… USs have health concerns, too, but not on this scale. The year is two months old and already in 2001 public opinion and public officials have been rattled by alarms over risks – proven and not – from genetically modified corn, hormone-fed beef and pork, 'mad cow' disease, a widely used measles vaccine, narrow airline seats said to cause blood clots and cellular phones said to cause brain damage* (Reid, 2001, p15).

Or, as the German sociologist Ulrich Beck put it in his book *World Risk Society*, published in 1999, we now live in a world which 'imposes on each of us the burden of making crucial decisions which may affect our very survival without any proper foundation in knowledge (Beck, 1999, p78).

Political developments

A second, related explanation for the change in European regulatory policies and institutions has to do with political developments within individual European countries. During much of the 1980s, support for strict environmental, health and safety regulations in Europe was geographically polarized. Often, Germany,

The Netherlands and Denmark favoured stricter and more risk-averse regulations, while the UK, France and Italy opposed them.[17] Much of EU environmental policy-making thus represented a struggle between the EU's three 'green' Member States, where constituencies representing civic interests enjoyed considerable public support and influence (the Green Party has played an important role in Germany since 1983), and the UK, France and Italy, where they did not. But while Germany, The Netherlands and Denmark continue to play a role as environmental 'pioneers' in the EU (subsequently joined in 1995 by Sweden, Austria and Finland), strong public interest and support for stricter health and environmental standards has spread south and west within Europe. This change has been particularly significant in the UK and France, which are no longer regulatory 'laggards' within Europe (see Chapter 10).

During the 1990s, UK public opinion became 'greener' and the UK's 'green' lobbies become more influential. This in turn has affected a number of UK policies. In 1990, as part of a broader re-examination of its environmental policies, the UK formally adopted the precautionary principle as one of the 'basic aims and principles supporting sustainable development' (Jordan and O'Riordan, 1995, pp70–71). The application of this principle has affected a number of UK regulatory policies, including the dumping of sewer sludge in the North Sea and domestic water pollution standards. It has also strained the UK's consultative regulatory style, challenging the ability of regulators to justify lax controls or regulatory delays on the grounds that they have inadequate knowledge of harm and forcing them to take preventive action in advance of conclusive scientific opinion.

The creation of the National Rivers Authority in 1989 and the Environment Act of 1995 allowed UK enforcement agencies to adopt a more arms-length relationship with operations and this new relationship has fostered a tough approach towards enforcement. The Environment Act of 1995 incorporated sustainable development into UK law and in 2000 the Prime Minister established the Sustainable Development Commission. This political shift within the UK has also changed its stance towards EU policy-making. For example, the UK played a leadership role in encouraging the EU to adopt a system of integrated pollution control and it was the strongest advocate of the EU's leg-trap ban. Flynn comments, 'Britain has clearly emerged from the more minimalist and hostile stance of the early 1980s to emerge as a medium-positioned state in the league of environmental leaders and laggards'. (Flynn, 1998, p696).

Within France a series of regulatory failures at the national level during the early 1990s, most notably the above-mentioned scandals associated with contaminated blood and asbestos, has increased citizen support for risk-averse regulatory policies. Corinne Lepage, the French environment minister under the Juppé government, was a leading public critic of GMOs, acting in opposition to the Ministry of Agriculture. In 1996 the French government formally adopted the precautionary principle and three years later it established a quasi-independent food safety agency. In 1997, following the election of Prime Minster Jospin, the Green Party joined the French government for the first time and the party's president, Dominique Voynet, became environment minister. In 2000, France became the second European nation to ban the use of meat and bone-meal (farines) for all farm animals to prevent further outbreaks of mad cow disease, a decision based on the precautionary principle since there was no evidence that they posed a danger to either public or animal health (*Le Monde*, 2000, p6). And French public opinion and public policy has been among the most hostile in Europe to GMOs.[18]

Moreover, Italy, responding to public health scares, was among the first nations to pressure for the beef hormone ban. More recently, the health hazards of electromagnetic transmissions have emerged as an important political issue, prompting a large-scale review of government regulatory policies.

In 1999 the Green Party was represented in four European governments: Germany, where it has historically been strong, and France, Italy and Belgium, where it previously was not. Moreover the party had nearly 150 members in 11 of the 15 EU national legislatures (McCormick, 2001, p61). In sum, while substantial national differences in regulatory priorities persist within the EU, political support for more stringent protective regulations has become more widespread in Europe.

The European Union

In addition to a series of regulatory failures, and related broadening and deepening of public support for more stringent regulatory polices within Europe, the emergence of the EU as a more important source of regulatory policy-making has also affected the stringency and scope of European regulatory policies. It is significant that the changes in European regulatory policies and politics described in this article began around the time of the enactment of the Single European Act (SEA) in 1987. This amendment to the Treaty of Rome, by enabling directives to be enacted by a system of qualified majority voting instead of unanimity, significantly accelerated the EU's regulatory competence. The EU has played a critical role in changing the dynamics of European regulatory policies: each subsequent revision of the Treaty of Rome has accorded civic interests greater weight in the policy process. Combined with growing public support for risk-averse policies, these revisions have had important policy impacts.

The SEA gave environmental policy a treaty basis for the first time, specifying that preventive action should be taken whenever possible and requiring that harmonized standards take as a base 'a high level of protection'. The Treaty on the EU (1993) made precaution a guiding principle of EU environmental policy: 'Community policy shall aim at a high level of protection taking into account the diversity of situations in the various regions of the Community. It shall be based on the precautionary principle and on the principles that preventive action should be taken' (Jordan and O'Riordan, 1995, pp68–69). The Treaty of Amsterdam (1997) called upon the Council and the Parliament to achieve high levels of health, safety, environmental and consumer protection in promulgating single market legislation and Article 153 explicitly defined consumer policy and health protection as 'rights'. It also extended the precautionary principle to consumer protection.

As Majone has noted, the EU is primarily a regulatory state: issuing rules is its most important vehicle for shaping public policy in Europe (Majone, 1996). Notwithstanding frequent criticisms of the EU's 'democratic deficit', its institutions have played an important role in strengthening the representation of civic or diffused interests. The influence of consumer and environmental pressure groups on the Commission remains limited and they typically enjoy less access than representatives of business (Grant et al, 2000, Chapter 2). There are, however, exceptions: the European Consumers Union did lead a successful campaign calling for the EU to ban beef hormones, while Greenpeace worked with Green Parties to mobilize public and political opposition against the approval of GMOs in Europe. In addition, the 'European Court of Justice has often played a crucial role in promoting civic interests' and has been repeatedly willing 'to be influenced by consumer and civic concerns in reaching its judgments' (Young and Wallace, 2000, p19).

EU treaties have also steadily expanded the role of the European Parliament, a body in which consumer and environmental interests have been relatively influential, in shaping European legislation.[19] The SEA granted Parliament legislative power under 'co-operation' procedures, and these were expanded by the Maastricht Treaty which established 'co-decision' procedures, thus giving the Parliament and the Council of Ministers co-responsibility for writing legislation (see Chapter 6). The Parliament's purview over environmental legislation was expanded by the Amsterdam Treaty. 'Despite the limitations of co-decision, its use as the legislative procedure for environmental measures considerably strengthens the Parliament's role in the adoption of new environmental legislation' (Grant et al, 2000, p35). The Green Party has been an important political presence in the European Parliament since 1989, when it captured 37 seats; following the June 1999 election it again had 37 members. The Parliament has often been an effective source of pressure on the Council for the adoption of more stringent regulations.

The EU's structure has also magnified the influence of the 'greener' Member States. As Héritier argues, an important key to understanding the dynamics of EU policy making lies in the logic of diversity, 'which initiates a spontaneous acceleration of policy-making by regulatory competition and mutual learning' (see Chapters 8 and 10; Héritier, 1999). Formally, EU policy is highly centralized: directives are approved in Brussels and then the Member States are obliged to transpose them into national law and then enforce them. But in fact EU policy-making is highly fragmented. If supporters of more stringent regulatory standards can persuade decision-makers in one or more Member States that their ideas have merit, 'these policy-makers will carry this point of view into the EU process' (Zito, 2000, p23). Accordingly, 'the significant participation of the Member States means that the various ideas that circulate at the national level may in turn diffuse into the EU level' (ibid, p23). This is also the case when Member States unilaterally enact more stringent regulatory standards – which often results in placing these standards on the EU's agenda. This dynamic has often contributed to a 'trend toward higher and tougher standards by Brussels' (Young and Wallace, 2000, p9). For example, both the EU's Packaging and Electronics Recycling Directives were influenced by Member State regulations, as were the EU's vehicle emission requirements (see Chapter 10).

The EU's quasi-federal structure, along with the fragmentation of authority among the Commission, the Council, the European Parliament and the ECJ has provided representatives of civic interests with multiple points of access. An entrepreneurial coalition favouring more stringent regulatory standards 'needs ready access to only one part of the EU system (as long as that structural position provides a visible and vocal platform for the coalition's cause). Because EU institutions encompass such a wide array of interests, finding one sympathetic access point is relatively easy' (Zito, 2000, p192). A fragmented political system also provides opponents of policy change with multiple veto points. The EU's constitutional structure does not automatically privilege civic interests any more than does the fragmented US system. But, as the US experience of the 1970s illustrates, the multiple points of access offered by a fragmented political system, when combined with a highly mobilized and risk-averse public, can lead to a significantly strengthening and broadening of regulatory standards.

Finally, the strengthening of regulatory standards at the European level has also been affected by the dynamics of the single market. An important consequence of the single market has been to make European consumers increasingly dependent on, and thus vulnerable to, the regulatory policies of all 15 Member States as well as Brussels. This has increased political pressures on the EU to promulgate stricter European-wide rules since regulatory failure in any Member State endangers the single market as a whole. In addition, protecting the health and safety of Europeans as well as the European environment has become critical to the EU's legitimacy and its claim to represent the broader interests and concerns of Europeans. As Breyer and Heyvaert suggest:

> [Regulatory centralization] may be the expression of a growing feeling of unity among the citizens of Europe, of a growing desire to protect the common European heritage across national boundaries, and of a rising expectation among Europeans that, when they move from one country to another, they will benefit from the same high level of health and environmental protection (Breyer and Heyvaert, 2000, p327).

The European Present and the American Past

There are a number of similarities between regulatory policies and politics in Europe since the mid-1980s and those in the US from the early 1960s through around 1990. During these three decades, an influential segment of US elite and public opinion became more risk averse, often focusing on the dangers of new technologies rather than their potential benefits. One UK journalist wrote in 1971: 'We saw the Americans thrashing around from one pollution scare to the next, and we were mildly amused. One moment it was cyclamates, mercury the next, then ozone, lead, cadmium – over there they seemed set on working their way in a random manner through the whole periodic table' (Johnson, 1971, pp170–171). A UK social scientist observed in 1979, 'Americans seem to have taken an excessively strict interpretation of risk, reducing "reasonable risk" practically to "zero risk"'.[20] Douglas and Wildavsky wrote in *Risk and Culture*, published in 1982:

> *Try to read a newspaper or news magazine... on any day some alarm bells will be ringing. What are USs afraid of? Nothing much, really except the food they eat,*

the water they drink, the air they breathe… In the amazingly short space of 15 to
20 years, confidence about the physical world has turned into doubt. Once the
source of safety, science and technology has become the source of risk (Douglas
and Wildavsky, 1982, p10).

The argument in the US against public funding of a supersonic passenger air-
plane is similar to that made by many Europeans against regulatory approval for
genetically modified agricultural products nearly a quarter of a century later: in
both cases, a significant segment of the public saw no benefits associated with the
proposed new technology, only increased environmental and health risks. The
political salience of the issue of ozone depletion in the US during the 1970s parallels the high level of European concern over global climate change during the
1990s. The political setbacks experienced by the US chemical and automotive
industries during the 1970s and 1980s are similar to those experienced by agricultural biotechnology firms in Europe over the last decade.

In both the US in the 1970s and 1980s and Europe since the mid-1980s,
public preferences and concerns have played an important role in shaping both
the regulatory agenda and specific regulatory policies. Significantly, a number of
US regulatory policies implemented in the 1970s and 1980s and European policies since the mid-1980s have been similarly criticized for being too risk averse
and rooted more in public fears than scientific evidence.[21] In 1997, responding
to the European demands for the separation of GM and non-GM foods, US Secretary of Agriculture Dan Glickman declared that 'test after rigorous scientific test
has proven these products to be safe. Sound science must trump passion' (Urry,
1997, p4). But during the 1970s and 1980s, many USs were as sceptical as many
contemporary Europeans of relying on 'sound science' to dictate risk management policies.[22]

The US, like Europe, also experienced a series of widely publicized regulatory
failures, and accusations of regulatory failures whose cumulative effect was to
increase public support for more effective and stringent regulation. The thalidomide scandal (1962), Rachael Carson's *Silent Spring* (1962), Ralph Nader's exposé
of the health industry, *Unsafe at Any Speed* (1965), Love Canal (1977) and Three
Mile Island (1979) were the US counterparts to Europe's Chernobyl, the contamination of the Rhine, mad cow disease, dioxin in the food supply and contaminated blood. The significant membership expansion and increased political influence of public interest lobbies in the US during the 1970s parallels the increased
influence of representatives of civic interests, including Green Parties, in Europe
during the 1980s and 1990s. And the centralization of regulatory policy-making
in Brussels parallels the federalization of regulatory policy-making in the US. On
both sides of the Atlantic institutional changes made regulatory policy-making
more exposed to public scrutiny and pressure, which in turn strengthened the
influence of pro-regulation constituencies and reduced the ability of business to
dictate regulatory outcomes.[23] Significantly, the fragmented constitutional structure of the EU, with its quasi-separation of powers and quasi-federal division of
regulatory responsibilities more closely resembles the US than it does any Member State.

What Happened in the US?

This raises a critical question: what happened to US regulatory politics and policies after 1990? After all, EU regulations could have become more stringent and comprehensive, while the US also continued to enact relatively stringent and comprehensive regulations, thus producing policy convergence. Or each could have adopted more stringent and innovative policies in different areas, with the result that on balance, the consumer and environmental standards adopted since 1985 or 1990 would have been no more or less stringent or innovative on either side of the Atlantic. But neither has occurred. Why?

Before addressing this question, it is important to note that the relatively stringent and comprehensive statutes enacted in the US through 1990 have not been repealed. Indeed, some highly risk-averse regulations continue to be issued pursuant to these laws including, for example, the 1997 ozone national ambient air standards promulgated by the Clinton administration and the Bush administration's 2001 standards for arsenic in drinking water. There have also been a number of additional controls over the tobacco industry by both the courts and in a number of states. What has changed is the rate at which significant new federal regulatory laws have been adopted. For example, between 1993 and 2002, encompassing the eight years of the Clinton administration (1993–2000), and the first two years of the second Bush administration (2001–2002) Congress passed only four environmental or consumer protection laws: the Food Quality Protection Act, the Safe Drinking Water Act Amendments, the Transportation Equity Act and the Small Business Relief and Brownfields Revitalization Act. This represents fewer new laws than were enacted during any previous decade since the 1960s. And of these, only the Food Quality Protection Act, which adopted a new approach to regulating pesticides, can be considered a significant regulatory policy innovation (Kraft, 2002, pp127–150).

The last major legislative expansion of environmental regulation in the US took place in 1990. That year saw the enactment of three statutes: the Oil Pollution Act of 1990, the Pollution Prevention Act of 1990 and the Clean Air Act Amendments of 1990. The last-mentioned was particularly significant: it established a cap and trade system to reduce emission of sulphur dioxide and nitrogen oxides, required stricter emission standards for motor vehicles and cleaner fuels, required emission limits to be set for all major sources of toxic or hazardous air pollutants, listed 189 chemicals to be regulated, prohibited the use of CFCs, and phased out other ozone-depleting chemicals.

It is primarily with respect to the environmental agenda that has emerged since 1990 that the US has become a regulatory laggard. Here the contrast with the EU is particularly striking. It is not that US federal standards regarding eco-labelling, packaging wastes, automobile and electronic recycling and carbon emissions are less stringent than those of the EU; in each of these areas *US federal regulation is non-existent*. And in the critical case of GMOs, European standards are notably more stringent than in the US. Why, then did the US hare start moving like a tortoise?

The slowdown in the rate of new regulatory policy initiatives in the US during the 1990s stems in large measure from the absence of major regulatory failures in the US. (The last major regulatory failure in the US was the 1989 *Exxon Valdez* oil spill, which, however, affected only a narrow range of policies.) There have been periodic consumer safety and environmental crises since then, but unlike in Europe their policy impact has been limited. In part due to the absence of such failure, USs are now more trusting of government regulation than Europeans. Thus while 90 per cent of Americans believe the US Department of Agriculture's statements on biotechnology, only 12 per cent of Europeans trust their national regulators (Enriques and Goldberg, 2000, p103). The degree of public anxiety about the pervasiveness of threats to public health, safety and the environment coupled with a lack of faith in the capacity of government adequately to protect public health and environmental quality from business, has diminished in the US over the last 10 to 15 years, at the same time as it has increased in much of Europe. This may partially explain the degree of public acceptance of GMOs – a technology which, if it had been introduced into the US two decades earlier, might well have received a more sceptical public reception. According to one polling firm, the US's faith in major corporations rose in the 1980s and 1990s, helping to 'produce a politics that has been reluctant to impose new regulatory burdens on business that might diminish corporate profits (Callahan, 2000, pA23).

Moreover, the Republican Party's control of one or more Houses of Congress since 1994, combined with the growing conservatism of Republican legislators, has significantly enhanced the influence of business over regulatory policies. In addition, business itself became more politically effective – a process that began in the late 1970s but became particularly significant after 1990 in the area of environmental policy.[24] Business pressures played a critical role in shaping US opposition to both the Biosafety and Kyoto Protocols (Falkner, 2001, pp157–177). US non-governmental organizations (NGOs) spent the six years after 1994 fighting to prevent the rolling back of existing statutes. While this effort by and large succeeded, it came at the cost of lost momentum to advance new regulatory goals. The election of President Bush in 2000 continued this pattern: in 2001 and 2002 the efforts of NGOs primarily focused on maintaining the regulatory status quo rather than expanding the scope of consumer or environmental protection.

Conclusion

After comparing a wide range of US and European regulatory standards, Weiner and Rogers argue that the notion 'of a precautionary Europe and a risky America (or a general flip-flop in relative precaution across the Atlantic) is unpersuasive' (Weiner and Rogers, 2002, p333). They cite, for example, the US decisions made in 1989 and 1991 to ban imports of UK beef and the 1999 decision of the Food and Drug Administration to reject blood from any donor who had spent more than six months in the UK between 1980 and 1996. By contrast, they note that the EU lifted its ban on UK beef in 1998 and has imposed no restrictions on blood donors based on their prior residency in the UK.

It is true that on balance Europe is not more precautionary than the US, since virtually all the relatively risk-averse statutes enacted by the US before 1991 are still in effect. Nor is it the case that all European regulations issued since 1990 are more stringent or comprehensive than in the US. It is rather that the most powerful determinant for the relative stringency or innovativeness of consumer and environmental regulations in the US and Europe is the time frame during which they were enacted. For the most important consumer and environmental regulations enacted prior to the mid-1980s in which US and European policies were divergent, US policies were more likely to be either more stringent or innovative. Examples include automobile emission standards, chemical approval and renewal policies, regulations governing food additives, drug approval policies and restrictions on CFCs. For regulations which emerged on either the European or US regulatory agenda after 1990, European regulations are more likely to be either more stringent or comprehensive. Important examples include the approval and labelling of genetically modified foods and seeds, the recycling of packaging, automobiles and electronic products, restrictions on international trade in hazardous wastes, animal protection and cutbacks on carbon emissions. Policies enacted in the interim, namely between 1985 and 1990, present a more mixed pattern. Some were more stringent in the US, such as the 1990 automobile emission standards, while others were more stringent in Europe, such as the 1985 ban on growth hormones for cattle.

In an essay published in 1990, entitled 'American Exceptionalism and the Political Acknowledgement of Risk', Jasanoff writes that while 'the US process for making risk decisions impressed all observers as costly, confrontational ... and unusually open to participation', in Europe, 'policy decisions about risk, remained, as before, the preserve of experienced bureaucrats and their established advisory networks' (Jasanoff, 1993, pp63, 66). Her generalization about European and American policy styles and policy consequences that flow from them are echoed in virtually every comparative regulatory study published during the 1970s and 1980s.[25] This generalization must now be re-examined, a process which Jasanoff her to show signs of impermanence (ibid, p77). Over a decade later, it is now much clearer that the 'US approach' to health, safety and environmental regulation is no longer as distinctive as it appeared to scholars writing during the 1970s and 1980s.[26]

But nor is it the case that 'deep-rooted cultural' differences drive, for example, European and US policies on global climate change due to Americans being 'more individualistic, more concerned about their lifestyles than about the environment, and more ideologically averse to regulations' (Levy and Newell, 2000, p10). The issue of global climate change has been more politically salient in Europe than in the US for more than a decade, and, unlike in the US, European policy-makers have enacted restrictions on carbon emissions. But this hardly can reflect 'deep-rooted cultural' differences between Europe and the US, since during the 1970s and 1980s, the US enacted a wide range of more risk-averse, innovative and comprehensive environmental and consumer regulations – including restrictions on CFCs – than did any European country or the EU.

We are now in a better position to generalize about the dynamics of regulatory policy-making on both sides of the Atlantic. Consumer and environmental regulations are likely to become more innovative, comprehensive and risk averse as a response to a widespread public perception of regulatory failures. These regulatory failures have a spillover effect: they both make public opinion more sensitive to the risks associated with new technologies and undermine public confidence in existing regulatory institutions. They also increase the political influence of political constituencies who favour more stringent regulatory policies and reduce the influence of business. Two policy consequences flow from this dynamic. First, policy-makers become more likely to adopt more comprehensive and risk-averse policies, even when these policies adversely affect the financial interests of important industries. Secondly, regulatory policy-making itself changes: it becomes more open, more transparent and more accessible to non-industry influences.

The US experience suggests that this policy dynamic can persist for an extended period of time. It persisted for nearly three decades in the US and the momentum for increased regulatory stringency in Europe has now lasted more than 15 years. It, however, does not last indefinitely. As new procedures for making regulatory policies are established and appear to be functioning reasonably effectively, the political salience of consumer and environmental regulation declines and public pressures for more stringent standards diminish. At the same time, the influence of industry on regulatory policy-making again increases as policy-makers become more sensitive to the costs of relatively stringent standards. As long as the institutional changes that made policy-making more open and publicly accessible remain in place, the result is not so much a rolling back of existing consumer or environmental regulations, but rather policy gridlock. This took place in the US after 1990 and will at some point occur in Europe.

Notes

1   See Marsha Echols, 'Food Safety Regulation in the EU and the US', *Columbia' Journal of European Law*, Vol.4 (1998), pp525–543.
2   Quoted in Vogel, p158.
3   Quoted in Vogel, p172.
4   For a more extensive discussion of the differences between European and US regulations of GMOs, see Thomas Bernauer and Erika Meins (2001) 'Scientific Revolution Meets Policy and the Market: Explaining Cross-National Differences in Agricultural Biotechnology Regulation', unpublished paper, Adelaide University, Centre for International Economic Studies; Mark Pollack and Gregory Shaffer, 'The Challenge of Food Safety in Transatlantic Relations', Mark Pollack and Gregory Shaffer (eds) (2001) *Transatlantic Governance in the Global Economy*, Oxford: Bowman & Littlefield, pp162–70; and David Vogel (2002) 'Ships Passing in the Night: GMOS and the Politics of Risk Regulation in Europe and the US', INSEAD: Centre for the Management of Environmental Resources Working Paper.
5   See Kurk Eichenwald, Gina Kolata and Melody Peterson (2001) 'Biotechnology Food: From the Lab to a Debacle', *New York Times*, 25 January. According to this article, 'the control this nascent industry exerted over its own regulatory destiny ... was astonishing'.
6   See Vogel, pp46–52.
7   For a detailed discussion of each of these trade disputes, see Vogel (1997).

8   Communication from the European Commission on the precautionary prin-
    ciple, 2 February 2000, p15.
9   (Translation by author). For a collection of essays generally sympathetic to
    this position, primarily by USs, see Carolyn Raffensperger and Joel Tickner,
    eds, *Protecting Public Health and the Environment-Implementing the Precau-
    tionary Principle* Washington, D.C.: Island Press, 1999. For a wide-ranging
    critique of the precautionary principle as both law and philosophy, see Julian
    Morris, ed., *Rethinking Risk and the Precautionary Principle* Oxford: Butter-
    worth, 2000.
10 There is an extensive literature on this subject. See, for example, Scott Ratzan
    (ed) *The Mad Cow Crisis: Health and the Public Good,* New York: New York
    University Press, 1998.
11 The links are observed by journalists in titles such as 'Mad Coke disease', see
    John Lanchester, *New York Times Magazine,* 14 July 1999.
12 See Graham Chambers, 'The BSE Crisis and the European Parliament', in
    Christian Joerges and Ellen Vos, (eds) *EU Committees: Social Regulation, Law
    and Politics,* Oxford: Hart Publishing (1999).
13 See the other contributions in Joerges and Vos (eds) *EU Committees.*
14 For an extended discussion of this issue, seem Francis Chateauraynaud and T.
    Didier (1999) *Les Sombres Precurseurs (the Dark Forerunners)* Paris: Editions
    de l'Ecole des Hautes Etudes en Sciences Sociales, Chapters 3–7.
15 The extensive literature on this issue includes Michel Setbon, *Pouvoirs contra
    Sida,* Paris: Editions du Seuil (1993); Blandine Kriegel, *Le Sang, la justice, la
    politique,* Paris: Plon (1999); and Olivier Beaud *Le Sang contaminé,* Paris:
    Behemoth (1999). It should be noted that many scholars believe the scandal
    has been overblown and the prosecution of government officials for it was
    both ethically and legally problematic. But this point of view has not
    affected public perceptions.
16 For a discussion of the origins of French policies towards GMOs, see David Vogel
    and Olivier Cadot (2001) 'France, the United States and the Biotechnology
    Debate', Washington, DC: The Brookings Institution, Foreign Policy Studies.
17 See Andersen and Liefferink (1997).
18 See, for example, Pierre-Benoit Joly and Claire Marris (2001) 'Les Americans
    ont-ils accepté les OGM? Analyse compare de la construction des OGM
    comme problème public en France et aux Etats-Unis', Centre for Manage-
    ment of Environmental Resources, INSEAD, Workshop on Regulating
    Genetically Modified Food.
19 See Elizabeth Bomberg (1998) *Green Parties and Politics in the EU,* London:
    Routledge.
20 Quoted in Vogel (1986).
21 For the US, see, for example, Michael Fumento (1993) *Science Under Siege,*
    New York: William Morrow; and Aaron Wildavsky (1995) *But Is It True? A
    Citizens' Guide to Environmental Health and Safety Issues,* Cambridge, MA:
    Harvard University Press. For Europe, see Frank Furedi (1997) *Culture of Fear,*
    London: Cassell, and Durodie (2000).
22 See, for example, Harvey Sapolsky (ed) (1986) *Consuming Fears: The Politics
    of Product Risk,* New York: Basic Books; and Wildavsky, *But Is It True?*

23 The changes in the US are explored in detail in Vogel, *Fluctuating Fortunes*, Chapter 5.
24 For business political activity during the 1970s and 1980s, see Vogel, *Fluctuating Fortunes*, Chapters 7, 8; for a historical overview of business and environmental politics, see Norman Vig (2002) 'Presidential Leadership and the Environment' in Vig and Kraft (eds), *Environmental Policy*, Washington, DC: Congressional Quarterly Press, pp103–26.
25 See, in addition to Brickman et al (1985): Lundqvist, (1980); Vogel (1986); Joseph Badaracco Jr (1986) *Loading the Dice: A Five Country Study of Vinyl Chloride Regulation*, Boston, MA: Harvard Business School; Steven Kelman (1981) *Regulating the US, Regulating Sweden*, Cambridge, MA: MIT Press; and Graham Wilson (1985) *The Politics of Safety and Health: Occupational Safety and Health in the US and the UK*, Oxford: Clarendon Press.
26 Breyer and Heyvart make a similar point in a more recent comparison of US and European institutions for managing risk.

References

Andersen, M. S. and Liefferink, D. (eds) (1997) *European Environmental Policy: The Pioneers*, Manchester: Manchester University Press.
Applegate, J. (2000) 'The Precautionary Preference: An American Perspective on the Precautionary Principle', *Human and Ecological Risk Assessment*, Vol.6, pp413–443.
Arp, H. (1993) 'Technical Regulation and Politics: The Interplay Between Economic Interests and Environment Policy Goals in EC Car Legislation', in Liefferink, J. D., Lowe, P. D. and Mol, A. P. J. (eds) *European Integration and Environmental Policy*, London: Belhaven Press.
Beck, U. (1999) *World Risk Society*, Cambridge, England: Polity.
Benedict, R. E. (1998) *Ozone Diplomacy*, Cambridge, MA: Harvard University Press.
Blanford, D., Bureau, J.-C., Fulponi, L. and Hensen, S. (2002) 'Potential Implications of Animal Welfare Concerns and Public Policies in Industrialized Countries for International Trade', in Krissoff, B., Bohman, M. and Caswell, J. (eds) *Global Food Trade and the Demand for Quality*, New York: Kluwer Academic.
Bomberg, E. (1998) *Green Parties and Politics in the European Union*, London: Routledge.
Breyer, S. and Heyvaert, V. (2000) 'Institutions for Managing Risk', in Revesz, R., Sands, P. and Stewart, R. (eds) *Environmental Law, the Economy and Sustainable Development*, Cambridge, England: Cambridge University Press.
Brickman, R., Jasanoff, S. and Ilgen, T. (1985) *Controlling Chemicals: The Politics of Regulation in Europe and the United States*, Ithaca, NY: Cornell University Press.
Burros, M. (1999) 'US Plans Long-term Studies on Safety of Genetically Altered Foods', *New York Times*, 14 July.
Callahan, D. (2000) 'Private Sector, Public Doubts', *New York Times*, 15 January.
Cameron, J. (1999) 'The Precautionary Principle', in Sampson, G. and Chambers, W. B. (eds) *Trade, Environment and the Millennium*, New York: United Nations University Press.

Consumer Voice (2000) 'Back to the Future', Special Edition.

Cookson, C. and Houlder, V. (1999) 'An Uncontrolled Experiment', *Financial Times*, 13/14 February.

Douglas, M. and Wildavsky, A. (1982) *Risk and Culture*, Berkeley: University of California Press.

Durodie, B. (2000) 'Plastic Panics: European Risk Regulation in the Aftermath of BSE', in Morris, J. (ed) *Rethinking Risk and the Precautionary Principle*, Oxford: Butterworth Heinemann.

The Economist (1999) 'Genetically Modified Food: Food for Thought', 19 June.

Enriquez, J. and Goldberg, R. (2000) 'Transforming Life, Transforming Business: The Life Science Revolution', *Harvard Business Review*, March-April, pp94–104.

Falkner, R. (2001) 'Business Conflict and US International Environmental Policy: Ozone, Climate and Biodiversity', in Harris, P. (ed) *The Environment, International Relations, and US Foreign Policy*, Washington, DC: Georgetown University Press.

Flynn, B. (1998) 'EU Environmental Policy at a Crossroads? Reconsidering Some Paradoxes in the Evolution of Policy Content', *European Journal of Public Policy*, Vol.5, p691–696.

Godard, O. (1997) 'Social Decision-Making Under Conditions of Scientific Controversy, Expertise and the Precautionary Principle', in Joerges, C., Ladeur, K.-H. and Vos, E. (eds) *Integrating Scientific Expertise into Regulatory Decision-Making: National Traditions and European Innovation*, Baden-Baden: Nomos Verlagsgesellschaft.

Grant, W., Matthews, D. and Newell, P. (2000) *The Effectiveness of European Union Environmental Policy*, London: Macmillan.

Haverland, M. (1999) *National Autonomy, European Integration and the Politics of Packaging Waste*, Amsterdam: Thela.

Herman, R. (1988) 'An Ecological Epiphany', *Washington Post National Weekly Edition*, 5–11 December.

Héritier, A. (1999) *Policy-Making and Diversity in Europe,* Cambridge: Cambridge University Press.

Jasanoff, S. (1993) 'American Exceptionalism and the Political Acknowledgement of Risk', in Burger, E. (ed) *Risk,* Ann Arbor: University of Michigan Press.

Jasanoff, S. (1997) 'Civilization and Madness: The Great BSE Scare of 1996', *Public Understanding of Science*, Vol.6.

Jasanoff, S. (2000) 'Technological Risk and Cultures of Rationality', in *Incorporating Economics, and Sociology in Developing Sanitary and Phytosanitary Standards in International Trade*, Washington, DC: National Academy Press, pp65–86.

Johnson, S. (1971) *The Politics of the Environment: The UK Experience*, London: Tom Stacey.

Jordan, A. and O'Riordan, T. (1995) 'The Precautionary Principle in UK Environmental Law and Policy', in Gray, T. (ed) *UK Environmental Policy in the 1990s*, London: Macmillan.

Kraft, M. (2002) 'Environmental Policy in Congress: From Consensus to Gridlock', in Vig, N. and Kraft, M. (eds) *Environmental Policy*, Washington, DC: Congressional Quarterly Press.

Lepage, C. and Query, F. (2001) *La Politique de Precaution*, Paris: Presses Universitaires de France.

Levy D. and Newell, P. (2000) 'Business Responses to Global Environmental Issues in Europe and the United States', *Environment*, Vol.42, No.9.

Libby, R. (1998) *Eco-Wars: Political Campaigns and Social Movements,* New York: Columbia University Press.

Lundqvist, L. (1980) *The Hare and the Tortoise: Clean Air Policies in the United States and Sweden*, Ann Arbor: University of Michigan Press.

Majone, G. (1996) *Regulating Europe,* London: Routledge.

Mann, M. (2002) 'Brussels Acts Over Missed Scrap Car Deadlines', *Financial Times*, 30 July.

McCormick, J. (2001) *Environmental Policy in the European Union,* New York: Palgrave.

Millstone, E. (2000) 'Comment and Analysis', *Financial Times*, 6 October.

Le Monde (2000) 'Le Gouvernement Peaufine un Plan d'Interdiction des Farines Animates', 12–13 November.

Paarlberg, R. (1999) 'Lapsed Leadership: US International Environmental Leadership Since Rio', in Vig, N. and Axelrod, R. (eds) *The Global Environment*, Washington, DC: Congressional Quarterly Press.

Reid, T. R. (2001) 'Be Careful What You Eat, Where You Sit and ...' *Washington Post National Weekly Edition*, 12–18 May.

Scott J. and Vos, E. (2002) 'The Juridification of Uncertainty', in Joerges, C. and Dehousse, R. (eds) *Good Governance in Europe's Integrated Market,* Oxford: Oxford University Press.

Stecklow, S. (2001) 'Despite Assurances, US Could Be at Risk for Mad-Cow Disease', *Wall Street Journal*, 18 November.

Tait, N. (1999) 'EPA Sued Over Genetic Crop Approval', *Financial Times*, 19 February.

Thompson, M. (1983) 'A Cultural Basis for Comparison', in Kunreuther, H. et al, *Risk Analysis and Decision Process: The Siting of Liquefied Energy Gas Facilities in Four Countries,* Berlin: Springer-Verlag.

Urry, M. (1997) 'Genetic Products Row Worsens', *Financial Times*, 20 June.

Vehicle Emission Reductions (2001) Paris: European Conference of Ministers of Transport.

Vogel, D. (1986) *National Styles of Regulation: Environmental Policy in Great Britain and the United States,* Ithaca, NY: Cornell University Press.

Vogel, D. (1989) *Fluctuating Fortunes*, New York: Basic Books.

Vogel, D. (1990) 'When Consumers Oppose Consumer Protection', *Journal of Public Policy*, Vol.100, pp449–470.

Vogel, D. (1995) 'Trading Up Consumer and Environmental Regulation in a Global Economy', Cambridge, MA: Harvard University Press.

Vogel, D. (1997) *Barriers or Benefits? Regulation in Transatlantic Trade,* Washington, DC: Brookings Institution Press.

Weiner, J. and Rogers, M. (2002) 'Comparing Precaution in the United States and Europe', *Journal of Risk Research*, Vol.5, pp317–349.

Weiss, R. (1999) 'No Appetite for Gene Cuisine', *Washington Post National Weekly Edition*, 3 May.

Williams, N. (1998) 'Plant Genetics: Agricultural Biotech Faces Backlash in Europe', *Science*, 7 August.

Young, A. and Wallace, H. (2000) *Regulatory Politics in the Enlarging European Union*, Manchester: Manchester University Press.

Zito, A. (2000) *Creating Environmental Policy in the European Union*, London: Macmillan.

14

Emissions Trading at Kyoto: From EU Resistance to Union Innovation

Chad Damro and Pilar Luaces Méndes

Introduction

The 1997 Kyoto Protocol on climate change continues to be a target of pointed praise and condemnation from a variety of actors in domestic and international environmental policy-making.[1] As a result, the Kyoto Summit has been the subject of close scrutiny by a diverse group of scholars.[2] However, most of this literature overlooks interesting questions related to the political dynamics surrounding the emergence and implementation of a new environmental policy instrument (NEPI) at the international level – a greenhouse gas emissions trading system.[3]

While the 11-day Kyoto Summit was an extremely well-attended international conference, it is particularly productive to analyse the negotiations in terms of the conflicting positions of two central actors, the European Union (EU) and the United States of America (US). Such an analysis generates two interesting questions related to NEPIs: (1) how and why was a new emissions trading system incorporated into an international environmental agreement, and (2) to what extent do post-conference, NEPI-adoption discussions reflect an ongoing process of policy innovation in the EU and US?

Investigating these questions may provide specific insights into the domestic politics and international negotiations that surround the complex adoption and implementation of similar NEPIs. To do so, this chapter employs a detailed analysis of primary and secondary documents on EU and US climate change policies. Central to the analysis, two conflicting policy paradigms are identified: US free-market environmentalism and EU risk-prevention leadership (cf Chapter 13). These paradigms were transformed at Kyoto into a US demand for an emissions trading system and EU calls for binding commitments and fixed timetables for emissions cuts.

In addition to exploring the ways in which conflicting EU and US positions were overcome, this study investigates the post-Summit promotion of the Kyoto NEPI by the formerly resistant EU. Following the Summit, the adoption of an emissions trading system appears to have failed as an act of policy innovation in the US. However, while the EU initially opposed the inclusion of this particular NEPI in the final agreement, policy innovation remains under way in the Union. Unlike in the US, the Kyoto Protocol now appears to function as an external source of EU policy change.

Competing Explanations of Policy Innovation

The emergence of emissions trading has been a significant innovation in international environmental policy-making. In the scholarly literature, such innovations generally stem from diverse sources and occur in different degrees. Both dimensions produce different (albeit frequently complementary) explanations about why policy innovation occurs in a particular policy area and/or jurisdiction.

In general, policy innovation may originate from sources internal and external to a jurisdiction. Studies emphasizing the causal role of internal sources frequently argue that policy innovation occurs via numerous intra-territorial processes, usually prompted by significant alterations in socio-economic conditions, governing coalitions and groups, or policy decisions adopted in other policy domains. They can also result from routine policy evaluation and new information. Any of these factors may foster policy-oriented learning, which Sabatier and Jenkins-Smith understand as relatively enduring alterations of thought and behavioural intentions that result from experience and/or new information, and that are concerned with the attainment or revision of policy objectives within a policy area (Sabatier and Jenkins-Smith, 1995). For Sabatier and Jenkins-Smith, policy learning is more likely when there is an 'informed' level of conflict between two 'advocacy coalitions' without affecting the core beliefs of either coalition.[4]

Such alterations can be instrumental or can shape core attributes of a policy. In the first case, policy learning involves a new understanding of policy instruments underpinning the policy design (May, 1992). Policy learning affects the core attributes of a policy when the process 'involves a greater understanding of the policy problem and the very goals become affected' (May, 1992). In these cases, the set of ideas and standards within which policy-makers customarily work reveals crucial anomalies that lead to the alteration and redefinition of policy goals, policy instruments and the techniques to provide policy solutions. For Sabatier and Jenkins-Smith this process is likely to occur in the presence of significant alterations outside of the policy area.

Hall (1993) has referred to this process as change in the policy paradigm. Similarly, in this chapter, we hypothesize that the EU's policy paradigm affects the way innovation is taking place in Europe. EU climate change policy is embedded in an ongoing internal process that gradually revealed the limitations of command-and-control policy instruments. This process was gradual because earlier voices calling for an 'economization' of policy instruments encountered resistance from three deeply entrenched ideas within the policy area: a commitment to stringent emissions reductions, a need to protect the internal market's international competitiveness, and a growing internal demand for EU leadership in international climate change policy.

In contrast to internal learning, alternative explanations highlight the causal influence of external sources in policy innovation. These explanations argue that external sources can induce policy innovation through a variety of transnational processes. For example, a state's participation in international organizations or interaction with other states through less formal transnational processes may create the conditions for adopting policies, practices, programmes or policy instruments already operating in other jurisdictions (Page, 2000). This chapter hypothesizes that the source of policy innovation was external to the EU and occurred through a transnational process.

Analyses of policy innovation resulting from sources external to a governmental jurisdiction often focus on the processes and patterns through which innovation is adopted. This is the case in *policy diffusion* studies, which mainly investigate US cases (Stokes Berry and Berry, 1999). Such studies are concerned with identifying patterns of diffusion and demonstrating that policy innovations travel across borders due to geographical proximity or interaction among national officials. These diffusions are likely to occur among adjacent authorities with similar resources. However, scholarly work on policy diffusion pays little attention to the process of transfer and its agents. Thus, policy diffusion studies are often considered 'agentless' (Dolowitz and Marsh, 2000).

Another explanation of policy innovation that emphasizes external sources comes from studies of *lesson-drawing*. The lesson-drawing literature stresses the importance of understanding the conditions under which policies or practices operate in one jurisdiction and whether and how similar conditions may be created in another jurisdiction (Page, 2000). This approach suggests that the application of a policy occurs through conscious emulation (Jordan et al, 2000; Rose, 1993). The emphasis on conscious emulation suggests that innovation occurs as a voluntary process.

Finally, policy transfer studies focus on understanding the decision-making process through which a policy operating in one jurisdiction is identified and adopted in another country, focusing on the reasons leading to this decision and the actors involved (Page, 2000; Dolowitz and Marsh, 2000). In contrast to lesson-drawing, policy transfer may range from a coercive to a totally voluntary process. Understanding the precise reasons and circumstances through which transfer proceeds may shed light on the 'success' or 'failure' of transferred policies.[5]

This chapter argues that the introduction of an emissions trading system in EU environmental policy stems from a process of policy transfer, derived from the negotiations between the US and the EU at the Kyoto Summit. The policy transfer literature offers the most useful set of analytical devices for elucidating why the EU has introduced a market-oriented emissions trading system into its climate change policy. Since lesson-drawing focuses heavily on 'emulation', it seems an insufficient analytical option for understanding the decision-making process – which varies considerably from that found in the US – through which emissions trading is being introduced in the EU.

Rather than focusing on the process of innovation, lesson-drawing stresses how conditions under which a policy operates in an 'exporter' jurisdiction may be created in an 'importer' jurisdiction (Page, 2000). Similarly, policy diffusion studies assume that exogenous innovation is likely to occur among adjacent jurisdictions with similar resources, a condition not present in the Kyoto case.

This chapter hypothesizes that, far from being an 'obligation', this policy transfer has been a voluntary process driven by the EU's perception of necessity. Policy transfer focuses on the very basic questions of who, what, where, how and why a transfer occurs. Each dimension helps to deepen our understanding of the decision-making process in the transferring jurisdiction and whether the transfer will succeed or fail.

While almost any policy can be transferred from one political system to another, it is useful to identify exactly what is being transferred. In other words, is an entire policy being transferred or just parts of a policy – goals, contents and/or instruments (Dolowitz and Marsh, 2000, p12)? As Pressman and Wildavsky (1973) argue, marginal changes in instruments or contents are more likely than overall transfers of policies, which imply changes in underlying ideas. Thus, we may expect the ideas upon which policies are based to be quite resistant to change, with marginal changes in instruments and contents more likely to occur. In the Kyoto case, the evidence suggests that the transfer of a single policy instrument – an emissions trading system, not an entire policy – has facilitated the process of innovation in the EU.

Innovation through policy transfer is also eased when it follows certain timing patterns. The shorter the time period, the more an innovation is likely to be perceived as an alien import. But if the time period is extended, innovations become domesticated as the relationship between existing institutions and policies shapes their development (Page, 2000, p5). Clearly, the EU understands timing as a crucial variable. The EU initiated its internal work programme on this NEPI in 1999, in order to implement gradually an EU emissions trading system by 2005. This target date is seven years before the global system will come into operation.

A voluntary process of transfer might vary according to the degree to which the transfer is a collectively organized procedure or a more 'casual' process (Page, 2000, p7). The conscious collective effort of the Commission to co-operate with stakeholders[6] reveals a deliberate and planned process of innovation, which seeks to overcome uninformed or incomplete innovations through transfer. Furthermore, the analysis of how transfer proceeds should investigate the extent to which transfer respects the policy's overall goals. This chapter shows that the transfer of emissions trading after Kyoto has left the overall goals of EU climate change unaltered. For the EU, a strong commitment to stringent reductions and the protection of the internal market's international competitiveness accompanied by a determination for global leadership are necessary components of any proposal on the establishment of an emissions trading system.

Whereas these dimensions enlighten the process of innovation through transfer, they do not fully address the reasons why countries borrow from one another. Page (2000, pp5–6) posits three main reasons, arguing that a jurisdiction may (1) need to develop innovations quickly, (2) adopt a policy if there is a fad or fashion for introducing certain changes in a given policy area, or (3) adopt an external innovation as a way to add weight or support to policies that have little or nothing to do with what is being evoked. The first and second arguments are echoed here, while the third appears slightly complemented.

A Kyoto NEPI: The Emissions Trading System

This section provides a brief description of the Kyoto NEPI – an emissions trading system (Article 17, Kyoto Protocol). The NEPI was introduced based on the US's 'very positive experience with permit trading in the acid rain program, [which reduced] costs by 50 per cent from what was expected, yet fully serving our environmental goals' (Eizenstat, 1998, p4). As such, the mechanism in the Kyoto Protocol resembles the American 'pollution permits' scheme for reducing domestic sulphur dioxide and lead output (Banks, 2000, p488). More specifically, tradeable permits resemble the system developed in the US Clean Air Act Amendments of 1990, the Southern California Air Quality Management District's Regional Clean Air Incentives Market and the South Coast Air Basin (Johnston, 1998).[7]

The idea of an emissions trading system is a new approach to the problem of climate change. Dobes provides a useful general description of the mechanics behind this NEPI:

> *Tradeable permits …represent a right granted by a government to the permit holder to emit a specified quantity of gases. By issuing only a limited number of permits governments can control the total quantity of gas emitted, on a local, national or international level. Because permits are usually limited to a quantity that is less than the amount of gas that would normally be emitted, the right to emit becomes a valuable commodity. If trading of permits is allowed, then a market price will be established. Those wishing to emit the specified gases beyond permitted levels must either reduce their emissions or purchase permits to emit. Polluters able to reduce their emissions relatively cheaply will do so, rather than purchase permits. Those polluters who face higher abatement costs will tend to buy permits to satisfy government requirements. In this way, reductions in emissions are made by those polluters who can do so at least cost, being compensated by polluters who face higher costs of abatement* (Dobes, 1999, pp81–82).

While a number of concerns surrounded the establishment of an emissions trading system at the international level, proponents of the system convincingly argued for the NEPI at Kyoto. Indeed, 'concerns that such a system was not practical, that there was not enough time to set it up, or that administrative requirements would be too onerous, proved hard to sustain' (Grubb et al, 1999, p92). Nevertheless, the uncertainty and complexity of this market-based NEPI reflects its relative newness as a policy instrument and prefigures the subsequent scepticism and outright resistance encountered at Kyoto.

The US Position at Kyoto: Free-Market Environmentalism

This section describes the US position at the actual Kyoto negotiations. A crucial insight of the following discussion is the pervasiveness of the dominant US policy paradigm at Kyoto, confidence in market-based solutions to the problem of climate change. Prior to Kyoto, the US government announced its position on some of the most contentious issues relating to climate change via the Climate Action Report (1995). This report signalled US determination to pursue market-based solutions to climate change. As Campbell (1998) argues:

> *By its own admission, the US government is focusing the majority of its efforts on market incentives and voluntarism, with a lesser emphasis on regulation and R&D. Numerous references are made [in the report] to the outstanding industry response to voluntary programmes, and their superiority over mandatory programmes, which are considered more time consuming to enact and are subject to limited compliance. In the context of climate change, two regulatory shifts in environmental policy are emphasized: first, that from end-of-pipe regulation to pollution prevention through voluntary agreements, particularly in the area of energy efficiency; second, from command-and-control methods to tradeable emissions permits notably through the Clean Air Act amendments of 1990* (Campbell, 1998, p162).

The focus of the US negotiating position on market-based mechanisms was strongly supported by the international business community.[8] Such support is not particularly surprising given that market-based mechanisms typically reflect and encourage strong incentives for business. By enhancing the pursuit of profit, a market-based mechanism is preferable for the business community because it 'creates a tradeable asset: the permit or allowance... [Whereas a tax] extracts revenue from the firm without adding any compensating value' (Grubb et al, 1999, p90). In other words, the regulatory flexibility inherent in the Kyoto NEPI could replace environmental taxation with greater corporate control over the pursuit of profit.

The US position at Kyoto was built on three separate but consistent objectives. Speaking before the US Senate Foreign Relations Committee, the head of the US delegation to Kyoto, Under Secretary of State Stuart Eizenstat, outlined the three objectives that guided the US position. The first US objective was to attain 'realistic targets and timetables for reducing greenhouse gas emissions among the world's major industrial nations' (Eizenstat, 1998, p3). By 'realistic', the US negotiators meant a flexible, multi-year time frame instead of a fixed, single-year target. The perceived benefit of such an approach was that it would allow the averaging of emissions reductions over five years. Such flexibility, it was argued, would lower public and private costs and 'smooth out the effects of short-term events such as fluctuations in the business cycle and energy demand, or hard winters and hot summers that would increase energy use and emissions' (Eizenstat, 1998, p3).

The second US objective was to initiate flexible, market-based mechanisms for achieving the agreed upon targets. The central component of this objective was the introduction of an emissions trading system, which was viewed as a cost-effective, market-based incentive to attain the maximum level of emissions reductions. Eizenstat declared the ultimate inclusion of the emissions trading system a 'major victory for us', because 'The commitment we made in Kyoto would not have been made – could not have been made – were it not for the flexibility mechanisms that were also agreed there' (Eizenstat, 1998, p4). Thus, the concept of flexible, market-based solutions was a core principle of the US negotiating position. Without it, support from important congressional and business interests would have been lost.

The last US objective was to require meaningful participation in emissions reductions by developing countries. This objective was strengthened by the pressure of the Byrd-Hagel Resolution, which passed in the US Senate prior to the Kyoto Summit by an impressive margin of 95–0. While Byrd-Hagel was a non-binding resolution, it did announce the Senate's intent not to ratify any agreement that lacked meaningful commitments by developing countries. While the US acknowledged that industrialized countries accounted for 70 per cent of greenhouse gases, the objective grew out of concerns over future sources of greenhouse gases. According to Eizenstat, 'by around 2015 China will be the largest overall emitter of greenhouse gases, and by 2025 the developing world will emit more greenhouse gases in total than the developed world' (Eizenstat, 1998, p4).

While Eizenstat argued that the US negotiating team achieved the first two objectives, the third was viewed as a continuing aim of post-Kyoto negotiations. Indeed, Eizenstat admitted as much when he unambiguously stated 'The Kyoto agreement does not meet our requirements for developing country participation' (Eizenstat, 1998, p5). The US negotiating team did attempt to rectify this apparent shortfall by supporting a Brazilian proposal for a clean development mechanism (CDM).[9] Nevertheless, even with the CDM, the failure to attain the third objective in the Kyoto Protocol would prove a critical element in the US Senate's failure to ratify the Protocol.

The EU Position at Kyoto: Risk-prevention Leadership

This section identifies the basic EU position at Kyoto, a position that was gradual and complex in its development. Particular attention is given to the EU's position on emissions trading. A crucial insight of the following discussion is the existence of the dominant EU policy paradigm at Kyoto: risk-prevention leadership. This paradigm is based on a serious commitment to stringent CO_2 reductions, fierce protection of the internal market's international competitiveness and a desire for leadership in global climate change policy. Risk-prevention leadership refers to the adoption of CO_2 reductions stringent enough to prevent global warming – regardless of clear and consensus-based scientific evidence – coupled with enough flexibility to avoid the Summit's failure.

The EU has largely developed its environmental policy on the basis of product and process regulation (Majone, 1996, p81). By imposing uniform and detailed directives within the EU, both the Member States and the Commission overcame environmental dumping, the transaction costs associated with settling environmental issues (for example, gathering information, bargaining) and the credibility problems associated with policing at the national level. Within the context of avoiding market failures, EU environmental goals have been inspired by the prevention rather than resolution of problems 'at the source' and application of the polluter-pays principle.[10] Thus, the EU endorses regulatory approaches that sustain the environment without harming economic competitiveness, both important elements of the EU's policy paradigm.

At Kyoto, the EU position was to defend a 'bubble concept' of shared responsibility for emissions reductions within the EU and to pursue common and coordinated policies and measures as the main mechanisms to cut EU emissions.[11] The EU also had a clear preference for mandatory emissions cuts in all Annex I countries.[12] In order to understand the EU's position, it is critical to focus attention on the actors that defined the EU position and their basic goals before the Kyoto negotiations.[13]

EU climate change policy was initiated in the 1980s[14] and gained momentum in 1990 with the first commitment to reduce CO_2 emissions by the year 2000 to 1990 levels.[15] Climate change policy was based on the common understanding that this global issue should be managed at the international level and – in line with the so-called precautionary principle – that uncertainty should not limit intervention (Huber, 1997, p143). Two main features determined the initial development of EU climate change policy.

First, the thrust of EU climate change has reflected a desire to claim EU leadership, both externally and internally, in the policy field. A general belief existed in Europe that industrialized countries had specific responsibility to reduce their CO_2 emissions and bear the costs of stringent regulations. While the Commission was a primary proponent of this position, additional pressure to play such an external leading role also came from the European Parliament and the European Environmental Bureau. This call for leadership inevitably arose before international meetings. The aspirations for external leadership, though, also required the EU to persuade Member States to co-operate internally with stringent reduction objectives rather than to free-ride. In internal debates, leadership in reducing CO_2 emissions was understood as economically beneficial if, parallel to strong commitments, incentives for developing environmentally sound technology could be provided. Hence, internal compromise over climate change policy could create a niche for environmentally sound technology before the arrival of US and Japanese firms.

Second, the complex interrelatedness of economics and climate change was believed too difficult to steer by traditional command-and-control devices alone. In response, an 'economization' of EU environmental policies was needed – besides focusing on the efficacy of regulations to tackle environmental issues, policy instruments should also consider the economic efficiency of measures. This is especially obvious in that reductions of CO_2 emissions pertained to all energy-intensive sectors. For climate change policy, the former DG II (economic analysis) carried out the conceptualization of economic instruments. Much of the research and solution-oriented work of DG II initially focused on tradeable emissions permits. However, after a decision by the Environment Council of Ministers in 1990 to develop a Community tax to deal with CO_2 (1997) rightly posits, the stabilization goal initially failed because it lacked an explicit set of rules to manage distributive inequalities resulting from the burden of reducing CO_2 emissions and bearing the costs of paying the tax. The cohesion countries – Spain, Portugal, Greece and Ireland – along with the UK were the first to question the sharing of emissions reductions (Haigh, 1996). The UK and Spain were especially sensitive to the possibility of shifting co-ordination and research competencies to the national level while leaving the Commission with no internal basis of authority to conduct foreign relations (Huber, 1997).

The issue of 'who should do what' remained unanswered through 1996. The Irish and Italian presidencies considered targets for negotiation without discussing target-sharing. This position upset the cohesion countries who feared that these specific targets would restrict their economic growth. The first proposal on sharing emissions reductions was issued by the Commission as a 'non-paper', which failed to gain the necessary sponsorship and lost much of its credibility.

Nolin argues that the eventual adoption of the 'bubble concept' as the EU climate change goal owes a great debt to the Dutch presidency (1999, p178). The Dutch took advantage of the knowledge accumulated since 1995 about each Member State's CO_2 emissions objectives. They were also aware of the special treatment being demanded by the cohesion countries and the emissions declines being experienced by Germany and the UK, due to factors such as economic restructuring in new German Länder and moderate economic growth rates in Britain. In addition, the Dutch presidency had to consider the impact of Member States switching from petroleum to natural gas and new national policies in the energy and industrial sectors.

The Dutch presidency expanded its scientific resources by enhancing close links between its own national Ministry of Housing, Spatial Planning and Environment and academic and other non-governmental experts. This array of cognitive resources gave a definitive boost to the bubble proposal, which distributed the level of emissions reductions/increases by sectoral and national criteria. The Environment Council of Ministers (March 1997) adopted commitments for each Member State, initially as a 15 per cent reduction. The Member States' burdens are provided in Table 14.1.

Different reasons explain the clear preference of the EU for common and co-ordinated policies and measures (CCPMs). CCPMs refer to actions at the community level that are adopted by all Member States usually in the form of a directive or other legal measure. Although the Commission recognized the inadequacy of regulatory instruments to deal with emissions problems, EU climate change policy was largely based upon regulatory emissions limitations, technical standards and incentives to use environmentally sound technology. Climate change policy has also introduced new environmental instruments, such as environmental agreements and eco-schemes, as shown in Table 14.2. CCPMs can be viewed as an encompassing chain of policy instruments aimed at reducing emissions, whether through air quality standards or emissions limits, as stated in the IPPC Directive.[17] These CCPMs and the earlier failed attempts to economize EU climate change policy increased EU resistance to the introduction of a new environmental policy instrument along the lines of the proposed Kyoto emissions trading system.

The final EU position prior to the Kyoto Summit is unambiguously stated in the 'Commission communication on climate change: EU strategy towards Kyoto conference'. The Commission recognized that it would only be possible to reduce emissions if Kyoto participants assumed a shared responsibility.[18] This is reflected in a proposal for a 15 per cent reduction for the EU below levels of 1990 by 2010

Table 14.1 *Greenhouse Gas Emissions in the EU (CO_2, CH_4, N_2O)*

	Share of EU emissions in 1990	CO_2 emissions in 1990 (in million ton equivalents)	Per capita emissions in 1990 (in million ton equivalents)	Evolution from 1900 to 1994 (% change)	Evolution from 1990 to 1995 (% change)	Burden sharing (%)	Burden sharing of CO_2 (in million ton equivalents)
Austria	1.7	74	9.2	-1.3	0.6	-13	64
Belgium	3.2	139	13.7	4.1	4.4	-7.5	129
Denmark	1.7	72	13.7	15.2	10.0	-21	57
Finland	1.7	73	14.2	-3.6	-0.5	0	73
France	14.7	637	11.0	-2.9	-1.1	0	637
Germany	27.7	1201	14.7	-12.1	-12.3	-21	949
Greece	2.4	104	9.9	3.2	4.6	25	130
Ireland	1.3	57	16.0	2.6	4.3	13	64
Italy	12.5	542	9.5	-2.9	1.7	-6.5	506
Luxembourg	0.3	14	34.7	-10.2	-45.0	-28	10
Netherlands	4.8	208	13.5	3.4	7.5	-6	196
Portugal	1.6	69	7.0	6.0		27	87
Spain	7.0	301	7.6	4.0	8.0	15	347
Sweden	1.6	69	7.9	-2.6	-3.3	4	72
UK	17.9	775	13.3	-6.9	-8.4	-12.5	678
Total EU	100	4334	13.1			-8	3998

Source: Council Conclusions 16 June 1998.

Table 14.2 *Primary Common and Coordinated Policies and Measures*

Measure	Reference	Goal
Reducing CO emissions for passengers cars	COM (95) 689	+/– 15% of total emissions reductions under Kyoto. 80-90 million tons.
Reducing CO_2 emissions from freight transport by road	COM (97) 242, COM (97) 243, COM(95)691	40% equivalent decrease in CO_2 emission from freight
Taxation of aircraft fuel/kerosene	COM (97) 30	Not yet determined
Common action progressively to reduce/remove fossil fuel and other subsidies, tax schemes and regulations, which counteract an efficient use of energy	Decision 36/32/93/ECSC	Reduction in CH_4 emissions. Promotion of domestic less carbon-intensive fuels
Promoting energy efficiency	Council Decision 96/737 (SAVE FT), followed by COM (97) 69	Reduce growth in energy intensity around 20% of total current energy consumption.
Improved technical performance and design of appliances and equipment	92/42/EC, 95/57/EC	Electricity saving of 10%.
IPPC	96/61EC	Implementation of BAT
Promote an increased use of renewables in the EU	COM (97) 599. ALTENER II	400m ton of CO_2 saved per year.
Promotion of environmental agreements	COM (96) 561	Not determined yet
Measures to promote the increased use of combines heat and power (CHP) generation	COM (97) 514	Double use of CHP by 2010 (from 9 to 18%)

Source: Derived from material in COM (99) 230 final

on a basket of three gases – CO_2, N_2O and CH_4. The Commission pushed for similar reductions for all industrialized states:

> ... *it only would be possible to reverse the emission trends in the framework in a global regime of shared responsibility and comparable commitments. The EU position ... is based upon the supposition that all the industrialized countries must and can act in the same way (p20)... The impact on international competitiveness in certain sectors would be substantial if the rest of the industrialized countries do not assume comparable commitments* (COM (97) 481 final, p18).

This last statement is the basis of the EU's demand for so-called quantified emissions limitations and reduction objectives (QELROS) in all Annex I countries. In addition, the EU initially proposed a fixed date for emissions reductions. Moreover, reduction targets would have to be accompanied by CCPMs for achieving the fixed objectives. This position was based on the assumption that global coordination of policies and measures would facilitate the implementation of cost-effective policy instruments and would diminish political resistance by spreading a sense of symmetry regarding the implementation of the Protocol. While the EU supported flexible mechanisms linked to voluntary agreements, EU representatives were wary of the multiple loopholes linked to them, which could render compromises meaningless. For this reason, the EU linked emissions trading systems to the acceptance of binding targets and fixed timetables, and required them to be complementary to measures already taken at the national level.

Based on these objectives, the EU position encountered strong opposition from the US and other supporters of the Kyoto NEPI. Nevertheless, the EU firmly defended its position. For the EU, a final agreement at Kyoto would be acceptable only if it included assurances for sustainable development through regulatory approaches to binding targets, fixed timetables and CCPMs. The same emphasis created scepticism toward new flexible mechanisms, in particular the market-based emissions trading system.

The Kyoto Negotiations

While the emissions trading system created a clear divide at the Summit, other issues of contention soon emerged. To determine how the NEPI was incorporated into an international environmental agreement, this section emphasizes the opposition at Kyoto to the EU's bubble concept and binding QELROS. Very early, Canada (and the US) challenged the EU bubble as inequitable because it would allow for wide differentiation within the EU while denying differentiation among other parties to the Protocol. Moreover, it was not clear to what extent the EU would be able to achieve its commitment after EU enlargement. The EU was a vocal opponent of stretching flexibility in QELROS too far. Instead, it proposed the creation of 'burden-sharing groups', such as the EU, to achieve credible reduction commitments. Because it was unclear how the EU might achieve its commitment jointly through the bubble, the concept was ultimately criticized by most parties at the negotiations (Grubb et al, 1999, p86).

The question of QELROS ended up in gridlock on the last day of negotiations. The EU – along with some non-Annex I countries, mainly China and the G77 (Group of 77 developing countries) – claimed QELROS as a sine qua non condition for reaching any type of agreement. This tough stance was bolstered in response to the US demand for emissions trading. The EU was facing a clear disadvantage because its own system was completely unfamiliar with implementing this type of NEPI. In addition, the EU's heavy dependence on regulatory instruments imposed sunk costs on its climate change policies and served to solidify opposition to the emissions trading system. Thus, the EU argued that the acceptance of the NEPI without binding QELROS would encourage the practical non-commitment of some developed countries. For example, the US could achieve its obligations through buying permits/credits from other countries.

Despite these concerns, the EU moderated its position on the Kyoto NEPI. While the EU emphasized a regulatory approach, as long as the EU lacked competence in crucial areas of fiscal and energy policies, concerns remained about its ability to promote emissions cuts through fiscal measures.[19] In addition, the Fifth EAP had already recognized the limitations of a purely regulatory approach to tackle the climate change problem and had declared that a broader range of instruments was required for emissions reductions.[20] The combination of these factors and the very real threat of the possible failure of the Kyoto Summit contributed to the EU's ultimate acceptance of the Kyoto NEPI.

Toward the end of the negotiations, the US linked its emissions cuts with the creation of a trading system, which might start to work just after the Kyoto Summit. For its part, the EU pointed out that its scope for flexibility, whether on targets, timetables or the use of market-based instruments was contingent upon QELROS numbers. Once the exact numbers were agreed, the EU and US reached a compromise.

The Power of Policy Paradigms

This chapter uncovers insights into the broader category of policy change, as defined by Sabatier (1993). Some aspects of long-term theories of policy change are useful (1) to determine the extent to which both parties' positions were eventually affected by the final agreement, (2) to identify causal chains that could explain the final agreement, and (3) to delimit analytically the introduction of emissions trading within the EU as an act of policy transfer (Dolowitz and Marsh, 1996, 2000).

Hall argues that policy paradigms can be identified because 'Policy-makers customarily work within a framework of ideas and standards that specify not only the goals of policy and the kind of instrument that can be used to attain them, but also the very nature of the problems that they are meant to be addressing' (Hall, 1993, p279). Applied to change in policy-making, Hall asserts that dysfunctions and anomalies on the dominant policy paradigm can affect the settings of available policy instruments (first-order changes), the basic techniques to provide policy solutions (second-order changes) and, eventually, the overarching goals behind the policy or programme (third-order changes). Only in the last case has a change in paradigm occurred.

This concept seems especially useful for analysing international negotiations over the Kyoto NEPI and for explaining the influence of the US Senate as well as the EU Commission's mixed competence and influence over Member State positions. This analytical approach to the influence of ideas in the policy process suggests that the initial gridlock during the Kyoto negotiations might be the result of translating environmental policy paradigms into non-negotiable positions. Specifically, the US translated 'free-market environmentalism' into the sine qua non condition of introducing an international emissions trading system. In the same manner, the EU transformed its 'risk-prevention leadership' paradigm into a non-negotiable position for binding targets, fixed timetables and burden-sharing reductions for all Annex I countries, very much according to its strong commitment to protecting the internal market's international competitiveness.

Regulation and harmonization – the traditional EU environmental policy devices – are reflected in the EU position at Kyoto for establishing binding QELROS for all Annex I countries. The clear preference for uniform measures to achieve these goals is based upon the assumption that multiple loopholes could be created through the use of flexible instruments – mainly the fact that the US could achieve its QELROS by purchasing permits without actually cutting domestic emissions. This would create international competitive disadvantages, which the EU has historically tried to avoid within its own burden-sharing agreements. These disadvantages would clearly harm EU economic interests and would discredit EU claims for global leadership within the EU itself. In addition, emissions trading was an unfamiliar policy instrument for the EU. The Union found it much more convenient to try to extend its traditional regulatory approach than to change the traditional CCPMs by which climate change policy had been instituted.

Post-Summit Emissions Trading: A Case of Policy Transfer?

This section provides a discussion of the post-Kyoto development of an emissions trading system in the EU and investigates a potential explanation for this apparent policy innovation. The central issue under investigation is to what extent post-conference NEPI adoption reflects an ongoing process of policy innovation in the EU and/or the US.

In the US, the Kyoto Protocol requires ratification by two-thirds of the Senate to become legally binding.[21] The Clinton administration did not submit the final Protocol to the Senate for ratification because it did not require adequate participation by developing countries. The failure of the Senate to ratify the agreement seriously undermined the post-Summit process of policy innovation in the US. The US Environmental Protection Agency (EPA) summarized the status of the Kyoto Protocol at the end of the Clinton administration: 'Because of a Congressional prohibition, the US government has not undertaken any domestic regulatory actions to implement the Protocol, nor has it begun to prepare for its implementation' (USEPA, 2001). The new administration of George W. Bush dealt policy innovation on the NEPI a further blow in the US. Reversing a campaign pledge, the Bush administration pulled out of the Kyoto process and failed to contribute to COP-7 in Marrakech, Morocco, from 29 October to 9 November (Environment Watch, 2001). Instead, the White House issued an alternative plan on 14 February 2002. By replacing the previous agreements on the NEPI with a new 'cap and trade' system that does not include CO_2, the Bush administration has dampened, if not eliminated, the process of policy innovation in the US. The story is quite different in the EU.

The EU's post-Summit position on the Kyoto NEPI displays clear signs of policy change. Shortly after the Kyoto Protocol was signed, the EU began producing numerous documents directly and indirectly related to the implementation of its burden-sharing agreement and the establishment of an EU emissions trading system.[22] The final agreement at Kyoto included the possibility of creating an international emissions trading system that would come into force in 2008 (Article 17, Kyoto Protocol). In the meantime, the Commission has repeatedly pointed out that 'the best preparation for the Community and its Member States might be to develop their own emission trading experience.'[23] This Kyoto mechanism, though, is fundamentally different from the way the EU and its Member States have organized their environmental policy in recent decades. Therefore, why is the EU so attentive to this new policy instrument? Is the EU currently engaged in a process of policy innovation as a result of an international compromise? Might this be a process of policy transfer?

The very subject of this study – the international acceptance and ex-post consideration of an emissions trading system in the EU – seems to indicate 'a process by which knowledge of policies, administrative arrangements, institutions and ideas in one political system (past or present) are used in the development of policies, administrative arrangements, institutions and ideas in other political system' (Dolowitz and Marsh, 2000, p5). Accordingly, the apparent change in the EU's post-Kyoto strategy appears to be a process of policy transfer. The current study adopts the definition of Dolowitz and Marsh because it is not dealing with adjacent authorities across which innovations diffuse. Furthermore, the role of the actors involved in the process is crucial to understanding the decision-making through which the emissions trading system has been introduced in the EU. The Commission had discouraged this climate change policy instrument in the early 1990s. However, interaction in a transnational process at Kyoto prompted the EU to reconsider the use of this policy device, a decision that was neither an emulation nor an obligation. Because this process seems to be a voluntary one driven by the perception of necessity, policy transfer variables help to explain how innovation is operating in EU climate change policy.

The acceptance and subsequent introduction of an emissions trading system in EU climate change policy is nothing more than the introduction of an instrument to deal with already established policy objectives without casting doubt on them. The emissions trading scheme does not challenge the goals that have guided climate change policy, mainly, a belief in stringent emissions reductions, the protection of the internal market and the need for EU leadership. Moreover, the adoption of this market instrument satisfies voices calling for an economization of EU climate policy. Whereas the perception of 'failure' of old instruments facilitated the transfer, the EU's risk-prevention leadership paradigm is limiting its impact in the policy area to instrumental alterations.

The timing of relevant Commission documents (1998, 1999, 2000 and 2001) reveals a step-by-step approach that softens the potential misfit this new policy instrument could otherwise create. The long transfer period allows the Commission to introduce this new policy instrument gradually. In fact, the Commission expects that the initial functioning of the system will provide lessons for its permanent establishment from 2005–2008 (Commission, 2001, p3). The seven-year period in which the EU system will operate before the international system comes into force becomes a strategic factor allowing the EU to adopt gradual changes in climate change policy without challenging measures (CCPMs) or goals (mandatory emissions reductions) already in operation.

The policy transfer literature also suggests that a voluntary process of innovation varies according to the degree to which the transfer is either a collectively organized process or a more 'casual' one (Page, 2000, p7). Moreover, this variable might be related to the failure or success of transferred policies, as collectively organized processes are more likely to avoid inappropriate or uninformed transfers.[24] The gathered empirical evidence shows signs of a collectively organized process of innovation in the transfer of this NEPI. The current Commission proposal (COM (2001) 581) is the result of extensive consultations with industry, governments, non-governmental environmental organizations and other stakeholders – up to 62 groups.

The question of how to organize the emissions trading system is closely related to the burden-sharing agreement under the 'EU bubble' (Article 4, Kyoto Protocol). Trading requires a high degree of certainty on monitoring actual emissions for both initially allocating quotas and for having an overview of progress in reductions, accounting for transfers, adjusting assigned amounts, and verifying emissions units and certified reductions (Commission, 1998, p22). Each member state will be allowed to allocate permits on the basis of its overall commitment under the burden-sharing agreement (Council Conclusions, 16 June 1998). The instrument is crucially based on the existence of a system of linked national registries of both emissions and allowances. This system is based on the experience of the allowance tracking system under the US sulphur-trading regime and in the guidelines on national registries under the Kyoto Protocol. The system seeks to protect the credibility of the instrument and its commitment to stringent emissions reductions. Hence, installations that have not had their emissions reports verified as accurate would lose their right to transfer allowances until they are in compliance with the requirements of the emissions trading system. The transfer process carefully identifies ways to protect the internal market while implementing this innovative climate change policy instrument. If Member States were allowed to distribute initial emissions allowances to certain enterprises for free or without imposing conditions, it would constitute state aid that was inconsistent with EU competition rules. In addition, even when emissions targets are established, Member States might be tempted to set low sectoral targets, since allocation not only will depend on how much a sector pollutes, but also on how much it costs to achieve a certain target. This would also constitute potentially distortionary aid that could counter EU competition rules (Commission, 2000, p18).

To avoid these effects, and after consulting with stakeholders, the Commission has proposed that Member States will grant emissions permits for free, avoiding distortions that might arise if some Member States would opt for auctions and others for grandfathering.[25] The credibility of the system is assured through monitoring and electronic tracking of allowance exchanges and verification of compliance. Again, following the design of the US sulphur-trading scheme, the EU emissions trading system establishes a non-compliance penalty of either €100 per excess ton or twice the average market price during a certain period, whichever is higher. This evidence suggests that the design of the EU emissions trading system is inspired by some features of the US sulphur scheme that are considered particularly effective. But the Commission is being extremely careful in designing the system so that it does not jeopardize the functioning of the internal market.

Lastly, the EU's reasons for borrowing an environmental policy instrument from another jurisdiction cannot be explained simply by understanding what is transferred, the timing of the process and how the transfer is being developed. Rather, the ultimate decision about importing this policy instrument seems to reflect a multifaceted bounded-rational decision. First, the instrument provides the required flexibility in the policy area over a fairly long period of time. Second, the EU responds to demands long expressed by other actors and even international organizations (mainly the OECD), reflecting a 'fashion' or 'fad' regarding the use of NEPIs in environmental policy. Yet, the EU has been able to maintain its old commitment to strong emissions reductions through technological investment and long-term competitive advantages in the use of environmentally sound technologies. This policy goal is satisfied because the EU emissions trading system will benefit those companies that are energy efficient and/or environmentally friendly. At the same time, the EU is gaining credibility as a leader in international climate change policy and in its ability to fulfil international compromises. Therefore, as Page (2000) has suggested, innovation through transfer has the ability to add weight to issues that have little to do with what is being evoked, a reason that might influence the transfer process as much as the need to overcome former policy failures.

Conclusions

This chapter investigates the introduction of an interesting and innovative policy instrument in international and domestic environmental policy-making – an emissions trading system. In the US, the process of policy innovation regarding the NEPI appears to have largely stalled, while in the EU, the process continues. This is a surprising outcome given the EU's initial opposition to the emissions trading system.

During the Kyoto process, domestic environmental policy paradigms emerged as important explanatory factors of how the US and EU defined their initial positions and interests. Before and after the Kyoto Summit, the US made clear its opposition to binding targets through mandatory measures. The US translated its free-market environmentalist paradigm into a non-negotiable demand to create an emissions trading system that would preserve existing domestic flexibility. Yet, before and during the Summit, the EU manifested its distrust of flexible instruments, which could hide industry hypocrisy and be held hostage by government procrastination (Golub, 1998, p23).

The positions and interests also interacted at the international level. For example, while the EU's bubble concept evolved and had to be domestically implemented according to previous CCPMs, it also had to be defended internationally. Although it is difficult to demonstrate the causal path that links domestic ideas in a policy area with national interests at an international conference, it is still possible to recognize the 'domestic policy legacies' of both actors, not only in the preferred instrument, but also in defence of the overall goals that ought to guide climate change policy. It also seems that these domestic policy paradigms shape the process of policy transfer.

The question of whether the instrument would have been adopted in the absence of the Protocol remains partially unanswered. While the Commission had rejected a similar instrument in the early 1990s, the EU's decision at Kyoto seems to be based on bounded rationality: emissions trading provides the needed flexibility for EU climate change policy and, by opting for a common proposal, the Commission seems to be trying to avoid harmonization issues that would harm the internal market. In this way, the overall goals that inspire the EU's risk-prevention leadership in climate change policy remain unaltered.

In conclusion, the current study identifies the important role of domestic policy paradigms for both shaping the formation of national interests in international arenas and determining the contours of the process of policy transfer. Moreover, within the emerging literature on policy transfer, it may raise questions about the role of policy paradigms for explaining why political systems transfer policies and programmes, rather than emulate them. Further research is encouraged to answer more fully these questions and to determine the precise nature and extent of the EU's ongoing process of policy innovation regarding the Kyoto NEPI.

Notes

1   Much of this attention was initiated and significantly amplified at the 1992 Earth Summit in Rio de Janeiro. The Rio Summit established a follow-up working group, the Conference of the Parties (COP). The COP's first meeting, COP-1, was held in Berlin in 1995. The next meeting, COP-2, was held in Geneva, Switzerland in 1996. The COP-3 meeting – the central issue of this chapter – was held in Kyoto in December 1997.

2   For example, see Banks (2000), Dawson (1999), Dobes (1999), Worika et al (1999), Johnston (1998), Missfeldt (1998), Schneider (1998), Trexler and Kosloff (1998), Yamin (1998).

3   For useful discussions of NEPIs in Europe, see Jordan et al (2000) and Golub (1998).

4   Advocacy coalitions are conceived of as groups of people from different governmental and private organizations who share a set of normative and causal beliefs and engage in a non-trivial attempt at co-ordinated activity over time (Sabatier and Jenkins-Smith, 1999, p120).

5   In this sense, Dolowitz and Marsh understand policy success as 'the extent to which policy transfer achieves the aims set by a government when they engaged in transfer, or is perceived as a success by the key actors involved in the policy area' (Dolowitz and Marsh, 2000, p17).

6   The publication of Commission document COM (2000) 87 initiated extensive consultations with stakeholders, including industry (more that 60 industry associations and companies), governments and non-governmental organizations. These dialogues are the basis of the *Proposal for Establishing a Framework for Emissions Trading Within the EU*, COM (2001) 581.

7   See Banks for a discussion of the history of the tradeable permit system (2000, p487).

8   The International Chamber of Commerce's statement on Kyoto reflects this faith in market-based environmentalism (1997). For more on the business perspective on the Kyoto Protocol, see Carr and Thomas (1998).

9   For more on the CDM, see Parson and Fisher-Vanden (1999), Werksman (1998). The CDM is often referred to as the 'Kyoto Surprise' because it was not included in the pre-Summit negotiating text.

10 These principles were first recognized in the Fourth Environmental Action Programme (EAP).

11 As a regional integration organization, the EU's position is complex. The EU was a signatory to the Protocol, but so too were its Member States because international environmental policy-making is an area of 'mixed competence'. The legal complexities of relations between the EU and Member States lead to numerous questions on the part of third parties about which actor – the EU or each Member State – is responsible for implementation. This complex arrangement of competency resulted in a certain degree of ambiguity over whether the EU individually or the Member States jointly would be responsible for meeting the Kyoto emissions targets (Macrory and Hession, 1996, p114). However, the EU's position at the Summit is rather more easily determined because of the pre-Kyoto negotiating position agreed by the Member States. While the EU Presidency and the Member States played active roles at the Summit, their positions reflected the pre-Kyoto guidelines decided by the Council of Ministers, via a detailed 'burden-sharing' agreement. For discussions that clarify the evolution of the EU's negotiating capacity at international environmental conferences, see Sbragia with Damro (1999), Jupille and Caporaso (1998).

12 The Annex I countries appear in the first annex to the Kyoto Protocol. These countries have agreed to stabilize emissions reductions by 2000 to 1990 levels. Included in Annex I are most Organisation for Economic Co-operation and Development (OECD) members, the Eastern European countries, Ukraine and Russia.

13 To analyse EU climate change policy in the period 1988–1996, this chapter strongly relies on the work of Huber (1997).

14 European Commission (1988), 'The greenhouse effect and the Commission', Commission work programme concerning the evaluation of policy option to deal with the greenhouse effect, COM (88) 656.

15 Joint Council of Energy and Environment Ministers, Oct 1990.

16 For Huber, the failure resulted from a 'cost-free leadership' strategy (1997, p150). The Commission could not provide internal support for the tax on a zero-cost assumption, so its strategy was extended to other OECD countries. The result was that the EU could only act if, and after, the US and Japan also

introduced a (comparable) energy tax. This limited the feasibility of the proposal for a CO_2/energy tax.

17 Directive 96/61/EC, on Integrated Pollution Prevention and Control. The IPPC Directive does not deal with diffuse emissions sources such as the transport, tertiary, household and agriculture sectors. Nonetheless, the investment programmes that steered EU climate change policies sought to encourage the use of new technologies for the sake of eventual emissions reductions. This was the case with the ALTENER, SAVE, THERMIE or the Fifth Framework Programme for Research and Technological Development.

18 This strategy recalls the attempt developed by the EU in the mid-1990s, when it adopted a 'cost-zero leadership' strategy (Huber, 1997) through which it tried to persuade other OECD countries to reduce their CO_2 emissions through an energy tax comparable to the one that the Commission was trying to introduce in the European agenda.

19 The attempts to establish an EU CO_2 tax were opposed by the UK. After that, the Commission decided to encourage Member States to establish national taxes on a product-by-product basis. See COM (96) 217, COM (97) 30.

20 Energy programmes, such as ALTENER II or SAVE II, establish financial assistance to develop and adopt best available technologies (BAT) in order to improve energy efficiency.

21 Internationally, for the Protocol to enter into force, it must be 'ratified by enough countries to account for at least 55 per cent of the industrialized world's carbon dioxide emissions' (USEPA, 2001). This hurdle was addressed at UN climate talks (COP-7) in Marrakech (29 October–9 November) when participants agreed to an 'operational rulebook' that will allow ratification of the Protocol (Environment Watch, 2001).

22 For example, see COM (99) 230 final; COM (98) 353, COM (99) 676, COM (00) 87, COM (00) 88, COM (00) 576.

23 EU Commission (1999), 'Preparing for implementation of the Kyoto Protocol'. Commission communication to the Council and the Parliament, COM (99) 230 final.

24 Insufficient information about the policy instrument may lead to uninformed transfer, whereas insufficient attention to the economic, social and political context would lead to 'inappropriate' transfer (Dolowitz and Marsh, 2000, p17).

25 In fact, the Commission was initially very concerned with this issue and expressed its preference for auctioning. For further details, see COM (2000) 87 final.

References

Banks, F. E. (2000) 'The Kyoto Negotiations on Climate Change: An Economic Perspective', *Energy Sources*, Vol.22, pp481–496.

Brack, D., Grubb, M. and Vrolijk, C. (1999) *The Kyoto Protocol: A Guide and Assessment*, London: Earthscan.

Campbell, K. (1998) 'From Rio to Kyoto. The Use of Voluntary Agreements to Implement the Climate Change Convention', *RECIEL,* Vol.7, No.2, pp159–169.

Carr, D. A. and Thomas, W. L. (1998) 'The Kyoto Protocol and US Climate Change Policy: Implications for American Industry', *RECIEL,* Vol.7, No.2, pp191–201.

Dawson, G. (1999) 'Market Exchange, Social Contract and the Kyoto Protocol', *Risk Decision and Policy,* Vol.4, No.3, pp63–77.

Dobes, Leo (1999) 'Kyoto: Tradable Greenhouse Emission Permits in the Transport Sector', *Transport Review,* Vol.19, No.1, pp81–97.

Dolowitz, D. and Marsh, D. (1996) 'Who Learns What from Who?' Political Studies, Vol.XLIV, pp343–357.

Dolowitz, D. and Marsh, D. (2000) 'Learning from Abroad: The Role of Policy Transfer in Contemporary Policy Making', *Governance,* Vol.13, No.1 (January) pp5–24.

Eizenstat, S. (1998) 'Statement before the Senate Foreign Relations Committee', Washington, DC, 11 February, State Department web page archive (www. state.gov), printed 23 January 2001.

Environment Watch (2001) 'Operational Rulebook For Kyoto Protocol Agreed at Marrakech', *Environment Watch: Europe,* Vol.10, No.22 (23 November) pp1–2.

Golub, J. (ed) (1998) *New Instruments for Environmental Policy in the EU,* London: Routledge.

Haigh, N. (1996) 'Climate Change Policies and Politics in the European Community', in O'Riordan and Jager (1996).

Hall, P. (1993) 'Policy Paradigms, Social Learning and the State: The Case of Economic Policy Making in Britain', in *Comparative Politics,* Vol.25, No.3, pp275–296.

Huber, M. (1997) 'Leadership in European Climate Policy: Innovative Policy Making in Policy Networks', in Liefferink, D. and Andersen, M. S. (eds) *The Innovation of EU Environmental Policy,* Copenhagen: Scandinavian University Press.

International Chamber of Commerce (1997) 'Statement by the International Chamber of Commerce, the World Business Organization, at the Conclusion of the Third Conference of the Parties to the Framework Convention on Climate Change', Kyoto, 11 December.

Johnston, J. L. (1998) 'Emissions Trading for Global Warming', *Regulation: The CATO Review of Business and Government,* Vol.21, No.4 (Fall), pp19–23.

Jordan, A., Wurzel, R. and Zito, A. (2000) 'Innovating with "New" Environmental Policy Instruments: Convergence or Divergence in the European Union?' paper presented at the Annual Meeting of the American Political Science Association, 31 August – 3 September.

Jupille, J. and Caporaso, J. (1998) 'States, Agency and Rules: The European Community in Global Environmental Politics', in Rhodes, C. (ed) *The European Union in the World Community,* Boulder, CO: Lynne Rienner.

Macrory, R. and Hession, M. (1996) "The European Community and Climate Change: The Role of Law and Legal Competency', in O'Riordan and Jager (1996, p106–154).

Majone, G. (1996) *Regulating Europe,* London: Routledge.

May, P. (1992) 'Policy Learning and Failure', *Journal of Public Policy*, Vol.12, No.4, pp331–354.

Missfeldt, F. (1998) 'Flexibility Mechanisms: Which Path to Take After Kyoto', RECIEL Vol.7, No.2, pp128–139.

Nolin, J. (1999) Time and Sponsorship: The Research to Policy Process and the European Union's Kyoto Proposal', *Minerva*, Vol.37, pp165–181.

O'Riordan, T. and Jager, J. (eds) (1996) *Politics of Climate Change: A European Perspective*, London: Routledge.

Page, E. E. (2000) 'Future Governance and the Literature on Policy Transfer and Lesson Drawing', paper prepared for the ESRC Future Governance Programme Workshop on Policy Transfer, London.

Parson, E. A. and Fisher-Vanden, K. (1999) 'Joint Implementation of Greenhouse Gas Abatement Under the Kyoto Protocol's "Clean Development Mechanism": Its Scope and Limits', *Policy Sciences*, Vol.32, pp207–224.

Pressman, J. and Wildavsky, A. (1973) *Implementation*, Berkeley, CA: University of California Press.

Rose, R. (1993) *Lesson Drawing in Public Policy: A Guide to Learning Across Time and Space*, Chatham, NJ: Chatham House Publishers.

Sabatier, P. (ed) (1993) *Theories of the Policy Process*, Boulder, CO: Westview Press.

Sabatier, P. and Jenkins-Smith, H. C. (1993) *Policy Change and Learning: An Advocacy Coalition Approach, Boulder*, CO: Westview Press.

Sbragia, A. with Damro, C. (1999) 'The Changing Role of the European Union in International Environmental Politics: Institution Building and the Politics of Climate Change', *Environment and Planning C, Government Policy*, Vol.17, pp53–68.

Schneider, S. H. (1998) 'Kyoto Protocol: The Unfinished Agenda', *Climate Change,* Vol.39 pp1–21.

Stokes, B. F. and Berry, W. D. (1999) 'Innovation and Diffusion Models in Policy Research' in Sabatier (ed) (1999).

Trexler, M. C. and Kosloff, L. H. (1998) 'The 1997 Kyoto Protocol: What Does It Mean for Project-Based Climate Change Mitigation?' *Mitigation and Adaptation Strategies for Global Chang*, Vol.3, pp1–58.

US Environmental Protection Agency (USEPA) (2001) 'The Kyoto Protocol – Introduction', 26 Feb, www.epa.gov/globalwarming/publications/reference/kyoto/.

US Government (1995) *Climate Action Report: Submission of the United States of America Under the United Nations Framework Convention on Climate Change*, Washington, DC: US Government Printing Office.

Werksman, J. (1998) 'The Clean Development Mechanism: Unwrapping the "Kyoto Surprise",' *RECIEL*, Vol.7, No.2, pp147–158.

Worika, I., Lucky, T. W., Brown, M. and Vinogradov, S. (1999) 'Contractual Architecture for the Kyoto Protocol: From Soft and Hard Laws to Concrete Commitments', *RECIEL*, Vol.8, No.2, pp180–190.

Yamin, F. (1998) 'The Kyoto Protocol: Origins, Assessment and Future Challenges', *RECIEL*, Vol.7, No.2, pp113–126.

EU primary documents

Council Conclusions (1998) '2106 Council Meeting of Environment', Luxembourg, 16–17 June 1998, Pres/98/205 in www.eel.nl/counciy2106.htm.

EC Commission (1988) The Greenhouse Effect and the Commission', COM (88)656.

EC Commission (1991) 'Commission Strategy to Limit Carbon Dioxide Emissions and to Improve Energy Efficiency', SEC (91) 1744 final.

EC Commission (1992) 'Proposal for a Council Directive Introducing a Tax on CO_2 Emissions and Energy', COM (92) 266.

EU Commission (1996) Communication from the Commission under the UN Framework Convention on Climate Change', COM (96) 217 final.

EU Commission (1997) 'Proposal for a Council Directive Restructuring the Commission Framework for the Taxation of Energy Products', COM (97) 30 final.

EU Commission (2002) 'Report from the Commission under Council Decision 93/389/EEC, as amended by Decision 99/2966/EC for a Monitoring Mechanism of EU Greenhouse Gas Emissions', COM (02) 702 final, in www.europa.eu.int/comm/dgs/environment.

European Commission (1997) Climate Change: EU Strategy Towards the Kyoto Conference', COM (97) 481 final. Brussels, 1 Oct. 1997.

European Commission (1998) Climate Change: Towards a Post-Kyoto Strategy', COM (98) 353, in www.europa.eu.int/comm/dgs/environment.

European Commission (1999) EC Economic and Development Cooperation: Responding to New Challenges of Climate Change', COM (99) 676.

European Commission (1999) 'Preparing for the Implementation of the Kyoto Protocol', COM (99) 230 final, in www.europa.eu.int/comm/dgs/environment.

European Commission (2000) 'Green Paper on Greenhouse Gas Emission Trading within the EU', COM (00) 87, in www.europa.eu.int/cornm/dgs/environment.

European Commission (2001) 'Proposal for a Directive of the European Parliament and of the Council Establishing a Framework for Greenhouse Emission Trading within the European Community and Amending Council Directive 96/61/EC', COM (01) 581, in www.europa.eu.int/comm/dgs/environment.

Note: Those documents that do not have a link have been found in *EUR-Lex*.

Part 5
FUTURE CHALLENGES

15

EU Environmental Policy and the Challenges of Eastern Enlargement

Stacy D. VanDeveer and Jo Ann Carmin

With each wave of expansion, the European Union (EU) does not simply get bigger, it also changes. The EU enlarged significantly in 2004 when countries from Central and Eastern Europe (CEE) joined the EU. This expansion required tremendous efforts on the part of the new accession states. Following the fall of the communist regimes in 1989, the goal of EU membership often served to guide these countries as they developed new agencies and adopted widespread environmental policy reforms. Citizens and officials alike grappled with adjustments in their relationships with each other, with state authority, and with market dynamics. Although the goal of accession was generally accepted in countries in CEE, it met with mixed reactions within the rest of the EU, which is now struggling to adapt to various changes wrought by enlargement. Supporters argued that enlargement would help stabilize the region's new political and economic systems, reinforce Europe's ability to compete in a globalizing economy, and foster improvements in environmental protection and quality throughout CEE and continental Europe. Although proponents maintained that EU enlargement would have numerous benefits, environmental critics believed that it would hinder environmental policy development, reduce environmental quality, and lower environmental standards and their implementation right across Europe (Homeyer, 2004; Holzinger and Knoepfel, 2000).

Despite the presence of variable support for membership of the formerly communist countries, accession proceeded. In May 2004, when the EU formally expanded from 15 to 25 Member States, new and old members as well as EU institutions faced a myriad of challenges. While significant social, political, and environmental changes have been achieved in CEE since 1989, the transformation continues as these countries strive to transpose additional EU directives and implement those already in place. Thus, the 2004 enlargement presents challenges and opportunities for the new Member States, at the same time as it alters the economic, political, and cultural dynamics within the EU as a whole.

The EU has undergone a number of enlargements since its founding, but the 2004 expansion is by far and away the biggest and most complex. After summarizing the accession process, this chapter considers several of the major environmental policy challenges facing the new Member States and the EU. While adopting EU law and regulation has proceeded quickly in CEE, progress in implementation and enforcement has been more difficult. This is due in part to limitations in agency capacity, the need to sort through mixed messages and conflicting priorities emanating from the EU 15, and a weak civil society that is often not recognized as a potential source of innovation, ideas, information, and expertise by officials from within the region. The expanded EU must also navigate numerous challenges as it attends to the present enlargement and looks toward the next wave of expansion. For the EU to realize its potential as a regional and global environmental leader, environmental policy must be more consistently implemented and enforced in all Member States. At the same time, the current trend of a one-way flow of information from East to West must be replaced by one of mutual respect, learning and exchange that draws on the lessons learned by the EU 15, as well as on the socialist past and transition experiences of the new accession countries.

Eastern Expansion of the European Union

In the wake of the collapse of the communist systems, accession to the EU became one of the early and pre-eminent goals of many countries in CEE. Though enlargement engendered debate, expansion was not impeded by it. In 1998, formal accession negotiations began with the Czech Republic, Estonia, Hungary, Poland and Slovenia. Negotiations were subsequently opened with Bulgaria, Latvia, Lithuania, Romania, Slovakia and Croatia, resulting in 11 CEE countries formally initiating their push toward EU membership. Countries from CEE were accompanied by the Mediterranean states of Cyprus, Malta, and Turkey and the south-eastern states of Bosnia and Albania in their pursuit of EU membership.

In order to join the EU, the new Member States in CEE had to transpose the *acquis communautaire into domestic law and policy, and begin implementing and enforcing these provisions.* The *acquis* consists of 31 chapters, each detailing EU laws, regulations, norms, and standards for different substantive policy arenas. The environmental chapter contains over 300 regulations and directives. These include framework legislation, measures on international conventions, biodiversity protection, product standards, and provisions to ensure reductions in national, transboundary, and global pollution (Europa, 2002). Though accession countries had developed environmental policies in many of these areas in socialist times and in the period immediately after the fall of communism, most had to be redeveloped and realigned with those in the *acquis*.

In December 2002, accession negotiations were provisionally closed for eight of the countries in CEE (the Czech Republic, Estonia, Hungary, Latvia, Lithuania, Poland, Slovakia, and Slovenia) and two Mediterranean countries (Malta and Cyprus). The Accession Treaty was signed in April 2003 and by September of that year all ten accession countries had approved their entry into the EU (most by referendum). These ten states formally joined the EU in May 2004, in time to participate in the European Parliament elections of June 2004 (see Chapter 6). The 2004 accession brought EU membership to 25, with formal accession discussions continuing with Bulgaria, Croatia, Romania, and Turkey.

For the new Member States, the transposition, implementation and enforcement of environmental laws and regulations specified in the *acquis* was difficult to achieve, and in some cases this process remains incomplete. Between 1998 and 2004, the eight new Member States transposed the vast majority of the *acquis* into their domestic law. In contrast to previous expansions where candidate countries were granted compliance periods to achieve harmonization, for CEE it was a precondition of membership. While transposition was achieved fairly rapidly, implementation of this massive body of law and regulation is proceeding more slowly. For governmental and non-governmental actors in CEE, the challenge of implementing such a huge body of law and regulation in just a fraction of the time it took to construct and implement in Western Europe, is enormous.

Implementation Challenges within the Accession Countries

Communism left the countries of CEE with a legacy of significant environmental degradation (see DeBardeleben, 1993; DeBardeleben and Hannigan, 1995; Pryde, 1995; Vari and Tamas, 1993; McCuen and Swanson, 1993; Simons, 1990). While a number of early reports emphasizing significant problems were overstated, they accurately reported that the region was plagued with widespread pollution, local ecological disasters, inferior environmental technology, and serious and identifiable threats to public health (see Andrews, 1993; Albrecht, 1987). If their desire to join the EU was to become a reality, the CEE countries had to remediate much of the existing damage, adopt EU laws, establish new agencies, and create sound provisions for implementation and enforcement.

In the period leading to accession, the countries in CEE achieved improvements in environmental quality and made significant changes in environmental policies (see Archibald, Banu and Bochniarz, 2004; HELCOM, 1998, and Selin and VanDeveer, 2004). For example, the expansion of water treatment capacity was accompanied by improvements in waste-water discharges and surface water quality, while the closure or reduction in emissions from many polluting plants has contributed to improvements in air quality (Gutner, 2002; HELCOM, 2001; OECD, 1997; Pavlínek and Pickles, 2000). Further, new bodies of environmental policy have been developed and ministries and environmental agencies have been formed or reformed with the goal of making them more effective. Despite these and other strides, countries in CEE still face significant challenges in sustaining their progress and in implementing and enforcing the body of EU laws and regulations that have been transposed. Three critical challenges that these countries face in the wake of accession are: developing and sustaining agency capacity; responding to mixed messages and conflicting priorities emanating from EU institutions and the EU 15; and realizing the full potential of civil society actors.

Developing and sustaining agency capacity

The environmental aspects of the transition away from Soviet-style socialism and towards EU membership required different skills, information, and social and political institutions from those prevalent in communist times. To foster these changes, as well as promote the development of environmental policy and improvements in environmental quality, international assistance from various national, intergovernmental, and non-governmental donors was directed at the region (VanDeveer and Carmin, forthcoming). During the decade of accession negotiations and preparations, an emphasis was placed on harmonizing law and regulations in CEE with the *acquis*. As a result, a great deal of environmental capacity-building assistance was dedicated to this goal. For instance, funding was provided to facilitate the translation of EU directives and regulations, educate and train policy-makers from the region on EU requirements, and draft environmental legislation and regulations.

In the early days of the transition period, bilateral assistance was offered by most West European states, the US, Canada, and Japan, by intergovernmental organizations, and by a host of non-governmental organizations. Together, international governments invested over 3 billion ECU in the early 1990s, with Germany and Denmark taking the lead among European donors with combined contributions of over 500 million ECU (Kolk and van der Weij, 1998). Between 1990 and 1994, the World Bank provided loans totalling US$788 million for environmental projects (Connolly et al, 1996). At the same time, many states, agencies, foundations, non-governmental organizations (NGOs) and firms also contributed to the development of environmental capacity by providing scientific, technical, and policy guidance (Baker and Jehlika, 1998; Gutner, 2002). During this period, international actors provided support for NGOs, the advancement of democracy, and a wide variety of civil society development programmes (Carmin and Hicks, 2002; Quigley, 2000; Kolk and van der Weij, 1998; Carmin and VanDeveer, 2004).

The EU made significant contributions to developing the environmental capacity of CEE states. Many of these efforts were dedicated at 'harmonizing' national policy and practice with EU directives and regulations (Carius et al, 2000). The PHARE twinning programme was one of the more important programmes in this era. Initially oriented to assist in the development of democratic institutions and aid the economic transition by enhancing the capacities of public organizations, over time it began to focus on environmental assistance. Although many states rushed to provide support in the early days of the transition, as accession drew closer, many donors and agencies withdrew from the region. By the late 1990s, this left the EU as the primary source of funding for environmental issues in CEE.

The capacity-building efforts that took place in the 1990s contributed to the development of new bodies of environmental law and policy across the region. They also contributed to the development of greater levels of public, NGO, and private sector environmental expertise in states and societies in CEE than was present in socialist times or even during the early days of accession negotiations. However, a number of critical gaps in agency capacity remain. One of the more critical and visible lies within environmental ministries, national government research and enforcement institutes. Being poorly staffed and underfunded, they struggle to keep pace with the demands of implementing and enforcing an ever-growing body of laws and regulations (Jehlicka and Tickle, 2004). Just as national agencies and officials are encountering difficulties, so too are those at the regional and local levels. Many of these bodies are responsible for monitoring, enforcing and implementing numerous complex and expensive policies (Carmin and VanDeveer, 2004). In short, the challenges of implementing and enforcing the environmental *acquis* in the new Member States will persist long after accession.

Navigating mixed messages and conflicting priorities

As countries in CEE move from an era of institution-building (ie 1989–2004) to an 'era of implementation' (ie 2004 onward), officials and the public find themselves faced with mixed messages and conflicting priorities communicated by the EU 15. Overall, the EU has been a major advocate of high environmental standards and more sustainable development (see Chapter 1). However, as countries in CEE attempt to implement the *acquis,* they encounter numerous gaps between the rhetoric and the reality of policies related to sustainability. In areas such as nuclear power and radioactive waste disposal, traffic and transport policies that foster pollution, and urban development patterns that lead to urban sprawl, EU policies contradict the basic premises of sustainable development (Carius et al, 2000; Princen et al, 2002; Auer and Legro, 2004; Carmin and VanDeveer, 2005). Consequently, as states and societies in CEE implement EU policies and become more like their neighbours to the west, they find that some of their previously sustainable practices are being undermined.

Mixed messages and conflicting priorities have a direct impact on institutions such as the legal system. For instance, adopting EU laws and shifting to a policy where national law is superseded by Community law creates tensions in domestic legal cultures and practices. While some implementation difficulties are due to capacity deficiencies within the existing legal system, they also stem from the often vague and contradictory content and nature of EU law itself (Kružíková, 2004). Conflicts are not limited to institutions, but are present within a number of policy arenas. For example, EU economic policies promote 'Western style' consumption and its reliance on disposable products, while EU environmental policies support waste minimization through recycling and reuse (Gille, 2004). Mixed messages also appear in the form of divergent purposes across different policy domains. For instance, the EU has developed agricultural and rural policies designed to build local capacity and enhance environmental quality. Yet these goals are often undermined by other EU goals, programmes and funding (Beckmann and Dissing, 2004).

The tensions arising from contradictions are not limited to processes that take place within a single state, but extend to transnational relations and policy variations among Member States. The ongoing processes and decisions associated with the Temelín nuclear power plant in the Czech Republic and the international politics that have surrounded it, illustrate how such tensions can emerge across the EU and between older members and the new accession countries (see

Axelrod, 2004). Because EU Member States have such divergent views on nuclear power, they are unable to agree on any significant pan-European regulation. Not only do new members receive contradictory messages and incentives from older members, but EU law offers them little additional guidance.

Differential purposes and messages are not restricted to states and state decision-making. Civil society actors also face many dilemmas that are not of their making. For example, while the EU espouses the importance of public involvement, these views often diverge from the types of participatory practices that are actually being promoted and implemented. The EU signed the Aarhus Convention, an international treaty, in 1998 and the European Parliament adopted its stated provisions on access to information and public participation in environmental decision-making, with the goal of implementing these by 2005. Further, in 2004, the EU issued the Directive on strategic environmental assessment that contained provisions for greater openness in planning procedures and opportunities for civil society actors to influence environmental plans and programmes. Though the intent to foster involvement may be present, it appears that some officials in Brussels are trying to distance themselves from advocacy and activist organizations, instead preferring to limit their interactions to NGOs that conduct research and provide technical expertise (Hallstrom, 2004). These patterns send contradictory messages to NGOs and to the new Member States about EU preferences for promoting, supporting, and sustaining civic engagement in environmental decision-making.

Realizing the potential of civil society

Environmental movements and movement organizations were visible and influential in the period leading up to the fall of the communist regime. As a result, there were high expectations that members of these groups would assume influential political positions and that environmental organizations would be included in all facets of decision-making. For a while, it appeared that these visions would be realized. However, as environmental concerns were gradually eclipsed by economic priorities, the visibility and levels of engagement of environmental activists and organizations soon began to wane (Fagin, 1994; Slocock, 1996). Since 1989, environmental organizations in CEE have experienced variations in popularity, differing degrees of integration into the policy process, and variable access to resources (Carmin and Hicks, 2002; Jancar-Webster, 1998).

But greater political openness in the period immediately following the fall of the communist regimes offered civil society actors and organizations greater access to the transnational and international arenas. New opportunities to participate in international conferences, commissions, and networks emerged. Organizations experienced an influx of resources as many sources of international aid funded democracy-building and environmental programmes (Jancar-Webster, 1998; Wedel, 1998; Quigley, 2000; Carmin and Hicks, 2002; Mendelson and Glenn, 2002; Cellarius and Staddon, 2002). As with government funding, the exodus of many donors from the region left the EU as one of the few remaining sponsors of NGOs and civil society initiatives in the region (Carmin and Hicks, 2002).

The scarcity of financial resources has shaped the activities and capabilities of environmental organizations in CEE. However, there are a number of additional social and political forces that are creating constraints and placing limitations on these groups. The historically weak engagement of civil society in CEE continues (Howard, 2003). As a result, not only are many national environmental organizations struggling to operate on limited funding, they are also having difficulty recruiting new leaders, generating popular support for their work and mobilizing the broader public (Auer, 2004; Beckmann et al, 2002; Brzel, 2000). The accession process and post-accession period have also placed limitations on environmental organizations. In the period leading up to accession, many organizations found that although their research skills were valued, their activist agendas were regarded as disruptive by officials. As a result, they had difficulty gaining access to decision-making processes and officials in Brussels (Hallstrom, 2004). At the same time, as adoption of the laws and regulations specified in the *acquis* becomes the main driving force of national environmental policy, many of these groups have found that their agendas are being dominated by EU goals rather than by national priorities (Hicks, 2004).

The EU has influenced the agendas and activities of many environmental NGOs in CEE. However, these organizations have the potential to play critical roles in the implementation and enforcement of environmental policies that are as yet unrealized (Bell, 2004). At the local level, nature conservation organizations, including those that were active in communist times, are actively engaging in conservation and land management activities. In a number of instances, these groups have also become active in promoting and implementing rural sustainable development initiatives (Carmin et al, 2003; Beckmann and Dissing, 2004). While a great deal of policy implementation plays out in local communities, national organizations have the potential to make significant contributions to the policy process. Although their potential remains unrealized, environmental organizations can be a source of ideas, innovation, information and expertise, all of which can contribute to agenda-setting as well as policy development, implementation and monitoring (Bell, 2004). But their contributions often go unrecognized or are marginalized by government officials.

Challenges and Opportunities in an Expanded Union

After decades of the Cold War and its associated ideological divisions, a deeply embedded pattern is to think of Europe in East–West terms. At a time when the accession states are becoming more like their Western European neighbours, this division is less meaningful than in the past. In particular, it ignores the presence of substantial differences in environmental policy-making, monitoring and implementation that are emerging across the 15 (pre-2004) EU Member States (Holzinger and Knoepfel, 2000; Jordan et al, 2004; Jordan and Liefferink, 2004; Knill and Lenschow, 2000). Additionally, notable variations in national policy style, risk perception and domestic institutional structures among the EU 15 have significant implications for national environmental policy choices, effectiveness, and implementation levels (see O'Neill, 2000; Skjaerseth, 2000; Jordan, 2002). In other words, although in theory there is one *acquis*, there continues to be a host of inter-pretations of its contents and a wide array of institutional models directed toward implementation both in older and newer EU countries (see Chapters 8 and 10).

All the EU Member States encounter difficulties related to policy implemen-tation and in making internationally designed law and regulation fit in to their domestic institutional and organizational settings. Just as all the individual states face challenges, so too does the EU as a collective body. At the same time, an expanded EU presents myriad new opportunities. Although present across numerous areas of environmental policy, these limitations and opportunities are clearly seen. They have important implications with regard to environmental pol-icy-making processes, intra-EU learning and information exchange, and the EU's role in global environmental policy-making.

Environmental quality and policy-making

An EU of 25 states is inherently more difficult to manage than one of 15, hence the need for treaty reform (see Chapter 3). Consequently, much of the debate at and since Nice has focused on national 'voting' weights and decision rules in an enlarged EU (Schreurs, 2004). Decision-making difficulties are not restricted to rules of voting, as accession is also accompanied by the potential for policy-making paralysis to arise. For example, the lower level of economic resources in CEE may make these states cautious, if not sceptical, of expensive new EU-level policy proposals. Further, because the new accession countries generally lack an actively engaged polity and NGOs that continuously challenge and monitor government action, implemen-tation of the many procedurally based EU environmental policies such as those related to environmental assessment, eco-audits and integrated pollution and pre-vention, may not have sufficient support from civil society (Homeyer, 2004).

Though concerns were expressed that countries from CEE would work together and hinder the policy-making process in the EU, to date there is no evi-dence that policymakers from CEE are attempting to co-ordinate their environ-mental positions with one another (Jehlika and Tickle, 2004). It is still possible that voting patterns that reflect the limited financial and civil society capacity in the new accession countries could paralyze the entire EU as minorities of Mem-ber States take action to block policies and protect sovereign authority of smaller states from domination by larger ones (see Homeyer, 2004). However, it seems more likely that variability in institutions as well as in the priorities of individual states will result in countries from CEE taking independent action that addresses their own interests (Homeyer, 2004).

The pre-2004 debate about the ramifications of enlargement often focused on the concern that countries from CEE would join the so-called environmental 'laggard' EU states by slowing the development – or attempting to reverse – the progressive nature of EU environmental policy (see Holzinger and Knoepfel, 2000; Jehlicka and Tickle, 2004; see also Chapter 10). There are many reasons to be sceptical of these blanket assumptions. For one thing, the CEE states often have very different interests, so the assumption that they will forge a coherent bloc may not be a realistic one. Also, the states and societies of CEE are not devoid of environmental concern or policy activity. Most were anxious to redesign their environmental policies and implement new legislation. The redevelopment of the industrial sector holds the promise of bringing new technologies that are 'greener' and cleaner than those found in other parts of Europe. Further, the new accession states are not alone in their struggle to implement the *acquis*. A number of studies demonstrate that older and wealthier EU Member States are also having difficulty implementing the existing *acquis* (Knill and Lenschow, 2000; McCormick, 2001; Skjaerseth, 2002; European Commission, 2003).

Rather than consistently lagging or having difficulties, there are instances where the countries from CEE are taking the lead and bringing new ideas to the EU. For example, the accession countries have been innovative with their pollution and resource extraction taxes, and with the operation of national environmental funds. 'Green' taxes, subsidies, and market-style policy instruments have been discussed in Western Europe and North America (Chapter 17), but appear to be more widely practiced in former socialist states (Carmin and VanDeveer, 2004; Holzinger and Knoepfel, 2000; VanDeveer and Carmin, forthcoming; Schreurs, 2004). Similarly, despite the talk about sustainable agricultural policy, the EU has not taken a leadership role in this area (see Chapters 14 and 17). These patterns suggest that environmental leaders and laggards are not within one country or region, but can be found in all parts of the EU.

Previous expansions in EU membership have demonstrated that integration and harmonization can provide new opportunities for innovation and collaborative approaches to environmental problem-solving. They also show that enlargement can enhance the policy capacity of both the EU and that of most Member States' environmental policy capacity (Schreurs, 2004). In fact, the years leading up to 2004 saw an expansion of EU environmental policy across a variety of issue areas (see Chapter 9). As a result, all 25 EU Member States have important new policies to implement in the coming years, not just the ten new ones.

Intra-EU learning and information exchange

The accession process was largely framed as a one-way transfer of institutions, ideas and expertise from West to East. Yet, 15 years of transition and the subsequent accession of the countries from CEE have revealed some of the limits of this thinking. For example, a Brussels-driven approach has not created a means for indigenous knowledge and environmentally friendly practices (such as bottle reuse, minimal packaging and a reliance on public transportation) to be integrated into EU practices or policies. In general, EU dominance of the environmental policy agenda in CEE has marginalized non-EU-generated ideas and institutions. It has also shaped what policies and practices from the past could be kept or adapted (Carmin and VanDeveer, 2005). While state socialism had a poor environmental record, countries from the East may be able to bring important insights and experience to the EU.

Just as the communist past can bring innovative policies and practices, the transition offers a number of important lessons that can be used to guide EU environmental governance (Carmin and VanDeveer, 2004). For instance, the rapid harmonization and transition processes have highlighted some of the contradictions in EU policy areas (see Chapter 16), and raised questions about how these might be undermining environmental quality. Further, while many of the environmental problems from the socialist era remain, this history can be mined for policy lessons (Gille, 2004).

The advantages and disadvantages of centralization in Brussels and in national capitals have not yet been fully considered (Golub, 1998a; 1998b; Holzinger and Knoepfel, 2000). As membership expands, the EU is becoming simultaneously more integrated and more institutionally complex. All the EU members, both East and West, need to develop organizational structures that are suited to their unique situations. As a result, a balance may need to be achieved between centralization and decentralization so that Member States can make different choices about the ways they choose to accomplish the same environmental goals.

Pan-EU environmental and institutional variability has the potential to produce policy experiments, challenges and innovations at local and national levels across the continent (and beyond). Simply asking 'how do domestic institutions and actors change in response to EU action?' (Jordan and Liefferink, 2004), is too narrow a question to capture the diversity of factors shaping environmental policy change and environmental outcomes across the EU 15 (Carmin and VanDeveer, 2005). Even as European environmental politics and policy change, common challenges faced by both newer and older EU members suggest that innovation and learning will need to be transnational and multi-directional. States, citizens, ideas and experiences from CEE are likely to be needed across Europe if the pan-EU challenges of environmental policy implementation and sustainability are to be met.

Global environmental leadership

The EU of 15 was influential in international negotiations (see Chapter 12), but an EU of 25 members may provide even more avenues of influence (and numbers of votes) in regional and global environmental co-operation fora. The EU and many Member State officials have grown increasingly engaged and active in – and politically and financially supportive of – regional and global environmental agreements and organizations (Carmin and VanDeveer, 2005). EU officials have worked to harmonize regional environmental governance around and across Europe and its peripheries. This has included active engagement in shaping international and national policies through the 'Environment for Europe' process and the United Nations Economic Commission for Europe. EU members are presently party to over 60 international environmental treaties and this number is likely to continue to expand (VanDeveer, 2003). In addition, just as EU officials regularly work to harmonize regional treaties and programmes with EU law and policy, they also pressure and fund programmes directed at post-Soviet and North African countries to encourage them to ratify and implement them as well (Carius, 2002; Carmin and VanDeveer, 2005). Thus, regional fora may be increasing EU influence both in new Member States, aspiring Member States, and those well beyond the Union's borders.

EU enlargement also has global ramifications for international environmental governance. An EU of 25 or more may act in global environmental politics either unilaterally, multilaterally, or through trade accords (Garvey, 2002). EU actors may also choose to lead by example or to use access to their markets to push environmental goals and to construct and promulgate certain environmental standards, policy ideas, norms and principles (Carmin and VanDeveer, 2005; Mitchener, 2002). Internal standards may help to improve the environmental performance of firms and governments (see Andonova, 2003). At the same time, well-designed public policy can shape markets in more environmentally sensitive ways through the use of 'green' taxes, investment incentives, public information-sharing and product standards.

EU officials are demonstrating an increased willingness to use foreign assistance and issue-linking strategies to pursue their global environmental policy goals. For example, environmental aid and capacity-building assistance are extended to EU applicants, neighbours and less-developed countries around the globe. As of 2004, it appears that EU officials were able to broker a deal on climate change with Russian officials. The EU, it seems, offered its support for Russia's bid to enter the World Trade Organization in return for it ratifying the Kyoto Protocol. A larger EU, if its officials are committed to global environmental leadership, may be able to create more such opportunities to support and shape regional and global environmental co-operation and better compete, when necessary, with the global influence of the US.

In sum, in order to meet the challenges posed by a host of transnational and global environmental problems, a larger and growing EU has increased potential to exercise global influence and leadership around international environmental issues, negotiations and organizations (Carmin and VanDeveer, 2005). If an EU of 25 or more can act and negotiate as a bloc in international fora, the global influence of the Union could be greatly increased across many issue areas, including climate change, chemical regulation, biodiversity protection and international trade.

Conclusions: Future Challenges and Remaining Questions

Environmental law and regulations, and the domestic and transnational politics around them, have been dramatically redrawn and transformed in the eight new Member States of CEE. The transposition of the environmental *acquis* has largely been achieved. Consequently, officials from these countries have enacted a stunning array of new legal acts and issued thousands of new regulations. Also, the region's citizens and NGOs now operate in a radically changed legal environment as a result of the general political transitions in the region that enact new rights, laws, and rules for public participation and access to information. In other words, 'on paper' almost everything has changed. On the ground, some things have also changed substantially. Many ecological improvements have been achieved, including reductions in many forms of air water pollution and in the use and emissions of many hazardous and toxic substances (Pavlínek and Pickles, 2000). These environmental improvements stem from multiple sources, including market transformation and privatization as well as legal and regulatory change.

However, significant challenges continue to face the new Member States (and those still aspiring to join the EU). Chief among these is the problem of how to find ways to realize and capitalize on the potential of civil society actors. More pressing is the inadequate institutional, organizational, and human resource-related capacity to implement the thousands of new laws and standards. And yet, while it may appear that countries in CEE are the only ones struggling to implement EU environmental policy, the problem is widespread. EU members old and new continue to grapple with the challenges of overcoming the existing 'implementation gap' (Jordan, 2002).

Officials from the EU 15 and those in Brussels must be credited with making environmental issues and policies a priority in the accession debates and negotiations and keeping these issues on the table after 1989. Few doubt that the massive environmental policy changes seen across CEE prior to enlargement would have been achieved without regulatory pressure and funding from the EU. Yet, it is clear that the EU continues to send very mixed messages to actors in the new (and also the older) Member States. As argued above, EU policies and funding priorities around issues such transport, agriculture, and economic development often serve to undermine or overwhelm the environmental policy transformation occurring in CEE. That specific areas of law and regulation can be Europeanized, making them more like those emanating from Brussels, is clear (see Chapter 10; Jordan and Liefferink, 2004). What is also becoming clear, however, is that the limitations and contradictions of EU environmental policies and practices can also be exported.

Environmental policies in the new Member States are beginning to look more and more like those in the older Member States. Consequently, the new EU members may eventually come to be seen as being as able to produce environmental innovations as the older Member States. Post-2004, the EU is likely to need greater regulatory and institutional flexibility to accommodate its great institutional and economic variability. Rather than being framed as a problem or a burden for the older EU Member States, it may be time to look upon the new members as untapped resources and laboratories for environmental policy experimentation and innovation. Because of their lower level of economic development, for example, countries in CEE have even greater incentives than those in the EU 15 to design cheaper and more efficient means of achieving compliance with high EU standards. A generation of more efficient, less costly policies could benefit new and old members alike.

Lastly, a new and enlarged EU of 25 or more members offers multiple opportunities to exercise greater European environmental leadership beyond the Union's borders. The 2004 enlargement sets the stage – and raises the bar – for subsequent rounds of enlargement. The new entrants from CEE demonstrated what many doubted, namely that they could transpose the extensive and ever-expanding EU *acquis* into law and regulation. The accession states must now demonstrate that they can achieve high levels of implementation, even though this has yet to be achieved by many of the EU 15. The larger aspiring Member States such as Bulgaria, Romania and Turkey, as well as the smaller states of southeastern Europe, will do well to emulate the environmental accomplishments of the new Member States from CEE.

References

Albrecht, C. (1987) 'Environmental Policies and Politics in Contemporary Czech-oslovakia', *Studies in Contemporary Communism*, Vol.20, pp291–302.

Andonova, L. (2003) *Transnational Politics and the Environment: EU Integration and Environmental Policy in Central and Eastern Europe*, Cambridge, MA: MIT Press.

Andrews, R. N. (1993) 'Environmental Policy in the Czech and Slovak Republic', in Vari, A. and Tamas, P. (eds) *Environment and Democratic Transition: Policy and Politics in Central and Eastern Europe*, Dordrecht: Kluwer Academic Publishers.

Archibald, S. O., Banu, L. E. and Bochniarz, Z. (2004) 'Market Liberalisation and Sustainability in Transition: Trends and Turning Points in Central and Eastern Europe', *Environmental Politics*, Vol.13, pp266–289.

Auer, M. R. (2004) *Restoring Cursed Earth: Appraising Environmental Policy Reforms in Central and Eastern Europe and Russia*, Boulder, CO: Rowman & Littlefield Press.

Auer, M. R. and Legro, S. (2004), 'Environmental Reform in the Czech Republic: Uneven Progress after 1989', in Auer, M. (ed) *Restoring Cursed Earth: Appraising Environmental Policy Reforms in Central and Eastern Europe and Russia*, Boulder, CO: Rowman & Littlefield Press.

Axelrod, R. (2004) 'Nuclear Power and EU Enlargement: The Case of Temelin', *Environmental Politics*, Vol.13, pp153–174.

Baker, S. and Jehlika, P. (1998) 'Dilemmas of Transition: The Environment, Democracy and Economic Reform in East Central Europe – An Introduction', in Baker, S. and Jehlika, P. (eds) *Dilemmas of Transition: The Environment, Democracy and Economic Reform in East Central Europe*, London: Frank Cass Publishers.

Beckmann, A., Carmin, J. and Hicks, B. (2002) 'Catalysts for Sustainability: NGOs and Regional Development Initiatives in the Czech Republic', in Filho, W. L. (ed) *International Experiences on Sustainability*, Bern: Peter Lang Scientific Publishing.

Beckmann, A. and Dissing, H. (2004) 'EU Enlargement and Sustainable Rural Development in Central and Eastern Europe', *Environmental Politics*, Vol.13, pp135–152.

Bell, R. G. (2004) 'Further Up the Learning Curve: NGOs from Transition to Brussels', *Environmental Politics*, Vol.13, pp194–215.

Brzel, T. A. (2000) 'Improving Compliance through Domestic Mobilization? New Instruments and the Effectiveness of Implementation', in Knill, C. and Lenschow, A. (eds) *Implementing EU Environmental Policy: New Directions and Old Problems*, Manchester: Manchester University Press.

Carius, A. (2002) 'Challenges for Governance in a Pan-European Environment: Transborder Cooperation and Institutional Coordination', in Crisen, S. and Carmin, J. (eds) *EU Enlargement and Environmental Quality: Central and Eastern Europe and Beyond*, Washington: Woodrow Wilson International Center for Scholars.

Carius, A., Homeyer, I. and Bar, S. (2000), 'Eastern Enlargement of the European Union and Environmental Policy: Challenges, Expectations, Multiple Speeds and Flexibility', in Holzinger, K. and Knoepfel, P. (eds) *Environmental Policy in a European Union of Variable Geometry? The Challenge of the Next Enlargement*, Basel: Helbing & Lichtenhahn.

Carmin, J. and Hicks, B. (2002) 'International Triggering Events, Transnational Networks, and the Development of the Czech and Polish Environmental Movements', *Mobilization*, Vol.7, pp305–324.

Carmin, J., Hicks, B., and Beckmann, A. (2003) 'Leveraging Local Action: Grassroots Initiatives and Transnational Collaboration in the Formation of the White Carpathian Euroregion', *International Sociology*, Vol.18, pp703–725.

Carmin, J. and VanDeveer, S. D. (2004) 'Enlarging EU Environments: Central and Eastern Europe from Transition to Accession,' *Environmental Politics*, Vol.13, pp3–26.

Carmin, J. and VanDeveer, S. D. (2005) *EU Enlargement and the Environment: Institutional Change and Environmental Policy in Central and Eastern Europe*, London: Routledge.

Cellarius, B. A. and Staddon, C. (2002) 'Environmental Nongovernmental Organizations, Civil Society and Democratization in Bulgaria', *East European Politics and Societies*, Vol.16, pp182–222.

Commission of the European Communities (2003) 'Fifth Annual Survey on the Implementation and Enforcement of Community Environmental Law', Brussels.

Connolly, B., Gutner, T. and Berdarff, H. (1996) 'Organizational Inertia and Environmental Assistance in Eastern Europe', in Keohane, R. O. and Levy, M. (eds) *Institutions for Environmental Aid*, Cambridge, MA: MIT Press.

DeBardeleben, J. (1993) *To Breathe Free: Eastern Europe's Environmental Crisis*, Washington, DC: Woodrow Wilson Center Press/Johns Hopkins University Press.

DeBardeleben, J. and Hannigan, J. (1995) *Environmental Security and Quality after Communism*, Boulder, CO: Westview Press.

Europa (2002), 'Enlargement: Negotiations of the Chapter 22: Environment', available online at http://europa.eu.int/comm/enlargement/negotiations/chapters/chap22/index.htm.

Fagin, A. (1994) 'Environment and Transition in the Czech Republic', *Environmental Politics*, Vol.3, pp479–494.

Garvey, T. (2002) 'EU Enlargement: Is it Sustainable?' in Crisen, S. and Carmin J. (eds) *EU Enlargement and Environmental Quality: Central and Eastern Europe and Beyond*, Washington, DC: Woodrow Wilson International Center for Scholars.

Gille, Z. (2004) 'Europeanizing Hungarian Waste Policies: Progress or Regression?', *Environmental Politics*, Vol.13, pp114–134.

Golub, J. (1998a) *New Instruments for Environmental Policy in the EU*, London: Routledge.

Golub, J. (1998b), *Global Competition and EU Environmental Policy*, London: Routledge.

Gutner, T. L. (2002) *Banking on the Environment: Multilateral Development Banks and Their Environmental Performance in Central and Eastern Europe*, Cambridge, MA: MIT Press.

Hallstrom, L. (2004) 'Eurocratising Enlargement? EU Elites and NGO Participation in East Central European Environmental Policy', *Environmental Politics*, Vol.13, pp175–192.

HELCOM (Helsinki Commission) (1998) *Final Report on the Implementation of the 1988 Ministerial Declaration*, Baltic Sea Environment Proceedings No.71, Helsinki: HELCOM

HELCOM (Helsinki Commission)Project Team on Hazardous Substances (2001) *The Implementation of the 1988 Ministerial Declaration on the Protection of the Marine Environment of the Baltic Sea Area with regard to Hazardous Substances*, Helsinki: HELCOM, May.

Hicks, B. (2004) 'Setting Agendas and Shaping Activism: EU Influence on Central European Environmental Movements', *Environmental Politics*, Vol.13, pp216–233.

Holzinger, K. and Knoepfel, P. (2000) *Environmental Policy in a European Union of Variable Geometry? The Challenge of the Next Enlargement*, Basel: Helbing & Lichtenhahn.

Homeyer, I. (2004) 'Differential Effects of Enlargement on EU Environmental Governance', *Environmental Politics*, Vol.13, pp52–76.

Howard, M. M. (2003) *The Weakness of Civil Society in Post-Communist Europe*, Cambridge: Cambridge University Press.

Jancar-Webster, B. (1998) 'Environmental Movement and Social Change in the Transition Countries' in Baker, S. and Jehlika, P. (eds) *Dilemmas of Transition: The Environment, Democracy and Economic Reform in East Central Europe*, London: Frank Cass.

Jehlika, P. and Tickle, A. (2004) 'Environmental Implications of Eastern Enlargement: The End of EU Progressive Environmental Policy?' *Environmental Politics*, Vol.13, pp77–98.

Jordan, A. (2002) *Environmental Policy in the European Union: Actors, Institutions and Processes*, London: Earthscan

Jordan, A. and Liefferink, D. (eds) (2004) *Environmental Policy in Europe: The Europeanization of National Environmental Policy*, London: Routledge.

Jordan, A., Liefferink, D. and Fairbrass, J. (2004) 'The Europeanization of National Environmental Policy: A Comparative Analysis' in Barry, J., Baxter, B. and Dunphy, R. (eds) *Europe, Globalisation and Sustainable Development*, London: Routledge.

Knill, C. and Lenschow, A. (2000) *Implementing EU Environmental Policy: New Directions and Old Problems*, Manchester: Manchester University Press.

Kolk, A. and van der Weij, E. (1998) 'Financing Environmental Policy in East Central Europe' in Baker, S. and Jehlika, P. (eds) *Dilemmas of Transition: The Environment, Democracy and Economic Reform in East Central Europe*, London: Frank Cass.

Kružíková, E. (2004) 'EU Accession and Legal Change: Accomplishments and Challenges in the Czech Case', *Environmental Politics*, Vol.13, pp99–113.

McCormick, J. (2001) *Environmental Policy in the European Union*, New York: Palgrave.

McCuen, G. E. and Swanson, R. P. (1993) *Toxic Nightmare in the USSR and Eastern Europe*, Hudson: Gary E. McCuen Publications.

Mendelson, S. E. and Glenn, J. K. (2002) *The Power and Limits of NGOs: A Critical Look at Building Democracy in Eastern Europe and Eurasia*, New York: Columbia University Press.

Mitchener, B. (2002) 'Standard Bearers: Increasingly, Rules of Global Economy are Set in Brussels', *Wall Street Journal*, 23 April, ppA1, A10.

OECD (1997) *Environmental Data Compendium 1997*, Paris: OECD.

O'Neill, K. (2000) *Waste Trading among Rich Nations: Building a New Theory of Environmental Regulation*, Cambridge, MA: MIT Press.

Pavlínek, P. and Pickles, J. (2000) *Environmental Transitions: Transformation and Ecological Defense in Central and Eastern Europe*, London: Routledge.

Princen, T., Maniates, M. and Conca, K. (2002) *Confronting Consumption*, Cambridge, MA: MIT Press.

Pryde, P. R. (1995) *Environmental Resources and Constraints in the Former Soviet Republics*, Boulder, CO: Westview Press.

Quigley, K. F. F. (2000) 'Lofty Goals, Modest Results: Assisting Civil Society in Eastern Europe', in Carothers, T. and Ottaway, M. (eds) *Funding Virtue: Civil Society Aid and Democracy Promotion*, New York: The Carnegie Endowment.

Schreurs, M. (2004) 'Environmental Protection in an Expanding European Community: Lessons from Past Accessions', *Environmental Politics*, Vol.13, pp27–51.

Selin, H. and VanDeveer, S. D. (2004) 'Baltic Hazardous Substances Management: Results and Challenges', *AMBIO: Journal of the Human Environment*, Vol.33, pp153–160.

Simons, M. (1990) 'Eastern Europe: The Polluted Lands', *The New York Times Magazine*, 29 April, pp30–35.

Skjaerseth, J. B. (2002) *North Sea Co-operation: Linking International and Domestic Pollution Control*, Manchester: Manchester University Press.

Slocock, B. (1996), 'The Paradoxes of Environmental Policy in Eastern Europe: The Dynamics of Policy-making in the Czech Republic', *Environmental Politics*, Vol.5, pp501–521.

VanDeveer, S. D. (2003) 'Green Fatigue', *Wilson Quarterly*, Autumn, pp55–59.

VanDeveer, S. D. and Carmin, J. (forthcoming) 'Sustainability and EU Accession: Capacity Development and Environmental Reform in Central and Eastern Europe' in Cohen, G. B. and Bochniarz, Z. (eds) *Environment and Sustainability in the New Central Europe*, New York: Berghahn Books.

Vari, A. and Tamas, P. (1993) *Environment and Democratic Transition: Policy and Politics in Central and Eastern and Europe*, Dordrecht: Kluwar Academic Publishers.

Wedel, J. R. (1998) *Collision or Collusion: The Strange Case of Western Aid to Eastern Europe 1989–1998*, New York: St. Martin's Press.

16

New Regulatory Approaches in 'Greening' EU Policies

Andrea Lenschow

Introduction

For about 30 years, the European Union (EU) has developed an increasingly comprehensive environmental policy. Although the EU has a primary commitment to building a common market, and may therefore be expected to focus on the removal of trade-inhibiting environmental regulations, EU environmental policy has proved to be quite resistant against such a 'race to the bottom' and actually improved the level of regulatory protection in many instances (Scharpf, 1998; Eichener, 1996). Despite these efforts, and despite the relatively high technological, financial, and administrative capacities in Europe, the actual impact of the EU environmental policy remains disappointing. Notwithstanding some success stories, such as measures for the protection of the ozone layer, the ecosystems in Europe and biodiversity remain threatened. In a recent publication, the European Environment Agency finds the European state of the environment 'far from satisfactory' (European Environment Agency, 1999).

Two basic factors are responsible for this deplorable state of affairs. First, many EU environmental policies are implemented poorly in the Member States, hence high protective standards remain ineffective on the ground (CEC, 1996; European Parliament, 1996; Collins and Earnshaw, 1992; Knill and Lenschow, 2000). Second, progress in the environmental policy field is counteracted by developments in other policy fields. In the EU – and in most of its Member States – sectoral polices such as agricultural policy, transport policy, energy policy, cohesion policy, fiscal policy and so on are formulated in disregard of their environmental impact. In other words, environmental policy is not treated as a horizontal policy feeding into all relevant policy decisions of the EU. As a consequence, the EU's environmental policy has shown only limited effectiveness.

In recent years, the EU has become increasingly aware of both deficits – the implementation gap, and the failure to achieve environmental policy integration

(EPI) – and in responding to these problems, the EU is experimenting with new forms of governance. In short, the EU is rethinking its institutionally fragmented, hierarchical, and legalistic style of policy-making and introducing more flexible, participatory, and decentralized regulatory forms. We witness the emergence of so-called new instruments; procedural rules meant to encourage the wide reflection on policy goals and approaches are drawn up to complement the previously dominating environmental standards. Furthermore, the EU is attempting to develop a policy-making structure that allows for deliberation and learning across policy fields, and across the various levels of governance, hence within an open network structure (cf Kohler-Koch, 1999).

In this chapter, I focus on the EU's attempts to improve its performance in integrating environmental concerns in sectoral policies. The two following parts trace the concept of EPI in the history of EU environmental policy-making and describe the current 'new governance' efforts to achieve EPI. This review will also reveal a certain evolution of new governance forms in this area. Maybe ironically, top-down guidance and even pressure have furthered the acceptance of EPI in the Member States and among sectoral policy actors. While it would be too early to evaluate the recent efforts in terms of their impact on the state of the environment, in the fourth part I will comment on the overall experience concerning EPI with a few cautioning remarks. Both the neo-institutionalist and the rational choice literature point to important constraints to learning that must not be neglected in designing new forms of governance.

EPI as an Emerging Policy Objective

As already indicated, the acceptance of the need for a more integrative approach was partly triggered by a gloomy internal assessment of past policy practices. Traditionally, the EU has treated the protection of the environment as the sole responsibility of environmental policy-makers in the Commission's Environment Directorate General and the national environment ministries, rather than as a common responsibility. In this framework, the EU made use of regulatory, mostly 'command-and-control', policy instruments. But, neither the general state of the environment nor the implementation of concrete EU regulations give convincing evidence that the EU is on the right path with this strategy. Present efforts to establish the environment as a horizontal policy matter and to build a cross-sectoral 'Partnership for Integration' (CEC, 1998a) reflect the lessons drawn from policy failure.

At the same time, these lessons borrow recipes from the international discourse on sustainable development. The core idea of 'sustainable development' is that environmental protection, economic growth, and social development are mutually compatible, rather than conflicting, objectives. Environmental protection ensures that the very foundation for economic activity and the human existence are not destroyed. Economic and social development, in turn, are considered possible without further depleting non-renewable resources and reducing biodiversity. The publication of the Brundtland Report broadened this perspective to the social and political sphere, and firmly established the concept on the European political agenda. The report defined sustainable development as 'a process of change in which the exploitation of resources, the direction of investment, the orientation of technological development, and institutional change are made consistent with future as well as present needs' (WCED, 1987, pp8–9). The introductory note that '[o]ur message is, above all, directed towards people, whose well-being is the ultimate goal of all environment and development policies' (pxiv) and the compatibility assumptions behind the concept resonate well with the economic mainstream, while equally responding to the emerging environmental concerns in Western Europe. 'Sustainable development' represents an idea able to facilitate political consensus; it offers a story that is attractive to many actors because it provides a conceptual foundation for the pursuit of widely accepted ethical values (intergenerational equity, alleviation of poverty, environmental protection) at seemingly low financial and political costs.[1]

The concept of sustainable development gained particular currency in EU circles, where the problem of squaring the objective of economic competitiveness with the goal of environmental protection had resulted in increasingly controversial debates, which even resulted in several court cases dealing with the priority or compatibility of economic and environmental objectives (Koppen, 1993). The old regulatory-based approach began to face a serious legitimacy crisis, as it seemed to impose high costs on economic actors without producing the desired environmental improvements. It is therefore hardly surprising that the new 'no trade-off' conceptualization of the economy–environment relationship and the related 'softening' of the top-down regulatory approach found increasing acceptance.

Clearly implicit in the notion that environmental, economic and social objectives may be achieved in a mutually compatible way is the integration principle. In Angela Liberatore's words:

> *The relevance of integration for moving towards sustainable development is straightforward: if environmental factors are not taken into consideration in the formulation and implementation of the policies that regulate economic activities and other forms of social organization, a new model of development that can be environmentally and socially sustainable in the long term cannot be achieved* (Liberatore, 1997, p107).

Put differently, EPI represents a first-order operational principle to implement and institutionalize the idea of sustainable development, which assumed an increasingly central role in the EU's *acquis*.

The EPI principle in the Environmental Action Programmes (EAPs) of the EU

The growth of a general concern for environmental protection is reflected in the series of EAPs of the EU. Already the First EAP hinted at the need for an integrated approach that argued that 'effective environmental protection requires the consideration of environmental consequences in all technical planning and decision-making processes at national and Community level' (OJ, 1973, p6). This was made more explicit in the Third EAP in 1983, which stated:

> *[T]he Community should seek to integrate concern for the environment into the policy and development of certain economic activities as much as possible and thus promote the creation of an overall strategy making environmental policy part of economic and social development. This should result in a greater aware- ness of the environmental dimension, notably in the fields of agriculture (includ- ing forestry and fisheries), energy, industry, transport and tourism (OJ, 1983, Section I, p8).*

The Fourth EAP of 1986 (OJ, 1986) devoted a whole subsection to discussing 'Integration with other Community Policies' (Section 2.3) and announced that the 'Commission will develop internal procedures and practices to ensure that this integration of environmental factors takes place routinely in relation to all other policy areas' (paragraph 2.3.28). The Fifth – and most recent – EAP, which came into force in 1993 (CEC, 1992), placed great emphasis on the integration principle. It identified five key areas – industry, energy, agriculture, transport and tourism – where policy integration seemed most urgent, and developed an approach of dialogue and joint responsibilities to pursue the sustainable develop- ment agenda. Rather than attempting to regulate integration, the Fifth EAP hoped to involve policy-makers and stakeholders in a co-operative *process* that would result in the penetration of the idea of sustainable development and EPI into all sectors of society and public policy – an aspect I will return to below. The Fifth EAP was also most explicit in pointing to the limits of top-down regulation and the promise of 'soft law' to achieve the desired attitude change. In the words of the Commission:

> *the basic strategy therefore is to achieve full integration of environmental and other relevant policies through the active participation of all the main actors in society (administrations, enterprises, general public) through a broadening and deepening of the instruments for control and behavioural change including, in particular, greater use of market forces (CEC, 1992, p49).*

Evolution of the treaty base for sustainable development and EPI

The EAPs are reflections of the policy-planning process within the formal agenda- setter of the EU: the European Commission. Legally, however, the EAPs are non- binding and they may amount to little more than a wish list of ambitious policy- makers. In the case of the EPI principle, the publication of new EAPs, however, was paralleled – responding to Commission initiatives, in particular – in the treaty evolution of the EU. The Single European Act, which entered into force in June 1987, first established a legal basis for environmental policy in general, and formulated the objective of integrating environmental considerations into other policies at all levels in the new environment title of the EC Treaty (Title VI, Arti- cle 130r EC). The Treaty on European Union (TEU), which was ratified by late 1993, strengthened Article 130r by requiring that 'Environmental protection *must* be integrated into the definition and implementation of other Community policies' (Article 130r(2) TEU, emphasis added). It also approached the 'sustain- able development' language by inserting a new Article 2 into the Treaty that read:

'The Community shall have as its task ... to promote throughout the Community a harmonious and balanced development of economic activities, sustainable and non-inflationary growth respecting the environment'. Despite the much-criticized phrasing, calling for 'sustainable ... growth', this article moved the environmental objective to the front of the Treaty and hence added weight to it. This process was continued in the Treaty of Amsterdam that elevated in Article 6 the integration principle to a guiding objective of the EU. Furthermore, the achievement of sustainable *development* becomes a fundamental objective of the EU, mentioned in the preamble and Article 2 of the Treaty.

From the conception and legal institutionalization to the operation of EPI: hard or soft law?

Considering the emergence of the EPI principle as a Treaty obligation, hence a binding commitment, it may seem strange to examine the principle in the context of new governance methods. In fact, the drafters of the recent amendments to the TEU seemed to believe that the previous failure to integrate environmental concerns into sectoral policies can be solved by imposing an integration commitment through law, from the top down.[2]

Despite this appearance of 'hard law', I suggest that the recent application of the EPI principle justifies its interpretation as an element of 'new governance'. In developing this argument, I will draw on Andre Nollkaemper's legal analysis of the EPI principle (2002). Nollkaemper points out the ambiguity of the legal meaning of EPI and suggests that the integration principle could play three alternative roles in European environmental law:

> *Firstly, it [could] serve as an objective that underlies and inspires more specific environmental law. As such, the principle is unobjectionable, though not distinguishable from environmental policy proper. Secondly, the integration principle can, as a rule of reference, be used as a vehicle to encourage the Community and other international institutions to comply with relevant norms of international law in their various activities* (p31).

In neither case, the EPI principle carries any autonomous meaning apart from existing environmental law – be it of the traditional 'top-down' or the more flexible and participatory kind emphasizing procedure over substantive regulation. Both as an objective and as a rule of reference, its main function is to call extra attention to the environmental law and to underscore the applicability of environmental principles outside the narrow realm of the treaty's environment title.

More interesting, for our purposes, is the third interpretation of the EPI principle. Here, the integration principle may come to play a role as an *autonomous normative principle* with a procedural and as well as a substantive component. 'With regard to the procedural function, the principle requires, at a very minimum, that *interests of environmental protection are considered in decision-making procedures*' (Nollkaemper 2002, p30, emphasis added). Substantively, 'the integration principle provides a means of balancing two competing norms' (ibid); more specifically, it is a norm to reconcile economic development with the protection of the environment. In this third meaning, therefore, the EPI principle implies procedural norms that permit a highly reflexive form of problem-solving in a modern world where it is difficult to authoritatively establish a clear hierarchy of norms or truths. While neither the first nor the second meaning of EPI add anything new to the already existing environmental *acquis* of the EU, this third meaning directs EU policy-makers towards the adoption of a new governance style. In this perspective, EPI is more than a reminder of legal obligations in the environmental *acquis* of the EU; it is about the introduction of structures and procedures that facilitate a dialogue across policy sectors and governmental levels to reconcile conflicting interests. Whether the EPI principle will play this third more far-reaching role, Nollkaemper writes, 'depends upon the identification of normative space and the development of criteria to evaluate integration. This will be an area where much will depend upon the energies and activities of interested actors to make the principle effective and practicable' (p31). Looking at some of the recent developments towards giving the EPI an operational meaning, we can observe exactly this trend.

The Path to and from 'Cardiff'

Looking back at the history of EPI in the EU, until recently it was far from representing an autonomous normative principle with any independent procedural or substantive consequence. For a long time, the principle served as a policy objective that moved nobody to rethink established practices. Efforts to move from a superfluous rhetoric towards a meaningful principle and governing norm began only in the early 1990s with the drafting of the Fifth EAP. Two dimensions can be distinguished in the application of the EPI principle – an administrative challenge and new forms of state–society relations. In administrative terms, the EPI principle implied the end of organizational structures that encouraged a sectorally highly segmented policy-making process. Although there may be good reasons to divide the organizational structure of government into directorate generals, councils, committees or – on the national level – ministries, EPI calls for organizational channels and procedures that facilitate a regular dialogue and exchange between policy fields, encouraging not only co-ordination and cohesion but common problem-solving involving the reconciliation of policy objectives and norms in a world of uncertainties.

Such reconciliation of policy objectives is not only an organizational question; it depends on societal acceptance and support. Both public authorities and private actors in the Member States need to implement EPI, yet implementation involves more than a traditional implementation perspective suggests. While there may be certain rules and procedures to follow (and obey), a general normative principle such as EPI is dependent on triggering a *multiplying* effect on the ground. It aims to facilitate (thinking about) reforms on the lower levels of governance that were not prestructured on the EU policy arena. It provides a general framework for domestic initiative from the 'bottom up'. For this to work, the application of EPI is dependent on a wider societal dialogue and the inclusion of societal actors in modern governance.

Such new forms of state–society relations must not be mistaken as a governance form without state or governance through the market. New governance, soft or procedural law, while resonating with the deregulatory intentions of the neo-liberal paradigm, needs to be held clearly distinct. In a framework of new governance, the role of the state (or the equivalent institutions in the EU) is not to stay away and *laissez-faire* as the neo-liberal school would have it, rather the role of the state has changed into that of an 'activator' and 'facilitator' (Kohler-Koch, 1999, Kooiman, 1993). In other words, new governance implies some activity from above, even though this activity is quite different from the traditional 'authoritative allocation of value.'

Returning now to the development of the EPI principle in the EU, we will see that these institutional questions, as well as the modification of state–society relations, offer a wide field for experimentation. EU efforts have evolved in terms of scope and emphasis. More importantly, however, we observe a change in the new governing style and, more specifically, in the role of the state. In brief, in the last year, or so, the EU has begun to develop a central 'activator role', building a framework for a mutual learning process across sectors and across Member States. I shall suggest that these efforts at *active guidance* were necessary to move EPI on an effective path. The last year in the evolution of EPI on the general level, as well as some more precise policy cases, suggest that the substantive objectives that are targeted by the EPI principle depend on the presence of a (legitimated) 'master of procedure'.

The pre-Cardiff phase

The EU's initial attempts to apply the EPI principle were cautious and followed a pure 'bottom-up' approach, meaning that influence rather than formal power was applied to change the attitude and behaviour of the stakeholders in non-environment sectors (cf Wilkinson, 1997). The Fifth EAP provided the general framework for these first activities. But, even though the action programme addressed all levels of government (from the local to the EU level), and private as well as public actors, even proposing actions, targets, and timetables, only the European Commission followed up on its own invitation and made deliberate efforts to put the EPI principle into operational practice. The Commission's integration arrangements were set out in an internal communication (CEC, 1993a), drafted under the leadership of the Environment Directorate General (DG XI) and adopted by all Commissioners in May 1993. It included the following measures:

- A new *integration unit* was placed in DG XI, reporting directly to the director-general.
- Each directorate general was to designate an *integration correspondent*, who would liaison between his/her DG and DG XI and ensure that environmental concern would be given proper account.
- Policy proposals with significant environmental effects would be signified with a *green star* in the annual legislative programmes of the Commission and be subject to an environmental appraisal.
- Each DG was called to conduct an *annual evaluation* of its environmental performance.

- A *code of environmental conduct* was to be drawn up for the Commission itself.

Even though these internal procedures were incorporated into the Commission's internal manual of operational procedures, their impact on the practices in the non-environment directorate generals was disappointing. Dialogue between the DGs proved difficult, with only few exceptions (cf Lenschow, 1997, on the regional policy area). Dialogue groups degenerated to talking shops, reporting obligations were frequently perceived as bureaucratic burden, and many so-called new instruments were implemented as poorly as old-style policies. In 1997, in the context of the publication of the Commission's work programme for 1998, Environment Commissioner Bjerregaard admitted that the internal measures to improve integration 'have not been particularly effective' even though progress had been achieved in areas such as regional spending, development policy, transport, and energy (EWWE, 1997, p14). Assessments conducted by the EEA, such as the Dobris Assessment, followed the Commission's self-critique.

As a result of these reviews, the Commission renewed its commitment to adapt its internal procedures to the task of EPI by reinforcing old measures and adding new ones. It proposed an analysis of the environmental impact of funding from the EU budget. It also attempted to strengthen the overall process by introducing an independent evaluation of the EPI process conducted by the Environment Directorate General and the development of training programmes for Commission staff on environmental appraisal and integration (EWWE, 1997, pp14–15; ENV Press, 1997). This first response to initial failure represented a (partial) return to old, authoritative steering. Disappointed by the lacking responsiveness in many policy sectors, the Environment Directorate General considered a return to a policing role, applying its own criteria in evaluating the reform progress in the neighbouring DGs. It soon realized that such a strategy suffered from low legitimacy – what gives the Environment Directorate General the right to control in an open conflict of norms? Furthermore, the Environment DG was not yet equipped with the substantive criteria and indictors guiding an evaluation. In both regards, the EU Council meeting in Cardiff became a turning point, directing the EPI story towards the development of legitimate guidelines.

Cardiff and beyond

From a sectoral standpoint, EPI – conceived as a balancing and reconciliating tool – cannot be imposed only from one side and hope to gain broad acceptance. As we have seen, the EPI principle is intrinsically bound to a deliberative practice, bringing together all sides in a conflict of norms. In our modern age with ample uncertainties, there exists no a priori truth that sets the value of nature conservation before the value of free individual mobility or – maybe less controversially – before the value of employment. As EPI depends on a process that listens both ways, such a process also needs to be controlled from both sides. In order to bring both sides together, a 'third party' may have to act as an activator or facilitator. This third party needs to be perceived as legitimated and neutral.

This at least is the one lesson that can be learned from the spell of activity that followed the Cardiff Summit in June 1998. During this summit meeting, the national chiefs of government represented in the European Council assumed that facilitating role, shifting leadership from an actor that was perceived as partial and hence poorly legitimated to a more neutral, yet influential, ground. With EPI being upgraded to a chief concern in the EU, the strategy in pursuing integration changed from a rather passive, purely bottom-up approach to a guided learning approach, which established a formal framework for the integration process.

More specifically, the mobilization of the European Council for a more active EPI agenda developed after the so-called northern enlargement of the EU that brought Austria, Finland, and Sweden – three 'pioneers' in the area of environmental policy (Andersen and Liefferink, 1997) – into the EU. With the help of these countries, first the integration clause was strengthened in the Amsterdam Treaty. At the 1997 Luxembourg Summit, the current less legalistic and more process-oriented approach to EU environmental policy integration was launched on the basis of a Swedish initiative. Maybe surprisingly, the following UK presidency placed the environmental integration project at the top of its agenda. Besides organizing the first-ever joint council of environment and transport ministers and raising environmental concerns in other councils such as energy and fisheries, the UK supported and gave weight to a new Commission strategy on EPI (Jordan, 1998b). The Commission's communication 'Partnership for Integration' (CEC, 1998a) was prepared for and adopted by the European Council in Cardiff. This document, which continues to be the general reference point for present EPI initiatives, implied a transformation of the previous cautious and inward-oriented approach towards a more guided process with clearly assigned tasks. It explicitly called on the Council of Ministers and the European Parliament to take responsibility in the integration process.[3] While the Commission still hopes to improve its implementation of the internal rules that had been agreed by 1997, the councils are now asked to:

- collect experiences and evidence of *best practices* of EPI in the Member States and develop a basis for improved Community procedures;
- *identify a set of priority actions* in order to incorporate environmental requirements and to foresee effective mechanisms for *monitoring* their implementation;
- ensure that environmental requirements are explicitly reflected in their decisions on new proposals;
- commit themselves to *review their current organizational arrangements* to ensure effective implementation of this integration strategy.

The summit meetings that followed the publication of this latest EPI strategy seem to indeed indicate a strengthened commitment from the European Council and some real progress in the stocktaking of past activities and a targeting of procedure at substantive advancement. Most relevant sectoral councils were assigned to review their integration performance of the past and develop an EPI strategy for the future (see Table 16.1).

In addition to assigning responsibilities within a politically legitimated framework, the lesson learned from previous unresponsiveness was that progress

Table 16.1 *EPI at the Summits*

December 1997	Luxembourg Summit	Work on the current process of EU environmental policy integration launched.
June 1998	Cardiff Summit	*'The European Council welcomes the Commission's submission of a draft strategy* [for integration of the environment into other EU policies] *and commits itself to consider it rapidly in view of the implementation of the new Treaty provisions. It invites the Commission to report to future European Councils on the Community's progress'* (Cardiff European Council, 1998, paragraph 32). European Council invites all relevant sectoral councils to establish their own strategies for integrating the environment and sustainable development. Transport, energy, and agriculture are asked to start this progress and provided reports to the Vienna Summit.
December 1998	Vienna Summit	Transport, agriculture and energy councils produce initial reports. Further integration plans are invited from development co-operation, internal market, and industry councils for Helsinki.
June 1999	Cologne Summit	European Council called upon the fisheries, general affairs and Ecofin (finance) councils to report on the EPI process and sustainable development in 2000.
December 1999	Helsinki Summit	European Council calls on nine Councils of Ministers (energy, transport, agriculture, development co-operation, internal market, industry, general affairs, Ecofin, and fisheries) to complete work on environmental policy integration and to submit comprehensive strategies by June 2001. The European Commission is invited to prepare a long-term policy proposal on sustainable development by June 2001.
June 2001	Gothenburg Summit	The European Council takes stock of progress in the nine sectors and policy areas that were asked to review their activities and proposes a comprehensive integration strategy for the future.

towards EPI depends on an opening of both cognitive and institutional boundaries, and that such opening does not 'just emerge'. The initial 'directing' of the dialogue process on the part of the Commission proved not only questionable in terms of its legitimacy (see above) but also too passive. The invitation to dialogue was blocked institutionally and old organizational routines persisted; equally, there was little evidence that the frame of reference for sectoral policy-makers changed and took account of environmental objectives. Recalling the most recent and also most devastating review of the EPI process until 1999, the Commission's 1999 *Global Assessment* of the Community's Fifth EAP laments:

> *the commitment by other sectors and by Member States to the Programme is partial, and the patterns of production and consumption in our countries prevent us from achieving a clean and safe environment and protecting the world's natural resources... [W]ithout a reinforced integration of environmental concerns into economic sectors to address the origins of environmental problems and without a stronger involvement and commitment by citizens and stakeholders, our development will remain environmentally unsustainable overall* (CEC, 1999a, pp2–3).

In view of the lessons of institutionalist scholarship in political science or organizational theory, this is hardly surprising. Policy and institutional change – and especially that of a paradigmatic nature – faces many constraints ranging from organizational inertia to the impact of sunk costs that make reforms unattractive or unfeasible, especially in the short term.[4] The early EPI strategy offered neither the incentives that might encourage rational actors to alter past practices, nor were sectoral frames of reference actively challenged. Although policy crises served as a 'substitute' for an active political strategy in some areas (regional policy and, to some extent, agriculture; cf Lenschow, 1999), the Cardiff process finally reacted to this lack of active guidance and currently, both procedural and substantive guidelines for EPI are being developed. Procedural guidelines, such as the conduct of environmental impact assessment, force sectoral policy-makers to consider environmental norms in their activities. Such impact assessments, if compared to mutually agreed environmental benchmarks, reveal the level of adaptational pressure for sectoral policy-makers. They also reveal the level of conflict with existing sectoral norms. In order to avoid a high level of resistance at this stage (as institutional analysis would predict), additional learning tools and processes are developed. Indicators – once worked out – will assist in pinpointing the main problem areas in a way sensitive to regional and economic context and, hence, help to weigh policy options to respond to environmental needs. During the Helsinki Summit the Commission submitted a report on 'Environment and Integration Indicators' (CEC, 1999b); this report relies in part on experiences gained by the Organisation for Economic Co-operation and Development (OECD), which also influences parallel efforts at the European Environment Agency. Several Directorate Generals in the Commission have reported own efforts to develop sectoral environmental indicator systems to guide their policies (eg CEC, 2000a, on agriculture, and CEC, 2001a, on transport and energy). This process encourages policy ideas to be exchanged. Member States are called to share models of 'best practice'. The first such market of ideas was organized during the German presidency in Bonn (cf Buck et al, 1999, for a brief review).

In sum, two features characterize the so-called Cardiff process. First, EPI has been declared a 'chief concern' with the heads of state or government assuming the role to activate the integration process. Commission communications, strategy papers, and guidelines have been discussed and adopted in the various European Summit meetings since Luxembourg, and therefore gained the legitimacy that was absent in previous attempts to put the EPI principle into practice (for instance in the context of implementing the Fifth EAP). Second, increased efforts are made to facilitate the dialogue, especially between sectoral and environmental policy-makers. Though still at an early stage, efforts to develop mutually agreeable and process-guiding EPI indicators were intensified and the exchange of 'best practice' models organized. These and the regular reporting commitments are supervised and evaluated in the framework of the European councils, holding the learning process on track and ensuring regular feedback. In short, the initial mere bottom-up process has been placed in some sort of authoritative context with the aim to guide and push the learning process towards 'greening' sectoral policies.

The example of regional policy

The following brief review of the environmental reforms of the EU's regional policy will further illustrate the crucial role of procedural guidance (for the full story, see Lenschow, 1997, 2002).

In the 1980s, the European Regional Development Fund (ERDF) went through several reforms, including an environmental dimension. Yet, the administrative reforms of 1993 are considered a breakthrough with respect to environmental policy integration. The reforms targeted poor planning and monitoring performance, the limited eligibility criteria for environmental programmes or projects, and the tendency to support so-called end-of-pipe[5] projects. The revised regulations reinforced the EPI by requiring that:

> *development plans ... must in the future include an appraisal of the environmental situation of the region concerned and an evaluation of the environmental impact of the strategy and operations planned, in accordance with the principles of sustainable development and in agreement with the provision of Community law in force. The plans must also mention the arrangements made by the Member States to associate their competent environmental authorities in the various stages of programming* (CEC, 1993b, p29, referring to Article 7 of the new Framework Regulation, emphasis added).

The legal evolution was paralleled by procedural changes leading towards fuller integration. The Commission developed an *aide memoire* (known as the environmental profile) for the Member States to clarify what information was to be supplied under the revised regulations. Although this profile had no legal standing, it served to assist public authorities to follow legal procedures. It also facilitated the harmonization of the national information submitted to the Commission. While the profile was targeted at the regional plans, a questionnaire was drawn up for the same purpose and directed at large operational projects. A list of indicators and a handbook were prepared with the intention of assessing the environmental impact of the regional programmes and its associated costs (Lenschow, 1997, 1999).

At the turn of the 20th century, the EU structural policies came up for another round of reforms in the context of devising the 'Agenda 2000' that would facilitate the further narrowing of the disparities in income between, and within, the Member States. As these reforms aim at the challenges implied in the future enlargement of the Community to East and Central Europe, it is not surprising that most of the political battles preceding the reforms focused on the distribution of the resources among the Member States, rather than on the quality of the spending. Nevertheless, the Commission further pursued its aim to ensure that the environment and sustainable development would be considered as a horizontal principle governing spending decisions (CEC, 1998b, 1999c). The final Council Regulation laying out the general provisions on the structural funds (Regulation 1260/1999 of 21 June 1999) includes a number of provisions furthering the integration of environmental consideration within the operations of the funds.

As is evident from the above description, the emphasis in the reforms lay on the operational side. The Commission – the Environment and the Regional Policy Directorate Generals – had made an effort to assist and guide the local adjustment processes. Environmental interest groups on the ground have quite favourably evaluated this strategy. However, practical experience shows that the implementation of the principle is not yet wholly successful. In the Member States and on the local level, environment groups still find evidence of poor consideration of environmental risks. This may become even more marked, as the latest reforms have begun to shift the 'mastery of procedure' from the EU level back to the Member States.

In the framework of the revised 1999 Regulation, the Commission is called to take a more decentralized, or hands-off, approach. National and regional 'managers' of the fund are to be informed of the principles and guidelines set out in the legislation and 'various working papers will be produced on sensitive or difficult issues ... to operators so as to facilitate their tasks: subjects will cover the application of the environmental directives' (CEC, 2000b). In other words, compared to the pre-1999 era, the Commission adopts a more indirect steering role, relying on a positive take-up in the Member States and regions.

Already on the general policy level (Fifth EAP), we saw the limits to this indirect approach, relying on the responsiveness from the bottom up. And also with respect to this particular development in regional policy, the Commission had immediate doubts with respect to such a hands-off approach. In view of some poor implementation of the EPI principle, Environment Commissioner Wallstrom reflected: 'In the long run I would prefer to be more of a consultant or advisor to Member States, but until then I will have to be more of a policewoman' (Harding, 1999). And indeed, the Commission seems to be steering a harder course again in enforcing the EPI principle, circumventing the limitations on active guidance imposed by the Regulation. Wallström warned that if governments breached EU environmental laws, 'they risked delays in receiving billions of Euro in regional aid from Brussels' (ibid) and she received backing from Commissioner Barnier, responsible for the regional policy portfolio, and the rest of the Commission (Smith, 2000).

More Limitations

The preceding discussion may have given the impression that I was advocating a return to traditional, top-down governance forms through the back door. In fact, I did argue that the application of the EPI principle, which can involve fundamental reforms in terms of procedure and substance, depends on the presence of legitimate and active leadership. Importantly, however, the – partly authoritative – leadership role refers to the mastery of procedures. Reporting, monitoring, evaluating, and exchanging are playing central roles. Here, the recent announcements in the regional policy context reflect only a second-best solution, chosen due to a reduced space for procedural guidance. With regard to the substantive policy changes that might follow from EPI, the leadership role can be limited to providing general orientation. The publication of best practice models is becoming quite fashionable in this context; the development of guiding indicators is proceeding more slowly, though slowly accelerating.

In this last part of the chapter, I shall argue that the EU may continue to underestimate the task of achieving EPI and hence follow too narrow – or too inconsistent – a strategy. The return to the stick in the regional policy case may be of only limited use as a 'model' because the withdrawal of funds is rarely applicable elsewhere. In fact, the return to authoritarian governance forms may be the least promising reaction to deficiencies in the new model. Rather, I see some evidence that the EU may not take the new governance approach seriously or far enough by neglecting society's role in applying the integration principle. Furthermore, and somewhat paradoxically, the EU may place too much hope in the power of dialogue and – implicitly – the malleability of interests and preferences and may have to complement deliberative governance methods with other tools. With respect to EPI, the EU needs to realize that policy integration does involve costs (for some) and that therefore the process will encounter limits to learning. Hence, the implementation of the principle may require a return to very traditional forms of governance – at least in Europe – namely (re)distributive measures.

Taking the societal link seriously

The concept of sustainable development is considered a new paradigm in public policy. While sectoral policy-makers are used to perceiving environmental policy as a constraint, forcing them to trade off economic gain for some illusive environmental objective, the sustainability paradigm assumes the objectives of economic development, social equity and environmental protection to be reconcilable. EPI is the means to find such reconciliation, involving reforms in organizational structure and routines, and behavioural changes on the part of producers as well as consumers. The acceptance of EPI as a political and procedural principle is closely linked to the acceptance of the new policy paradigm; hence, it is part and parcel of a process of paradigmatic learning.

The literature on policy change and policy learning hints at the relevant mechanisms responsible for, and may inform our evaluation of, the EU strategy of EPI. Policy learning involves a cognitive and reflective process in which policy-makers adapt their beliefs and positions in view of past experiences (lesson drawing), experiences of others (diffusion), new information, or technological developments and apply it to their subsequent choices of policy goals or techniques. Traditionally, policy learning has been applied to communities of policy elites (epistemic communities, governmental officials and experts) who 'puzzle' on society's behalf (Heclo, 1974). Recalling the Community's efforts at EPI, most efforts focus on facilitating such puzzling of the policy elites, despite all rhetoric to involve the general public in the process. The Commission was concentrating initially on its internal reforms; dialogues with representatives of societal interests were conducted as add-ons without much consequence. Also, the Cardiff process focuses on the activities of the directorates general, the technical councils, and the Member State governments. Will a paradigmatic shift come about in the context of such collective puzzling? Peter Hall (1993) provides us with a more differentiated and sceptical picture. He argues that such elite learning may be responsible for lower-level changes (involving the choice of policy instruments or precise settings), whereas paradigm shifts depend also on the mobilization of societal actors and a reshuffling of elites, hence on powering. The immediate – and possibly premature – hypothesis following from Hall's analysis is the following. Governance forms that aim to facilitate a paradigm shift towards sustainable development and EPI in theory and practice need to adopt a strong(er) societal focus (furthering the mobilization of supporters from the bottom up). Also, they may need some powerful help.

While there is no case evidence yet that could support this hypothesis with respect to the Cardiff process, some earlier examples suggest that societal pressure from below does indeed play a crucial role for EPI. I have argued elsewhere that the regional policy reforms described above were due to a very effective environmental alliance, which succeeded to fully discredit previous funding practices of the ERDF (Lenschow, 1997). Lauber's case study on freight transport across the Alps comes to similar conclusions. In all three regions involved (Switzerland, Tyrol, and Trentino-Alto Adige), 'environmental concerns were taken into account in transport policy primarily due to public pressure by those directly affected by the negative impacts of trucking. These impacts extend to individual persons, landscapes, natural and urbanized surroundings and sometimes even people's economic standing' (Lauber, 2002, p171). In a political context, in which the environmental implications of economic activities continue to elude the sectoral policy-makers – not least due to underdeveloped methodologies for assessing such implications – the input of locally affected people will close a gap in policy planning. Considering the EU's formal commitment to 'shared responsibility' (cf Fifth EAP), it seems strange that the European Court of Justice has, in the past, denied environmental NGOs *locus standi* to represent local environmental interests against the Commission (funding regional development programmes). Local people who feel the environmental impact of economic activities, especially in the context of large construction projects, are rarely capable of entering into expensive and time-consuming legal battles. If the wish for 'broadly based and active involvement' is to be taken seriously, access to the courts needs to be widened.

But even access to the courts may not be sufficient to ensure the public's involvement. It has become common knowledge that not all types of interests are equally capable of organizing. Also, there may be regional differences in the mobilization of public interests. Hence, new forms of governance may have to go even further than providing court access in levelling the playing field, as it would be in the interest of a balanced approach to problem-solving. A recent publication of the Commission's think-tank – the Forward Studies Unit – goes in that direction, suggesting that:

there will be attendant need to ensure that those coming into the process for the first time are not disadvantaged by their relative lack of organization and resources.

> *If this issue is not addressed, the result would be similar to many current consultation processes where there is a formal universal right to participate which nevertheless presupposes a certain minimum level of material and cognitive resources possessed in fact only by certain actors. New forms of governance, therefore, will at the most basic level need to take account of any inequality of resources and make allowances accordingly. Beyond that most basic level it may also be appropriate to consider the ways in which active steps may be taken to compensate less well-resourced stakeholders, perhaps by offering material help or perhaps by providing access to neutral expertise* (Lebessis and Paterson, 2000, pp23–24).

In short, besides the widely heard request for more openness and transparency in the governing processes, procedural equity is another prerequisite for the balancing of norms in modern society.[6]

Taking interests seriously

The previous remarks have hinted at the power structure in society that will influence the process and direction of learning. One approach at enabling a balanced reconciliation of interest is the strengthening of the weaker part (see above). Another approach is to target the structurally more powerful interest. It would be naive to think that powerful interests can be fully balanced through procedural reforms, not least because powerful interests are likely to prevent such reforms in the first place.

In the discussion of sustainable development and the associated principle of EPI, there is a tendency to reduce the conflict of interests to the cognitive dimension and, as a result, to place a particular emphasis on influencing the cognitive dimension in order to bring about change. And indeed, in economic practice, we observe that the costs of unsustainable practice often remain elusive. Sectoral policy-makers are overtaxed in assessing the environmental impacts of their programme and projects, and in evaluating sustainable practice. Several new instruments, like eco-audits or eco-taxes, aim at correcting the cost–benefit analysis of producers and hence to allow for the perception of environmental factors. The development of sustainability indicators and targets (benchmarks) serve a similar primarily cognitive function.

However, there exists a gap in the 'story' of sustainable development with rather serious implications for political strategy. The emphasis of the sustainability concept and EPI on 'win–win' scenarios, with regard to the environment and the economy, is only persuasive from an aggregate and long-term perspective. There is little doubt that environmental degradation today will impose restrictions on the economic opportunities of future generations; this is most obvious with respect to the extraction of natural, non-renewable resources or soil erosion. But, this win–win logic often breaks down on less aggregate levels. The sustainable development paradigm implies a restructuring of the economy with redistributive effects, where not every producer, farmer, or consumer will gain.

In political terms, this means that the EPI principle is more likely to gain acceptance on the 'general expert level' and among heads of state or government, or Commission officials, but it will face resistance where immediate trade-offs are felt. In other words, the 'weapon' of the sustainability story often loses power on the ground. The very slow 'greening' process of agricultural policy is a commonly known example showing that concerns with the immediate costs of reforms prevail over responsibilities for a common good. Even the argument that intensive farming methods may destroy the very basis for future farming, namely unpolluted soil, has proven insufficient to convince the average farmer of the need to restructure production. Equally, the variation in the acceptance of the EPI concept is closely related to short-term economic consequence.

This does not mean that EPI always breaks down on the ground. The story of mutual gains has inspired creative minds in political and economic planning, and more sustainable solutions were found for many economic activities. The development of new, less resource-intensive materials, recycling techniques, ecological housing projects, or eco-tourism represent only a few examples of 'green' niches in economic activities. Nevertheless, such niches are not always easy to find. To name a few more examples – in recent years the outspoken Austrian stand towards restricting road traffic across the Alps, especially for heavy lorries, diminished once it became clear that local (Tyrolian) traffic could not be easily exempted from the costs because such discriminatory policy would violate against internal market principles (Lauber, 2002). Christian Hey (2002) provides a similar example, tracing the 1993 Eurovignette Directive, among other things, to a significant fall in oil prices, allowing the introduction of an eco-tax without imposing new costs on the transport sector. While the latter case points to an economic window of opportunity for institutionalizing an environmental policy instrument, both examples show the economic limits on 'greening' sectoral policies – at least when the potential losers happen to be politically influential and powerful.

What is the political consequence of this constraint to balancing interests? I suggest that win–win solutions need to be constructed. In other words, individual losers of 'greening' measures need to be compensated, typically by subsidizing their adaptation processes. Subsidies, although controversial in the current political discourse, have the advantage that they allow for a steering of the restructuring processes, establishing clear incentives and disincentives. The agri-environmental measures of the EU agricultural policy move in this direction. By contrast, the ongoing attempts to liberalize the energy and transport markets point to the political difficulty of 'internalizing' environmental costs and of subsidizing providers of environment-friendly energy or modes of transport. In this context, and once again, political will is necessary in order to find sustainable solutions.

In sum, the EPI case suggests to me that it may not suffice to differentiate between different regulatory approaches. Procedures aimed at deliberation, mutual learning, and consensus-seeking should not lead us to believe that there will not be winners and losers in shifting from one to another paradigm. Especially in the field of environmental policy integration, sectoral producers or employees may incur considerable cost. The willingness for reform is likely to be linked not only to the cognitive dimension and learning (or generational change) but also to material compensation, hence redistributive measures.

Four Conclusions

The story of EPI in the EU shows the dangers of pursuing 'new governance' as something opposite to 'old governance'; it shows the limits of dichotomous thinking. EPI – and I would argue 'new governance' – does not mean the end of state intervention; it does not even imply a shift from top-down to bottom-up policy-making; and least of all does it pitch one policy field against another. Rather, policy-making in a world of uncertainty and a multitude of often-conflicting objectives can only be effective and legitimate if it is successful in linking participation and guidance with the aim to learn within, across and beyond policy sectors. The following four concluding lessons will once again stress this challenge to modern policy-making – a challenge that may not only be applicable to the case of EPI, but for problems of co-ordination in general:

- EPI depends on a politically backed 'mastery of procedure' and operational guidance. Guidance serves to build capacity on the ground and hence, avoid one of the main reasons for poor implementation.
- Especially in a multilevel governance context as in the EU, new governance forms depend on the involvement of society. Otherwise, the dialogue will be limited to elites and be effective, if at all, only during the policy formulation and decision phase, and risk implementation failure.
- The involvement of societal actors with the aim to balance the policy discourse is insufficient if the approach merely focuses on the provision of open access and transparent procedures. Rather, it needs to be actively enabling and mobilizing.
- New governance forms must not ignore the role of interested actors whose interests are only partly malleable through deliberation. The mediation and reconciliation of conflicts may depend on (re)distributive policies as well.

Notes

1   The concept's ambiguity with respect to the true costs and demand for change implied by achieving sustainable development has been criticized as allowing actors to share in the political correctness of the term without changing behaviour (Richardson, 1997). I shall return to this aspect when discussing the constraints to applying the EPI principle in the second half of this chapter.

2   Not surprisingly therefore, the process of institutionalizing this legal principle had involved plenty of conflict (cf Jordan, 1998a; Verhoeve et al, 1992).

3   This process goes hand in hand with pressures emanating from the United Nations Conference on the Environment and Development (UNCED) process, begun in Rio in 1992, that requires all participating states to develop strategies for sustainable development.

4   The literature is too vast to be reviewed at this stage. See Peters (1999) for an overview.

5 Dealing with emissions at the end of an otherwise unchanged production process.
6 While the White Paper on Governance is focusing a great deal on openness and transparency, it does not go beyond these goals (CEC, 2001 b).
7 I am grateful to Charles Sabel for making this point so pointedly during the workshop on 'Law and New Approaches to Governance in Europe' at the European Union Center of the University of Wisconsin-Madison on May 29–30, 2001.

References

Andersen, M. S. and Liefferink, D. J. (eds) (1997) *European Environmental Policy: The Pioneers,* Mancester: Manchester University Press.

Buck, M., Kraemer, R. A. and Wilkinson, D. (1999) 'Der "Cardiff Prozess" zur Integration von Umweltschutzbelangen in andere Sektorpolitiken', *Aus Politik und Zeitgeschichte* B48/99. pp12–20.

Cardiff European Council (1998) 'Cardiff European Council, 15 and 16 June 1998, Presidency Conclusions', http://europa.eu.int/council/off/conclu/jun98.htm#C31

Commission of the European Communities (CEC), (1992) *Towards Sustainability. A European Community Programme of Policy and Action in Relation to the Environment and Sustainable Development,* COM(92) 23/fin, Brussels: CEC.

CEC (1993a) *Integrating the Environment into Other Policy Areas Within the Commission,* Communication to the Commission from Mr Paleocrassas and Mr van Miert, Brussels: CEC.

CEC (1993b) 'Community Structural Funds: 1994–1999'. *Revised Regulations and Comments,* Brussels: CEC.

CEC (1996) *Thirteenth Annual Report on Monitoring the Application of Community Law,* Brussels: CEC.

CEC (1998a) *Partnership for Integration. A Strategy for Integrating Environment into EU Policies. Cardiff – June 1998,* Communication from the Commission to the European Council, COM(98) 333, Brussels: CEC.

CEC (1998b) *Proposal for a Council Regulation (EC) Laying Down General Provisions on the Structural Funds,* 98/0090 (AVC), Brussels: CEC.

CEC (1999a) *Europe's Environment: What Directions for the Future? The Global Assessment of the European Community Programme of Policy and Action in Relation to the Environment and Sustainable Development, 'Towards Sustainability',* Communication from the Commission, COM(1999) 543 final, Brussels: CEC.

CEC (1999b) *Report on Environment and Integration Indicators to Helsinki Summit,* Commission Working Document, SEC(1999) 1942 final, Brussels: CEC.

CEC (1999c) *The New Programming Period 2000–2006: Technical Papers by Theme. Technical Paper 1: Application of the Polluter Pays Principle. Differentiating the Rates of Community Assistance for Structural Funds, Cohesion Fund and ISPA Infrastructure Operations.* 6 December, Brussels: CEC.

CEC (2000a) *Communication from the Commission to the Council and the European Parliament. Indictors for the Integration of Environmental concerns into the Common Agricultural Policy,* COM(2000) 20 final, 26 January, Brussels: CEC.

CEC and the Directorate-General for Regional Policy (2000b) *Directorate-General for Regional Policy Working Programme for 2000*, Brussels: CEC.

CEC (2001a) *Integrating Environment and Sustainable Development into Energy and Transport policies: Review Report 2001 and Implementation of Strategies*, Commission Staff Working Paper, SEC(2001) 502, 21 March, Brussels: CEC.

CEC (2001b) *European Governance: A White Paper*, COM(2001)428, 25 July, Brussels: CEC.

Collins, K. and Earnshaw, D. (1992) 'The Implementation and Enforcement of European Community Environment Legislation', *Environmental Politics*, Vol.4, No.1, pp213–249.

ENV Press (1997) *The Commission Renews its Commitment to Integrate the Environment in its Policy-Making*, IP/97/636, http://europa.eu.int/comm/environment/press/ip97636.htm

Eichener, V. (1996) 'Die Rückwirkung der europäischen Integration auf nationale Politikmuster', in Jachtenfuchs, M. and Kohler-Koch, B. (eds) *Europäische Integration*, Leske and Budrich, pp249–280.

European Environment Agency (EEA) (1999) *Environment in the European Union at the Turn of the Century*, Environmental Assessment Report No.2, Copenhagen: EEA.

Environment Watch Western Europe (EWWE) (1997) *EU Executive Renews Bid to Integrate Environment into Other Policies, Own Operations*, Arlington, MA: Cutter Information Corp, 1 August.

European Parliament (EP) Committee on the Environment, Public Health and Consumer Protection (1996) *Working Document on Implementation of Community Environmental Law* (Rapporteur: Ken Collins), PE 219,240, Brussels: CEC.

Hall, P. (1993) 'Policy Paradigms, Social Learning and the State. The Case of Economic Policymaking in Britain' *Comparative Politics*, Vol.25, pp75–296.

Harding, G. (1999) 'Wallstrom Vows to "Name and Shame" Environmental Laggards', *European Voice*, 10–17 November, Vol.2.

Heclo, H. (1974) *Modem Social Politics in Britain and Sweden*, New Haven: Yale University Press.

Hey, C. (2002) 'Why Does Environmental Policy Integration Fail? The Case of Environmental Taxation for Heavy Goods Vehicles', in Lenschow, A. (ed) *Environmental Policy Integration. Greening Sectoral Policies in Europe*, London: Earthscan.

Jordan, A. (1998a) 'Step Change or Stasis? EC Environmental Policy after the Amsterdam Treaty', *Environmental Politics*, Vol.7, pp227–236.

Jordan, A. (1998b) 'European Union: Greener Policies', *Oxford Analytica Daily Brief*, Vol.4, 14 July, pp12–14.

Knill, C. and Lenschow, A. (eds) (2000) *Implementing EU Environmental Policies: New Directions and Old Problems*, Manchester: Manchester University Press.

Kohler-Koch, B. (1999) "The Evolution and Transformation of European Governance', in Kohler-Koch, B, and Eising, R. (eds), *The Transformation of Governance in the European Union*, New York: Routledge, pp14–35.

Kooiman, J (ed) (1993) *Modem Governance. New Government-Society Interactions*, Thousand Oaks, CA: Sage.

Koppen, I. (1993) 'The Role of the European Court of Justice', in Liefferink, J. D., Lowe, P. D. and Mol, A. P. J. (eds) *European Integration and Environmental Policy*, Belhaven Press, pp126–149.

Lauber, V. (2002) 'The Sustainability of Freight Transport Across the Alps: European Union Policy in Controversies on Transit Traffic', in Lenschow, A. (ed) *Environmental Policy Integration. Greening Sectoral Policies in Europe*, London: Earthscan.

Lebessis, N. and Paterson, J. (2000) *Developing New Modes of Governance*, European Commission, Forward Studies Unit, Working Paper, Brussels.

Lenschow, A. (1997) 'Variation in EC Environmental Policy Integration: Agency Push Within Complex Institutional Structures', *Journal of European Public Policy*, Vol.1, No.4, pp109–127.

Lenschow, A. (1999) 'The Greening of the EU: the Common Agricultural Policy and the Structural Funds', *Environment and Planning C: Government and Policy*, Vol.17, pp91–108.

Lenschow, A. (2002) 'Dynamics in a Multilevel Polity: Greening the European Union Regional and Cohesion Funds', in Lenschow, A. (ed) *Environmental Policy Integration. Greening Sectoral Policies in Europe*, London: Earthscan

Liberatore, A. (1997) 'The Integration of Sustainable Development Objective into EU Policy-making. Barriers and Prospects', in Baker, S., Kousis, M., Richardson, D. and Young, S. (eds) *The Politics of Sustainable Development. Theory, Policy and Practice Within the European Union*, New York: Routledge, pp107–126.

Nollkaemper, A. (2002) 'Three Conceptions of the Integration Principle in International Environmental Law', in Lenschow, A. (ed), *Environmental Policy Integration. Greening Sectoral Policies in Europe*, London: Earthscan.

Official Journal of the European Communities (OJ) (1973) *Declaration of the Council of the European Communities and the Representatives of the Governments of the Member States Meeting in the Council of 22 November 1973 on the Programme of Action of the European Communities on the Environment*, C112, 20 December.

OJ (1983) *Resolution of the Council of the European Communities and of the Representatives of the Governments of the Member States Meeting Within the Council of 7 February 1983 on the Continuation and Implementation of a European Community Policy and Action Programme on the Environment (1983–1986)*, C46 (17 February.

OJ (1986) *Resolution of the Council of the European Communities and of the Representatives of the Governments of the Member States Meeting Within the Council of 19 October 1987 on the Continuation and Implementation of a European Community Policy and Action Programme on the Environment (1987–1992)'*, C328, 7 December.

Peters, G. B. (1999) *Institutional Theory in Political Science. The 'New Institutionalism'*, Pinter, London.

Richardson, J. J. (1997) 'The Politics of Sustainable Development', in Baker, S., Kousis, M., Richardson, D. and Young, S. (eds) *The Politics of Sustainable Development. Theory, Policy and Practice Within the European Union*, New York: Routledge, pp43–60.

Scharpf, F. W. (1998) 'Die Problemlosungsfahigkeit der Mehrebenenpolitik in Europa', in Kohler-Koch, B. (ed) *Regieren in entgrenzten Raumen* (PVS Sonderheft 29/1998), Wiesbaden: Westdeutscher Verlag, pp121–144.

Smith, M. (2000) 'EU States' Aid at Risk over Environment', *Financial Times*, 17 March.

Verhoeve, B., Bennett, G. and Wilkinson, D. (1992) *Maastricht and the Environment,* IEEP, London.

Wilkinson, D. (1997) 'Towards Sustainability in the European Union? Steps within the European Commission Towards Integrating the Environment into other Policy Sectors', in O'Riordan, T. and Voisey, H. (eds) *Sustainable Development in Western Europe: Coming to Terms with Agenda 21,* Frank Cass, London pp153–173.

World Commission on Environment and Development (WCED) (1997) *Our Common Future,* Oxford: Oxford University Press.

17

European Governance and the Transfer of 'New' Environmental Policy Instruments (NEPIs) in the European Union

Andrew Jordan, Rüdiger Wurzel, Anthony R. Zito and Lars Brückner

Introduction

Since the 1980s, the European Union (EU) has sought to become an innovator and leader in international environmental policy. Part of its bid has involved the development of ambitious controls in areas such as climate change and the promotion of themes such as sustainable development in international arenas including the United Nations (UN) and the Organisation for Economic Co-operation and Development (OECD). Another dimension in its global effort is the creation of 'new' environmental policy instruments (NEPIs); these include instruments that emphasize the role of information (such as eco-labels) and that manipulate market incentives (such as eco-taxes). This chapter assesses how the EU has shaped NEPI innovation in its Member States, focusing particularly on NEPIs that do not draw on 'command-and-control' legislation, or at least retain a relatively high degree of flexibility concerning policy goal achievement. The three types of instruments discussed in this chapter vary in coerciveness. Eco-labels constitute the 'softest' and eco-taxes the 'hardest' instrument. Voluntary agreements (VAs) are somewhere in between although they are generally closer to the former as regards their degree of coerciveness.

Three main research questions guide this chapter. What are the reasons for NEPI adoption? How systematic has the use of these NEPIs been in the EU? What impact has the EU institutional and ideational systems had on the adoption and implementation of softer policy instruments? The section that follows explores the different roles that the EU may perform in the policy transfer process. Next we describe the theoretical framework and how it explains NEPI adoption. This is followed by an analysis of why EU environmental policy has followed certain paths concerning policy instrument choices and an assessment of EU efforts to adopt NEPIs in three areas: taxation, voluntary agreements and eco-labels. The Conclusion provides an overall analysis of the EU role based on the preliminary research presented in this chapter.

Defining types of instruments

Policy instruments are the various techniques that governments use to achieve their policy objectives (Howlett and Ramesh, 1993). Bemelmans-Videc et al (1998) categorize environmental instruments according to the degree of constraint that the instrument imposes on target groups: carrots, sticks and sermons. The 'carrots' are the economic instruments which manipulate market incentives and processes in a way that constrains choice to a more moderate degree than traditional 'command-and-control' legislation which constitutes the 'stick', as they highly constrain the target groups' choices (OECD, 1998). 'Sermons' imply few constraints as they usually present the target actors with information about the implications of particular choices. Market instruments such as eco-taxes still retain a substantial element of imposition through the price mechanism. In practice, researchers must apply such typologies flexibly as it is difficult to fit certain instruments, for example voluntary agreements, neatly into the Bemelmans-Videc et al typology. Moreover, different governments may not use the identical policy tools in the same fashion (Hood, 1983).

EU Policy Transfer Roles

Within the EU, a chief determinant of NEPI use is policy transfer (PT). PT focuses on the process by which knowledge (about NEPIs) at a particular time and place is used at another time or place in a different governance setting (Dolowitz and Marsh, 1996). In assessing the EU's influence, we consider a range of possible PT roles and develop a typology of EU influence vis-à-vis the Member States. These roles are not mutually exclusive; the EU process may foster NEPI innovation through several of these roles simultaneously: (1) passive arena; (2) facilitating arena; (3) harmonization arena; (4) competitive arena; and (5) independent actor.

The first role implies that Member State convergence occurs without Europeanization. The next three roles all suggest that the EU creates strong incentives for Member State convergence while the fifth suggests a 'top-down dynamic' where the EU supranational institutions push Member States into NEPI innovation.

1   *Passive arena*: in this role, policy innovation and transfer within and between Member States occur with no substantive contribution from the EU institutions. Member States with relatively similar policy problems and resources will seek to emulate key aspects of each other's successful policies (Bennett, 1991). For example, Germany's eco-label, which is the earliest national scheme

worldwide, influenced similar schemes in other Member States prior to EU adoption of its own scheme.

2   *Facilitating arena*: this role postulates that the complex EU web of policy actors and processes creates the conditions in which ideas and experience will more quickly diffuse and be transferred across Member States. The EU structure enhances the creation of networks of EU and Member State actors. The EU efforts to develop a common carbon/energy tax have highlighted the differences in Member State approaches, leading to a sharing of ideas and experiences. The arena also enables Member State representatives to showcase their approach to other Member States and to define the EU agenda. Dutch environmental officials figured heavily in the formulation of the Fifth Environmental Action Programme (EAP), which resembled the Dutch Environmental Policy Plan.

3   *Harmonization arena*: this role concentrates on the impact of the Single European Market (SEM). At least prior to the 1987 Single European Act (SEA), NEPIs had to be justified in terms of, and be in harmony with, the SEM project. Much of the pre-1987 environmental legislation had the aim of protecting the SEM and reducing market distortion, even though 'non-market' justifications (such as quality of life and amenity reasons) increased, as can be seen in the example of the Bathing Water Directive (Jordan, 1999a; Wurzel, 2002). The economic motivation remains important. For example, the impact of the German Packaging Waste Ordinance on the SEM triggered the EU Packaging Directive (Golub, 1996b). The Commission justified the launch of the EU eco-label scheme by arguing that an increasing number of competing national eco-labels could lead to market distortions.

4   *Competitive arena*: here the EU creates the conditions under which Member States compete for economic advantage and try to minimize regulatory adjustment costs. Because EU integration has required a significant adjustment of national environmental policies and standards, Member States have an incentive to stay ahead of EU regulations and regulatory intentions in their national policies. Member governments which have imposed regulations with significant costs on industry may seek to ensure that other Member States adopt similar legislation (Héritier, 1996). Member States with higher standards will try to shape the EU agenda in order to avoid having to adjust national legislation.

One example is the negotiations that led to the adoption of the Eco-Management and Audit System (EMAS). Environmental management systems are voluntary schemes and set out basic principles of environmental practice to guide business operations (Zito and Egan, 1998). The British government and other Member States that had adopted the British environmental management standard (BS 7750) promoted BS 7750 as the basis for the EU standard. Countries with their own standards (for example France) opposed this move.

5   *Entrepreneur*: EU actors may have an independent causal effect on Member State policies, making them converge. Supranational actors within the EU may seek to define the agenda for the Member States. Most commonly known is the Commission's role as an entrepreneur, seeking to expand its

influence by seeking opportunities to suggest new policy initiatives (Jordan, 1999a; Radaelli, 2000). In terms of NEPIs, the Commission's continued desire for a common energy taxation approach and an EU-wide emission trading system in order to facilitate compliance with the Kyoto climate change protocol suggests a combination of motives, such as the desire to expand the EU's international leadership position and to increase the influence of EU institutional actors on key environmental and economic issues involving taxation (see Chapter 14).

Theoretical Framework

Having laid out the potential EU avenues for influencing Member State convergence in NEPI selection, we turn to the theoretical factors that influence how EU actors select different types of NEPIs and how the EU structure shapes the adaptation process for individual Member States. The current debates in public policy list a large number of approaches, including institutionalist, large-n comparative, constructivist, punctuated equilibrium, policy diffusion and others (Sabatier, 1999, pp8–12; Radaelli, 2000). We have concentrated our analytical frame on three of these alternative approaches in order to discern how well their different perspectives and foci explain the case data.

The first perspective, ideational approaches, stands out in its strong change dynamic which may be important in explaining the evolution of instruments. In contrast, the institutionalist perspective emphasizes those factors that lead to continuity over time in the policy process, and this may prove to be the alternative finding for our study. The final approach, centred around Kingdon's multiple streams approach, provides a viewpoint the other two perspectives lack, with its focus on ambiguity in causal relations and the importance of random events and chance linkages (Radaelli, 2000). Such factors which create policy opportunities are often critical in the environment policy area. These approaches are summarized in Table 17.1.

Ideas-dominant approaches

This public policy literature focuses upon ideas as the driving force behind policy change. Applying this literature to the selection of policy instruments, it argues that ideas and beliefs drive the policy-makers' instrument selection. Policy instruments have a secondary, instrumental role in underpinning larger beliefs. Instrument selection is only one aspect of the wider policy process where social learning is a dominant force (Howlett and Ramesh, 1993). Policy change results from a cognitive struggle between groups of policy actors seeking to solve policy problems and apply the most suitable policy instruments (Hall, 1993). Normally instruments are simply fine-tuned to meet the current political demands, but sometimes policy crises open the policy area to substantial changes in explanatory frameworks and new instruments.

Hall (1993) and Sabatier (1998) offer parallel explanations for the learning process shaped by ideas, emphasizing its voluntary, rational nature. Hall views the

Table 17.1 *Theorizing the Transfer of Instruments and Policies within the EU*

	'Ideas' dominant	*'Settings' dominant*	*'Chaos' dominant*
Themes	Instrument choice driven by the conflict between competing ideas	National institutions shape the selection and implementation process	Instruments look for policies; policies look for instruments ideas
Role of instruments	Mainly instrumental: implement dominant ideas/ approaches	Embedded in institutional settings which shape the policy development /search process	Search process is ad hoc (whatever appears to work)
Key agents of policy transfer	Expert communities, advocacy coalitions, experts and scientists	National and/or supranational actors within the institutional structures	Pluralistic mix of actors
Search process	Rational and goal directed	Path dependency (to achieve 'goodness of fit')	Chaotic and highly pluralistic
Scope for innovation	Generally large	Small if goodness of fit poor (the 'stickiness' of adaptation); higher if the fit is better	Unclear a priori: context dependent
What is transferred?	Ideas, paradigms, policy goals	Mainly theories of stability rather than change: but crises?	Not clear a priori: possibly ideas, policy goals or instruments

role of policy-making and learning as occurring at three levels: (1) the design of existing instruments based on past experience; (2) the choice and usage of instruments to achieve particular objectives; and (3) the wider goals that the policy-making is pursuing (Hall, 1993, pp281–287). Change occurs because actors face new problems and anomalous events that challenge their current policy paradigms. While Hall focuses on the change of ideas, Sabatier's approach focuses more on how different actor coalitions, armed with distinct sets of core and secondary beliefs, compete to become the dominant coalition in the policy sector, or 'subsystem' (Sabatier, 1998; Howlett and Ramesh, 1993). Both Hall and Sabatier distinguish between major (the alteration of core aspects of a policy programme) and minor (secondary aspects, such as instruments) policy change. The secondary changes to instruments are likely to be much more frequent and involve much less political contestation than the larger strategic changes.

In the context of the EU and NEPIs, this approach emphasizes the role of particular policy principles and 'paradigms', such as sustainable development, and particular actor groups seeking to promote these worldviews and related policy instruments. These policy philosophies may conflict with other EU priorities, such as ensuring market efficiency and competitiveness.

Settings-dominant theories

These works argue that the political context in which decisions about instruments are made is critical in informing decision-makers' choices. The 'new' institutionalist approach focuses on 'the whole range of state and societal institutions that shape how political actors define their interests and that structure their relations of power to other groups' (Thelen and Steinmo, 1992, p2). Institutions contain standard operating procedures and norms that give preference to particular instruments. Actors select and modify instruments on the basis of what is appropriate to the institutional context, in terms of what is politically acceptable and what 'satisfies' the given policy problem.

In terms of environmental instruments, actors operating in institutions resist substantial change, preferring incremental alterations to fit the given policy context. Only when the sector faces a notable policy failure, such as an ecological catastrophe, will institutional settings be forced to open their policy processes to a wider selection of new ideas and associated policy instruments. Even in this context, the institutionalist notion of path dependence suggests that past decisions still shape new outcomes in a way that maintains existing arrangements. Instruments that fit the organizational pattern and routine of EU and Member State institutions are much more likely to be adopted than those that challenge these norms and structures. Moreover, once these new policies are adopted, the institutions are likely to filter policy characteristics as they proceed through the implementation stage (Majone, 1991).

Applying the settings perspective to the EU process, the traditional linkage of the environmental policy to the SEM is noteworthy as being one of the EU's most deeply embedded institutional norms. The complex structure of EU institutions also provides access points for different points of view and necessitates agreement being established across the entire set of EU institutions (Weale, 1996). Moreover, the EU operates at multiple levels, which means that Member State representatives and the supranational institutions must agree to policy solutions, which domestic political actors subsequently implement. Moving beyond the lowest common denominator in creating an EU instrument is difficult (although not impossible) and variation in how NEPIs are implemented is likely.

Chaos-dominant approaches

In contrast to the first two approaches, this policy literature views the policy process as unstable because preferences are unclear for actors who operate under conditions of uncertainty and who lack the time for comprehensive information searches. The policy process resembles less a rational, linear process than a 'garbage can' (Cohen et al, 1972). At any given time an unpredictable assortment of ideas, problems, solutions and decision-making priorities is present in the policy process, with no necessarily systematic policy pattern resulting. Policy solutions may precede and shape the definition of policy problems.

Kingdon (1984) argued that the policy process contains: (1) a stream of policy problems that demand policy attention; (2) a stream of available policies that are developed without necessarily one policy problem in mind; and (3) a stream of politics where actors compete for position and resources, shaping how policy problems are defined and solutions selected. These streams operate simultaneously, but they may interconnect. This interconnection leads to a 'policy window', where a compelling problem forces political recognition and opens an opportunity for specific policy solutions to seize the agenda. Because of the complexity and contingency of this system, success at defining the agenda depends on luck as well as power resources. This is where policy entrepreneurs take advantage of these opportunities to advance their agenda. Unlike the ideas approach, there may be opportunities for instruments to be designated as solutions without necessarily involving a systematic change in worldview within the policy subsystem.

The chaos-dominant perspective suggests that NEPIs are fitted fairly randomly into political problems when the opportunities are favourable. Because the problem stream can be unpredictable and because various advocates will be pushing their solutions in a rapidly moving political process, often including policymakers with extremely short-term perspectives, the policy picture is much more fluid. This fluidity exists in the EU system where it is difficult for actors to anticipate the behaviour of other subsystem actors. The multiple access points to the EU system give the opportunity for Commission and Member State entrepreneurs to shape instruments in particular ways. The chaos-dominant perspective would expect the Commission, with its fairly central location in the policy process, to seize the opportunities created by uncertainty on the part of other actors, in order to push for particular initiatives (Héritier, 1996).

Linking to EU roles

In terms of the EU roles outlined above, the variables outlined in all three theoretical lenses may be present in all of the roles. Nevertheless, to achieve the outcomes suggested in the EU roles, certain variables given more emphasis in one particular approach are likely to explain why change happens in NEPI adoption. Thus the study and emulation of ideas by Member States with possible transfers across networks of actors, fit with the passive arena scenario; the facilitating scenario gives the EU process the role in diffusing these ideas. Similarly, we can argue that behind the harmonization and competition roles are the institutional requirements of market harmonization. However, notions of harmonization and competitiveness are also dominant ideas in EU decision-making. Finally, the entrepreneurial focus of the Kingdon approach and Sabatier's concepts of an advocacy coalition promoting ideas fit with the idea of the Commission taking an independent, entrepreneurial role and seeking alliances.

Institutional Patterns in EU Environmental Policy

The historical pattern of EU environmental policy, and its decision-making process, are important to understanding the role the EU can play in facilitating and promulgating instruments. We compare the pattern of instrument adaptation prior to 1992 and afterwards using all three theoretical approaches. 1992 constitutes a turning point for the use of NEPIs in the EU because it saw the arrival of the Community-wide carbon/energy tax proposal, and the adoption of the Fifth EAP with its emphasis on new policy instruments. Of course, the EU considered NEPIs – including the carbon tax proposal and other softer instruments – before this date, but additional pressures for 'soft' instruments arose after the Maastricht Treaty fall-out in 1992. After noting this change, we explore the decision-making process and the factors promoting the subsequent changes in EU instrument selection.

Patterns of NEPI use prior to 1992

Up until the late 1980s, environmental policies in Western Europe primarily took the form of the traditional command and control legislation. Community-wide initiatives resembled the pervasive philosophical approach across the member states: instruments that reflected command-and-control principles. These were designed to deal with pressing visible pollution problems from point sources; there was a focus on remedial as opposed to preventive action and a problem definition that addressed issues in a single media (for example water), and in a non-holistic fashion. A few early NEPIs did exist in Member States, but these were usually supplementary instruments (for example the water pollution levies and tax incentives for less-polluting cars in The Netherlands and Germany, and the German eco-label).

The institutional constraints reinforced this ideational bias. Prior to the 1987 SEA, there simply was no explicit legal base for a common environmental policy. This posed an immediate institutional constraint, requiring EU environmental legislation to be justified primarily on the basis of economic harmonization (Jordan, 1999a; Wurzel, 2002; Zito, 2000). Another important institutional constraint was the fact that national policy styles and preferences for certain types of policy instruments existed within Member States and these often clashed on the EU level. One prominent example is the conflict between the UK and continental states over water pollution regulation.

The Commission's Directorate General for the Environment (DG Environment) was a relatively weak and junior partner, which meant that it had to aim for visible legislative accumulation (Jordan, 1999b). DG Environment had a further institutional constraint: many NEPIs (such as eco-taxes and VAs with industry) involved agreement with other DGs which had differing priorities and constituencies. These tensions surfaced when DG Environment proposed a carbon/energy tax (Zito, 2000). These constraints did not prevent the EU from adopting a raft of different and increasingly stringent measures that went beyond the requirements of protecting the SEM (Weale, 1996; Wurzel, 2002). However, it focused the Commission agenda on creating new legislation with less attention paid to assessing cost-efficiency requirements and implementation problems, and how NEPIs might perform. Moreover, it was only when EU and Member State environmental policies matured and after the most serious environmental problems had been tackled by command-and-control legislation that cost-efficiency questions gained in importance.

The institutional constraints led the Commission to pursue a strategy of 'negative integration' (which was largely based on the harmonization of national command-and-control legislation) in order to protect the SEM as opposed to 'positive integration', which involved creating generally new EU policies and/or the adoption of novel policy instruments (Majone, 1991).

The Commission also gradually gravitated towards proposing framework legislation, which only lays out the general regulatory principles (Héritier, 1996). As these framework proposals were likely to meet less resistance from national governments, their acceptance was easier and could start a process of gradual commitment towards more specific measures. Crucially, this usage of 'softer' framework legislation was a well-established practice before 1992. DG Environment started consulting with external actors in 1990 to draw up proposals for EMAS.

Patterns of NEPI use after 1992

Since 1992, there has been a substantial shift in the dominant regulatory philosophy of the Commission (Héritier et al, 1996, Friedrich et al, 2000). Much of the 'dirigiste' legislation remains in place, and has been difficult to revise in a way that reduces the command-and-control nature of EU environmental legislation. Nevertheless, EU policy innovation and instrument selection has witnessed a substantial change in focus (Golub, 1996a). In the Fifth EAP, the Commission noted its intent to consider market instruments and approaches emphasizing shared responsibility among public and private actors (CEC, 1993b). Weale (1996) argues that the Fifth EAP implied the greater use of VAs.

The EU has used mainly command-and-control instruments in order to bring about the SEM and to achieve other policy goals (Weale, 1996). Two pressures from below constrained the Commission from proposing new initiatives and provided policy windows for advocates of NEPIs. The post-Maastricht referenda fallout has pushed the Commission into a more reactive and defensive mode where it seeks to justify new policies by working to improve efficiency and implementation of already established policies. The Santer Commission's resignation has continued this trend. In this context, certain Member States, particularly Britain, strove to enshrine the subsidiarity principle within the Treaty (Golub, 1996a). Second, the wider European economy fell into recession in the 1990s, which encouraged actors to look for instruments that improved economic competitiveness (Weale, 1996). Third, EU environmental policy has matured and now requires a revision which takes into account a more systematic approach as well as cost-effectiveness considerations (something which represents the policy learning on the part of the actors involved in the process). However, it is difficult to achieve agreement between the core veto actors (that is, Member States). EU taxes can be adopted unanimously only by the Council and some Member States (such as Britain) have long opposed the adoption of EU taxes on sovereignty grounds.

Fourth, the Commission has recognized the need to broaden responsibility and involve industry more directly. By the 1990s the Commission had conducted studies which emphasized the need to improve current legislation and which raised concerns about cost-effectiveness (CEC, 1995; Delbeke and Bergman, 1998). These pressures have combined with the change in regulatory philosophy about instruments and the participation of other actors.

The reaction to political circumstances outside the environmental field and the endogenous evolution in policy thinking has given the Commission a strong incentive to propose legislation that is less intrusive while being based on the principle of shared responsibility – that is, wider stakeholder involvement (Jordan, 1999a). Framework directives therefore received considerable prominence as they allow Member States greater scope during the implementation process. The Commission has concentrated more of its effort on 'soft law' instruments (for example, legally non-binding resolutions as well as White and Green Papers) to cajole the Member States towards general principles and best practices.

It also gives the Commission the incentive to create instruments that involve stakeholders in a non-conflictual way. Informational instruments fulfil this requirement. The Commission has pushed EMAS among industrial actors as a means of getting them to engage voluntarily in the self-regulation process via the information incentive (Héritier, 1996). In the early 1990s, the EU also agreed the eco-label scheme and the 'Access to Information' Directive. During this time the Commission also created the Consultative Forum – which aims to involve a wide range of stakeholders by consultations – prior to the publication of new policy proposals.

Commission officials also used the increasing arguments about global competitiveness to expand the use of economic instruments. They gained wider credibility within the Commission with the publication of the Commission's White Paper on 'Growth, Competitiveness and Employment' (CEC, 1993a). This document promoted the use of market-based instruments as a means of shifting the financial burden away from the employment of labour towards the consideration of environmental costs.

Adopting NEPIs

The patterns established before and after 1992 are reflected in the EU's NEPI innovation. This section examines the pattern of NEPI innovation and how the EU has affected the adoption of individual instruments at the national level with respect to three categories of instruments, environmental taxes, voluntary agreements and eco-labels.

Environmental taxes

The most prominent instrument in this category is the unsuccessful attempt to adopt a common carbon energy tax. In terms of policy selection, the story reflects characteristics in all three theoretical frames laid out in this chapter (Zito, 2000). There was an advocacy coalition – the Commission Environment and Energy Directorates – that pushed forward the EU carbon/energy tax idea. In line with the fifth role (that is, the EU as independent actor) and the chaos-dominant approach, there was also a clear element of policy entrepreneurship with actors attempting to seize a window of opportunity. One can also view the Commission alliance of the Environment and Energy Directorates as a coalition, but it is debatable whether this alliance constituted a fully fledged advocacy coalition, although certain Member State governments strongly supported the idea. The study and use of environmental taxes was becoming stronger in EU Member

States such as Denmark and The Netherlands, as well as external states such as Finland and Sweden who also pushed for the widespread use of eco-taxes. There was a distinct element of the EU arena serving as a forum for exchange, but a larger exchange was occurring beyond EU corridors. The Environment Commissioner of the time, Ripa di Meana, and DG Environment used the impending 1992 Rio Earth Summit as well as increasing concerns about climate change to focus on this particular solution, which had the institutional benefits of increasing the EU's global role and the Commission's scope of influence and might serve (through the bringing of international pressures into the equation) as a way of overcoming the likely Member State veto point in the Council (Zito, 2000). The Commission advocates received the support from Member States (such as Germany) which favoured the adoption of EU-wide eco-taxes because they were concerned about the competitive impact of unilateral eco-tax measures.

However, the momentum for this proposal was quickly up-ended by the fundamental institutional constraints operating against EU environment actors. First, DG Environment had to compromise with other Commission directorates. More significantly, the EU institutional context (that is, the adoption of supranational taxes requires unanimity within the Council) gave a set of opposing states, motivated for different reasons as seen in the case of the UK (sovereignty fears) and Spain (development fears), the ability to block the proposed tax.

The Commission subsequently repackaged the instrument in a far less ambitious form. In 1997, the Commission introduced a proposal emphasizing the need to harmonize Member State taxation on energy products, particularly fossil fuels (CEC, 1997). However, again the proposal had been frozen, in large part due to Spanish opposition. In 2001 the Swedish EU presidency managed to get general agreement on the basic principles of this Directive (*ENDS Daily*, 19 March 2001 and 23 April 2001).

After a considerable amount of negotiating, particularly on the part of the Spanish 2002 presidency, the EU finance ministers finally reached an agreement on the Framework Directive on 20 March 2003. It conforms with the traditional norm associated with EU environmental protection, that is, enhancing market harmonization by ensuring a consistent taxation policy (for each fuel) in all the Member States. The Energy Products Directive forces national measures towards a minimal convergence on price levels on minerals (already an EU policy), coal, natural gas and electricity while also raising minimum rates for oil products. The Directive includes a significant number of derogations and transition periods for particular countries and economic sectors (*ENDS Daily*, 21 March 03). The final outcome of the Directive suggests the continued importance of EU institutional constraints and norms, which limit the scope of supranational entrepreneurship, particularly in the politically sensitive area of taxation. The slow progress on the EU level, which was due to the unanimity rule, led to informal meetings between like-minded countries that had already adopted national energy taxes (for example Denmark) or were pushing for EU-wide versions (for example Germany). Although such meetings took place in the 1990s, this group of countries made little headway in achieving an EU-wide acceptance of the carbon dioxide tax.

Voluntary agreements

The picture of EU action over VAs shows a different pattern. The Fifth EAP contributed to the momentum of instituting these instruments. The experience of VAs in The Netherlands and Germany gave some impetus to the Commission effort (suggesting the importance of the EU as arena for sharing ideas). The debate about the subsidiarity principle played an important role in creating a policy window for the Commission concerning this instrument. The emphasis of this discussion on less interventionist instruments, which was promoted by particular Member States, including the UK, allowed DG Environment to place this instrument on the EU agenda. Because voluntary agreements had no legal standing in the Community treaties, the Commission issued a legally non-binding Communication which allowed it to avoid veto points (that is, the EP) since it does not have to be discussed. Despite gaining approval, by late 2001 little more than one dozen of EU voluntary agreements have been adopted (Mol et al, 2000; interviews, 2001).

In 1996, the Commission announced its aim of promoting the use of 'effective and acceptable' environmental agreements as a means of supplementing traditional regulation (CEC, 1996). One year earlier, the Molitor Report argued that the EU's command-and-control regulations put European businesses at a competitive disadvantage (CEC, 1995). The mixed coalition of Commission officials (some oriented to enhancing internal market and others promoting ecological modernization) and industry promoting VAs has not yet created a new and genuine model; rather, the EU VAs take characteristics from various Member State approaches as well as including novel supranational elements. The variation in Member State approaches has created tensions for the EU concerning the appropriate VA design. For example, the Dutch tradition of VAs emphasized the need for a formal instrument while the German approach is often informal, albeit closely linked to the threat of legislation. Moreover, some Member States (such as Britain) have no national tradition of making use of VAs.

Doubts have been raised about the legitimacy, legality and transparency of creating an EU instrument (interviews, 2001; Mol et al, 2000; Friedrich et al, 2000; CEC, 1996a). The lack of an explicit treaty base and consultation, especially with the EP, has made the adoption of EU-level VAs controversial.

One notable example of a Commission-negotiated agreement concerns the voluntary fuel economy standards negotiated with the automobile industry. Reacting to the 1991 Auto-oil Programme which regulated vehicle emissions and fuel standards but excluded carbon dioxide reduction measures, the Commission entrusted a group of national officials and motor industry representatives to draw up policy proposals to limit these emissions (ibid, 2001). Initially the group proposed tax solutions, which DC Environment strongly supported but the Commission Directorate for Indirect Taxation rejected. DG Industry proposed the VA solution, which DG Environment accepted after initial reluctance (ibid, 2001). The automotive industry had been pushing for these instruments at the start of the EU process, but lost enthusiasm as the negotiations progressed.

After several years of haggling with the manufacturer's association, the Commission in 1998 secured an agreement for industry to institute a 25 per cent fuel economy improvement by 2005 (ibid, 2001). The Commission has subsequently also adopted VAs on fuel economy with the Japanese and Korean automobile manufacturers. The agreements have faced considerable criticism from environmental groups for being unambitious. Perhaps most serious was the issue of transparency. The Council and especially the EP were kept out of the negotiations and merely briefed about the outcome: moreover, there is no explicit treaty basis for non-binding agreements. Although the political context of subsidiarity provided some favourable conditions, the lack of a strong coalition outside DG Industry for this instrument suggests that this case is more the outcome of an absence of well-considered alternatives by the Commission. However, there are also institutional reasons why the Commission has recently favoured VAs. It allows the Commission to expand its powers (especially vis-à-vis the EP which had gained considerably in power from recent treaty amendments) without relying on formal legislation.

As was the case with tax instruments, EU aims and legislation (the institutional setting) can have a significant constraining effect on Member State usage of VAs. However, it would be wrong to argue that the EU has abandoned traditional (command-and-control) regulatory measures. There are a few examples of EU legislation actually replacing Member State VAs. For example, the EU End of Life Vehicles (ELV) Directive, which regulates manufacturer obligations to take back scrapped cars, replaced VAs in Austria and Germany. The 1994 EU Directive on Packaging and Packaging Waste rendered void a Dutch covenant with packaging manufacturers (Lauber and Ingram, 2000, pp30–37). The Dutch actors were pleasantly surprised when the Commission approved a new VA version agreed by the various parties as a means of implementing the EU Directive.

In July 2002, the Commission has sought to give new scope to VAs by proposing 'a half-way house' for VAs on the EU level 'that would see objectives and timetables fixed in law with businesses given freedom to decide how to meet them' (*ENDS Daily*, 17 July 2002; CEC 2002). Climate change and waste management are likely test grounds for the Commission's new emphasis on VAs although their wider use on the EU level is opposed by the EP which remains largely excluded from the decision-making process of non-legislative policy instruments. The Commission's 2002 proposal would entail a significant expansion of self-regulation and the formal introduction of 'co-regulation' on the EU level. Co-regulation would allow the EP and Environmental Council to legislate targets and timetables while leaving it up to industry how to achieve the objectives within the specified time period.

Eco-labels

Eco-labels are legally non-binding voluntary policy tools. They are relatively soft policy instruments which rely mainly on moral suasion. Eco-labels exert only very moderate constraints on market actors, especially when compared with traditional command and control legislation, but also in comparison to market instruments such as eco-taxes and tradeable permits (CEC 2001; Jordan et al, forthcoming). Eco-labels are informational devices which can act as market instruments if their uptake is high for a certain product/service group in a market (segment) in which consumer behaviour reflects a high degree of environmental awareness. On the other hand, eco-labels can also be used to promote public environmental awareness although this requires considerable public resources. Germany acted as a pioneer when it adopted the first nationwide eco-label in 1978. Twenty years later more than a dozen national and multinational eco-labels were established around the globe (Kern et al, 2001). The establishment of the supranational EU eco-label was to a large degree a reaction to the rapid proliferation of national and multinational eco-label schemes. The Commission used this opportunity to press for the adoption of an EU-wide eco-label. The Commission and, although to a lesser degree, the EP justified the setting up of an EU-wide eco-label scheme by pointing out that the increasing number of competing national schemes could trigger market distortions and lead to consumer confusion. Export-oriented European producers generally supported this line of argument although they opposed the adoption of stringent national eco-labels while favouring instead a wide uptake of the EU label (*ENDS Daily*, 25 June 2002). Thus we see the Commission taking an entrepreneurial role and taking advantage of the institutional dynamics of harmonization within SEM. However, there does not seem to be a coalition of actors beyond the Commission and EP; the Commission created its own window of opportunity by emphasizing potential harmonization conflict. However, Member States, such as Germany, which had already had well-functioning national eco-label schemes, remained sceptical.

From its beginnings, the 1992 EU eco-label scheme was dogged with problems (Eiderström, 1998). It suffered from a cumbersome and non-transparent decision-making process and relatively high fees. It achieved only a very low degree of acceptability among producers and consumers. The EU eco-label also came under attack from non-European companies which exported to the EU's SEM (Vogel, 1998).

During the first four years of the scheme's existence only six product groups applicable for eco-labels were established. By early 1999, the number of product groups had risen to 18. However, during the first seven years only 41 EU eco-labels had been awarded (Haigh, 1999, section 11.7). This figure compares with almost 4000 national eco-label awards by the German eco-label for much of the late 1990s. Unsurprisingly, the 1992 EU eco-label scheme had little impact on consumer choices and producer behaviour; however, producers, although they did not formally apply for the EU label, started to use it as a benchmark.

The revision of the EU eco-label scheme was originally scheduled for 1997 but had to be postponed until 2000 because of disagreements between the Commission, Member States and the EP (*EWWE*, 22 January 1999, pp7–8). The Commission's revised proposal in 1996 was unacceptable to both the Environmental Council and the EP because it suggested: (1) the phasing out of national eco-labels; (2) the creation of an independent eco-label organization (ECO); and (3) the replacement of the pass/fail system with a graded label. Institutional rivalries and fears about the dilution of nationally more stringent criteria were the main reason why the revision had to be postponed.

A graded eco-label system would have had the advantage of taking account of different environmental conditions in various Member States (and importer countries). It was strongly favoured by the British government and some MEPs. However, member governments and MEPs opted to retain the simple pass/fail system because of fears that a more complex graded system could lead to consumer confusion (interviews, 2001).

The majority of MEPs initially supported the phasing out of national eco-label schemes although they demanded more stringent criteria for the EU scheme than had been proposed by the Commission. However, the EP in the end joined the majority of member governments which pressed hard for the continued co-existence of EU and national labels (*ENDS Daily*, 3 July 2000). Thus instrument reform encountered difficulties in overcoming the elaborate institutional process with its veto points representing various interests.

In July 2000, the Environmental Council and the EP finally adopted a Regulation (1980/2000/EC), which introduced the following major changes (CEC 2000): (1) establishment of the EU eco-labelling board (EUEB) which is composed of the national competent authorities and thus ensures that Member States continue to play a decisive role within the revised scheme; (2) enhanced transparency; (3) expanded scope of the label also to cover services; (4) stronger involvement of consumer and environmental groups; (5) a ceiling for the fees which allows a discount for small businesses that make use of the EU's Eco-Management and Audit System (EMAS).

The EU eco-label became explicitly linked to other soft policy instruments (ie EMAS). The Dutch government has long suggested that eco-labels should form part of a wider range of different NEPI mixes which could be tailored to deal with particular policy problems in different market segments. The EU's recent emphasis on integrated product policy (IPP) and soft instruments may provide a lifeline for the flagging EU eco-label scheme (CEC, 2001). However, the EU eco-label scheme is unlikely to become a successful policy instrument if it fails to gain stakeholder support, something which is difficult to achieve because environmental NGOs demand stringent eco-label criteria while businesses often demand less environmental dogmatism (*ENDS Daily*, 25 June 2002). The 2000 revision has gained greater acceptance from member governments and consumer/environmental groups (interviews, 2001). Since 2001, the number of applications for EU eco-labels rose by 150 per cent (*ENDS Daily*, 25 June 2002). However, industry largely remains sceptical about the scheme's viability and it is still not widely known among consumers, who generally have better knowledge about national schemes. Member States with national eco-labels have done little to divert scarce resources for the promotion of the EU eco-label.

Conclusion

An increased proportion of EU time and attention is being devoted to NEPIs and soft instruments. Nevertheless, the evidence indicates that these new instruments have not supplanted traditional (command-and-control) legislation. In the three cases cited the actual policy impact the EU instruments have made is quite limited. The EU failed to adopt the least 'soft' of the NEPIs assessed in the chapter (ie eco-taxes) because of sovereignty and national interest concerns that were able to prevail due to the required unanimity rule; only a substantially less ambitious directive that harmonized certain national taxes was possible. In the areas of VAs and eco-labels, the EU has moved past the decision-making stage. However, the uptake of these instruments at the supranational level has been limited, although there has been a marked increase in recent years.

The EU has given greater weight to the use of more flexible instruments that exert 'suasion' on their target actors. While this may constitute a change in the balance of 'hard' and 'soft' instruments in EU policy outputs, strategy papers and framework directives have played a significant role in EU policy since the 1970s.

The changes that have occurred do reflect a philosophical shift in the use of instruments in the early 1990s. This is partially due to policy learning concerning the problems (in terms of costs, implementation failure and the growing perception of the importance of integrating policies) of traditional (command-and-control) instruments and the need for policy-makers to consider other alternatives. However, a critical factor was increased political pressure resulting from questions about the EU's legitimacy, the balance of responsibilities between the Member States and the EU institutions (subsidiarity), and the concerns about economic competitiveness.

In terms of the three instruments assessed and the three analytical approaches, the EU has played an important but limited role. Ideational forces have made an impact on the EU agenda because of the ability of the EU process to serve as an arena for Member States to gain information about activities and experiences of their counterparts (for example the German and the Dutch covenants). At the same time, institutional dynamics provided a constant contraint on both the possibility for the instruments to be on the agenda and their acceptance in the process. The layers of interests contained in the EU process in the end served to kill the EU tax proposal in its original form and to severely shape the nature of eco-label reform. The EU (and especially the Commission) has tried to act as a harmonizing force which suggests the path-dependent push of the EU institutional system. This dynamic has become a key justification for a common framework concerning the taxation of energy products and the proposed abolition of national eco-labels. The case studies reveal the limitations of the EU's role and the limitations of using the single market justification.

Part of the obstacle to, rather than a motivation for, NEPI adoption was found in the institutional process that hinged on the issue of competitiveness. Countries such as Germany have been reluctant to abandon their successful national eco-label in favour of an EU scheme that is not widely known among consumers. Nevertheless, in the tax case, concerns about protecting competitiveness in the EU institutional context have led certain Member States to push for an EU-level eco-tax although other states exercised their veto on sovereignty grounds.

The entrepeneurial attempt of EU institutions, especially the Commission, to increase their influence is clear in the case of taxation; it is arguably less of a driving force in the other two cases although still present since the Commission did seize the window of opportunity created by the subsidiarity discussions with respect to VAs and the need to avoid undermining market competitiveness by having a single label. We can detect an interactive effect between the Kingdon and the institutional approaches as the Commission had both an interest and opportunity created by the institutional dynamics, but still had to exert entrepreneurship and make the policy links to put it on the agenda.

While we see indications of elements for all three (ideas-, settings- and chaos-dominant) approaches in the three cases, the impact of the institutional factors is strongest in affecting instrument choice. The EU continues to rely on a great deal of traditional environmental regulation with the new instruments being used mainly in a supplementary function. A traditional institutional motivation for EU environmental legislation, the protection of the SEM, continues to play a very important role. The tension between the Environment and the Economic DGs remains an influence in the Commission decisions about the use of ('soft') NEPIs, as does the need to build consensus with member governments.

As has been already noted, there is evidence of an ideas shift within EU environmental policy. An advocacy coalition within the Commission did promote the carbon/energy tax, but a change in institutional and external circumstances thwarted its efforts. The voluntary agreements case and the impact of the subsidiarity debate suggest the concept of policy windows (chaos-dominant approach) providing opportunities for actors with specific instruments in mind. The eco-tax case, if one views the Commission alliance as a coalition, fits with the ideational approach as well as the chaos-dominant approach. Nevertheless, national interests focused on protecting competitiveness and sovereignty have exploited the institutional rules to resist common initiatives. EU innovation in this area has also been limited by the traditional approaches to instruments found in the Member States and which they are reluctant to replace.

The case studies in this chapter suggest that the use of 'soft' NEPIs at the EU level reflected more a continuity and sporadic innovation than a revolution in policy instrument use. The most significant strides in the use of 'soft' NEPI innovation seem to be occurring in particular Member States (see also Mol et al, 2000).

Acknowledgements

The research for this chapter was generously funded by the Economic and Social Research Council's (ESRC) Future Governance Programme (L216252013). An earlier version was presented at the 2001 Biennial ECSA Conference in Madison, Wisconsin, US. The authors would like to thank the two anonymous referees and Renaud Dehousse for their helpful comments.

References

Bemelmans-Videc, M., Rist, R and Vedung, E. (1997) *Carrots, Sticks and Sermons: Policy Instruments and Their Evaluation.* New York: Transaction Publishers.

Bennett, C. (1991) 'What is Policy Convergence and What Causes it?', *British Journal of Political Science*, Vol.21, pp215–233.

CEC (Commission of the European Communities) (1993a) *Growth, Competitiveness and Employment: The Challenges and Ways Forward in the Twenty First Century*, EC Bulletin, Supplement 93–6, Brussels: CEC.

CEC (1993b) *Towards Sustainability: A European Community Programme of Policy and Action in Relation to the Environment and Sustainable Development*, Official Journal, No. C 138 of 17 May, pp5–98, Brussels: CEC.

CEC (1995) Report of the Group of Independent Experts on Legislative and Administrative Simplification, *COM(95)288 final*, 21 June, Brussels: CEC.

CEC (1996) *Communication from the Commission on Environmental Agreements, COM (96) 561 final*, Brussels: CEC.

CEC (1997) *Proposal for a Council Directive Restructuring Community Framework for the Taxation of Energy Products* (http://europa.eu.int/scadplus/leg/en/lvb/127019.htm).

CEC (1998) *Development of a Strategy for the Promotion of the European Eco-label award Scheme*, Report for the European Commission. Brussels: CEC.

CEC (2000) *Regulation (EC) No. 1980/2000 of the European Parliament and of the Council of 17 July 2000 on a revised Community eco-label award scheme*, Official Journal, No. L 237 of 21 September 2000, 1–12, Brussels: CEC.

CEC (2001) *Proposal for a Directive of the European Parliament and Council Establishing a Scheme for Greenhouse Gas Emission Trading within the Community and Amending Council Directive 96/61/EC, COM (2001) 581 final*, 2001/0245. Brussels: CEC.

CEC (2002) *Communication from the Commission. Environmental Agreements at Community Level within the Framework of the Action Plan on the Simplification and Improvement of the Regulatory Environment*, COM (2002) 412 final, 17 July 2002, Brussels: CEC.

Cohen, M., March, J. and Olsen, J. (1972), 'A Garbage Can Model of Organisational Choice', *Administrative Sciences Quarterly*, pp1–25.

Delbeke, J. and Bergman, H. (1998) 'Environmental Taxes and Charges in the EU', in Golub, J. (ed) *New Instruments for Environmental Policy in the EU*, London: Routledge, pp242–260.

Dolowitz, D. and Marsh, D. (1996) 'Who Learns from Whom?', *Political Studies*, Vol.44, pp343–357.

Eiderström, E. (2000) Ecolabels in EU Environmental Policy', in Golub, J. (ed) *New instruments for environmental policy in the EU*, London: Routledge, pp190–214.

ENDS Daily (various years), Daily email service. London: Environmental Data Services, email: envdaily@ends.co.uk.

Friedrich, A., Tappe, M. and Wurzel, R. (2000) 'A New Approach to EU Environmental Policy-making? The Auto-oil Programme' *Journal of European Public Policy*, Vol.7, pp593–612.

Golub, J. (1996a) 'Sovereignty and Subsidiarity in EU Environmental Policy', *Political Studies*, Vol.44, pp686–703.

Golub, J. (1996b) 'State Power and Institutional Influence in European Integration: Lessons from the Packaging Waste Directive', *Journal of Common Market Studies*, Vol.34, pp313–339.

Hall, P. (1993) 'Policy Paradigms, Social Learning, and the State: The Case of Economic Policymaking in Britain', *Comparative Politics*, April, pp275–296.

Héritier, A. (1996) 'The Accommodation of Diversity in European Policy-making and its Outcomes: Regulatory Policy as a Patchwork', *Journal of European Public Policy*, Vol.3, pp149–167.

Héritier, A., Knill, C. and Mingers, S. *Ringing the Changes in Europe: Regulatory Competition and the Transformation of the State*, Berlin: Walter de Gruyer.

Hood, C. (1983) *The Tools of Government*. London: Macmillan.

Howlett, M. and Ramesh. M. (1993) 'Patterns of Policy Instrument Choice', *Policy Studies Review*, Vol.12, pp3–24.

Jordan, A. (1999a) 'Editorial Introduction: The Construction of a Multilevel Environmental Governance System', *Environment and Planning C: Government and Policy*, Vol.17, pp1–17.

Jordan, A (1999b) 'The Implementation of EU Environmental Policy: a Policy Problem without a Political Solution?', *Environment and Planning C: Government and Policy*, Vol.17, pp69–90.

Jordan, A., Wurzel, R., Zito A. and Bruckner, L., forthcoming. 'Consumer Responsibility-taking and Eco-label Schemes in Europe', in Micheletti, M. et al (eds) *The Politics Behind Products. Using the Market as a Site for Ethics and Action*. New Brunswick: Transaction Press (in press).

Keay-Bright, S. (2001) 'A Critical Analysis of the Voluntary Fuel Economy Agreements, Established between the Automobile Industry and the European Commission, with Regard to their Capacity to Protect the Environment.' Paper presented at the ECPR Joint Session Workshops, Grenoble, 6–11 April.

Kern, K., Kisslin-Naf, I., Landmann, U. and Mauch C. (2001) 'Ecolabelling and Forest Certification as New Environmental Policy Instruments. Factors which Impede and Support Diffusion', paper presented at the ECPR Joint Session Workshops, Grenoble 6–11 April.

Kingdon, W. and (1984) *Agendas, Alternative and Public Policies*. New York: Harper Collins.

Lauber, V. and Ingram, V. (2000) 'Packaging Waste', in Mol, A., Lauber, V. and Liefferink, D. (eds) *The Voluntary Approach to Environmental Policy*, Oxford: Oxford University Press, pp105–155.

Majone, G. (1991) 'Cross-national Sources of Regulatory Policy Making in Europe and the US', *Journal of Public Policy*, Vol.11, pp9–106.

Mol, A., Lauber V. and Liefferink D. (2000), *The Voluntary Approach to Environmental Policy*, Oxford: Oxford University Press.

Radaelli, C. (2000) 'Policy Transfer in the EU', *Governance*, Vol.13, pp5–43.

Sabatier, P. (1998) 'The Advocacy Coalition Framework: Revisions and Relevance for Europe', *Journal of European Public Policy*, Vol.5, pp98–130.

Sabatier, P. (1999) *Theories of the Policy Process*. Boulder, CO: Westview Press.

Thelen, K. and Steinmo, S. (1991). 'Historical Institutionalism in Comparative Politics', in Steinmo, S., Thelen, K. and Longstreth, F. (eds) *Structuring Politics: Historical Institutionalism in Comparative Analysis*. Cambridge: Cambridge University Press, pp1–32.

Vogel, D. (1998) 'EU Environmental Policy and the GATT/WTO', in Golub, J. (ed), *Global Competition and EU Environmental Policy*. London: Routledge, pp 142–60.

Weale, A. (1996) 'Environmental Rules and Rule-making in the European Union', *Journal of European Public Policy*, 3, pp594–611.

Wurzel, R. (2002) *Environmental Policy-making in Britain, Germany and the European Union. The Europeanisation of Air and Water Pollution Control*. Manchester: Manchester University Press.

Zito, A. (2000) *Creating Environmental Policy in the European Union*. Basingstoke: Palgrave Macmillan.

Zito, A. and Egan, M. (1998) 'Environmental Management Standards, Corporate Strategies and Policy Networks', *Environmental Politics*, Vol.7, pp94–117.

18

European Environmental Policy by Stealth: The Dysfunctionality of Functionalism?

Albert Weale

Consider the following (paradoxical) features of European Union (EU) environmental policy:

1   The EU is an international organization founded on liberal principles, including the free movement of goods, services, capital, and people. Yet in its approach to environmental policy it has made little use of economic instruments; less use indeed than have some countries more closely identified with social democracy than with economic liberalism.
2   The European Commission is formally and legally independent with respect to Member States. Yet in practice it is heavily dependent on those Member States both for the development of particular policy measures and for the enunciation of general policy principles.
3   The European Parliament is a latecomer to the EU institutional scene. Yet it has had more influence on environmental measures than is typically true for more well-established national parliaments.
4   Rational principles of institutional design would suggest that the EU should concentrate on the protection of environmental public goods at an international level. Yet the EU has often been active in policies for the protection of subnational local public goods such as urban air quality, bathing water, and drinking water. How are we to understand these paradoxes?

In answer to this question my thesis in this chapter can be easily stated. All four features are related to one another as the effects of a common cause: European political unification 'by stealth' (Hayward, 1996), as implied by the Monnet method of institution building. If this thesis is true, then it carries implications for the way in which we study European environmental policy. It is often said (indeed, I have said it myself) that, if it is to be successful, environmental policy needs to be integrated with other sectors of public policy, as environmental problems are typically the by-product or runoff of otherwise legitimate activities (industry, transport, and agriculture). We also need to consider reverse influences, however. What effect does spillover from other policy sectors have on the shape and character of environmental policies? A central feature of the Monnet method of European integration is the establishement of conditions producing spillover of concerns from one policy sector to another. As a result, environmental policy in Europe needs to be studied as much as effect as cause.

The remainder of this chapter has three sections. In the first, I set out a characterization of the Monnet method, examining its effect on the development of EU environmental policy. In the second I look at how the four paradoxes can be understood in the light of the Monnet method. In a brief concluding section I consider the implications for institutional redesign suggested by the first two.

European Unification by the Monnet Method

The present EU system of environmental governance emerged from the Monnet method of European integration. This method is one of integration by stealth. Instead of confronting the major questions of constitutional principle involved in the integration of European societies, the Monnet method requires policy-makers to focus upon apparently technical matters of a 'low-politics' variety in order to advance greater political co-operation among Member States. From this beginning it then posits: issue linkage and spillover from one policy sector to another; the indeterminate extension of such spillovers; the creation of a shared system of authority in which Member States are locked into a broad process of integration; and an emphasis upon continual momentum rather than the enjoyment of achievements (cf Schmitter, 1996). Although logically distinct from one another, these elements all share in common an emphasis upon process rather than end state.

At the European level the Monnet method has been remarkably successful. In retrospect it is easy to lose sight of the fact that, at the time when the European Coal and Steel Community (ECSC, the forerunner of the EU) was founded, there were a great many movements and projects offering models for European integration, including the European Union of Federalists, the International Committee for a Socialist United States of Europe, the United Europe Movement, the European League for Economic Cooperation, the European Parliamentary Union, and the proposals for the European Political Community and the European Defence Community (see Griffiths, 1995, pp14–28; Mazey, 1996, pp24–39). That the Monnet method emerged as the most successful approach in this highly competitive environment presumably says something about the way that its presuppositions and implications suited the political realities of the time.

As is well known, Monnet's own view was that European integration required a piecemeal pragmatic approach, rather than the implementation of a previously conceived grand design, and it was this belief that lay behind the stress on putting technical issues first. In his own memoirs, he stressed that the starting point for European integration had to be limited achievements, leading to de facto 'solidarity' from which a federation would grow. The notion of 'solidarity' appeared, for Monnet, to be defined in terms of the existence of common interests, created for example in the 'pooling' of coal and steel resources. He wrote that the ECSC provided for a breach in national sovereignty that was 'narrow enough to secure consent, but deep enough to open the way towards the unity that is essential to peace' (Monnet, 1978, p296). In this view, European integration had to be achieved by small incremental steps in policy sectors where issues of national sovereignty were not likely to be raised, rather than in the high politics of defence and foreign policy (cf Mazey, 1996, p29). Indeed, this was the main feature of Monnet's method that marked it out from contemporaneous attempts at European federalism.

As Hayward (1996, p252) has pointed out, this method has its origin in a French political system in which politicians had only a short expectation of high office in any government and in which bureaucrats were more used to inertia than to innovation. In Hayward's view, such origins led to the founding of the European Union by a few self-conscious agents of change. In these circumstances, elite non-elected leadership, focusing upon apparently technical questions of economic harmonization, could accomplish much, establishing what Wallace (1996) has called 'government by committee', subsequently solidified in the EU's system of 'comitology'. European integration is thus a process of dealing with the 'low-politics' issues of the harmonization – more recently the mutual recognition – of standards to create the conditions for market integration. Conversely, and by implication, it is an important feature of this approach that large constitutional questions should be avoided or sidestepped.

Unification by stealth led to government by appointed officials chosen for their technical competence rather than for their political representativeness. Both Monnet and Hallstein stressed the importance of making the high authority of the ECSC independent of elected representatives in contrast to those who, like Dirk Spierenburg, wished for greater political control (Laursen, 1996). Hayes-Renshaw (1996) points out that the technocratic bias of the European Union is reinforced by much Council business being settled through negotiations in COREPER (the Committee of Permanent Representatives).

The Monnet approach also depends on the idea of issue linkage. In other words, integration is not only focused on technical matters, it also involves an issue dynamic (which we can define as the set of further questions and issues which a solution to a particular policy problem involves) drawing broader considerations into the decision-making process, perhaps without anyone ever seeing that they are involved. Thus, just as the creation of a single market had a logic leading to a single currency (Cameron, 1992, pp25–27), so it also had a logic leading to the strengthening of environmental policy (Weale and Williams, 1992). Just as Monnet himself stressed the potential for industry and agriculture to provide the basis for the common interests which the pooling of sovereignty in certain spheres would enable, so, even in specific areas of policy, Monnet saw the solution to specific problems as raising general concerns, most notably the need for better communications if prosperity was to be achieved. As I note below, the development of environmental policy is entirely consistent, at least in its origins, with this logic of spillover, based on the issue dynamic that is created by the original pooling of resources.

The Monnet method was not implemented in a pure form, however. In the negotiations in which the ECSC was set up, it was the smaller nations who insisted on the injection of political control though a council of ministers. As the pattern adopted for the ECSC was to form the basis of the institutional arrangements of the EU, the division of decision-making authority between the Commission and the Council of Ministers which derived from this original institutional bargain meant that the structure of European governance was superimposed on the political institutions of the Member States. It may well be the case, as Milward (1992) has argued, that this superimposition is itself built upon a logic through which national politicians seek to strengthen their own position domestically by displacing the costs of policies onto the European level. Yet, whatever the original motivation, the development of European institutions means that the pattern of policy-making authority is vertically complex, necessarily involving complex interactions between institutions at the European level and the Member States.

It is also horizontally complex. That is to say, it is characterized by a complicated pattern of inter-institutional processes at the EU level itself. It has always been an issue in the academic analysis of the EU to determine the exact extent to which it rests on an intergovernmental bargain or derives its legitimacy from the extent to which it is able to meet the felt needs of European citizens (for a good recent review, see Cram, 1996). Clearly, both elements are important. Yet, in the striving for greater popular legitimacy, the creation of the directly elected European Parliament in 1979 and the successive growth in its powers through the 1987 Single European Act, the 1992 Maastricht Treaty, and the 1997 Amsterdam Treaty have had important effects on decision-making processes. In particular, the growth of parliamentary power now means that the EU incorporates a principle of the separation of powers in its policy-making – a separation that is compounded by the role of the European Court of Justice over matters of compliance and implementation. Such a separation leads to horizontal complexity in the making of policy.

In addition, European integration following the Monnet method should be seen as an open-ended process, not as the implementation of a constitutional blueprint. The bicycle metaphor is the one that is frequently used in this connection: European unification is like riding a bicycle – you need to keep going forward in order not to fall off. The Monnet method thus rests upon the steady accumulation of powers at the supranational level, and not on a once-and-for-all constitutional bargain among contracting parties.

What are the consequences of the Monnet method for the decision-making structure of the European Union? In many ways, environmental policy can be regarded as a textbook illustration of the method at work. As Jordan points out in his editorial introduction (1999a), the Treaty of Rome did not find a place for environmental policy. Yet, even in the 1960s the harmonization of technical standards called for attention to environmental rule-making. By the early 1970s, with the rise in popular concern about the environment, heads of government decided to take the matter more seriously and the First Action Programme was developed. With the intense German interest in environmental policy in the early 1980s, the politics of the environment became important in EU relations and formal competence was incorporated into the Single European Act. Thus, environmental concerns were taken up into an institutionalized domain of policy in its own right. Completely unanticipated in 1957, environmental policy had moved from silence to salience within 30 years. This is not to say that functional spillover was the sole, or even prime, mover in the development of European environmental policy. Patterns of environmental policy are not be explained by the pure logic of spillover (Weale, 1996, pp602–606). Other pressures and trends associated more generally with the rise of international environmental politics as well as developments wholly within the realm of domestic politics have played their part. Yet, without the impetus of functional spillover, the domestic and European politics of environmental policy would have been different.

The Monnet Method and Environmental Policy

To say that the logic of the Monnet method underlies the development of EU environmental policy is not to say that the legacies of that logic are unexceptionable or without problems. Indeed, I suggest in this section that the original four paradoxes with which I began can be seen as consequences of the Monnet method and the subsequent processes of political integration to which it has given rise. I consider each of the four paradoxes in turn.

Illiberal instruments and liberal foundations

The basis upon which European political unification developed was economically liberal: the creation of a common market without barriers to trade in goods and services and allowing the free movement of capital and people. No doubt in the development of this orientation Monnet's own career background in international business was important, as well as his hostility to the traditional French policy of protectionism. Of course, economic liberalism is not the whole story, as the existence of the interventionist Common Agricultural Policy testifies. Nevertheless, the liberal elements were of crucial importance. Such a view of European integration must represent more than a personal vision on the part of Monnet himself. That Jacques Delors was able to revive the pace of European integration in the 1980s by stressing the importance of the completion of the single market, and the added impetus that the 1992 programme gave to integration, are likely to reflect important features of the underlying dynamic of the process. Enough Member States could see enough advantages over a suitably defined range of issues to give the completion of the single market priority. It is not evidence against this conclusion to note that the implementation of the programme has not been perfect and the protectionist sentiments have not been eliminated.

The pace of the development of environmental policy increased at the same time as the Single Market Programme was developed for reasons that were in part related to that programme, although there was no attempt to consider environmental effects arising from the single market at the time (Weale and Williams,

1992). There is, over a number of issues, a potential conflict arising from the completion of the internal market and the achievement of EU environmental goals, most obviously related to increased transport flows and the way in which waste is handled as a commercial product. Within this context Majone has identified the case for saying that there is a liberal argument for the EU developing a strong environmental policy, in order to correct for market failure (1996, pp28–31).

The essence of Majone's argument rests upon the claim that there is often a strong liberal argument for regulation by the political authorities in order to promote economic efficiency. In the case of environmental policy this argument arises because pollution can be seen as an economic externality. Such externalities exist when the full costs of production and exchange are not borne solely by the beneficiaries of the exchange, but fall in part upon third parties. For example, water pollution from agricultural runoff will adversely affect downstream fishing or water abstraction for human consumption, imposing costs on those who are not parties to the contract between farmers and those who buy from them. (The example is mine, not Majone's.) In these circumstances, a case for public intervention exists on grounds of economic efficiency alone. Correcting for the externality by forcing producers to internalize the costs will lead to a better use of resources. On such liberal grounds, the case is especially strong for the regulation of international environmental pollution by the EU, as its boundaries are extensive enough to ensure that externalities are internalized across the full extent of its authority, whatever national boundaries are involved.

It is common, though by no means universal, in neoclassical treatments of the externality problem to underline the extent to which regulation by means of economic instruments is superior, by the test of economic efficiency, to regulation by means of administrative rules (for a range of views see, inter alia, Brown and Johnson, 1984; Burrows, 1974; Dolan, 1990, Hanley et al, 1990). Such economic instruments include: taxes on emissions, usually by volume emitted; refund schemes for returnable items, ranging from cars to bottles; taxes on polluting substances, for example fuel oil or pesticides; and so on. The arguments favouring such measures are many and varied, depending on the case at hand. Such measures allow greater freedom for producers to find least-cost solutions to their pollution problems than do uniform emission limits. Economic instruments, such as taxes on pesticides, are likely to be more effective at dealing with dispersed, non-point sources of pollution. And where pollution arises from consumption rather than from production externalities, economic instruments are often only the effective instruments.

The merits of these arguments applied to any particular case are less relevant than is their appeal to those holding to liberal principles. If international conflict is to be constrained by the liberal policy of free trade within the boundaries defined by the treaty parties, then it would seem that a liberal approach to pollution control would be the logical corollary. In fact, the EU Commission and Council have long accepted the logic of the argument that an effective approach to pollution control requires the need to internalize the external costs arising from pollution. Acceptance of the polluter-pays principle, for example, is to be found in the First Action Programme on the Environment of 22 November 1973, and a 1983 memorandum by the Directorate General for the Environment (DG XI) to the House of Lords inquiry into the polluter-pays principle makes it clear that, in the Commission's thinking, acceptance of the principle rests upon economic grounds associated with the optimal allocation of resources (SCEC, 1983, p102). The 1987 Fourth Environmental Action Programme (EAP) took as one of its priority areas the 'development of efficient instruments such as taxes, levies, State aid, authorization of negotiable rebates' with the aim of implementing the polluter-pays principle (cited by SCEC, 1987, page 28), and the 1992 Fifth EAP asserted the importance of getting market prices right and the need to create market-based incentives for environmentally friendly economic behaviour (CEC, 1992, page 67).

Despite these commitments of principle, it is striking that little opportunity has been taken for making use of economic instruments in the attainment of environmental objectives. For example, in policies aimed at the reduction of sulphur dioxide emissions the sort of permit trading that has been developed in the US in order to achieve least-cost reductions has not been used. This is so despite the structural similarity of the problems on both sides of the Atlantic, as sulphur deposition both in Europe and in the US arises in large measure from spatially concentrated electricity-generating sources, often operating with old plant, and the regions which suffer the pollution are asymmetrically situated with respect to those causing it. Similarly, the Commission has not attempted to extend and make mandatory in all Member States the successful use of emissions charges relating to water pollution that exist in some. Most striking, perhaps, is the failure at the European level to develop economic instruments for the control of greenhouse gases, of which the failed carbon/energy tax is the clearest example.

Indeed, the failure to develop instruments is even more striking than these examples suggest, as the resistance to economic instruments can go as far as the Commission wishing to prevent Member States from using such instruments to meet their own pollution-control objectives. The clearest example here is probably provided by the Commission's opposition to the Dutch attempt, in the 1980s, to encourage cleaner cars. In the wake of the Council decision of 1985, which established the framework within which subsequent measures on emissions controls for cars were negotiated, the Dutch government introduced a subsidy to encourage the purchase of cleaner vehicles (Schrama and Klok, 1995). This stimulated opposition from other Member States, most notably France, which protested to the Commission about the measure. In 1989 there was even the threat of a European Court of Justice reference by the Commission, though it was not acted on in the end. Thus, we not only find little use of economic instruments, but we even find instances where there is opposition to their use at Member State level.

In large measures these restrictions stem from the legal constraints imposed by EU treaties. The effect of these treaty agreements is to give Member States veto powers over the development of taxed-based instruments for environmental protection at the European level. Under the Maastricht Treaty, the use of fiscal instruments for environmental policy objectives is subject to unanimous voting in the Council of Ministers, rather than qualified majority voting, thus giving veto power to any one Member State. A clear example of the use of such veto powers was seen in the opposition of the UK to the proposed carbon/energy tax.

Certainly, there were doubts about the wisdom of the tax in the UK environmental policy community (SCEC, 1992), but the UK government opposed the measure on the grounds of principle that the EU should not acquire more tax-raising capacity.

We have in this case, therefore, an indication of the inherent limits of functional integration. In order to avoid raising the large constitutional questions about sovereignty, the Monnet method adopts the approach of focusing on the low-politics issues of technical standards and market integration. However, if there is a need to use fiscal instruments in order to raise standards, it is impossible to avoid intruding on one of the responsibilities, tax policy, which by any definition is at the heart of the modern state. If we than embed the Monnet method in a system of decision-making which gives the Member States a privileged, if not all-powerful, place in the making of policy, the limits of functional integration are reinforced by the desire of Member States to preserve their own resources.

However, in addition to these inherent limits of the Monnet method (or rather the combination of the Monnet method and the institutional concessions granted to Member States in the original treaty bargains), there are other factors at work limiting the extent to which we might expect to see the development of economic instruments at the European level. One of these is the dependence of the Commission upon the Member States for the form and character of environmental measures. The general consequences of this dependence are touched on below. Here it is simply worth noting that emissions trading to control sulphur dioxide was unlikely to emerge at the European level, given that the original impetus for the measure came from Germany, a state which itself has shown little desire to experiment with the development of economic instruments in the field of air pollution control. Indeed, to the extent to which Germany has been a leader in European environmental policy (for contrasting evaluations, see Jänicke and Weidner, 1997; Pehle, 1997), we might expect its own preference for administrative regulation to be reflected in EU measures.

Political integration through market integration also has distinctive effects on patterns of environmental policy. It is striking that the Nordic states, strongly influenced by social democratic party ideology and principles, have nonetheless been among those countries who have most extensively developed the use of economic instruments (see European Environment Agency, 1996). With the exception of Denmark, these countries were outside the EU until 1995 (Norway and Iceland still are, of course) and so were not constrained in their choice of policy instruments by the Single Market Programme, with its inherent suspicion of environmental taxes and subsidies as a form of ecoprotectionism (see Weale and Williams, 1992). All this suggests that liberalism, as a set of principles for economic management, has an ambiguous significance for the development of environmental policy. On the other hand its endorsement of market integration, and the implication this has in turn for the development of environmental policy, suggest that functional spillover operated to link the single-market and environmental issues. On the other hand liberal economic policy, in the form of the creation of an integrated market, and in the absence of a political capacity to develop a full range of measures to correct for market failure, imposes limits on the development of environmental policy.

Yet there is also a large question begged in the above analysis: to what extent is European integration truly a liberal project? To be sure, the creation of the European single market and the emergent consequences of economic and mone-tary-union are the effective instruments of political integration. This does not mean, however, that the liberal credentials of the Single Market Programme are uncontested or have a uniform interpretation. It is clear that the support which Delors received from EU leaders for the pursuit of the Single Market Programme stemmed from a variety of motives, not all of which were compatible with one another (Garrett, 1992). On the other side were those who, like the UK govern-ment, favoured the project because they saw it as creating a free-trade area in Europe. On the other side were those who saw the single market as the necessary condition under which Europe could collectively take on the economic contest with the USA and Japan. This second group were more productivist and corpo-ratist in ideology than liberal, and there is no reason to expect them to be espe-cially sympathetic to an economic instrument such as eco-taxation as distinct from subsidies that might support infant eco-industries. In other words, the sin-gle market encapsulated the struggle of what Albert (1993) calls 'capitalism against capitalism'. In this context, it is not surprising that key economic instru-ments remain undeveloped at the European level.

The Dependent Supranational Commission

Independent supranational authority is intrinsic to the Monnet method, and its role is reinforced by various features of the formal, legal, and institutional arrangements of the EU. The Commissioners themselves, though nominated by the Member States, undertake to be independent of national affiliation and loy-alty. Their appointment and term of office is protected by their being, in effect, immune to parliamentary censure and removal. And the Commission is given the sole formal right to initiate measures, though in practice this has been qualified by the growth of various conventions which allow the Council and the Parlia-ment to bring to the attention of the Commission items which they want on the agenda. Moreover, the Commission operates according to the ethos of the conti-nental public functionary, from which Weber's (1947) picture of the bureaucrat was drawn: technically competent, careful of the rules, and deferential to the norms of legal-rational authority. This is not to say, of course, that these formal norms are always upheld in practice. It has been rumoured among the Commis-sion staff, for example, that a French Commissioner took a strong and partisan interest in protecting the interests of the French car industry during negotiations on exhaust emissions directives in the 1980s. But, if true, these would be venial human failings, not institutional characteristics.

Against this background it is striking that, in the development of proposals for environmental measures, the Commission is highly dependent upon the Member States. The clearest example to occur during the 1980s concerned the development of the Large Combustion Plant Directive. However, Héritier and her colleagues have shown that this is not an instance of a more general 'pioneer' role played by Germany but, rather, part of a pattern in which individual countries try, and sometimes succeed, to transpose their own domestic policy concerns and approaches onto the European stage (Héritier et al, 1994). Thus, the development of procedural measures, for instance directives on eco-audit or integrated pollution control, was heavily dependent upon the UK government's attempt to secure its approach within the EU. How does it come about, then, that the formal independence coexists with this de facto dependence?

Once again, the answer is the Monnet method: such de facto dependence is built into the policy process by the form which integration has taken. Monnet's own predilection, both when developing French economic planning and in the original staffing of the ECSC, was for a small-scale bureaucracy. In his view this both encouraged esprit de corps and, in the development of French planning, prevented other ministries from being envious of resources. This approach was transferred to the EU. As he rather nicely put it in his memoirs, Monnet's principle was that a few hundred European civil servants would be enough to set thousands of national experts to work (Monnet, 1978, p373). In addition, as Peters (1997, p28) has noted, the Commission is highly fragmented for a bureaucracy of its size, so that the staff of any one directorate general is likely to be small in relation to the tasks at hand. To be sure, DG XI has grown significantly in size from the mid-1980s, but a large part of this expansion is accounted for by temporary staff.

Moreover, as Scharpf (1994, p222) has noted (cited also by Hurrell and Menon, 1996, p391), the EU lacks those attributes which confer a high degree of policy-making autonomy on federal states: a relatively homogeneous political culture, a party system operative at the federal level, and a high degree of economic and cultural homogeneity. The lack of these characteristics would make for a weak centre in any system of governance, so it is hardly surprising that their effect is most keenly felt by the Commission as the body responsible for initiating European legislation. In the case of environmental policy, there is some offsetting pressure contrary to these centrifugal trends from the strong commitment which a number of observers have noted among staff in DG XI to the cause of the environment (Peterson, 1995, p482). However, common conviction in the importance of the issue you are dealing with does not of itself make for an autonomous policy-making capacity.

To some extent this problem highlights a flaw in the Monnet method itself. Monnet's own predilection for a small and committed staff made a great deal of sense in the immediate post-war context of French economic planning, where there was a need for a strategic core staff to promote economic reconstruction. It also made sense in the context of the ECSC, where there was a clearly delimited sphere of competence and it was important to live within the expectations of Member States. But in a system of multilevel governance like that of the EU, with an intrinsically heterogeneous issue like that of the environment, a small Commission staff becomes vulnerable to whatever parallelogram of forces is most active at the time, and it is made more vulnerable by the absence of the common 'formation' to which all civil servants would be subject if they were staffing national bureaucracies.

Moreover, the national pressures to which Héritier and her colleagues point are likely to become stronger, not weaker, with the development of EU environmental policy. In part, the motive for Member States to push their own priorities and approaches stems from the fact that implementation is made easier if EU legislation borrows from the pattern of one's own national system. Fewer changes in standard operating procedures need to be made and measures are likely to be less costly to implement if they are incremental changes from a national status quo. So, a relatively small Commission faces states with strong incentives to advance their own conceptions of environmental policy.

The European Parliament: The Power of the Parvenu

Regarded from the point of view of parliamentary systems in Europe, the powers of the European Parliament appear few. It is not the formal source of legislation. It does not appoint or overthrow governments. Its party alignments are not well established. It is less attractive than national parliaments to those for whom politics is a career rather than a form of early retirement. It does not have the last say on legislative matters. In short, it still has to make the transition fully from a consultative body to a legislative body holding the executive to account. Moreover, by comparison with the Council of Ministers, its formal powers are few. The EU system of governance is thus unbalanced, with what Lodge (1996, pp197–198) refers to as 'horizontal rivalry', involving imperfect bicameralism, imperfect parliamentary supervision of ministers, imperfect co-operation among the institutions, different interpretations of the decision rules, and inadequate information-sharing among the institutions.

There is much truth in this view. However, the more we accept it, the more we are presented with a paradox. The environmental rule-making and standard-setting process in national political systems is not one in which parliaments play a strong role once the legislative powers under which governments can set standards are in place. It is possible to find examples where there is a strong parliamentary influence in matters of environmental policy, for example the collapse of the Christian Democrat–Liberal coalition in The Netherlands in 1989 or the rejection by the UK Parliament of the proposals for VAT on domestic fuel at the standard rate, and in Germany the *Länder* are able to have their say on proposed measures in the *Bundesrat,* However, by and large the initiative for the changing of standards comes from the government, and typically involves bureaucratic, rather than parliamentary, activity.

The European Parliament, by contrast, has assumed significant environmental standard-setting capacity, particularly since it acquired more powers through the adoption of the co-operation procedure under the Single European Act in cases where environmental measures were implicated in single-market legislation. The clearest example was that of car exhaust legislation in 1989, in which the Parliament forced on the Council the acceptance of so-called 'US83' standards of emissions for all cars manufactured after 1992 (Arp, 1993). However, the Parliament was also important in placing the issue of poor implementation on the European political agenda, extending the powers of the European Environmental Agency (Judge, 1992) and most recently sending back to the Council draft directives on landfill and the control of auto oils (see *ENDS*, 1998a; 1998b, p41). In each case, the Parliament has taken a tougher pro-environment position than the common, or agreed, position of the Council. In the case of the last two, though the crucial decisions have still to be made at the time of writing, it seems as though the Parliament will succeed in strengthening the Directives in terms of environmental protection.

How does it come about that a 'weak' Parliament can exercise such strong powers? In part the answer to this question depends, as Tsebelis (1994) has explained, on the logic of the decision rules. According to the co-operation procedure, the European Parliament can amend a proposal coming from the Council, and if the Council wishes to reaffirm its original decision then it must do so by unanimity, even when the original decision was taken by a qualified majority (as most single-market legislation was). If there is a majority in the Council in favour of a move from a status quo point, then the Parliament can pull the whole Council further in the direction of stronger environmental measures than the Council would go on its own by presenting amendments to the Council's agreed position. It does this, in effect, by presenting the majority in the Council with a stark alternative: either some movement is accepted in the direction the Parliament wishes, or the status quo prevails. Faced with such a choice, the majority of the Council will sometimes concede to the Parliament, as it did on exhaust emissions.

Of course, in practice, the choice is never as simple or as stark as this explanation suggests. For example, with the Car Exhaust Emissions Directive there was a great deal of negotiation with the Commission before a text emerged which the Council could agree to (Judge, 1992, p202). Tsebelis's account, nonetheless, makes a great deal of sense of what would otherwise be obscure. In effect, he offers the theoretical explanation of what seasoned observers like Haigh have inferred from experience: since the Single European Act, 'the Commission and the Parliament acting together can put considerable pressure on the Council, since it can only change a revised proposal by unanimity' (Haigh, 1992, Sections 6.8–7).

In noting that the European Parliament does not control a government in the way that national parliaments do, we are simply committing a category mistake if we then infer that the Parliament's influence on environmental policy is weak. The correct comparison is not with the powers of national parliaments in Europe, but with a system like that in the US, in which there is a separation of powers between the executive and the legislature. To be sure, the European Parliament does not have the powers of the US Congress, but it would be surprising if it did after so short a period in its history. Even so, the co-operation procedure has, under some circumstances, given the Parliament important powers, and if the Treaty of Amsterdam is ratified it will be further strengthened in its veto power under the extension of the co-decision procedure.

The agenda-setting powers given by the existing rules are not the whole of the story with respect to the European Parliament, however. The Parliament had begun to flex its muscles in the early 1980s, before the Single European Act, in respect of the right of initiative, and had devised an informal procedure by which the Commission would follow up on its suggestions. Moreover, the Environment Committee is among the most important of the European Parliament's committees, and there is strong political interest in the selection of its chair, probably because, with party groupings relatively weak, it is possible for parliamentarians to form ad hoc coalitions on issues that are not captured along the single left–right spectrum of economic issues.

It would be a mistake to see the strength of the European Parliament as a direct consequence of the Monnet method. The attempt to secure political legitimacy for European integration through a directly elected Parliament came late in the development of European institutions. However, the power of the Parliament can be seen as an indirect consequence of Monnet's approach, as once the process of European integration had reached a certain level it was difficult not to attach the legitimacy of direct elections – the principal form of legitimacy in the modern world (Manin, 1997) – to the institutions of Europe.

Supranational Authority and Subnational Public Goods

The EU is clearly more than an international regime, even though it may be constrained in its development and freedom of manoeuvre by its constituent national states. The legal doctrine of the direct effect of Community law, its powers of implementation, and the extensive scope of the issues with which it deals all mark it out as a supranational authority of a distinct kind. However, this fact alone highlights our fourth paradox: how does it come about that a supranational body, which might be thought best tailored to the protection of international public goods, has spent a great deal of time and effort on matters concerned with local public goods, including urban air quality, bathing water, and drinking water? In other words, how has it come about that task assignment in EU environmental policy has taken the form that it has?

Task assignment involves the specification of functions and competences to different levels within a multilevel system of governance. If we were looking for a coherent rationalization of task assignment, then one obvious source would be within welfare economics and the utilitarian tradition more generally. According to this approach, policy competence and political authority should be placed at the level at which it will be most effective and efficient. In particular, jurisdictional competence for the protection of public goods should be set at the level at which the public authorities are large enough to internalize the relevant externalities (for example, see Peltzman and Tideman, 1972, p962; Rothenberg, 1970, p34; though most of the arguments were anticipated by Sidgwick, 1891, pp496–500). A contrast with this approach would be the principle of subsidiarity, according to which (in its most natural interpretation, at least), there should be a bias toward the local in the assignment of functions, and a distrust of centralization. Logically speaking, a proponent of the principle of subsidiarity ought to be prepared to countenance forgoing some of the benefits of centralization in order to preserve the advantages of local control. Whichever of these two views we take, however, neither would suggest that an international organization like the EU should be regulating the supply of subnational public goods. Kay (1994) put the point bluntly, but from the point of view of these two standard principles correctly, when he argued that regulation should be at the lowest feasible level and that 'If we [the UK population] choose to drink and bathe in dirty water, that is really our own business, and for Brussels to fine us when we admit to doing so is only to add public insult to private injury' (p14). The question, therefore, is whether it is simply an accident that 'interference' from Brussels should exist in matters of subnational environmental quality.

Once again, in answering this question, we need to look at the specific features of the Monnet method. Integration through functional interaction is bound to the logic of spillover. The solution to one set of problems leads on to the other problems. Just as the customs union led to the single market, which in turn led to economic and monetary union, so we cannot say in advance where the resolution of policy problems will lead. The efficiency secret of this approach, to use Bagehot's (1867) useful term, is the *acquis communautaire*. Roughly speaking, this means that having acquired a competence, the EU will not give it up. There is therefore no role in the constitutional politics of the EU for an equivalent to the tenth amendment of the US constitution, which states that powers not expressly granted by the states to the federal government remain reserved to the governments of the states. The *acquis* is central to the Monnet method of European integration, as it imparts a bias against the ability of Member States to reclaim their historic rights against the supranational authority of the EU (for water policy, see Jordan, 1999c).

Moreover, this distinctive feature of the constitution of the EU is reinforced by the form in which functions are assigned. In this respect, to the extent to which the EU is federal in form, it follows the logic of German federalism rather than US federalism. Scharpf (1988, p242) has argued that the EU is one of a class of political systems in which decision-making authority is not allocated in a zero-sum fashion between different levels of government, but is, instead, shared. Thus, the German federal government shares authority with the Länder through the need to secure a majority in the Bundesrat, and in many matters the division is not one of responsibility for policy sector but for stages of the policy process, with Länder governments having the responsibility for the implementation of policies agreed at the federal level. This pattern applies in environmental policy within the EU, as the typical mode of carrying out environmental measures is for the Member States to implement, according to their own procedures and laws, the measures that are contained in environmental directives (see Jordan, 1999b). So, rather than a neat division of sectors of policy between Europe and the Member States, we have the less clear-cut distinction of responsibility for different phases of the policy process.

Following the first Danish referendum on the Maastricht Treaty in June 1992, the British government secured an EU review of environmental legislation in an attempt to see whether some responsibilities could be repatriated (Jordan, 1999c). The argument was that the principle of subsidiarity, according to which functions should be carried out at the lowest feasible level, implied that the regulation of bathing-water quality, for example, should be a matter for the Member States and not for the EU. However, the review did not recommend a change of responsibility. As Flynn (1997) has shown in his review of the Commission's response to the Edinburgh decision, the application of the principle of subsidiarity was not used to reassign competences for particular issues of policy. Rather it was interpreted as an opportunity to assert the importance of 'soft law' approaches to environmental regulation. In place of the formal directives and regulations that had characterized environmental policy during the 1980s, there would be a greater stress placed on voluntary agreements, negotiated rule-making, and other nonlegal forms of environmental policy control. Significantly, not a single piece of legislation has been repealed and reform of the Drinking Water and Bathing Water Directives is taking a great deal of time.

Conclusion: Dysfunctional Functionalism?

There is a growing body of opinion that the Monnet method has run its course, and that in place of integration by stealth we should have an explicit constitutional contract that would refine and redefine the powers and principles under which European institutions should operate. We could imagine, for example, a constitutional convention, on the model of 1787 in the US, in which political representatives bargain and debate the shape and future of Europe. In any such constitutional process, environmental policy would obviously be a central topic of concern. It is politically important to European mass publics and there is a growing body of expert opinion to the effect that the protection of the environment involves large-scale and serious social and economic changes. Creating an institutional system in which the relevant issues could be properly debated and discussed is therefore an important priority. How much reform is required is, of course, an open-ended matter and would require discussion.

If we look at the history and character of environmental policy in the EU, it is easy to conclude that the functional method of European integration has been dysfunctional from the point of view of environmental policy. EU environmental policy may be thought too uniform in scope and form for the environmental diversity of Europe, with too much attention being paid to the post-materialist concerns of northern Europe and insufficient attention to the sustainable-development concerns of southern Europe. It can be charged with pursuing expensive solutions to marginal improvements to water quality, while ignoring the damage caused by water abstraction in the more arid regions of Europe. Some might think it intervenes too much at the subnational level, while being insufficiently vigorous on issues such as global climate change. Its decision-making procedures can be indicted for being slow and cumbersome, paying too much attention to special interests and not enough attention to the diffuse, but nonetheless real, interests of European citizens at large. Environmental policy is made by a bureaucracy in which the environmental right hand is ignorant of, or cannot control, the left hand of economic growth. In short, the Monnet method can be said to have yielded a system of environmental governance that is pervaded by pathologies.

All this may be true. It is equally true, however, that EU environmental policy has brought a degree of international accountability to the way in which national governments in Europe tend and manage their environmental resources that is unparalleled in any other part of the world among sovereign nation states. Moreover, the Monnet method has been one of the devices by which the countries of Western Europe have enjoyed more peace and stability in the last 40 years than they enjoyed in the previous 100. This is no small achievement. How far a constitutional convention would wish, after reflection and deliberation, to undo and refashion the achievements of the Monnet method in environmental policy is an intriguing, but perhaps unanswerable, question.

Acknowledgements

This chapter is drawn from the research project 'Environmental standards and the politics of expertise' funded by the Single European Market Programme (award No. W113 251 025) of the Economic and Social Research Council of the UK. I should like to thank my co-researchers in the project (Michelle Cini, Brendan Flynn, Dimitrios Konstadakopoulos, Geoffrey Pridham, Martin Porter, and Andrea Williams) for discussions and material relevant to this chapter. I am also grateful to Andrew Jordan and an anonymous referee for comments and suggestions. Remaining errors are my responsibility.

References

Albert, M. (1993) *Capitalism against Capitalism,* London: Whurr Publishers.

Arp, H. (1993) 'Technical Regulation and Politics: The Interplay between Economic Interests and Environmental Policy Goals in EC Car Emission Legislation', in Liefferink, J. D., Lowe, P. D. and Mol, A. P. J. (eds) *European Integration and Environmental Policy,* London: Belhaven Press, pp150–171.

Bagehot, W. (1867) *The English Constitution,* edited with an introduction by Crossman, R. H. S., 1963, London: Fontana/Collins.

Brown, G. M. Jr. and Johnson, R. W. (1984) 'Pollution Control by Effluent Charges: It Works in the Federal Republic of Germany, Why Not in the United States?' *Natural Resources Journal,* Vol.24, pp929–966.

Burrows, P. (1974) 'Pricing Versus Regulation for Environmental Protection' in Culyer, A. J. (ed) *Economic Policies and Social Goals,* Oxford: Martin Robertson, pp273–283.

Cameron, D. R. (1992) 'The 1992 Initiative: Causes and Consequences', in Sbragia, A. M. (ed) *Euro-Politics: Institutions and Policymaking in the 'New' European Community,* Washington, DC: The Brookings Institution, pp23–74.

CEC (1992) *Fifth Environmental Action Programme* COM (92) 23 final, Commission of the European Communities, Luxembourg.

Cram, L. (1996) 'Integration Theory and the Study of the European Policy Process', in Richardson, J. J. (ed) *European Union: Power and Policy-making,* London: Routledge, pp40–58.

Dolan, E. G. (1990) 'Controlling Acid Rain', in Block, W. (ed) *Economics and the Environment: A Reconciliation,* Vancouver, BC: The Fraser Institute, pp215–232.

ENDS (1998a) 'Parliament Declares War on Auto/Oil Standards' *Ends Report,* Vol.277, February, p44, London: Environmental Data Services Ltd.

ENDS (1998b) 'EC Climate Policy Takes Shape, Progress on Landfills, Air Pollution' *Ends Report,* Vol.288, March, pp39–41, London: Environmental Data Services Ltd.

European Environment Agency (1996) *Environmental Taxes: Implementation and Effectiveness,* Copenhagen: European Environment Agency.

Flynn, B. (1997) *Subsidiarity and the Rise of Soft Law,* Colchester, Essex: OP-40 Human Capital and Mobility Network.

Garrett, G. (1992) 'International Cooperation and Institutional Choice: The European Community's Internal Market', *International Organisation,* Vol.46, pp533–560.

Griffiths, R. T. (1995) 'The European Integration Experience', Middlemas, K. (ed) in *Orchestrating Europe: The Informal Politics of the European Union 1973–95,* London: Fontana Press, pp1–70.

Haigh, N. (1992) *Manual of Environmental Policy: The EC and Britain,* London: Catermill, release 12 November 1997.

Hanley, N., Hallett, S. and Moffatt, I. (1990) 'Research Policy and Review 33. Why is More Notice Not Taken of Economists' Prescriptions for the Control of Pollution?', *Environment and Planning,* Vol.22, pp1421–1439.

Hayes-Renshaw, F. (1996) 'The Role of the Council', in Andersen, S. S. and Eliassen, K. A. (eds) *The European Union: How Democratic Is It?,* London: Sage, pp143–163.

Hayward, J. (1996) 'Has European Unification by Stealth a Future?', in Hayward, J. (ed) *Elitism, Populism, and European Politics,* Oxford: Clarendon Press, pp252–257.

Héritier, A., Mingens, S., Knill, C. and Becka, M. (1994) *Die Veränderung van Staatlichkeit in Europa,* Opladen: Leske und Budrich.

Hurrell, A. and Menone, A. (1996) 'Politics Like Any Other? Comparative Politics, International Relations and the Study of the EU', *West European Politics,* Vol.19, pp386–402.

Jänicke, M. and Weidner, H. (1997) 'Germany', in Jänicke, M. and Weidner, H. (eds) *National Environmental Policies: A Comparative Study of Capacity-building,* Berlin: Springer, pp133–155.

Jordan, A. (1999a) 'Editorial Introduction: The Construction of a Multilevel Environmental Governance System', *Environment and Planning C: Government and Policy,* Vol.17, pp1–17.

Jordan, A (1999b) 'The implementation of EU environmental policy: a policy problem without a political solution?', *Environment and Planning C: Government and Policy,* Vol.17, pp69–90.

Jordan, A (1999c) 'European Union Water Standards: Locked In or Watered Down?', *Journal of Common Market Studies,* Vol.37, pp13–37.

Judge, D. (1992) 'Predestined to Save the Earth': The Environment Committee of the European Parliament', *Environmental Politics,* Vol.1, No.4, pp186–212.

Kay, J. 1994, 'Clever Trick but the Cracks Remain', *Financial Times,* 16 August, p14.

Laursen, F. (1996) 'The Role of the Commission', in Andersen, S. S. and Eliassen, K. A. (eds) *The European Union: How Democratic Is It?* London: Sage, pp119–141.

Lodge, J. (1996) 'The European Parliament', in Andersen, S. S. and Eliassen, K. A. (eds) *The European Union: How Democratic Is It?,* London: Sage, pp187–214.

Majone, G. (1996) *Regulating Europe,* London: Routledge.

Manin, B. (1997) *The Principles of Representative Government,* Cambridge: Cambridge University Press.

Mazey, S. (1996) 'The Development of the European Idea: From Sectoral Integration to Political Union', in Richardson, J. J. (ed) *European Union: Power and Policy-making,* London: Routledge, pp24–39.

Milward, A. (1992) *The European Rescue of the Nation State,* London: Routledge.

Monnet, J. (1998) *Memoirs,* translated by Mayne, R., London: Collins.

Pehle, H. (1997) 'Germany: Domestic Obstacles to an International Forerunner', in Andersen, M. S. and Liefferink, D. (eds) *European Environmental Policy: The Pioneers,* Manchester: Manchester University Press, pp161–209.

Peltzman, S. and Tideman, T. N. (1972) 'Local Versus National Pollution Control: Note', *American Economic Review,* Vol.62, pp959–963.

Peters, B.G. (1997) 'Escaping the Joint-decision Trap: Repetition and Sectoral Politics in the European Union', *West European Politics,* Vol.20, No.2, pp22–36.

Petersen, J. (1995) 'Playing the Transparency Game: Consultation and Policy-making in the European Commission', *Public Administration,* Vol.73, pp473–492.

Rothenberg, J. (1970) 'Local Decentralization and the Theory of Optimal Government', in Margolis, J. (ed) *The Analysis of Public Output,* New York: Columbia University Press, pp29–64.

SCEC (1983) 'Memorandum: The "Polluter Pays" Principle', in House of Lords, Select Committee on the European Communities. The Polluter Pays Principle Report 10, Session 1982–83, London: The Stationery Office, pp102–103.

SCEC (1987) *House of Lords Papers and Bills – Session 1986–87. Fourth Environmental Action Programme* HL 135, Select Committee on the European Communities, London: The Stationery Office.

SCEC (1997) *House of Lords Papers. Session 1991–92. Carbon/Energy Tax* HL 52, Select Committee on the European Communities, London: The Stationery Office.

Scharpf, F. W. (1988) 'The Joint-decision Trap: Lessons from German Federalism and European Institutions', *Public Administration,* Vol.66, pp239–278.

Scharpf, F. W. (1994) 'Community and Autonomy: Multi-level Policy-making in the European Union', *Journal of European Public Policy,* pp219–242.

Schmitter, P. C. (1996) 'Examining the Present Euro-polity with the Help of Past Theories', in Marks, G., Scharpf, F. W., Schmitter, P. C. and Streeck, W. (eds) *Governance in the European Union,* London: Sage, pp1–14.

Schrama, G. J. I. and Klok, P-J. (1995) 'The Swift Introduction of "Clean Cars" in the Netherlands, 1986–1992: The Origin and Effect of Incentive Measures', in Jänicke, M. and Weidner, H. (eds) *Successful Environmental Policy: A Critical Evaluation of 24 Cases,* Berlin: Edition Sigma, pp203–222.

Sidgwick, H. (1891) *The Elements of Politics,* London: Macmillan.

Tsebelis, G. 1994, 'The Power of the European Parliament as a Conditional Agenda Setter', *American Political Science Review,* Vol.88, pp128–142.

Wallace, W. (1996) 'Has Government by Committee Lost the Public's Confidence?', in Hayward, J. (ed) *Elitism. Populism and European Politics,* Oxford: Clarendon Press, pp238–251.

Weale, A. (1996) 'Environmental Rules and Rule-making in the European Union', *Journal of European Public Policy,* Vol.3, pp594–611.

Weale, A. and Williams, A. (1992) 'Between Economy and Ecology? The Single Market and the Integration of Environmental Policy', *Environmental Politics,* Vol.1, No.4, pp45–64.

Weber, M. (1947) *The Theory of Social and Economic Organization,* translated by Henderson, A. M. and Parsons, T., Oxford: Oxford University Press.

Further Reading

The European Union

Since the first edition of this book was published in 2002, the European 'turn' in politics and public policy analysis has continued apace. Consequently, there are even more good textbooks on the EU to choose from than three years ago. Currently, the best summaries are:

Bomberg, E. and Stubb, A. (eds) (2003) *The EU: How Does it Work?* Oxford: Oxford University Press.
Dinan, D. (1999) *Ever Closer Union* (2nd edn), Basingstoke: Palgrave.
Dinan, D. (2004) *Europe Re-cast: A History of the European Union,* Basingstoke: Palgrave.
George, S. and Bache, I. (2001) *Politics in the European Union,* Oxford: Oxford University Press.
Green Cowles, M. and Dinan, D. (eds) (2004) *Developments in the European Union 2,* Palgrave, Basingstoke.*
Hix, S. (2005) *The Political System of the European Union* (2nd edn), Basingstoke: Palgrave.
Nugent, N. (2002) *The Government and Politics of the European Union* (5th edn), Basingstoke: Palgrave.
Peterson, J. and Shackleton, M. (eds) (2002) *The Institutions of the EU,* Oxford: Oxford University Press.
Richardson, J. (ed) (2001) *European Union: Power and Policy Making* (2nd edn), London: Routledge.
Wallace, H., Wallace, W. and Pollack, M. (2005) *Policy Making in the European Union* (5th edn), Oxford: Oxford University Press.*

Some of these (*) contain a chapter on EU environmental policy, but the majority do not.

EU Policy Sectors/Issues

There are also more and more books coming onto the market that address particular parts or sectors of the EU. Without claiming to be exhaustive, the following list covers those which are especially relevant to EU environmental policy:

Grant, W. (1997) *The Common Agricultural Policy,* Basingstoke: Palgrave.
Holland, M. (2002) *The EU and the Third World,* Basingstoke: Palgrave.
Matlary, J. (1997) *Energy Policy in the European Union,* Basingstoke: Palgrave.
Nugent, N. (ed) (2004) *European Union Enlargement,* Basingstoke: Palgrave.
Stevens, H. (2004) *Transport Policy in the European Union,* Basingstoke: Palgrave.

Theories of the EU

Currently, the best reviews of the most popular theories of EU politics and European integration are:

Rosamund, B. (1999) *Theories of European Integration*, Basingstoke: Palgrave.
Wiener, A. and Diez, T. (eds) (2004) *European Integration Theory*, Oxford: Oxford University Press.

EU Environmental Policy

Nigel Haigh's annually updated looseleaf *Manual of Environmental Policy* describes each and every item of EU environmental policy and its impact on the UK:
Haigh, N. (2000) *Manual of Environmental Policy: The EU and Britain,* Leeds: Maney Publishing.

There are also at least two other good textbooks on EU environmental policy:
Barnes, P. and Barnes, I. (1999) *Environmental Policy in the European Union*, Cheltenham: Edward Elgar.
McCormick, J. (2001) *Environmental Policy in the European Union*, Basingstoke: Palgrave.

For more detailed analyses, the following are well worth consulting:
Bomberg, E. (1998) *Green Parties and Politics in the European Union*, London: Routledge.
Jordan, A., Wurzel, R. and Zito, A. (eds) (2003) *'New' Instruments of Environmental Governance: National Experiences and Prospects*, London: Frank Cass.
Jordan, A. and Liefferink, D. (eds) (2004) *Environmental Policy in Europe: The Europeanization of National Environmental Policy*, London: Routledge.
Jordan, A. and Schout, A. (2006) *The Coordination of the European Union: Exploring the Capacities for Networked Governance*, Oxford, Oxford University Press.
Lenschow, A. (ed) (2002) *Environmental Policy Integration*, London: Earthscan.
Lowe, P. and Ward, S. (eds) (1998) *British Environmental Policy and Europe*, London: Routledge.
Wurzel, R. (2002) *Environmental Policy Making in Britain, Germany and the EU*, Manchester: Manchester University Press.
Zito, A. (1999) *Creating Environmental Policy in the European Union*, Basingstoke: Macmillan.

Other Sources

Finally, academic journals such as *Environmental Politics*, the *Journal of European Public Policy, Environment and Planning A, Environment and Planning C,* and

European Environment, regularly carry articles on recent development in EU environmental policy. For up-to-date reviews of developments in policy and legislation, consult one of the many daily/monthly publications, such as *Environmental Data Services (ENDS) Report*, *ENDS Daily*, *Europe Environment*, *Agence Europe* and *Environment Watch: Western Europe*. Finally, the EU's primary web portal is: http://europa.eu.int/

Index